Cave monasteries of Byzantine Cappadocia

The 'pyramids' of Cappadocia (*Voyage du Sieur Paul Lucas . . .* (Paris 1712)).

Cave monasteries of Byzantine Cappadocia

LYN RODLEY

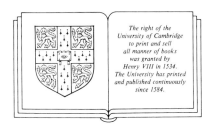

The right of the
University of Cambridge
to print and sell
all manner of books
was granted by
Henry VIII in 1534.
The University has printed
and published continuously
since 1584.

CAMBRIDGE UNIVERSITY PRESS

CAMBRIDGE
LONDON   NEW YORK   NEW ROCHELLE
MELBOURNE   SYDNEY

Published by the Press Syndicate of the University of Cambridge
The Pitt Building, Trumpington Street, Cambridge CB2 1RP
32 East 57th Street, New York, NY 10022, USA
10 Stamford Road, Oakleigh, Melbourne 3166, Australia

First published 1985

Filmset and Printed in Great Britain by BAS Printers Ltd,
Over Wallop, Hampshire

Library of Congress catalogue card number: 84-17485

British Library Cataloguing in Publication Data
Rodley, Lyn
Cave monasteries of Byzantine Cappadocia
1. Monasteries–Turkey–Cappadocia   2. Cave
churches–Turkey–Cappadocia   3. Architecture,
Byzantine–Turkey–Cappadocia
I. Title
726′.7   NA5869.C3
ISBN 0 521 26798 6

CONTENTS

List of figures   vii
List of plates   ix
Acknowledgements   xiv
Abbreviations   xv
Key to plans   xvii

1 **The background**   1
Introduction   1
Geography and history   2
Rock-cut architecture   5

2 **The courtyard monasteries**   11
Introduction   11
Hallaç Monastery   11
Bezir Hane   26
Şahinefendi Monastery   33
Kılıçlar Monastery   39
Soğanlı Han   45
Karanlık Kilise Monastery   48
Aynalı Kilise Monastery   56
Selime Kalesi   63
Direkli Kilise Monastery   85
Karanlık Kale   95
Eski Gümüş Monastery   103
Appendix : Other complexes   118

3 **Açık Saray**   121
Açık Saray No. 1   122
Açık Saray No. 2   125
Açık Saray No. 2a   129
Açık Saray No. 3   132
Açık Saray No. 4   137
Açık Saray No. 5   140
Açık Saray No. 6   142
Açık Saray No. 7   144
Açık Saray Churches Nos. 1 and 2   146
Function   148

4 **The refectory monasteries**   151
Yusuf Koç Kilisesi Monastery   151
The Archangel Monastery, Cemil   157
Göreme monasteries   160
Conclusion   182

5 **Hermitages**   184
Introduction   184
Hermitage of Niketas the Stylite   184
Hermitage of the Monk Symeon   189
Karabaş Kilise and complex   193
St Barbara, Soğanlı, and complex   203
Ayvalı Kilise   207
Tokalı Kilise   213

6 **The monasteries and their context**   223
Chronology   223
Architecture   224
 Technique   224
 Hermitages   225
 Monasteries   226
 Monastery churches   227
 Decoration and façades   236
The monasteries in use   237
 Monasticism   237
 Hermitages   239
 Monastery plans   240
 Courtyard monasteries   244
 Refectory monasteries   249
 Patronage   250

Conclusion   252

Select bibliography   255
Indexes
 Iconographic   259
 General   262

FIGURES

1   Map of volcanic valley area   10
2   Hallaç Monastery: plan   13
3   Hallaç Monastery: reconstruction of the vestibule north wall   15
4   Hallaç Monastery: painting in the main apse of the church   24
5   Bezir Hane: plan   27
6   Şahinefendi Monastery: plan   35
7   Kılıçlar Monastery: plan   40
8   Soğanlı Han: plan   47
9   Karanlık Kilise Monastery: plan (a) ground floor and church, (b) upper floor   49
10 Karanlık Kilise: donor images   54
11 Aynalı Kilise Monastery: plan (a) ground floor, (b) upper floor   58
12 Aynalı Kilise Monastery: painting and reconstruction of screen   60
13 Selime Kalesi: plan   64
14 Selime Kalesi: donor panel   73
15 Direkli Kilise Monastery: plan   86
16 Karanlık Kale: plan   96
17 Eski Gümüş Monastery: plan   104
18 Açık Saray: site (approximate locations of complexes)   121
19 Açık Saray No. 1: plan   122
20 Açık Saray Nos. 2 and 2a: plan   126
21 Açık Saray No. 3: plan (a) ground floor, (b) upper floor   133
22 Açık Saray No. 4: plan   138
23 Açık Saray No. 5: plan   141
24 Açık Saray No. 6: plan   142
25 Açık Saray No. 7: plan   144
26 Açık Saray No. 7: Room 1, south wall   145
27 Açık Saray Churches: (a) No. 1, (b) No. 2   146
28 Yusuf Koç Kilisesi Monastery: plan   152
29 Yusuf Koç Kilisesi: donor images   157
30 Göreme Park: site diagram   161
31 Çarıklı Kilise and complex (Göreme Unit 1): plan (a) upper floor, (b) ground floor   163
32 Göreme Refectories A to E   165
33 Göreme Refectories F to J   174
34 Hermitage of Niketas the Stylite: (a) plan of chapel, (b) plan of nearby chapel   185
35 Chapel of St Symeon: (a) plan, (b) site   190
36 Karabaş Kilise and complex: plan   194
37 Karabaş Kilise: images of monks   196
38 Karabaş Kilise: images of donors   199

39   St Barbara, Soğanlı, and complex: (a) plan, (b) site, (c) North Chapel screen   203
40   Ayvalı Kilise: (a) plan, (b) South Chapel, south wall   208
41   Ayvalı Kilise: images in the North Chapel   212
42   Tokalı Kilise: (a) plan, (b) plan of Lower Church   214
43   Karagedik Kilise: view from the northeast (after Restle)   230
44   Masonry-built churches: (a) Karagedik Kilise, (b) Çanlı Kilise, (c) Fisandon, (d) Çet Dağı, (e) Değile
       No. 35, (f) İbrala, (g) Ala Kilise   232
45   Çanlı Kilise, near Çeltek: view from the southeast (after Restle)   233
46   Fisandon Church: view from the southeast (after Eyice)   233
47   Ala Kilise, Ali Suması Dağı: south wall (after Bell)   234
48   Monastery of St Meletios, near Megara (after Orlandos)   240
49   Monastery of St Catherine, Mt Sinai (after Forsyth)   241
50   Monastery of St Euthymios, Palestine (after Chitty)   242
51   Monastery of Baramûs, Wadi'n Natrun, Egypt (after Evelyn-White)   243
52   Monastery of Id-Dêr, Syria (after Butler)   243
53   Monastery of Sameh, Syria (after Butler)   244
54   Alahan Monastery (after Gough)   245
55   Değile 35/45 (after Bell)   245
56   Değile 32/39/43 (after Bell)   246
57   Değile 33/36 (after Bell)   246
58   The Han, Kara Dağı (after Bell)   247
59   Monastery of Hogeac'vank' (after Thierry)   247

PLATES

The 'Pyramids' of Cappadocia (*Voyage du Sieur Paul Lucas . . . .* (Paris, 1712)) *frontispiece*

1	Volcanic valley area: Güllü Dere	3
2	Göreme valley: cones	3
3	Hallaç Monastery: site	12
4	Hallaç Monastery: northeast corner of courtyard	12
5	Hallaç Monastery: Area 1 (vestibule), view north	14
6	Hallaç Monastery: Room 2, view northwest	16
7	Hallaç Monastery: Room 3, northeast corner	16
8	Hallaç Monastery: Room 4, northeast corner	17
9	Hallaç Monastery: Room 4, southwest corner	18
10	Hallaç Monastery: Room 5, northeast corner	18
11	Hallaç Monastery: Room 5, detail of vault	18
11a	Hallaç Monastery: Room 5, detail of figure	19
12	Hallaç Monastery: Church, northwest view of vaulting	20
13	Hallaç Monastery: Church, southwest view of vaulting	20
14	Hallaç Monastery: Church, southwest capital	21
15	Hallaç Monastery: Church, northwest capital	21
16	Hallaç Monastery: Church, north wall, west end	21
17	Hallaç Monastery: Church, south wall, pilaster capital	22
18	Hallaç Monastery: Church, main apse	22
19	Hallaç Monastery: Church, tomb chamber, view southeast	23
20	Kızlar Kilise, Göreme: vaulting	25
21	Bezir Hane: exterior, northwest corner of vestibule	28
22	Bezir Hane: exterior, northeast corner of vestibule	28
23	Bezir Hane: Room 2, northwest corner	29
24	Bezir Hane: Church, dome and northwest corner	30
25	Bezir Hane: Church, west end	30
26	Bezir Hane: Church, St George	31
27	Bezir Hane: Church, Archangel Michael	32
28	Bezir Hane: Church, St Kosmas	32
29	Şahinefendi Monastery: site	34
30	Şahinefendi Monastery: façade and Room 1	34
31	Şahinefendi Monastery: Room 1, north wall	36
32a	Şahinefendi Monastery: Room 2, west wall, south end	37
32b	Şahinefendi Monastery: Room 2, west wall, north end	37
32c	Şahinefendi Monastery: Room 2, east wall, north end	37
33	Şahinefendi Monastery: Church, northeast pier	38
34	Kılıçlar Monastery: façade and Room 1	41

35	Kılıçlar Monastery: Room 1, east end	41
36	Kılıçlar Monastery: Room 1, northwest corner	42
37	Kılıçlar Kilise: entrance and side chapel	44
38	Soğanlı Han: site	46
39	Soğanlı Han: façade, view northwest	46
40	Soğanlı Han: façade, view northeast	48
41	Karanlık Kilise Monastery: vestibule, east end	49
42	Karanlık Kilise Monastery: vestibule, view southwest	51
43	Karanlık Kilise Monastery: vestibule, south wall, east end	51
44	Karanlık Kilise Monastery: Church, narthex tomb chamber	53
45	Karanlık Kilise Monastery: Church, narthex inscription	56
46	Aynalı Kilise Monastery: site	57
46a	Aynalı Kilise Monastery: façade, detail	57
47	Aynalı Kilise Monastery: Room 1, southeast corner	59
48	Aynalı Kilise Monastery: Church, narthex dome	61
49	Aynalı Kilise Monastery: Church, main apse and southeast corner	62
50	Aynalı Kilise Monastery: Church, northwest corner	62
51	Selime Kalesi: façade of Rooms 1–3 and porch (4a)	65
52	Selime Kalesi: Room 1, north wall	66
53	Selime Kalesi: Room 1, detail of ornament on south wall	66
54	Selime Kalesi: Room 1, detail of north wall recess	67
55	Selime Kalesi: Room 2, southeast corner	67
56	Selime Kalesi: Room 3, east end	67
57	Selime Kalesi: Room 4, ceiling and southwest corner	68
58	Selime Kalesi: Room 4, ceiling and north wall	69
59	Selime Kalesi: Church, entrance	70
60	Selime Kalesi: Church, north arcade and main apse	70
61a	Selime Kalesi: Church, south side of barrel vault, east end	72
61b	Selime Kalesi: Church, south side of barrel vault, west end	72
62	Selime Kalesi: Church, donor images on west wall	74
63a	Selime Kalesi: Church, porch inscription, north side	75
63b	Selime Kalesi: Church, porch inscription, south side	75
64	Selime Kalesi: Areas 11 and 10, view northeast	76
65	Selime Kalesi: Areas 11 and 10, view north	76
66	Selime Kalesi: Area 11	77
67	Selime Kalesi: Area 11, west wall	78
68	Selime Kalesi: Room 12, northwest corner	79
69	Selime Kalesi: Room 13, view northwest	79
70	Selime Kalesi: Room 18, southeast corner	80
71	Selime Kalesi: Area 21	81
72	Selime Kalesi: Area 23	82
73	Selime Kalesi: kitchen, with entrance to Room 25	83
74	Selime Kalesi: stable	83
75	Selime Kalesi: Room 28, lunette decoration	84
76	Direkli Kilise Monastery: site	86
77	Direkli Kilise Monastery: Room 1, west end	87
78	Direkli Kilise Monastery: Room 1, east end	87
79	Direkli Kilise Monastery: Church, narthex east wall	88
80	Direkli Kilise Monastery: Church, view towards main apse	88
81	Direkli Kilise Monastery: Church, entrance to side chapel	88
82	Direkli Kilise Monastery: side chapel, view east	89
83	Direkli Kilise Monastery: Room 5	90

84a Direkli Kilise Monastery: Church, north apse, conch   91
84b Direkli Kilise Monastery: Church, north apse, wall   91
85   Direkli Kilise Monastery: Church, St Sergios and St Bakchos   92
86   Direkli Kilise Monastery: Church, St Marina   92
87   Direkli Kilise Monastery: Church, St George   92
88   Direkli Kilise Monastery: Church, equestrian saint   93
89   Direkli Kilise Monastery: Church, artist's graffiti   93
90   Karanlık Kale: site   96
91   Karanlık Kale: Room 1, west end   97
92   Karanlık Kale: Room 1, east end   97
93   Karanlık Kale: Room 2, northwest corner   98
94   Karanlık Kale: Room 3, northwest corner   99
95   Karanlık Kale: Room 4, northwest corner   99
96   Karanlık Kale: Church, view west   99
97   Karanlık Kale: Church, view east   100
98   Karanlık Kale: corridor to Church   101
99   Karanlık Kale: corridor, detail of east wall   102
100 Karanlık Kale: side chapel   102
101 Eski Gümüş Monastery: north façade, west end   105
102 Eski Gümüş Monastery: north façade, east end   105
102a Eski Gümüş Monastery: north façade, detail   106
103a Eski Gümüş Monastery: east façade, north end   106
103b Eski Gümüş Monastery: east façade   107
104 Eski Gümüş Monastery: west façade   107
105 Eski Gümüş Monastery: south façade   108
106 Eski Gümüş Monastery: Room 1, east end   108
107 Eski Gümüş Monastery: Room 4, with pit   109
108 Eski Gümüş Monastery: steps to kitchen (7) from Room 4   110
109 Eski Gümüş Monastery: Room 21, northwest corner   111
110 Eski Gümüş Monastery: Church, northeast corner of narthex   113
111 Eski Gümüş Monastery: narthex, painting on east wall   113
112 Eski Gümüş Monastery: Church, northeast view of vaulting   114
113 Eski Gümüş Monastery: Church, tomb chamber in north wall   115
114 Eski Gümüş Monastery: Church, entrance to side chapel   115
115 Eski Gümüş Monastery: Church, north wall   116
116 Façade opposite Kılıçlar Kilise, Göreme valley   119
117 Açık Saray No. 1: façade   123
118 Açık Saray No. 1: Room 1, east end   124
119 Açık Saray No. 1: Church, east end   124
120 Açık Saray No. 1: Room 5, southeast corner   125
121 Açık Saray No. 2: Room 1, northwest corner   127
122 Açık Saray No. 2: Room 2, west arm   127
123 Açık Saray No. 2: Room 5, northwest corner   128
124 Açık Saray No. 2: stable entrance   129
125 Açık Saray No. 2a: Room 1   130
126 Açık Saray No. 2a: Room 6, view north   131
127 Açık Saray No. 2a: Church, view northeast   132
128 Açık Saray No. 3: façade   134
129 Açık Saray No. 3: Church, view northwest   135
130 Açık Saray No. 3: Church, view east   135
131 Açık Saray No. 3: Church, narthex vault   136
132 Açık Saray No. 3: Room 10, view southwest   136

133   Açık Saray No. 4: façade   137
134   Açık Saray No. 4: Room 1, view northeast   137
135   Açık Saray No. 4: Room 2, view northeast   139
136   Açık Saray No. 4: stable   140
137   Açık Saray No. 5: Room 1   141
138   Açık Saray No. 5: façade and Room 1   143
139   Açık Saray No. 6: Room 1   143
140   Açık Saray No. 7: façade   145
141   Açık Saray No. 7: Room 3   145
142   Açık Saray Church No. 1: northwest corner   147
142a Açık Saray Church No. 1: painting in main apse   147
143   Yusuf Koç Kilisesi Monastery: site, view southwest   153
144   Yusuf Koç Kilisesi Monastery: refectory   153
145   Yusuf Koç Kilisesi Monastery: porch leading to Room 3   154
146   Yusuf Koç Kilisesi Monastery: site, view northwest   154
147   Yusuf Koç Kilisesi Monastery: stable   155
148   Yusuf Koç Kilisesi Monastery: Church, entrance   155
149   Yusuf Koç Kilisesi Monastery: Church, St Demetrios and donor   155
150   Archangel Monastery: façade   158
151   Çarıklı Kilise Monastery: exterior   163
152   Çarıklı Kilise Monastery: Refectory A   165
153   Çarıklı Kilise: donor panel   166
154a Göreme Unit 2: site, with entrance to Chapel 25   167
154b Göreme Unit 2: site, with entrances to Refectory B, cavity (a) and Refectory C   168
154c Göreme Unit 2: site, with entrances to Refectory C, cavities (b) and (c)   168
155   Göreme Unit 2: Refectory C   169
156   Göreme Unit 2: Chapel 25, view of vaulting (central dome, south arm, corner bay)   170
157   Göreme Unit 2: Chapel 25, apse and chancel screen   170
158   Göreme Unit 3: Refectory D   171
159   Göreme Unit 3: site, with entrance to Chapel 27   171
160   Göreme Unit 3: site, with entrance to cavity (d) and Refectory D   172
161   Göreme Unit 4: entrance to Refectory E   173
162   Göreme Unit 5: entrance to Chapel 20   175
163   Göreme Unit 6: entrance to area (m)   176
164   Göreme: cavities (o) and (p), between Units 6 and 7   177
165   Göreme Unit 7: entrances to Chapel 18 and Refectory G   178
165a Göreme Unit 7: entrance to Refectory G   179
166   Göreme Unit 8: entrance to Refectory H   180
167   Göreme Unit 9: Refectory I   180
168   Hermitage of Niketas the Stylite: site   185
169   Hermitage of Niketas the Stylite: Chapel entrance and niche   186
170   Hermitage of Niketas the Stylite: Chapel (narthex, nave, apse)   187
171   Hermitage of Niketas the Stylite: Chapel, east wall   188
172   Hermitage of the Monk Symeon: site   189
172a Hermitage of the Monk Symeon: Chapel of St Symeon, entrance   190
173   Hermitage of the Monk Symeon: Chapel of St Symeon, northeast corner   191
173a Hermitage of the Monk Symeon: Chapel of St Symeon, detail of north wall   191
174   Karabaş Kilise complex: site, with opening to Room 1   194
175   Karabaş Kilise: entrance   195
176   Karabaş Kilise: east end   196
177   St Barbara, Soğanlı: entrance to Church and side chapel   204
178   St Barbara: military saints   205

179   St Barbara: St Theopiste and St Christopher   205
180   Ayvalı Kilise: site   209
181   Ayvalı Kilise: exterior   209
182   Ayvalı Kilise: North Chapel, north wall   210
183   Tokalı Kilise: Old Church, north wall   215
184   Tokalı Kilise: New Church, northeast view   217
185   Tokalı Kilise: north wall and niche   217
186   Tokalı Kilise: Lower Church, northwest corner   218
187   Tokalı Kilise: Lower Church, corridor in front of apses   219
188   Tokalı Kilise: steps to Lower Church   219

ACKNOWLEDGEMENTS

My first debt of gratitude is to two institutions, the Leverhulme Trust and Lucy Cavendish College, Cambridge, whose concurrent Research Fellowships provided me with the time and resources to write this book. I am also indebted to the Warburg Institute Library, the British Library and Cambridge University Library, and to their unfailingly helpful staff.

Parts of the text originated with my London University Ph.D thesis, supervised by Dr Robin Cormack and examined by Prof. Cyril Mango, both of whom are thanked for their very valuable advice and guidance; so too is Dr Robert Hillenbrand, who first pointed the way to Cappadocia.

Field work in Turkey was much facilitated by the kindness of Mr Gürbüz Ova, Director of the Ürgüp Museum, who gave a great deal of help in locating and gaining access to monuments, and by the people of the Cappadocian villages, whose hospitality so often mitigated the arduousness of long days in the sun.

I am particularly grateful to Charlotte Roueché, who gave considerable help with the Greek inscriptions in the monuments, and to other friends and colleagues who were generous with advice and assistance of various sorts: Clarissa Barton-Sayarer, Mary Cheney, John Haldon, Judith Herrin, John Higgitt, Jana Howlett, Ann Johnston, Stavros Mihalarias, Rosemary Morris, Valerie Nunn, Yıldız Ötüken, Andrew Palmer, Jonathan Shepard, John Smedley, Mary and Bernard Whiting, Stuart Spencer, Lesley and Altuğ Tahtakılıç, Helen Walker, John Wilkinson.

Finally, I wish to thank Nigel Rodley for giving up several summer vacations to act as photographer and field assistant, and for providing all the supportive services traditionally offered by long-suffering spouses.

ABBREVIATIONS

Budde, *Göreme*   L. Budde, *Göreme. Höhlenkirchen in Kappadokien* (Dusseldorf, 1958)

Epstein, 'Fresco Decoration'   A. W. Epstein, 'The Fresco Decoration of the Column Churches, Göreme
                                       Valley, Cappadocia', *CahArch* 29 (1980–1), 27–45

Epstein, 'Rock-cut Chapels'   A. W. Epstein, 'Rock-cut Chapels in Göreme Valley, Cappadocia: the
                                       Yılanlı Group and the Column Churches', *CahArch* 24 (1975), 115–35

Giovannini, *Arts of Cappadocia*   L. Giovannini, *Arts of Cappadocia* (Geneva, 1971)

Grégoire, 'Rapport'   H. Grégoire, 'Rapport sur un voyage d'exploration dans le Pont et en
                                       Cappadoce', *Bulletin de Correspondance Hellénique* 33 (1909), 1–169

Hild & Restle, *TIB* II   F. Hild and M. Restle, *Tabula Imperii Byzantini*, II: *Kappadokien*
                                       (Vienna, 1981)

Jerphanion, *Eglises*   G. de Jerphanion, *Une nouvelle province de l'art byzantin. Les églises
                                       rupestres de Cappadoce* (Paris, 1925–42)

Kostof, *Caves of God*   S. Kostof, *Caves of God. The Monastic Environment of Byzantine
                                       Cappadocia* (Cambridge, Mass./London, 1972)

Ramsay & Bell, *1001 Churches*   W. M. Ramsay and G. L. Bell, *The Thousand and One Churches* (London,
                                       1909)

Restle, *Studien*   M. Restle, *Studien zur frühbyzantinischen Architektur Kappadokiens*
                                       (Vienna, 1979)

Restle, *Wall Painting*   M. Restle, *Byzantine Wall Painting in Asia Minor*, trans. I. R. Gibbons
                                       (Shannon, 1969); first published as *Die byzantinische Wandmalerei in
                                       Kleinasien* (Recklinghausen, 1967)

Rott, *Denkmäler*   H. Rott, *Kleinasiastische Denkmäler aus Pisidien, Pamphylien,
                                       Kappadokien und Lykien* (Leipzig, 1908)

Strzygowski, *Kleinasien*   J. Strzygowski, *Kleinasien, ein Neuland der Kunstgeschichte.
                                       Kirchenaufnahmen von J. W. Crowfoot und I. I. Smirnov* (Leipzig, 1903)

Thierry, *Nouvelles églises*   N. and M. Thierry, *Nouvelles églises rupestres de Cappadoce. Région du
                                       Hasan Dağı* (Paris, 1963)

Dumbarton Oaks standard abbreviations are used, as follows:

AA   *Archäologischer Anzeiger*

ActaSS   *Acta Sanctorum Bollandiana*

AnalBoll	*Analecta Bollandiana*
AnatSt	*Anatolian Studies*
BAntFr	*Bulletin de la Société nationale des Antiquaires de France*
BCH	*Bulletin de Correspondance Hellénique*
BIABulg	*Bulletin de l'Institut Archéologique Bulgare*
BZ	*Byzantinische Zeitschrift*
CahArch	*Cahiers Archéologiques*
CahCM	*Cahiers de Civilisation Médiévale, Xe-XIIe siècles*
CMH	*Cambridge Medieval History*
CorsiRav	*Corsi di Cultura sull'Arte Ravennate e Bizantina*
CRAI	*Comptes-rendus des séances de l'Académie des Inscriptions et Belles-Lettres*
DOP	*Dumbarton Oaks Papers*
GRBS	*Greek, Roman, and Byzantine Studies*
IstMitt	*Istanbuler Mitteilungen*
JBAA	*Journal of the British Archaeological Association*
JÖB	*Jahrbuch der Österreichischen Byzantinistik*
JSav	*Journal des Savants*
JWarb	*Journal of the Warburg and Courtauld Institutes*
Mansi	J.D. Mansi, *Sacrorum Conciliorum nova et amplissima collectio*
MélUSJ	*Mélanges de l'Université Saint-Joseph, Beyrouth*
MonPiot	*Monuments et Mémoires*, publiés par l'Académie des Inscriptions et Belles-Lettres, Fondation E. Piot
OCP	*Orientalia Christiana Periodica*
PEFQ	*Palestine Exploration Fund, Quarterly Statement*
PG	Patrologiae cursus completus, Series Graeca, ed. J.-P. Migne
RA	*Revue Archéologique*
REArm	*Revue des Etudes Arméniennes*
REB	*Revue des Etudes Byzantines*
RQ	*Römische Quartalschrift für christliche Altertumskunde und [für] Kirchengeschichte*
Synaxarium CP	*Synaxarium Ecclesiae Constantinopolitanae. Propylaeum ad ActaSS Novembris*, ed. H. Delehaye (Brussels, 1902)
TM	*Travaux et Mémoires*
TürkArkDerg	*Türk Arkeoloji Dergisi*

KEY TO PLANS

It was necessary to invent a system of drawing conventions to deal with the peculiarities of rock-cut architecture; its principles are as follows:

Thick lines represent ground level; thin lines show features above ground level; thick broken lines indicate cavities at a level different from that of the main structure; thin broken lines show features no longer visible (because they are now lost or inaccessible) but which have been recorded by others; freehand lines show very crudely cut surfaces; dotted lines indicate curves, thus:

⋮⋮ = arch   ⋰⋱ = dome   ⊃ = conch   ▭ = barrel vault

Examples

A room with a flat ceiling above a cornice; a flat-backed, arched niche opens at ground level opposite the entrance, which is rectangular and opens from a façade with arched niches rising from ground level.

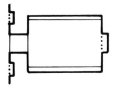

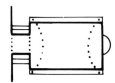

A barrel-vaulted room; ledges rise from ground level along the long walls; an apsidal niche opens above ground level opposite the entrance, which is arched and opens from a plain façade; windows flank the entrance.

A room with pilasters on one long wall, corbels on the other, linked by transverse arches. (Where a room has wall arches and/or transverse arches, implying the existence of a barrel vault, the dotted arcs normally used to show a barrel vault are omitted.)

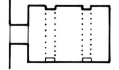

Modifications

A thin line crossed by an arrow shows a ground-level feature which precedes an overall rise in ground level, in the direction of the arrow:

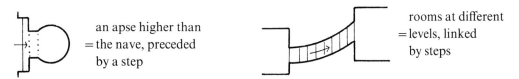

= an apse higher than the nave, preceded by a step

= rooms at different levels, linked by steps

Thin line is also used for the following:

⊗⊗⊗⊗ = masonry   ————⊃⊂⊃⊂⊃⊂⊃⌐——— = an opening sealed
                                                    by masonry   ⊂⊃ = grave pit

Many rooms have their walls pitted with rough secondary cavities. These have been drawn in only where they distort the original lines of the structure.

With only limited field-work time available, several factors made it impossible to produce precisely measured plans: the irregularities of rock-cut architecture, the difficulty of establishing the thickness of rock between cavities and the impossibility, in many cases, of taking measurements at ground level, since floors were so often deep in rubble. The plans that follow are, therefore, roughly measured sketch plans. Room size was estimated using a line marked in metres, or occasionally by pacing. Unless emphatically not so, corners were treated as right-angles and the rock between rooms as being of uniform width.

Note on spelling of proper names

The thorny problem of the rendering of Greek names in English has been stated several times elsewhere and has not been solved in the present work. Lacking a more satisfactory system, proper names have been transliterated according to the standard Greek system, except in cases where the anglicized or latinized form is so familiar that its displacement by a transliterated Greek form might cause confusion or irritation.

1

The background

Introduction

The tenth-century historian Leo the Deacon records a journey to Cappadocia made by Nikephoros Phokas shortly before he became emperor. Perhaps to recapture the attention of readers beginning to tire of troop movements he also offers a scrap of information about a curiosity of the region to which the emperor was heading: its inhabitants were once called troglodytes, because 'they went underground in holes, clefts and labyrinths, as it were in dens and burrows'.[1] This brief note was probably not based on first-hand knowledge but it might have been prompted by an awareness of the vast number of rock-cut cavities in an area to the west and southwest of Kaisareia (Kayseri of modern Turkey). Had Leo been more inclined to garrulous digression (or perhaps just better informed), he might have supplied more details of the troglodyte region and the task of bringing scholarly order to the hundreds of rock-cut monuments and other cavities in the area might have been much simpler.

As it is, our earliest description of the monuments comes long after the extinction of the Byzantine empire, in the early eighteenth-century accounts of the travels of Paul Lucas, who was sent by the French court to survey the lands around the Mediterranean. Lucas, straying slightly from the caravan with which he was travelling across Asia Minor, saw near the Halys river (Kızılırmak) a large number of 'pyramidical houses' with windows and entrances and paintings inside. Perceiving also what he took to be sculpted busts of hooded monks on the pinnacles of some pyramids and of the Virgin and Child on others, he thought at first that the curious houses might be the ancient dwellings of Christian hermits. He revised his opinion, however, on noticing that pagan subjects were also represented among the statues – some of them

indecent. Lucas had no opportunity to explore further, for he was called back to the caravan. There his travelling companions told him extraordinary tales: of a body cast out from a tomb but uncannily finding its own way back; of strange fires among the pyramids; of a monstrous beast whose peculiar laugh compelled those who heard it to follow, never to be seen again.[2]

In the nineteenth century, fable began to give way to fact as a series of European travellers brought back more accurate, if less entertaining, accounts of the region. Lucas' 'pyramidical houses' were recognized as natural cones of soft volcanic rock containing man-made cavities of various forms and functions, among them many churches; the 'sculpted busts' were the knobs of hard rock often found at the tops of such cones (cf. Frontispiece and Pls. 1 and 2). These brief travellers' tales led the way for the work of scholars such as Hans Rott and Henri Grégoire, who published accounts of individual monuments and their inscriptions in the early years of this century. At this time the region was still inhabited by a mixed population of Turkish-speaking Moslems and Greek-speaking Christians. The latter group left for Greece in the early 1920s, during an exchange of population minorities that was part of the radical social re-ordering initiated by Kemal Atatürk; they were replaced by Turks from Greece, mostly from Thrace. In the two decades before this upheaval, however, members of the local Greek population acted as guides to Guillaume de Jerphanion, who made several visits to the volcanic valleys and wrote his meticulous descriptions of many painted Byzantine rock-cut churches (*Une nouvelle province de l'art byzantin. Les églises rupestres de Cappadoce* (Paris, 1925–42)). This remains the principal source of information on the area and its monuments, but has been supplemented by the work of later scholars: a number of churches in

---

1 Leonis Diaconi, *PG* 117, *Historiae*, III, col. 713.

2 P. Lucas, *Voyage du Sieur Paul Lucas ... dans la Grèce, l'Asie Mineure, la Macédoine et l'Afrique ...* (Paris, 1712), I, 159–64.

Peristrema valley, not seen by Jerphanion, were published by N. and M. Thierry, *Nouvelles églises rupestres de Cappadoce. Région du Hasan Dağı* (Paris, 1963), and a survey largely concerned with technical data has been provided by M. Restle in *Die byzantinische Wandmalerei in Kleinasien* (Recklinghausen, 1967).[3] Accounts of further newly discovered churches have appeared in various journals since the 1950s; they are included in the bibliography at the end of this volume.

The extensive and often well-preserved wall-paintings of the Cappadocian cave churches have particular importance for the study of Byzantine art history because very little painting survives elsewhere in Anatolia. This, then, is the aspect of the cave churches to which the scholars mentioned above have directed most of their attention. The present text was generated by the opinion that little further progress can be made in either art-historical or historical study of the Cappadocian cave monuments without an attempt to elucidate the context of the cave churches, painted or otherwise. A step in this direction was taken by S. Kostof, in *Caves of God. The Monastic Environment of Byzantine Cappadocia* (Cambridge, Mass./London, 1972), in which an attempt was made to interpret the cave church material in the light of the principles of monastic life propounded by St Basil. This study was limited, however, by dependence for material evidence upon the authors cited above, whose main concern was, as noted, the wall paintings rather than the monuments as a whole.

It seems time, therefore, to take a wider view. In addition to the decorated cave churches there are a number of cave complexes which have received scant attention because their rooms contain little (or, more usually, no) wall painting. Further, there are several painted churches which have been recognized as belonging to hermitages, but while their paintings have been studied, their monastic context has been treated only superficially. The aim of the present text is therefore twofold: first to introduce detailed descriptions of the cave complexes, most of which are monasteries, and to assess their chronology and functions, and second to re-examine those cave churches which seem to have been associated with hermitages, giving attention to the sites as a whole rather than just to the paintings.

A problem encountered by students of Byzantine monasticism in Anatolia, particularly those concerned with material rather than spiritual culture, is that monasteries are known largely from documentary evidence, since very little, if anything, remains on the ground. Further, the documents seldom give bricks-and-mortar details of the lost structures. In Cappadocia this position is reversed. The architecture survives, but documents do not. Assessment of the size of population, the functions of monastery rooms and the motives of the founders must be approached from consideration of the material remains. The overall aim here, therefore, is to assemble the evidence for the whole range of monastic foundations in the volcanic valley region, with a view to defining the nature of the monastic presence.

Geography and history

The main concentrations of Byzantine cave monuments are in the region to the northwest and southeast of Ürgüp, and in a chasm known as the Peristrema valley, to the southeast of Aksaray, but scattered rock-cut monuments are also found at other sites (see p. 10). Those considered in this volume are within the boundaries of a rough triangle defined by the cities of Aksaray (Koloneia), Kayseri (Kaisareia) and Niğde (Nakida).[4]

The profusion of rock-cut architecture is made possible by the nature of the rock. In the recent geological past the volcano Erciyes Dağı (Mount Argaeus), some 20 km to the south of Kaisareia, laid down quantities of volcanic rock of various degrees of hardness. Over the centuries wind and rain have worn down the softer rock to leave a spectacular landscape, formed of hundreds of interlacing valleys lined by undulating and pinnacled rock (Pl. 1). Erosion has also produced the most conspicuous features of the landscape: tall, conical rock masses which occur both in close-packed groups and in loose clusters (Pl. 2). The soft rock occurs in a variety of pastel colours: white, cream, grey and pink, which adds to the unearthly appearance of the region.

At first sight, the land appears arid. The poor soil, made of the fine sand produced by the eroding rock, has little organic content and supports only sparse scrub and very few trees. There is, however, abundant water running in underground streams, breaking to the surface as springs in many of the valleys. Much of this water is produced when the heavy winter snows melt and, until the sun dries them in the summer, shallow streams run in many valley bottoms. Nevertheless, this is not an area propitious for agriculture: the lack of organic matter in the soil and the unevenness of the terrain limit agricultural activity to small orchards and vegetable patches in clearings among the cones.

At the beginning of the Byzantine period, Cappadocia

---

3 Translated into English by I. R. Gibbons and republished as *Byzantine Wall Painting in Asia Minor* (Shannon, Ireland, 1969).

4 Giovannini, *Arts of Cappadocia*, 48–9 (key 195–7) for a general map showing the locations of cave monuments, and 198–205 for detailed local maps.

1. Volcanic valley area: Güllü Dere.

2. Göreme valley: cones.

was embedded within the empire, and the main land routes between Constantinople and the east crossed it, converging on Kaisareia. Later, the Arab invasions, which began in the seventh century, caused the Byzantine frontier to retreat westwards across Asia Minor and left Cappadocia as an insecure and often embattled border zone until well into the ninth century. In the second half of the ninth century, however, there began a series of successful campaigns against the Arabs which initiated the re-establishment of Byzantine power in eastern Anatolia, but the border was not stable, and territorial gains and losses continued to fluctuate during the second half of the ninth century. The security of the empire was also threatened by an internal problem, the rebellion of the Paulicians, an heretical sect. The capture of its centre, Tephrike, in 872 and the absorption of its members into Orthodoxy, left the way clear for pushing the frontier gradually eastwards. This was accomplished by the campaigns of Basil I and Romanos I, and by the first half of the tenth century the major military events (the capture of Melitene in 931 and 934, of Amida in 942, the siege of Edessa in 943) happened well to the east of Cappadocia. The eastern campaigns continued during the reign of Nikephoros Phokas (963–9) and his successor, John Tzimiskes, who in 975 took Byzantine armies as far as Kaisareia in Palestine. There were shifts of population as the ravaged eastern regions were resettled by Syrian Christians and large numbers of Armenians. The newly re-occupied parts of the east were held by Basil II, and for some time after his death in 1025, but in the second half of the eleventh century another serious threat to the eastern part of the empire was presented by the Seljuk Turks, moving westwards from Mesopotamia. Kaisareia was sacked in 1067, and the critical battle of Manzikert lost in 1071; by 1085 much of Cappadocia was under the control of the Sultanate of Konya. In broad terms, therefore, Byzantine Cappadocia enjoyed a period of relative stability from the late ninth century to the late eleventh, when it was fairly securely in Byzantine hands, flanked by two phases of invasion, raiding and occupation, first by the Arabs and then by the Turks.[5]

The conditions of life in Cappadocia changed radically over the centuries, in accordance with this history. The early Christian period was the time of greatest stability and prosperity, with the administration of the old Roman empire still largely intact. In the fourth century Cappado-

cia was the area of ministry of three of the Church Fathers: St Basil and his brother Gregory of Nyssa, both born in Kaisareia, and Gregory of Nazianzos, whose birthplace was not far from the Peristrema valley.[6] Material evidence of the early Christian centuries is very fragmentary, but there survive, albeit in ruins, fine masonry churches of the fifth and sixth centuries: at Andabilis (Eski Andaval) and Diokaisareia (Tilköy), for example, and at several sites near Hasan Dağı. Virtually nothing remains of the Christian buildings of Kaisareia, and modern urban development has eclipsed the fragment of a large basilica there that survived until 1965. Some of its marble capitals, re-used in the nearby Hatuniye Medrese, remain to show the fine quality of this early architecture.[7]

The old order was lost as Arab raids and occupation encroached from the east, and it was never recovered. The border areas were now administered as military districts, the *kleisourai* and themes.[8] By the ninth century Cappadocia, like the rest of the eastern empire, was dominated by a military aristocracy: a small number of powerful families holding great tracts of land from whence a significant part of the Byzantine army was raised.[9] The great landlords were a source of recurrent anxiety to the court of Constantinople, since an emperor might be made or broken according to his standing with them. Indeed Anatolian family names – Phokas, Maleinos, Botaniates, Skleros – often appear in accounts of rebellions and usurpations.[10]

A rare glimpse of the style of life of some of these eastern magnates comes from the legendary epic of Basil the Border Lord (Digenes Akrites), said to have astonished the tenth-century inhabitants of eastern Anatolia with his Herculean capacity for hunting and fighting. Between bouts, he lived by the Euphrates, in a palace of cut stone, decorated with gold mosaic and polished marble, and set in a garden ornamented by tame peacocks.[11] Legendary though the account is, this description probably reflects the domestic setting of the more opulent of the aristocratic families.

A good distance, however, separates the onyx floors of the palace on the Euphrates and the rock-cut architecture of the volcanic valleys. It is necessary to remember that the volcanic region occupies only a relatively small area and that information on Cappadocia available from historical sources is not necessarily all to be applied to

5 Hild & Restle, *TIB* II, 70–111.
6 W. K. Lowther Clarke, *St. Basil the Great. A Study in Monasticism* (Cambridge, 1913), 43–62.
7 Restle, *Studien*, 36–42, 30–3, 23–8, 44–5.
8 J. Ferluga, 'Le clisure bizantine in Asia Minore', *Byzantium and the Balkans* (Amsterdam, 1976), 71–85, 82.

9 S. Vryonis, *The Decline of Medieval Hellenism in Asia Minor and the Process of Islamization from the Eleventh through the Fifteenth Century* (Berkeley/Los Angeles/London, 1971), 24–5, 72.
10 G. Ostrogorsky, *History of the Byzantine State* (2nd English edn., Oxford, 1968), 284–5, 306, 348, 299.
11 J. Mavrogordato, *Digenes Akrites* (Oxford, 1956), 218–20.

this small part of it. Members of one of the great aristocratic families, the Phokades, commissioned a cave church whose paintings include a portrait of the tenth-century emperor Nikephoros Phokas and his immediate family, but this is an isolated example.[12] Most of the names recorded in inscriptions in the cave churches are not those of the aristocracy and usually cannot be matched at all with historically documented figures.

The volcanic valley area was probably always sparsely populated, its people sustained by subsistence farming. There are neither material remains nor historical records of large centres there. Documentary information referring specifically to the region is very slight. The few medieval place names in the region that can be established are known only from scant references: one Elpidios, *Memorophylax* of Prokopios, who attended the Council of Chalcedon (451), may have come from Hagios Prokopios (now Ürgüp, but still called 'Prokopion' by the local Greek population in the early years of this century);[13] a tenth-century episcopal *notitia* (record of bishoprics) lists Hagios Prokopios, Sobesos (formerly Suveş, now Şahinefendi) and Dasmendron (now Ovacık, near Niğde); a later one includes Matiana (known until recently as Maçan, then as Avcılar).[14] Matiana is also mentioned briefly in the Acts of the early Christian martyr St Hieron, as is Korama (Göreme).[15]

Documents referring directly to the cave churches or monasteries are entirely lacking. There are no *typika* (foundation charters), inventories, letters or other material that can be associated with a Cappadocian cave monument. A group of manuscripts attributed to a 'Cappadocian school' cannot be linked with any institution and most of its members may well not even be Cappadocian.[16]

The military and trade routes linking Constantinople with the east converged on Kaisareia, about 60 km northeast of the volcanic valley area. Of the two roads

linking the *aplekta* (army gathering points) of Koloneia and Kaisareia, one rose to Zoropassos and then followed the Halys river (Kızılırmak) past Venasa (Avanos), thus running north of the main concentrations of cave monuments, and the other ran south, through Nazianzos, Malakopea and Kyzistra.[17] The volcanic valley region was therefore close enough to the important centres of western Cappadocia to have been known to travellers as a geographical curiosity, but far enough to demand a special expedition of some difficulty. Travelling with pack animals from Kaisareia to Hagios Prokopios (Ürgüp) might have taken more than a week, and the difficult paths among the cones to village and church sites still longer.

Rock-cut architecture

From some vantage points the volcanic valley landscape appears desolate: cones, ridges and chasms stretch into the distance showing little sign of human occupation, nor of vegetation. Elsewhere there are small patches of cultivated land and scattered cavities; elsewhere still, large rock masses are hollowed out to form labyrinths of interconnecting rooms. Cave churches and monasteries are also unevenly distributed: densely grouped in some areas, scattered in others.

It is necessary at the outset, therefore, to impose a rough classification on this vast number of cavities. Many of them were (and a few still are) peasant dwellings, cut into the sides of cliffs, massed cones or large outcrops of rock. Far from indicating degradation of their inhabitants, these dwellings should be seen as the necessary result of the scarcity of timber and a natural response to the local geological conditions. Such dwellings are quite easily cut in the soft rock, cost only labour and are well insulated against both the fierce summer heat of Anatolia and its freezing winters. Dense clusters of cavi-

12 L. Rodley, 'The Pigeon House Church, Çavuşin', *JÖB* 33 (1983), 301–39.

13 E. Schwartz, *Acta conciliorum oecumenicorum* ... (Berlin, 1914), II.1.2, 114 line 32.

14 J. Darrouzès, *Notitiae Episcopatuum Ecclesiae Constantinopolitanae* (Paris, 1981), 274 and 324. (But Rott, *Denkmäler*, 254, identifies Sobesos with Suvasa, 40 km west of Nevşehir.)

15 *ActaSS Novembris*, III, 329–39.

16 A group of seven Mss. is labelled 'Cappadocian' in K. Weitzmann, *Die byzantinische Buchmalerei des IX. und X. Jahrhunderts* (Berlin, 1935), 65–8. Five are of unknown provenance and are grouped together on the basis of the style of their (very simple) ornamental headpieces and initials. The anchors for the group are two Mss. in the British Library (London). One of these is BL Add. Ms. 39598 (a gospel lectionary), which has a colophon referring to a Metropolitan of Kaisareia. This Ms. was bought by Robert Curzon from the monks of St Saba, so the Kaisareia in question is almost certainly Kaisareia in Palestine. The other is BL Add. Ms. 39602 (Acts of

the Apostles, etc.), made for Stephanos, bishop of Kiskisos, a bishopric of the Metropolitanate of Kaisareia in Anatolia. Thus, only one of the group is definitely linked to Cappadocia (and still not certainly of Cappadocian provenance: Bishop Stephanos could have had his Ms. made elsewhere). In any case, since Kiskisos is to the south of Kaisareia, well away from the volcanic valley areas, even this sole survivor of the 'Cappadocian group' cannot be associated with the cave monasteries. A thirteenth-century Gospel book in Athens (Bibl. Genn. Ms. 1.5) has a colophon which places it in Kaisareia, the work of the scribe Basileios of Melitene: *Collection Hélène Stathatos.* 11: *Les objets byzantins et postbyzantins* (Limoges, 1957), 79; E. Zomarides, 'Eine neue griechische Hs. aus Caesarea vom J.1226 mit armenischer Beischrift' in *Studien zur Paleographie und Papyruskunde*, ed. C. Wessely, (Leipzig, 1902) II, 21–4.

17 F. Hild, *Das byzantinische Strassensystem in Kappadokien* (Vienna, 1977), 66–8; G. Huxley, 'A List of *Aplekta*', *GRBS* 16 (1975), 87–93, at 88–9.

ties form rock-cut villages, occurring usually in sites where large rock masses suitable for excavation are found together with access to reliable spring water; such is the case in, for example Ürgüp, Ortahisar, Üçhisar, Zelve and Çavuşin. Roughly rectangular, flat-ceilinged rooms usually occupy several levels in the rock mass. The levels are linked by terraced pathways, ramps and steps and by passages inside the rock. These passages occasionally contain, near their entrances, 'millstone' closing devices: each of these consists of a rock disc, resting on its edge, lodged in a narrow wall recess; the disc may be rolled forward to block the passage. The large number of rooms that honeycombs these village sites suggests that a sizeable population once inhabited this land, but the impression is misleading. The density must be partly attributable to the rock-cut habit: built structures that fall into disuse usually also fall into disrepair and ruin and are eventually cleared away. A rock-cut cavity is likely to remain – it may be damaged by erosion, but this natural process is neither as swift nor as thorough as human action. Thus many of the village sites probably began with a small number of dwellings which, with time, were vacated as erosion rendered them (or their access paths) unstable; they would then be replaced by new cavities in safer areas nearby. Such seems to have been the case in Çavuşin, for example, where a cliff shelters three stages of occupation: first, the remnants of a rock-cut village in the cliff itself; next, at the foot of the cliff a second stage, created when the cliff became dangerous, consisting of rock-cut rooms with built fronts or extensions. These were abandoned in recent times as falling rock from the cliff became a menace and the modern village, of masonry houses, was established at a short distance from the cliff, beyond the range of falling boulders.

Many dense concentrations of cavities are not, and never were, for human habitation. These are the large pigeon houses, an important element in local agriculture. Until the advent of artificial fertilizers, it was (and to a large extent, still is) local practice to supplement the sparse organic content of the dusty soil with pigeon droppings. Pigeons are, it seems, quite content to roost gregariously in dark, cool cavities if supplied with perches and nesting niches. Often a cliff or mass of cones is riddled with rough rooms: by boring vertical chimneys upwards from the ceilings of cavities, starting at ground level,

further rooms can be created at successively higher levels with no need to tackle the rock-face from the outside. Occasionally, when erosion strips away the rock-face, the honeycomb of cavities is revealed in section. Also with an agricultural function are other rough rooms, scattered about the valleys near areas of cultivation. These serve to stable a donkey and shelter the farmer and his family while at work on the land.

The cavities mentioned so far are all at or above ground level. A further category is needed for the small number of 'underground cities' such as those in Derinkuyu and Kaymaklı on the Nevşehir–Niğde road.[18] These are subterranean labyrinths of very rough interconnecting caves, often on several levels, linked by ramps and steps. In places their passages may be closed off by 'millstone' devices like those described above. References by ancient writers to troglodytes in other areas have been rather casually applied to Cappadocia, and are probably responsible for the identification of these complexes as dwellings.[19] I have examined the underground complexes at Kaymaklı and Derinkuyu only briefly, but find it difficult to accept that they were ever permanent dwellings. The small, totally dark, rough rooms would surely have been most unpleasant to live in, and, although ventilated by occasional vertical shafts, would quickly have become stale if full of people. If these 'cities' were inhabited, it can only have been a matter of bleak necessity in time of strife. Records do exist of people, elsewhere in Anatolia and in recent times, taking to underground hiding places when threatened by raiders, and perhaps such an explanation is applicable here.[20] This was probably not, however, their primary function: some rooms in the 'cities' contain large sunken pots, designed for the storage of foodstuffs, and storage in general would seem a more likely function than habitation.[21] That such areas be used occasionally for refuge is plausible, but perhaps usually for livestock, rather than people. When troubled by raiders, people can conceal themselves – especially in an erratic landscape like that of volcanic Cappadocia – but sheep and goats (very possibly the chief interest of raiders) cannot be relied upon to act likewise. Underground labyrinths into which they could be herded for short periods, and kept in by the millstone devices, might have been the solution. The lack of graffiti (other than those produced by the recent tourist boom) in the 'cities' supports this: frightened

18 H. Gürçay and M. Akok, 'Yeraltı şehirlerinde bir inceleme ve Yeşilhisar ilçesinin Soğanlıdere köyünde bulunan kaya anıtları', *Türk Ark Derg* 14 (1965), 35–59; Giovannini, *Arts of Cappadocia*, 76–7.

19 Giovannini, *Arts of Cappadocia*, 77, applies Xenophon's description of a cave-dwelling community in Armenia to Cappadocia (Xenophon, *Anabasis*, IV,v,25 (Loeb Classical Library), with translation by C. L. Brownson (Cambridge, Mass.), 308–10).

20 R. M. Dawkins, *Modern Greek in Asia Minor* (Cambridge, 1916), 15–16.

21 The modern tourist is encouraged to visit the underground caverns near Ortahisar and elsewhere, where citrus fruit grown on the south coast is brought for storage, the even, cool temperature of the chambers provides natural refrigeration. Possibly this modern procedure evolved from an older habit of underground storage.

people confined in uncomfortable underground spaces would surely have scratched their prayers (or, if illiterate, signs and symbols) on the walls.

The category of cavities that has most importance for Byzantine history and has been the main object of investigation is that of the cave churches. These are, like the village settlements, cut into the sides of cliffs or cone masses, or sometimes into solitary cones. Their interiors are finished to resemble built monuments of various architectural forms, complete with vaulting, columns, mouldings and other architectural details. The churches for which published descriptions exist are, for the most part, those with extensive painted decoration. There are many more, either with little polychrome painting or none at all, perhaps more than 600 in all.[22] As noted above, the distribution of cave churches is uneven. They occur scattered in some valleys, densely grouped in others, some are close to domestic settlements, others not. In addition to the churches, there is a much smaller number of monasteries which are the subject of the present work. Secular and ecclesiastical structures often overlap: the original disposition of Byzantine cave monuments is, in many sites, obscured by the presence of cavities excavated around them by the peasantry of the post-Byzantine centuries. Such distortion of many ecclesiastical sites has usually occurred because the monuments make fine pigeon houses. They are converted to this purpose simply by walling up the original entrances and windows, leaving only small pigeon-holes for the passage of the birds. Next, the area available for pigeons is enlarged by cutting extra cavities around the church or monastery, and many churches are thus surrounded by tiers of rough, flat-ceilinged rooms (easily mistaken, by the casual observer, for tiers of monastic cells).

Establishing a chronology for the rock-cut villages and their auxiliary agricultural structures is close to impossible, but a few tentative steps may be taken. Strabo, who describes troglodyte communities in Arabia and the Caucasus, does not mention any in Cappadocia. Further, he describes the lands around Mazaca (Kaisareia) as 'utterly barren and untilled, although they are level; but they are sandy and are rocky underneath. And, proceeding a little

further on, one comes to plains extending over many stadia that are volcanic and full of fire-pits.'[23] This is doubtless the source of one of the tales heard by Paul Lucas, but also suggests that the volcanic deposits around Erciyes Dağı were still not cool in classical antiquity.[24] Troglodyte communities probably did not therefore inhabit the area until more recent times. Strabo may, of course, be recycling an older tale, but Erciyes Dağı is only recently extinct and we should perhaps be wary of putting any of the volcanic valley caves into the remoteness of prehistory. At the other end of the time-scale, the large number of pigeon houses based on churches and monasteries must be placed in the post-Byzantine period, since it is unlikely that a Christian population would put even abandoned churches to this use. Between these two very tentative points lie at least a dozen centuries.

The troglodyte habit is often attributed to a need for places of refuge and concealment in troubled times, suggesting a chronology linked with either the Arab raids of the seventh to ninth centuries or the Turkish ones of the eleventh century. The habit itself does not, however, imply such a need. In fact, rock-cut villages often occupy conspicuous sites (the cliff of Çavuşin, or the towering masses of Ortahisar and Üçhisar, for example). Instead, as noted above, this mode of architecture should be seen as a logical response to the local conditions. The millstone closures, which appear formidably defensive to an eye accustomed to built architecture, must also be seen in this context: when timber is scarce and the soft rock easily worked, such a closing method for seldom-used storage cavities may be more efficient than a conventional door. The rock-cut villages cannot, therefore, be assigned with certainty to the periods of turmoil. There is certainly no question of concealment as far as the cave churches are concerned, since they are often located in prominent sites and many also have elaborate carved façades. Nor is there reason, therefore, for assigning the churches to periods of insecurity.[25]

Further, more reliable chronological indications are available for the cave churches, a few of which have dated or datable inscriptions.[26] Others may be dated by comparing the style and iconography of their decoration, and

---

22 My estimate of the number of churches, based on published lists and field observation, used to be 'around 300', but a recent count suggests that this number should be doubled: Y. Ötüken, *Kappadokya Bölgesi Bizans Mimarisi Araştırmaları* (Hacetteppe Universitesi, Ankara, 1981; Doçentlik Tezi). Dr Ötüken's catalogue (publication forthcoming) lists 703 Byzantine monuments in Cappadocia, not all of them cave monuments.

23 Strabo, *Geography*, XII.2.7 (Loeb Classical Library), translated by H. L. Jones (Cambridge, Mass., 1969); for troglodytes: XI.5.7, XVII.3.7.

24 *Catalogue of the Active Volcanoes of the World*, International Association of Volcanology (Rome, 1964), Pt 17, p. 4.

25 The opinion that the cave churches were the secret establishments of Christians during periods of persecution, occasionally encountered in nineteenth-century writing, is now very much out of date. It lingers, however, in popular literature, particularly guidebooks, to such an extent that it is perhaps worth noting that this is not the case.

26 The dated Cappadocian churches are listed and discussed in Jerphanion, *Eglises*, II, 389–95; see also J. Lafontaine-Dosogne, 'Nouvelles notes cappadociennes', *Byzantion* 33 (1963), 121–83, at 182–3, and R. S. Cormack, 'Byzantine Cappadocia. The Archaic Group of Wall Paintings', *JBAA* 30 (1967), 19–36.

sometimes the style of their architecture, with that of the monuments dated by inscription, or with that of datable work outside Cappadocia. The evidence thus derived suggests that a large number of cave churches may be placed in the Middle Byzantine period, particularly in the tenth and eleventh centuries. A small number of churches have been assigned to the early Christian, pre-Iconoclast and Iconoclast periods.[27] Most of the monuments concerned are small chapels with poor quality or rustic decoration, and none of them is firmly dated by inscription. While it is not intended here to deny the possibility that these attributions are correct, it must be said that the case is unproven. In addition to this 'rustic' group of churches, two large cave churches, St John the Baptist at Çavuşin and Durmuş Kilisesi in Avcılar, have also been assigned to early dates.[28] In both cases attribution to the pre-Iconoclast period depends largely upon the basilical form of the churches. Without further evidence, however, no firm conclusion may be reached and it is worthy of note that the cornices and mouldings in each church resemble those found in the basilical hall of Bezir Hane Monastery, for which an eleventh-century date is proposed below, based on the architecture and decoration of the monastery church. Three churches are dated to the thirteenth century by inscription.[29] These are, however, stylistically isolated from one another and from other Cappadocian painting, and probably represent only sporadic production of cave churches at this time.

The tentative chronology which may be established by using the dated monuments as anchors and grouping the other churches around them therefore suggests that the excavation and decoration of cave churches was sparse, at most, until the early tenth century and that the bulk of the monuments was produced between that time and the Turkish conquest of the late eleventh century. Thereafter, this activity seems to have declined and only a very

few cave churches were decorated. Thus, the majority of the cave monuments fall, as one might expect, into the period in which the area was reasonably securely under Byzantine control.

Whether or not the rock-cut villages are to be assigned to the same span is uncertain. It is possible that many of them belong, with the pigeon houses, to the post-Byzantine centuries. What is certain is that there is a very large number of churches in a rather sparsely populated area – too many to be accounted for as the places of worship of the populace. Observers of the riddled landscape, seeking to account for this, usually suggest that the volcanic valley area was the site of a monastic centre. Such an interpretation appears plausible when set against the example of early monasticism in Egypt where hermit monks in great numbers occupied cells in several semi-desert regions.[30] The context of early monasticism is also attractive given that the three Church Fathers mentioned above were Cappadocians and founders of monasticism. Indeed, it has been suggested that the excavation of cave churches in the volcanic valleys began under their influence.[31] There is, however, no evidence that this was so. While St Basil's monastic communities in Pontus and Kaisareia are known from documentary sources, there is no such evidence for establishments in the volcanic valley region. Further, the chronology proposed above for the churches strongly suggests a much later date for most of the rock-cut monuments.

The medieval Byzantine period also had monastic 'centres'. Some of these, like Mt Athos and Meteora, in Greece, function to the present day. Others, such as Mt Olympos in Bithynia and Latmos on the Carian coast, were abandoned as the empire crumbled. These perhaps offer a better parallel for the volcanic valley region.[32] However, in spite of centuries of abandonment, documentary records of these centres are preserved,

---

27 The case for pre-Iconoclast and Iconoclast decorations is put by N. Thierry in a series of articles: 'Eglise de Kızıl-Tchoukour: chapelle iconoclaste, chapelle de Joachim et d'Anne' (with M. Thierry), *MonPiot* 50 (1958), 105–46; 'Eglises rupestres de Cappadoce', *CorsiRav* 12 (1965), 579–602; 'Un décor pré-iconoclaste de Cappadoce: Açıkel Ağa Kilisesi', *CahArch* 18 (1968), 33–69; 'Peintures paléochrétiennes en Cappadoce: l'église No. 1 de Balkan dere', *Synthronon* (Paris, 1968), 53–9; 'Notes critiques à propos des peintures rupestres de Cappadoce', *REB* 26 (1968), 337–66; 'Les peintures murales de six églises du Haut Moyen Age en Cappadoce', *CRAI* (1970), 444–79; 'Art byzantin du Haut Moyen Age en Cappadoce: l'église No. 3 de Mavrucan', *JSav* (1972), 233–69; 'Iconographie et culte de la croix en Asie Mineure, en Transcaucasie et en Syrie et Mésopotamie byzantines', *Annuaire de l'E.P.H.E.* (1973–4), 209–12; 'Mentalité et formulation iconoclastes en Anatolie', *JSav* (1976), 81–119; 'L'église peinte de Nicétas Stylite et d'Eustrate Clisurarque, ou fils de Clisurarque, en Cappadoce', *Communications, 14e Congrès international des études byzantines, Bucharest 1971* (1976), 451–5.
28 N. Thierry, 'La basilique de S. Jean Baptiste de Çavuşin', *BAntFr*

(1972), 198–213, 212; *idem*, 'Quelques églises inédites en Cappadoce', *JSav* (1965), 626–35, 627–30.
29 These are: Karşı Kilise (1212), near Gülşehir (Jerphanion, *Eglises*, II, 1–16; Restle, *Wall Painting*, Cat. no. LI; Rott, *Denkmäler*, 243–5; J. Lafontaine-Dosogne, 'Nouvelles notes', 23–183); the Church of the Forty Martyrs of Sebaste (part of the programme dated 1216/17), Suveş (Jerphanion, *Eglises*, II, 156–74; Restle, *Wall Painting*, Cat. no. XLV) and St George (Kırk Dam Altı Kilise) (1283–95) in Peristrema valley (Thierry, *Nouvelles églises*, 201ff.; Restle, *Wall Painting*, Cat. no. LX).
30 N. Russell and B. Ward, *The Lives of the Desert Fathers* (London/Oxford, 1981), 50; M. Martin, 'Laures et ermitages du désert d'Egypte', *Mél US J* 42 (1966), 181–98, at 185ff.
31 H. F. Tozer, *Turkish Armenia and Eastern Asia Minor* (London, 1881), 145–7: Jerphanion, *Eglises*, II, 395.
32 F. W. Hasluck, *Athos and its Monasteries* (London, 1924); D. M. Nicol, *Meteora. The Rock Monasteries of Thessaly* (London, 1975); R. Janin, *Géographie ecclésiastique de l'Empire byzantin*. II: *Les églises et les monastères des grands centres byzantins* (Paris, 1975), 127–31, 216–20.

whereas none has survived from Cappadocia. Indeed, lack of documentary evidence, although a negative point, is significant: even given the poor survival rate of Byzantine archives, the absence of a single documentary reference to any monastery in the volcanic valley area definitely hinders its identification as an important centre, or one of long duration.

There is, then, something of a paradox. On the one hand documentary silence, on the other a very large number of cave monuments, some of them clearly identifiable as hermitages and monasteries, and far too many churches to be accounted for as the places of worship of a lay rural community. It is probably therefore acceptable as a generalization to attribute the bulk of the rock-cut monuments to a monastic presence, but its importance, duration and nature has yet to be established. As noted earlier, scholarship has so far concentrated on the style and iconography of the paintings which decorate many of the churches. This is an important pursuit, but unlikely to elucidate the broader social context of the monuments. For this the churches and other structures must be examined with a view to determining their function.

A first step towards clarification of the nature and chronology of monasticism in the area must be the examination of those cave structures identifiable as monastic. To date, publication and study of monasteries have been cursory, with attention given to their churches alone, and this only when they have paintings. The present study aims to provide detailed descriptions of the cave monasteries, together with an examination of dating evidence and assessment of their place in the history of the area.

Strictly speaking, the Greek *mone* (monastery) describes the dwelling of a monk or monks and so may be applied to anything from a single cell, accommodating a solitary, to a complex, housing a large community. A distinction has developed in English, however, wherein the term 'monastery' is generally reserved for larger establishments, while very small ones are called hermitages. Although imprecise, this distinction is used here. I have avoided the terms *coenobium* and *laura* when describing the cave monuments since these denote styles of monastic life, not simply the size of the foundation. An outline of the material culture of Byzantine monasticism is to be found in the final chapter.

The monasteries vary in size and detail, but fall into two general groups, albeit with some overlap between them. One type consists of a church and several rooms which are carefully carved to imitate built architecture, grouped in an orderly fashion, usually around a courtyard. For this reason I have called this the 'courtyard' type. In monasteries of the second type there is no formal arrangement of elements, but instead a loose grouping of church, refectory with rock-cut table and benches and a few randomly placed, roughly cut rooms; I have called this the 'refectory' type. A third group of monuments, which have no consistent architectural definition, supplies evidence of hermitages in the volcanic valley area. A group of monuments on a site known as Açık Saray (the Open Palace) is also described, after the courtyard monasteries which they resemble in many respects. I shall argue that these complexes are probably not monasteries, but justify their inclusion on the grounds that there is no detailed published description of them; since they have been called monasteries, and since some uncertainty as to their function remains, it is necessary to make the evidence available.

The descriptions that follow deal with each group in turn. They are as complete as limited field work could make them and are concluded in each case with a discussion of dating evidence. In cases where the description is long, the detailed account is followed by a short summary placed before the concluding discussion. These summaries, in conjunction with the appropriate plans and photographs, offer brief guides to the monuments for the reader not concerned with architectural detail. The monuments are not described in chronological order. As will be argued below, the hermitages, which come last in the series of descriptions, almost certainly pre-date the monasteries. The reason for this ordering is that I wish to present hitherto unpublished material before proceeding to a reconsideration of sites whose churches, at least, have been studied before. No great significance attaches to the order in which the monuments of a particular group are described. I have begun the section on courtyard monasteries with Hallaç Monastery since, of all the complexes, it seems to be most free from alteration or destruction and offers a view of the range of room-types found in these monuments.

The present text cannot be a complete record of rock-cut monastic architecture in the volcanic valleys of Cappadocia: other monuments doubtless exist, and it is hoped that this study will encourage the publication of newly discovered monasteries to complete the record.

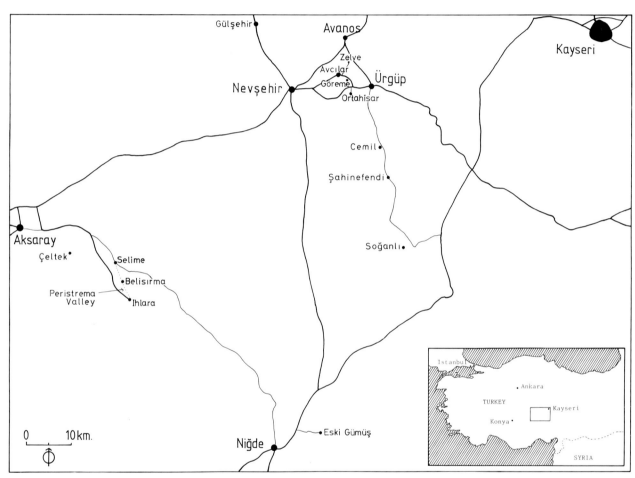

1. Map of volcanic valley area.

2

The courtyard monasteries

Introduction

In the complexes that I have called 'courtyard' monasteries, a church and several rooms, all carefully carved to imitate built architecture, are grouped in an orderly manner, usually around a courtyard. Often one large room runs the length of one side of the courtyard, forming a vestibule from which the other rooms are accessible. There is usually one room which is larger than the others – here called the hall – which opens either off the vestibule or directly off the courtyard. The terms 'vestibule' and 'hall' are used here for convenience and do not carry precise implications of function. It is not usually possible to know exactly what functions were served by the individual elements of a complex, except in the obvious cases of churches and kitchens. The issue of function will be considered in the final chapter.

The term 'courtyard monastery' is an imperfect one, since some of the monasteries in this group are without courtyards. I have used it nevertheless, in the absence of any other convenient term. 'Formally planned monasteries' would accurately describe all the monuments, but is too cumbersome. Further, most of the monasteries are in sites where natural rings or curves of cones could be cut back to form courtyards, whereas those which lack this feature are cut into sheer cliff faces. The absence of courtyards in these cases is probably, therefore, attributable to the limitations of their sites.

There are eleven courtyard monasteries, scattered over the volcanic valley region (Fig. 1). They are: Hallaç Monastery, near Ortahisar; Bezir Hane, in Avcılar (Matiana); Şahinefendi Monastery, near Şahinefendi (Sobesos); Soğanlı Han, in Soğanlı valley; Karanlık

Kilise Monastery, in Göreme valley; Aynalı Kilise Monastery, between Göreme and Ortahisar; Kılıçlar Monastery, between Avcılar and Göreme valley; Selime Kalesi, in Selime, to the north of Peristrema valley; Direkli Kilise Monastery, at the top of Peristrema valley, near Belisırma; Karanlık Kale, at the bottom of the valley, near İhlara; and Eski Gümüş Monastery, in Gümüşler, near Niğde.

Hallaç Monastery

The complex known as Hallaç Manastır is located a little more than 1 km north-northeast of the village of Ortahisar (Fig. 1).[1] It is cut into a large outcrop of rock visible from the road north of Ortahisar as a dark mass rising above the pink, cream and grey cones of softer rock in the valleys below the road (Pl. 3).

Courtyard and vestibule (Area 1) The core of the complex is a three-sided courtyard, entered from the open south side (Fig. 2 & Pl. 4). At some time after it ceased to function as a monastery the complex was made into a pigeon house. Entrances to rooms were blocked and the courtyard walls were re-cut to provide pigeon-holes as a means of access for the birds. The rock above the monastery is being eroded constantly and the silt thus formed has accumulated in the courtyard, raising its ground level so that the entrances to the rooms and church have only their tops visible. The ground level inside the complex is about 1.5 metres below that of the courtyard floor, so the silt must have accumulated after the entrances were blocked. It is retained within the court-

1 L. Rodley, 'Hallaç Manastır. A Cave Monastery in Byzantine Cappadocia', *XVI. Internationaler Byzantinistenkongress*, 1981. *Akten* 11/5, (*JÖB* 32/5) 425–34. Also mentioned briefly in N. Thierry, 'L'art monumental byzantin en Asie Mineure du XIe siècle au XIVe', *DOP* 29 (1975), 75–111, at 81, where it is also called Hasta-

hane. Photographs of the façade appear in Budde, *Göreme*, 28–31 and 33. The monastery is indicated on Plan 2, The Ürgüp Area, in Giovannini, *Arts of Cappadocia*, 198, where it is described simply as 'church, inscribed-cross plan' and numbered '4a'.

3. Hallaç Monastery: site.

4. Hallaç Monastery: northeast corner of courtyard.

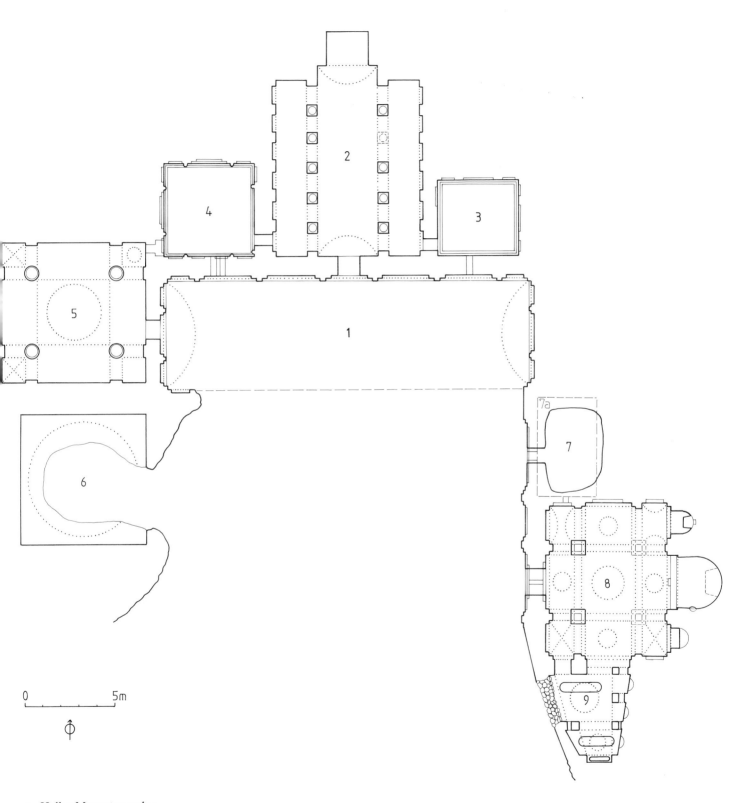

0   5m

2. Hallaç Monastery: plan.

yard area by a modern wall of rough masonry at the south side of the complex (see Pl. 3) and the courtyard is now used as a vegetable patch. The interior ground level is not much altered from its original state, for in all rooms containing columns or piers, the bases are still visible.

The courtyard now appears larger than it was when the monastery was first hewn, for the area at its north end (marked 1 on the plan) was originally a long rectangular barrel-vaulted room, of which the vault and south wall have collapsed (Fig. 2 & Pls. 4 & 5). This room formed an ante-room or vestibule, giving access to several other rooms of the complex. The depth of the room is defined by its east and west sides, which now form the northern extremities of the west and east walls of the present courtyard; several fragments of the springing of the barrel vault of the room are still visible on the north wall. Remains of the lower part of the south wall (its northern edge is indicated on the plan by a broken line) may exist below the accumulation of silt in the courtyard.

The north wall, which now forms a north façade to the courtyard, was decorated with blind niches and pilasters, now considerably damaged by the cutting of deep rectangular recesses housing pigeon-holes. The original decoration consisted of five wide horseshoe-arched blind niches separated by pilasters (Fig. 3). The central niche of the five contains the entrance to Room 2, and the

niched decoration is best seen in the bay to the right of this (Pl. 5). The five bays described are flanked by two smaller bays, which form the eastern and western extremities of the room. The east wall is decorated with two small niches flanking a large niche and separated from it by pilasters. Above the niches a cornice underlines the lunette, which bears the remnant of a relief cross. The north wall of this bay has a small horseshoe-arched niche (its arch springs from the same pilaster capital as the adjacent large niche arch of the north wall), with a gable moulding above it and a cornice above that; probably a cornice at this level ran the length of the room, above the large niches. At the west end the arrangement is similar but not identical: the lunette, outlined by a square-section moulding, is decorated with an equal-armed relief cross. Below this, on the west wall, a large central niche, which frames the entrance to Room 5, is flanked by a slightly smaller niche on the left and on the right a two-tier arrangement with a small, keyhole-shaped niche above a cornice with gable recess below. This last combination of motifs (niche with gable recess below) is also found on the north wall of this bay. The south wall, opposite, has a similar formula, with two small horseshoe-arched blind niches arranged vertically. This is the only remaining part of the south wall of Room 1.

The possibility should be noted that the east and west

5. Hallaç Monastery: Area 1 (vestibule), view north.

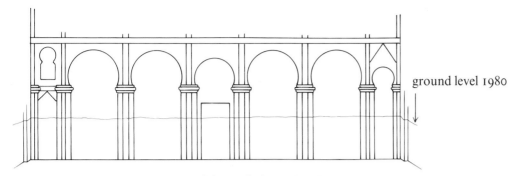

ground level 1980

3. Hallaç Monastery: reconstruction of the vestibule north wall.

bays just described were recesses in the courtyard façades, rather than the ends of a room. However, the traces of a barrel vault springing above the five-bay decoration of the north wall imply reconstruction of this area as a room. The blank area before the start of the east façade proper, which is wide enough to have accommodated a south wall, also argues for this. There is, moreover, a fragment of the northeast corner of the original north façade remaining in this area, above ground level. Possibly the south wall was pierced by several openings to admit light to the rest of the complex, making the vestibule virtually open-fronted. The pigeon-house phase noted above must have occurred after the fall of the vestibule, since the pigeon-holes have been cut into its north wall. Probably, therefore, the conversion took place long after the abandonment of the monastery.

Nothing remains of the wall surface at the west side of the courtyard, an area which has been badly eroded. On the eastern side of the courtyard, however, a decorated façade runs from the east wall of the vestibule to the tapering end of the rock face (Pl. 4). Once again, secondary cutting of the pigeon-house phase has partly obscured the original scheme. This consists of, from north to south: a pilaster (the lower part of it cut away); a rectangular recess enclosing a gabled recess, which houses the rectangular entrance to Room 7 (there is a square window above the point of the gable, flanked by groups of three keyhole-shaped blind niches, and above this register a cornice decorated with modillions); next, a pilaster the same height as the first, then a rectangular panel containing a decorated relief cross in a rectangular recess below a blind arcade of three keyhole niches; then another pilaster, shorter than the first two, followed by a further rectangular recess enclosing a gabled recess. This in turn encloses an arched niche housing the entrance to the church and a small keyhole-shaped window, now blocked. Once again, a blind arcade of keyhole-shaped niches and a modillion cornice surmount the rectangular recess. The façade decoration ends with another pilaster.

To the right of the façade is a short spur of undecorated rock, containing a short tunnel at its southern extremity. The tunnel is certainly secondary, since its floor is at the present ground level; it must have been cut after the courtyard was turned into a vegetable patch.

When I visited the site in 1982 I found that a deep hole had been dug in the west end of the vestibule floor, down to what appeared to be a rough cavity of uncertain extent. Possibly this is part of an underground storage area or perhaps a cistern.

Room 2 – the hall A large hall, Room 2, is reached through a rectangular entrance in the centre bay of the north wall of Room 1. This room has a form similar to that of a basilical church, but this is not its function: it has no apses, no liturgical furniture and is on a north/south axis. An arcade of six arches carried on five columns and two attached piers each side divides the hall into three aisles (on the east side the second column from the north end is largely gone) (Pl. 6). The columns stand on square bases and carry very simple slab capitals, decorated with carved and painted geometric patterns. The central aisle is barrel-vaulted, with the vault springing from a flat cornice which runs along the walls above the arcade and across the south wall. The narrow side aisles have flat ceilings. The long walls are decorated with shallow blind niches, six on each wall. The north end of the central aisle projects beyond the side aisles and is further extended by a rectangular recess with a barrel vault. This springs from a simple cornice decorated with triangular patterns cut in relief and picked out with red paint. The arch of the recess is outlined by a rim of simple hatched ornament and the back wall of the recess has a similar decoration of triangles.

Room 3 To the east of Room 2 is a small square room, Room 3, reached through a rectangular opening in the south end of the east wall of Room 2. The north wall is decorated with three blind niches – a large niche flanked

6. Hallaç Monastery: Room 2, view northwest.

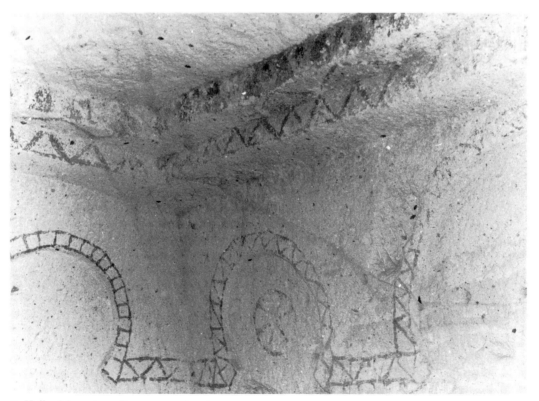

7. Hallaç Monastery: Room 3, northeast corner.

are cut to increase the space available for the pigeons, and this must be the case here.

Room 4 Room 4 is reached through the south end of the west wall of Room 2. It is a small square room with a flat ceiling and a rather elaborate decoration of very shallow blind horseshoe-arched niches and applied columns (Pls. 8 & 9). On the north wall (Pl. 8) the decoration consists of one large blind niche set in a rectangular recess, flanked by applied columns with block capitals and bases and then by two smaller blind niches. The central niche encloses a relief medallion containing a cross. The west wall is very similar, except that the small blind niche to the left, about 1 metre above floor level, frames a 'window' into Room 5 (Pl. 9). The east and south walls have a slightly different arrangement of ornament, since they accommodate the entrance to Room 2 and windows into Room 1 respectively. Reading from left to right, the east wall has a single niche, an applied column, then an area of wall which is plain except for a frieze at its top (made up of five compartments separated by relief uprights of double roll section), then another applied column close to the corner of the room (Pl. 8). The entrance to Room 2 is at the right end of this wall. The south wall has, from left to right: a blind niche, an applied column, two small blind niches with a two-light window above them, an applied column and a full-sized niche (Pl. 9). Above the applied column a two-stepped cornice meets the flat ceiling.

The capitals of the applied columns are decorated with simple geometric ornament in relief. Details of carved ornament are picked out in red paint and bands of simple geometric decoration – triangles and hatching – rim arches, recesses and cornices. The window to Room 1 is a double light with a central colonnette, and is now partly blocked. The window is visible on the north wall of Room 1 at the level of the cornice linking the arches of that wall. The pigeon-holes above and to the right of it do not, therefore, lead into Room 4, but into a cavity above the room, certainly a secondary development, as was suggested for the cavity above Room 3.

Room 5 A simple rectangular entrance in the west wall of Room 1 opens into a room of inscribed-cross plan, with a large dome carried on four thick columns with simple tapering block capitals (Pl. 10). Three of these are without ornament but the southwest capital has wedge-like projections at each corner. About 75 cm above each capital, about level with the tops of arches which spring from the walls to the columns, is a section of two-stepped cornice, forming a corner-bracket at the springing of the barrel vaults of the cross-arms. Small arches spring between the

8. Hallaç Monastery: Room 4, northeast corner.

by two smaller ones (Pl. 7). The niches are outlined in red paint and a painted border of chequer and zig-zag patterns runs around the arch of each niche and links the arches across the wall; the back wall of each niche is decorated with a medallion containing an equal-armed cross drawn in red paint, placed in the curve of the niche. The east wall has the same three-niche decoration, without the medallions. The west wall has a single blind niche at the right; its painted border extends to meet the painted borders of the north wall to the right and the entrance to Room 2 to the left. The ceiling is flat, met by a two-stepped cornice decorated with painted triangle ornament. This room is very dark at present, but probably once had a window to Room 1 – an opening in the south wall has been blocked.

The ceiling of this room is at about the level of the tops of the niches decorating the north wall of Room 1 (see Pl. 5). The pigeon-holes visible above this level do not, therefore, light Room 3, but must lead into a cavity above it. It is commonly the case, when a church or monastery is adapted for use as a pigeon house, that extra rooms

9. Hallaç Monastery: Room 4, southwest corner.

10. Hallaç Monastery: Room 5, northeast corner.

11. Hallaç Monastery: Room 5, detail of vault.

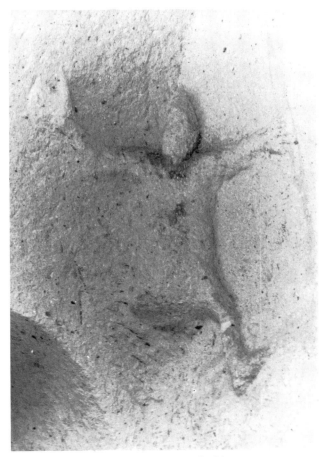

11a. Hallaç Monastery: Room 5, detail of figure.

columns and the walls, meeting shallow pilasters and rudimentary pilaster capitals which frame tiny corner bays. Northwest and southwest corner bays have cross vaults, the northeast bay has a small calotte and the southeast bay a flat ceiling. The columns have simple round bases. The dome is wide and quite shallow, its rim slightly above the level of the barrel-vaulted cross-arms which carry it; no attempt to reproduce pendentives has been made, but flat triangular spaces have been left between barrel vaults and dome (Pl. 11). The upper part of the dome has collapsed, leaving the room open to the sky. Very little painted decoration has survived the consequent weathering: there is some masonry pattern in the barrel vaults and a hatched and scalloped border around the rim of the dome.

In the northeast corner of the eastern arm of the cross is the only piece of human figure sculpture I have found in the Cappadocian cave monuments. This is a small figure, about 1.5 metres high, which seems to leap across the corner with arms outstretched (Pls. 10, 11 & 11a). The figure wears a short tunic of some sort and a pointed hat

or helmet. (The line that meets the figure's left hand is not, as may appear from the photograph, a spear, but is a discolouration of the wall caused by seepage of water down a crack.) Next to the figure is a small rectangular window through to Room 1; this is almost certainly secondary, since it cuts through the carved ornament on the west wall of Room 1, and lacks any moulding or other architectural detail. Another opening, the rectangular 'window' noted above, opens about 0.5 metres above the ground level, and links the northeast corner bay of Room 5 with Room 4. This may also be secondary, since it cuts into the pilaster to the right of it. Both 'windows' probably belong to the pigeon-house phase of the site.

Kitchen (6) To the south of Room 5 is a square room, slightly smaller than Room 5 and now largely lost to the weather because its vault has fallen. There remain parts of a wide, fairly steep dome rising above a deep overhang. Rooms of this type are found in other complexes (see below: Eski Gümüş, Selime Kalesi, Karanlık Kale and Açık Saray Nos. 2, 2a, 3 and 6), where their better state of preservation permits their identification as kitchens. This is doubtless the case here – a smoke hole would have been present at the summit of the dome.

Rooms 7 and 7a The first panel of the east façade to the south of Room 1 contains a rectangular opening of which only the top few centimetres are visible above the present ground level of the courtyard (Pl. 4). This opening leads into the room marked (7) on the plan. On inspection, the opening was found to be too small to enter, but enough of the interior could be seen from the outside to establish that this is a roughly cut room with low flat ceiling and no ornament. The delineation of this room on the plan, in broken thick line, is a very rough approximation of its form. The rectangular window visible on the façade above the gabled recess does not open into this room, but into a space above it. This is also inaccessible but is apparently another rough cavity (7a); its probable form is indicated on the plan by a thin broken line. To the right and above the window is a set of pigeon-holes opening into cavity (7a), which is also accessible by means of a crude secondary opening in the north wall of the church (see below).

It is possible that both (7) and (7a) are secondary cavities, but since the façade panel housing the window and entrance to (7) resembles the panel containing the church entrance, and since the window is outlined by a carved recess, it is also possible that the lower cavity (7) is evidence of an intention to cut another monastery room here, an intention which was never carried out to completion. The upper cavity (7a), accessible only via pigeon-

12. Hallaç Monastery: Church, northwest view of vaulting.

13. Hallaç Monastery: Church, southwest view of vaulting.

holes in the façade and the rough cavity in the church wall, must certainly belong to the pigeon-house phase.

Church (8) As noted above, the final large panel of the east façade contains the entrance to the church (Pl. 4). This is a rectangular opening with slightly gabled top. The church (8) is of inscribed-cross plan, with elaborate vaulting (Pl. 12). The crossing supports are in two stages: the central dome is carried on minor piers with simple two-step slab capitals; these in turn are carried on only slightly thicker main piers, only two of which survive complete. Arches spring between the minor piers, framing the vaulting of the centre bay. The southwest pier is decorated with a pilaster on each face and its capital is a rectangular block, decorated on each face with two stylized horned animal heads, with a raised zig-zag pattern below them (Pls. 13 & 14). The northwest pier has a square groove cut out of each corner, but no other decoration; it carries a squarish, bulbous capital with a square abacus and necking. Each corner of the capital is decorated with a much debased volute consisting of a wedge-shaped pro-

jection with an inscribed spiral on each face (Pls. 12 & 15). The northeast pier and capital are missing; the southeast pier is also lost and its capital badly eroded.

The four arms of the cross are covered by domes cut into shallow concave vaults. These spring from walls which rise above arches joining the main piers to wall pilasters (Pl. 13). Rudimentary arches spring between the minor piers and the walls, where they meet half-pilasters abutting the main pilasters. All the domes, including the central dome, are truncated, and there is no great difference in size among them; as in Room 5, no attempt to imitate pendentives has been made. The four corner bays are variously vaulted: the southeast and southwest bays have cross vaults, with bosses at the intersection, and the northern corner bays have barrel vaults: the vault of the northeast bay runs north/south, that of the northwest bay east/west.

Shallow blind niches decorate the walls: one in each of north and south walls and one in the centre bay of the west wall. In Pl. 16, showing the west end of the north wall, the elements visible in the centre of the plate are,

14. Hallaç Monastery: Church, southwest capital.

15. Hallaç Monastery: Church, northwest capital.

16. Hallaç Monastery: Church, north wall, west end.

from left to right: a horseshoe-arched blind niche in the west corner bay, the pilaster carrying the arch linking the wall with a main pier, the half-pilaster rising to the vaulting of the cross-arm and part of the blind niche of the centre bay. The secondary cavity visible in the west bay of the north wall is the opening to a vertical tunnel which leads into cavity (7a).

Pilaster capitals are block- or slab-shaped, decorated with carved geometric ornament or fluting, their details picked out in red paint. Three (north wall east, south wall west, west wall south) have horned animal heads carved on them, like the main capital of the southwest pier (Pl. 17).

The church has three apses, each two steps from the nave; the main apse is large and slightly horseshoe-shaped, the lateral apses are little more than absidioles (Pl. 18). The north apse has a shallow rock-cut altar projecting from its back wall, with a small round-headed niche above it; the south apse is partly blocked by a ledge about 1 metre high. In the main apse scars on the back wall and on the ground indicate that a rock-cut altar once

existed (shown on the plan with a broken line). A small shallow niche is let into the right side of the apse wall, and was perhaps a seat back (similarly placed niches are found at Eski Gümüş Monastery and Şahinefendi Monastery, for which see below). None of the apses had rock-cut chancel screens – there are no appropriate scars at their entrances. A pair of rudimentary corbels at the springing of the main apse arch may have held the upper beam of a tall wooden screen (Pl. 18).

Tomb chamber (9) To the south of the church is a tomb chamber of irregular form (9), reached through arched entrances cut in the centre and western bays of the south wall of the naos (Pl. 19). At the east side of the chamber a very narrow corridor is formed by the east wall and an arcade of three arches which rise from three free-standing piers and one attached pier (at the south end); the corridor tapers off to nothing at its south end. Apsidal niches are cut into the east wall, one in each of the three bays of the corridor; the niches have vertical grooves cut into them – doubtless a secondary modification to accom-

17. Hallaç Monastery: Church, south wall, pilaster capital.

18. Hallaç Monastery: Church, main apse.

19. Hallaç Monastery: Church, tomb chamber, view southeast.

modate wooden shelves, installed to provide pigeon nesting space. The main part of the tomb chamber has two small bays: the southernmost is covered by a dome carried on four arches springing from two attached piers in the south corners of the room, the southern pier of the corridor and a further free-standing pier opposite, close to the west wall (it is linked to the west wall by a narrow spur at capital level). A larger bay to the north of this, also domed, is framed by the south wall of the church, the west wall of the chamber, two arches of the corridor arcade and the north arch of the south bay. The west wall of the chamber has crumbled and been replaced by rough masonry. There are three grave pits in the floor, one below the northernmost dome, two in the south bay, one below the dome and the other between the corner piers. The grave pits are of a type common in the cave monuments: about 70 cm deep, long and narrow with slightly rounded ends.

Painting In the church details of carved capitals and bosses are picked out in red paint and faint red lines rim some of the arches. This simple decoration is more profuse in the tomb chamber, where borders of triangles, hatching and scalloping decorate the arches and rim the domes, and crude triangular ornaments are painted on the rudimentary pendentives of the southern bay.

At the top of the pilaster on the west face of the southwest pier in the church is a vertical inscription in red paint, beginning with a cross:

+IƷBACHΛH

Translation: [. .] Basil.

This is probably an invocation or description referring to St Basil, who appears in the painting in the main apse (see below).[2] To the right of the inscription, on the pier, is a crudely painted cross with each of its arms branching into three and the branches linked by a border.

The only polychrome painting in the whole complex is a single panel in the main apse of the church, just above the scar left by removal of the altar (Pl. 18). The paint is applied on a very thin layer of whitewash or plaster which has not masked the irregularities of the wall caused by the mason's tools.

The panel shows the Virgin and Child enthroned between an Archangel on the left and St Basil on the right

2 C. Roueché suggests that the letters before the name (IƷ) may represent the number 16 and if so perhaps have an isopsephic significance.

4. Hallaç Monastery: painting in the main apse of the church.

(Fig. 4). The Angel wears imperial dress, with a *loros* crossing over the chest, and carries a staff with a jewelled end in his right hand and an orb in his left. The figure of the Virgin is almost entirely obliterated, only her halo and the outline of her head remain. All that is left of the Child is a small area of the halo. The Virgin sits on a lyre-shaped throne, its back decorated with diamond pattern. A sausage-shaped red cushion on the throne is also clear. The best preserved figure is that of St Basil, who has black hair and beard and wears an *omophorion* decorated with crosses, over a purple chasuble and yellow *sticharion*. He carries a book with a jewelled cover in his left hand, and a white cloth (*encheiron*) falls from waist level over his left arm. An inscription, MP ΘV is still intact over the Virgin, and a fragment of the inscription to the left of St Basil also remains: ..ACHΛ. A dark shape between the Virgin's throne and the figure of St Basil may be the kneeling figure of a donor, but the painting is too much damaged to make this more than conjecture.

The inclusion of St Basil in the apse panel and the red-paint inscription of his name on the southwest pier suggest the dedication to St Basil of the church, and possibly the monastery as a whole.

Other structures on the site There are several other rooms cut into the rock a short walk beyond the courtyard complex: to the east, beyond the spur of rock that forms the southeast corner of the courtyard, are five roughly cut rectangular rooms with flat ceilings, placed at irregular intervals in the mass of rock which houses the monastery. The largest of these is about 6×4 metres; most have mangers cut into the walls. The tool marks on the walls of these rooms are much rougher than those in the monastery, and the rooms are entirely without ornament. These rooms are probably not to be associated with the monastery, but are post-Byzantine.

In the cliff above the monastery sets of pigeon-holes indicate the presence of a number of pigeon-house rooms. In this area there is also a smooth rectangular façade bordered by a heavy square moulding. In this, two sets of small arched windows or niches set into rectangular recesses (one group of three, another of four), flank a small rectangular entrance (Pl. 3). The façade and cavity behind it were probably part of the monastery, but could not be examined because the area is inaccessible.

Summary

Hallaç Monastery is laid out around an open courtyard (Fig. 2). It probably once had a vestibule (1) at one side of the courtyard, giving access to the hall (2) and a domed room (5); two small rooms (3 and 4) open off the hall. At the west side of the courtyard is a kitchen (6) and at the east side an unfinished room (7) and an inscribed-cross church (8) with a large tomb chamber (9). A painting and an inscription in the church suggest that it (or the monastery) was dedicated to St Basil.

The purposes to which the rooms were put may only be guessed at, except where it is obvious, as in the case of the church and the kitchen. In order to avoid fragmentary discussion of function, this aspect will be reserved for the concluding chapter.

Date

Every indication is that Hallaç Monastery was carved in one phase: the simple carved ornament on capitals, cornices and pilasters is uniform throughout and tool marks, still visible on all walls except exposed ones, where erosion has removed them, are of uniform appearance. The monastery is, therefore, still much as it was first laid out, apart from the crude alterations made to turn it into a

20. Kızlar Kilise, Göreme: vaulting.

pigeon house and the loss of the vault and south wall of the vestibule.

There is no direct evidence of date for Hallaç Monastery, but several indirect indications are available. First, the monastery has an inscribed-cross church. Although the origins of this form are controversial and its development only sketchily understood, it may, in the central Anatolian context, be assigned to the Middle Byzantine period (late ninth to twelfth centuries).[3] Next, Hallaç Church may be related to a group of churches in Göreme valley (about 2.5 km away), known as the Yılanlı group and thought to date to the mid to late eleventh century.[4] This is a group of churches of various architectural types, decorated with isolated panels of painting rather than with full programmes. It includes Göreme Chapels 10, 17, 18, 20, 21, 27 and 28. The affinity between Hallaç Church and the Yılanlı group is seen in several parallels of architectural form, detail and ornament. For example, the subsidiary domes of Hallaç Church, rising out of shal-

low concave vaults, have a parallel in Kızlar Kilisesi (Göreme Chapel 17) (Pl. 20). Here, too, the relationship of central dome and barrel-vaulted cross-arms is the same as in Hallaç Room 5, where recessed triangular spaces are left below the dome. The cornice and capital ornament of Hallaç Room 2 is paralleled in Göreme Chapel 21.[5] The small fluted pilaster capitals of Hallaç Monastery may be compared with corbels in Göreme Chapels 21 and 27.[6] In these two Göreme churches the corbels are apparently functionless, but may find an explanation in the pilaster capitals of the west wall of Hallaç Church, where their function is still apparent (i.e. the pilasters, almost vestigial at Hallaç, have been omitted entirely in the Göreme chapels). Proliferation of shallow horseshoe-arched blind niches as a decorative motif is found in several Göreme churches: the façades of Chapel 21 and Çarıklı Kilise, for example, where, too, there is a parallel for the blind arcade of small niches found on Hallaç east façade. Çarıklı Kilise, which is discussed in

3 See Chapter 6 for a discussion of the inscribed-cross church in Asia Minor. For the plan generally: R. Krautheimer, *Early Christian and Byzantine Architecture* (3rd edn, Harmondsworth, 1979), 359–60. (But note that Krautheimer refers to a rock-cut inscribed-cross (*quincunx*) church in Göreme bearing 'an iconoclast decoration of crosses. It is thus possible that its plan dates from before 843, if not from the eighth century.' It is not clear which of the Göreme churches is referred to, but the 'iconoclast' decoration is sure to

be of the simple aniconic red-paint type which is found in nearly all the cave churches and is definitely not to be associated with Iconoclasm. See Chapter 4, below, especially Göreme Chapels 20 and 25. This argument cannot, therefore, be used to give an Iconoclast date for the inscribed-cross plan.)

4 Epstein, 'Rock-cut Chapels', 116–20.

5 Jerphanion, *Eglises*, pl. 133.3.

6 Epstein, 'Rock-cut Chapels', 21.

Chapter 3, belongs to a second group of Göreme valley churches, known as the Column group, datable to the mid eleventh century.[7]

The decoration of the church with a single panel of painting conforms to the 'isolated panel' scheme of decoration found in the Yılanlı group churches, and the figure of St Basil at Hallaç resembles iconographically the figures of St Basil in Göreme Chapels 10 and 28.[8] Stylistic comparison is difficult, given the very poor condition of the Hallaç painting, but the tall, slim, rather small-headed figures are consistent with those of both the Yılanlı and Column group paintings.

The leaping figure of Room 5 and the animal-head decoration of some of the church capitals may also be of significance for dating. These carvings are without parallel in the Cappadocian cave monuments and human figures are rare in Middle Byzantine carved decorations generally. Such decoration does occur, however, in Armenian and Georgian churches. Specifically, the rudimentary volutes on capitals of Room 5 and in the church find a parallel at Parhal, a late tenth-century church, and the animal heads may be compared with the bull's heads of tetramorphs on a carved column at Osk Vank, of the third quarter of the tenth century. For the leaping man, no parallel offers itself, but the apparently casual use of secular motifs is a feature of Armenian and Georgian sculpted decoration.[9] The eleventh century saw a major movement of population from Armenia to parts of central Anatolia and may afford an explanation of these curious features of Hallaç Church. There is, however, no evidence for Armenian settlement in the volcanic valley area (there are, for example, no Armenian inscriptions) and, on the contrary, there is reason to believe that the limits of such settlement stopped short of this part of Cappadocia.[10] The possibility of an occasional Armenian mason coming into the region from the newly settled areas further north is, however, to be considered, and may account for this unique occurrence of figure sculpture. Such an hypothesis would support an eleventh-century date for Hallaç Monastery, but is offered only with great caution: perhaps the figure carvings at Hallaç, particularly the leaping figure, may as easily be explained as caprice on the part of a local mason.

Finally, some indication of date may be deduced from the pristine state of the monastery, which suggests that

it was abandoned shortly after its completion. Had it been in use for a long period, one would expect to find the single panel of painting supplemented by others, and a large number of pious inscriptions, of which there are none save the red-paint 'Basil', which was probably the work of a mason. There is also no sign of alterations to the structure that might be expected in a complex long inhabited: the only changes are those associated with the clearly post-Byzantine pigeon-house and vegetable garden phases. It is even possible that the monastery was never fully finished: as noted above, the east façade in front of cavities (7) and (7a) is decorated with motifs similar to those around the entrance to the church, suggesting that another room was planned, but not completed beyond the first rough stage of excavation. The most likely time for abandonment of the complex is the late eleventh century, in the face of the Seljuk incursions. If, at this time, the complex had not been occupied long, and may even have been unfinished, then, once again, a mid eleventh-century date for it is implied.

Bezir Hane

The monastery known as Bezir Hane is in Avcılar (Fig. 1). This village was known until the 1920s as Maçan, a name derived from Matiana, its name in the Byzantine period, appearing in episcopal *notitiae* and other sources.[11] The complex was seen by Jerphanion whose description, though brief, is of value because changes have occurred since his visit.[12] The complex was then in use as an oil press but has since been modified for use as a pigeon house: entrances and windows have been enlarged and then blocked up, leaving only pigeon-holes. There have been further losses due to weathering. The plan given here (Fig. 5) relies upon Jerphanion's plan for the church narthex, which was inaccessible when I visited the site in 1978 and 1980.[13]

In plan the complex resembles Hallaç Monastery in that it has a large basilical hall opening off a barrel-vaulted vestibule, the latter decorated with a series of large horseshoe-arched blind niches. The front of the complex is lost, so the presence or absence of a courtyard cannot be established.

Vestibule (1) A barrel-vaulted rectangular room forms a vestibule (1) from which the other rooms of the complex

7   Epstein, 'Fresco Decoration', 27 n.1.
8   Jerphanion, *Eglises*, pl. 39.4 (Chapel 10), pl. 134.4 (Chapel 28).
9   D. Winfield, 'Some Early Medieval Figure Sculpture from North-East Turkey', *JWarb* 31 (1968), 33–72; for Parhal: pl. 28c; Osk Vank, pl. 25b, 26; for secular figures, pp. 41–2.
10 G. Dédéyan, 'L'immigration arménienne en Cappadoce', *Byzantion* 45 (1975), 41–117, at 99.
11 The earliest reference to Matiana is in the Acts of St Hieron,

ActaSS Novembris, III, 333. See also Hild & Restle, *TIB* II, 231, also Chapter 6 of this text, note 128. Avcılar has recently been renamed Göreme, which causes some confusion, since this name has traditionally been applied to the Göreme valley, about 2 km away.
12 Jerphanion, *Eglises*, I. ii, 498–503; also mentioned in Kostof, *Caves of God*, 53.
13 Jerphanion, *Eglises*, pl. 137.

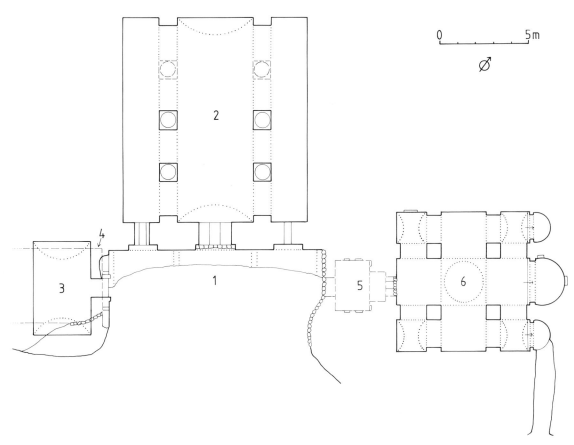

5. Bezir Hane: plan.

may be reached. The front of this vestibule was apparently intact until about 1900, but it had fallen by the time Jerphanion saw the site. The loss of this front (south) wall leaves the vestibule north wall as a false façade to the complex (Pls. 21 & 22). This north wall is decorated with three large horseshoe-arched blind niches; the arches are framed by simple mouldings which are linked horizontally by a two-step cornice; a similar cornice runs across the back of each niche at the springing of the arch (Pls. 21 & 22). Broad pilasters rise between the arches, from the cornice upwards, and extend into tranverse arches in the barrel vault. A further cornice, projecting more than the first, runs around the whole vestibule at the level of the springing of the vault. Jerphanion's photograph, taken before the vestibule was damaged by alterations of the pigeon-house phase, shows that each niche contained an arched window.[14] These windows have now been enlarged, then partly blocked, leaving small pigeonholes. Windows, arches and cornices were all decorated

with painted geometric ornament and there were several painted and incised inscriptions on the wall (see below). The west lunette is framed by a wall arch and divided into two by a pilaster (Pl. 21). Each division of the lunette contains a small keyhole-shaped window, now blocked. The east wall is badly damaged by erosion; it contains a large arched entrance, now blocked with rough masonry; the south side is lost.

Hall (2) The vestibule (1) opens to the north into a large hall of basilical plan, with the division into aisles made by four-arch arcades, each consisting of three columns and two attached piers. The northernmost columns of each arcade have been removed, leaving their capitals suspended (Pl. 23).[15] The arcades rest on simple tapering slab capitals and are decorated with running hood mouldings. The central aisle has a barrel vault and the side aisles flat ceilings. A simple cornice runs around the room at capital level and there is another cornice around the

14 *Ibid.* pl. 21.2.
15 Jerphanion's plan (*Eglises*, pl. 137) shows the southernmost (rather than northernmost) pair of columns lost and therefore contradicts my field notes. I have been unable to check the point but believe

this to be one of Jerphanion's very rare errors. Also shown in his plan are two apsidal extensions of the north wall – these are just irregular secondary cavities and I have omitted them.

21. Bezir Hane: exterior, northwest corner of vestibule.

central aisle, above the arcade, at the level of the springing
of the vault – this is also the level of the side aisle ceilings.
The room was originally lit by the three windows in the
vestibule north wall, one opening into each aisle. Several
irregular cavities have been cut into the walls and floor,
particularly at the north end, doubtless in the course of
the adaptation of the complex for agricultural purposes.

The present entrance to this room is a small rectangular
opening in the westernmost bay of the vestibule north
wall, which leads into the west aisle. This entrance is probably secondary, since it is roughly cut and has no trace
of surrounding moulding; the original entrance must
have been in the centre bay of the vestibule wall, leading
into the nave; the western niche was probably blind, like
the eastern one. The whole area of the central niche,
below the cornice, has been cut out and then blocked with
rough masonry. Jerphanion's photograph shows the
whole of the blocked area occupied by a rectangular
opening which was probably an enlargement of an original narrower opening.

Room 3 The west wall of the vestibule contains a rectangular entrance framed by a broad plain moulding.
This opens into a small room with a barrel vault on a
north/south axis. The room was filled with hay when
inspected, so no further details could be recorded.

Room 4 The western end of the complex (Pl. 21) is much

22. Bezir Hane: exterior, northeast corner of vestibule.

23. Bezir Hane: Room 2, northwest corner.

damaged and it is difficult to establish the full extent of the monastery. There appears to be another room, above Room 3, marked (4) on the plan. The south wall of this room has fallen away and the room has been blocked on this side with modern masonry. Pigeon-holes have been left in this wall, and the only other entrance is a small rectangular opening cut into the west lunette of the vestibule, to the right of the keyhole window. The broken lines on the plan indicate the probable form of the room. Its original entrance must have been in its south side, somewhat forward of the modern masonry, and access was presumably by means of a ramp or steps. Extra rooms are often cut around churches and monasteries when they are converted for use as pigeon houses, but in this case the two keyhole-shaped windows in the west lunette of the vestibule suggest that the room was an original part of the complex.

Church (6) The church, at the east side of the complex, was once entered by means of an opening in the east wall of the vestibule; this area is now blocked by rough masonry (Pl. 22). The church is in use as a store room; several modern rooms (the dwelling of the farmer who owns the site) have been built in front of it. The only entrance to the church at present is a passageway between these added rooms which leads into, and has partly destroyed, the south apse.

The naos is of inscribed-cross plan: the cross-arms have barrel vaults, springing from a plain cornice which circuits the naos; four square piers with chamfered corners and very simple, two-step slab capitals carry a tall central dome; four corbels project from the rim of the dome, one above the crest of each of the cross-arm barrel vaults (Pl. 24).[16] Arches spring from the piers to the walls, where they meet shallow pilasters and frame small corner bays; each corner bay has a barrel vault on an east/west axis.

The main apse is slightly horseshoe-shaped and there are vestiges of low chancel slabs at its opening; there are two arched blind niches in the apse wall, one at the north side and one at the back, both starting about two metres above floor level. There is no sign of an altar, but this may be lost, since the back of the apse has been extensively damaged. The side apses are about half the size of

16 They are not half-colonnettes or ribs, as described by Jerphanion (*Eglises*, I. ii, 502 and pl. 137).

24. Bezir Hane: Church, dome and northwest corner.

25. Bezir Hane: Church, west end.

the main apse, and also slightly horseshoe-shaped. Nothing remains of chancel slabs or altars, but Jerphanion's plan shows rock-cut altars in main and north apses. These have evidently been removed relatively recently. (The altar of the south apse would have been destroyed when the present entrance to the church was cut, which was before Jerphanion's visit.)

The original entrance to the naos, now blocked, is in the centre bay of the west wall, placed slightly off-centre, towards the south (Pl. 25). This is a rectangular entrance with an arched window, also blocked, above it. According to Jerphanion's plan the church has a small rectangular narthex with a decoration of blind arcading. This is inaccessible since both its entrances, from the naos and from the vestibule, are blocked – it is therefore indicated on the plan with broken lines.

Painting In the naos a red and white chequer pattern outlines the arches and there is hatching around the rim

of the dome. A red masonry pattern decorates the arches springing from the west wall to the crossing piers. This painting is on the rock surface, without plaster, a familiar feature of cave monuments and already noted in Hallaç Monastery. There is also a series of polychrome panels on the piers and on the pilasters flanking the apse. These are in very poor condition, with much of the paint scraped away. The panels are rectangular, extending across the faces of the piers and onto the chamfered corners. Each bears a standing figure with a name inscription placed to left and right of the head (O ΑΓΙΟC on the left, the name to the right). The palette used includes red, green, blue, yellow, brown, black and white; each panel has a bluish-grey ground and is bordered with thin lines of black, then white, then by a broad band of red. The lower part of the slab capital above each panel is decorated with polychrome ornament. The inscriptions are given below as recorded by Jerphanion; most of them have since deteriorated.[17] The panels are as follows:

17 Jerphanion, *Eglises*, I. ii, 502.

26. Bezir Hane: Church, St George.

Northwest pier (east face): St George, in military dress, carrying a circular shield and a sword in the left hand and a spear in the right. The saint is beardless, has short hair and wears a diadem (Pl. 26). Like the saints of all the other panels, George has a halo with a 'jewelled' border of alternating rectangles and double rows of white 'pearls'. Above the panel, on the first step of the capital, is a zig-zag pattern. Inscription: O ΑΓΙΟΣ ΓΕΟΡΓΙΟΣ.

Northwest pier (north face): a badly damaged painting of a young beardless saint wearing long robes. Jerphanion recorded the inscription ΔΑΝΙΗΛ for this figure, but this is no longer legible. The saint faces St Kosmas on the southwest pier, which makes it likely that the inscription was misread and that the saint represented is Damianos, since these two saints are usually represented as a pair.[18] The slab above is decorated with a simple white border.

Southeast pier (north face): Archangel Michael, wearing imperial dress with a *loros* crossed over the chest; the position of the arms of the figure is not clear, but he does not appear to carry a staff or standard (Pl. 27). Inscription: ΜΗΧΑΙΛ. The slab above is decorated with

alternating rectangles and groups of white dots, to represent jewelling.

Southwest pier (north face): St Kosmas, a youthful, beardless figure in ornate long robes, holding a phial (Pl. 28). Inscription: O ΑΓΗΟΣ ΚΟΣΜΑ[ς]. On the slab above is an elongated meander pattern.

Apse piers (east faces): flanking the main apse are panels showing two bishop saints, both bearded and wearing the *omophorion*. Jerphanion records inscriptions O ΑΓΗΟΣ ΒΑΣΙΛΗΟΣ for the north-pier figure and O ΑΓΗΟΣ ΝΗΚΟΛΑΟΣ for the south-pier figure; neither inscription survives. The decoration of the slab above is in each case damaged beyond definition.

There is no trace of painting in the apses, but the wall surface has been very badly damaged, probably by the seepage of water through the rock; it is likely that there was once painting here.

Inscriptions in the vestibule (1) Jerphanion noted that many inscriptions, in crude script, were visible on the north wall of the vestibule. The collapse of the front has permitted weathering of the north wall and none of these survives. Some inscriptions were in red paint, others

18 *Ibid.* II, 506–7, hagiographical index, for the list of examples in the cave churches.

27. Bezir Hane: Church, Archangel Michael.

28. Bezir Hane: Church, St Kosmas.

slightly incised; traces of them are visible in Jerphanion's plates. None appears to have been a formal inscription and most were too fragmentary to be reconstructed. Since they were higher than is usual for graffiti, they were probably executed by the masons who carved the complex. One of them, in the spandrel to the left of the entrance to Room 2, reads:

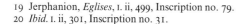

Ρ̄ Μ̄ / 'Εν ὀνόματη / Θ(ε)ο͂ ἐτελήοθη / δηά́δρομος / τοῦτος ὑπὸ / μαήστουρο(ς) / Νηκή́τα χό/ρηον τῦ ἀγί/υο Θεοδόρο[19]

Translation: 'In the name of God this passage was completed by Maistor Niketas, (estate or village?) of St Theodoros.'

This seems, therefore, to supply the name of one of the masons who worked on the monastery. The title *Maistor* is not common in Cappadocian inscriptions, but it does occur in Tokalı Kilise, New Church, in Göreme, where it also seems to apply to a mason.[20] *Chorion* in this context is problematic, since it may mean either 'estate' or 'village'.[21] Jerphanion, favouring 'estate', understood the last words of the inscription to mean that the monastery was that of St Theodoros. If this is so, however, then it is curious that no image of this saint appears in the church; it would seem necessary to suppose a lost painting of St Theodoros possibly in one of the apses. Alternatively, if *chorion* means 'village', then the village of St Theodoros must be that from which *Maistor* Niketas came, rather than the village in which Bezir Hane is situated, since this is one of the few Cappadocian sites whose ancient and medieval name (Matiana) is known.

Summary

Bezir Hane (Fig. 5) may or may not have had a courtyard – the front part of the complex is lost. A long vestibule

19 Jerphanion, *Eglises*, I. ii, 499, Inscription no. 79.
20 *Ibid.* I. ii, 301, Inscription no. 31.

21 For discussion of *chorion*, see E. Patlagean, *Pauvreté économique et pauvreté sociale à Byzance, 4e–7e siècles* (Paris, 1977), 241–2.

(1) gives access to a basilical hall (2), a small side-room (3) and an inscribed-cross church (6). Other rooms may have existed, at least on the west side of the complex. In the church painted panels on the nave piers bear images of saints and angels. Part of the monastery was carved by *Maistor* Niketas.

Date

As was the case with Hallaç Monastery, there is no direct evidence of date for Bezir Hane, so the same oblique method of dating must be employed. There is nothing to suggest other than that this complex was carved in a single phase of work: the quality and style of carving is consistent throughout; the decoration of running hood mouldings seen in the vestibule is repeated in Room 2; the simple slab capitals of the church piers match those of the Room 2 piers at each end of the arcades and both have the same form as the cornice linking the horseshoe-arched niches of the vestibule. The whole monastery may therefore be dated by its church. The inscribed-cross plan supplies a general Middle Byzantine bracket and, since it is reasonable to suppose that the painted decoration was undertaken shortly after excavation was completed, this bracket may be narrowed by attributing a date to the paintings.

The programme, consisting of single panels depicting saints, resembles the 'isolated panel' formula typical of the Yılanlı group, mentioned above in connection with Hallaç Church, for which a mid/late eleventh-century date has been proposed.[22] A rather closer parallel for the arrangement of decoration is found in Direkli Kilise, near Belisırma, which is the church of a monastery to be described below. Here the painted programme consists chiefly of panels depicting saints, placed on the piers of an inscribed-cross church; the parallel extends even to the chamfered corners of the piers. Further comparison is difficult, given the very poor condition of the Bezir Hane paintings, but there does seem to be some iconographic and stylistic proximity between the two programmes (compare, for example, Kosmas of Bezir Hane (Pl. 28) with Sergios and Bakchos at Direkli Kilise (Pl. 85) and note in particular the unusual jewelled haloes). The paintings of Direkli Kilise are datable by inscription to 976–1025, and their style places them towards the end of this period. A date in the eleventh century may therefore be proposed for the Bezir Hane paintings and hence for the monastery as a whole.

Finally, as noted above, Bezir Hane has several features in common with Hallaç Monastery: there is a general similarity of layout, with a large basilical hall opening off a vestibule and with an inscribed-cross church at the east side of the complex. The architectural form of the vestibule and its decoration with wide horseshoe-arched blind niches, pilasters and cornices, is very similar in each case. Nothing suggests that the two monasteries should not be regarded as approximate contemporaries.

Şahinefendi Monastery

Şahinefendi is on the road from Ürgüp to Soğanlı (Fig. 1), and has in the past been known also as Söviş or Suveş; it is usually identified with Sobesos, which appears in episcopal *notitiae*.[23] Before reaching the village, the road curves around a hillside which is crested by a cliff and has a scatter of cones at its foot. Halfway up the hill the façade of Şahinefendi Monastery is visible (Pl. 29).[24] The monastery is about 500 metres from the Church of the Forty Martyrs, but there is no evidence for close association between the two.[25] The site is very much damaged by erosion and partly buried by the rock debris that has fallen down the hillside. What now remains is a room complex fronted by a decorated façade, with a church to the east of it (Fig. 6). It is probable that a formal connection originally existed between the two: the disposition of the rooms and church suggests that the monastery had a courtyard (area A on the plan); a fragment of wall, projecting from the west end of the surviving façade, supports this.

Façade The left (west) side is all that remains of the decorated façade. This was articulated by heavy pilasters of which only two remain, plus the small corner pilaster at the left side, which starts the sequence (Pl. 30). The pilasters have simple slab capitals and support an architrave decorated with small semicircular blind niches. The base of the façade has been eaten away by erosion. Between the pilasters are tall horseshoe-arched blind niches, their arches double-recessed. Narrow arched openings are cut into the westernmost two such niches: the right one of these is a window, the other a deep recess.

The surviving section of façade occupies less than half the space across the front of the complex, so the original façade probably had a single central entrance with four pilasters and three niches on each side, and the architrave running across the whole front. Small areas of plaster remain on the pilaster capitals and on the upper parts of the large horseshoe-arched niches; probably the whole

22 See note 4.
23 Hild & Restle, *TIB* II, 285. See also Chapter 6, note 128.
24 A photograph of this monastery appears in Restle, *Wall Painting*,

I, 92, but it is otherwise unpublished. I have seen this monastery only once, very briefly, so this account is necessarily cursory.
25 Jerphanion, *Eglises*, II, 156–74.

29. Şahinefendi Monastery: site.

30. Şahinefendi Monastery: façade and Room 1.

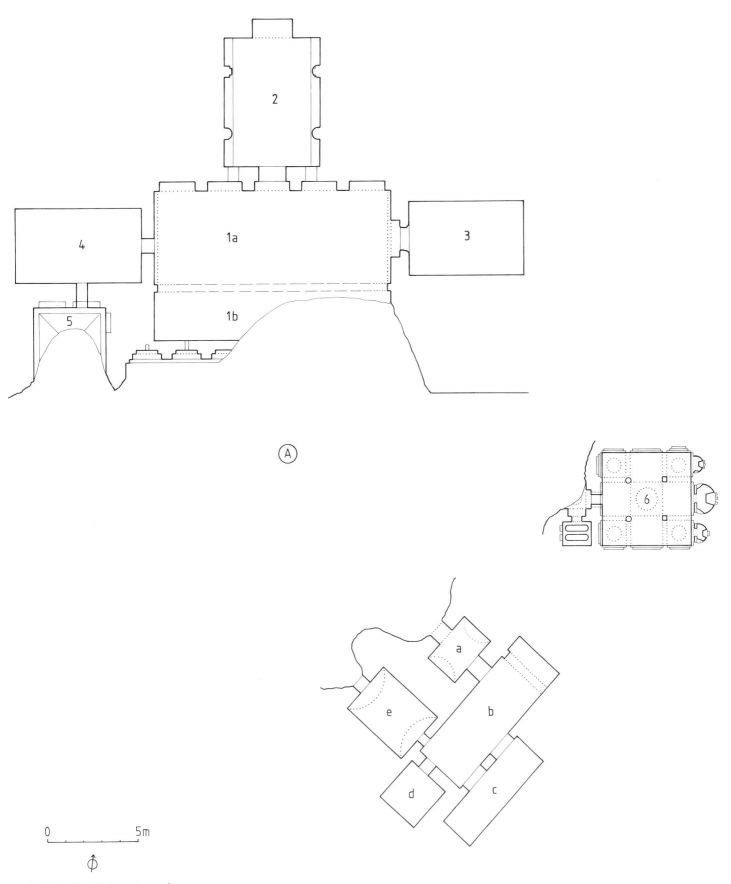

6. Şahinefendi Monastery: plan.

façade was originally thus treated. On the pilaster capitals there are also zig-zags and hatching in red paint. To the west of the façade is a short area of wall projecting at right angles to it, probably a fragment of the west side of the courtyard.

Vestibule (1a and 1b) Behind the façade, the vestibule is a large rectangular room of two sections: the front (south) part of the room (1b) has a flat ceiling and the back part (1a) a barrel vault. The two areas are separated by pilasters on each of the short walls. These pilasters are badly eroded, but each retains parts of a capital, from which springs an arch; the arch fragment attached to the west wall has a plain moulding rimming its south side. It seems, therefore, that an arcade, of which all further trace has been lost, once separated the two sections of the room (its position is shown in broken thin line on the plan). The barrel vault of the back section (1a) springs above a simple cornice which continues across the end walls to cut off lunettes, which are also outlined by wall arches.

The north wall of the room contains five deep arched recesses (Pl. 31). In each the arch springs from a simple cornice. The cornices are linked across the back wall of the recess by a horizontal moulding cutting off a lunette,

which is also rimmed by a moulding. The arches of the five recesses are also rimmed and linked by running hood mouldings, and on each spandrel is a pilaster, rising from the horizontal moulding to the upper cornice, where it splays out to form a rudimentary pilaster capital (Pl. 31). A second horizontal moulding, below the first, also has a pilaster below it. The central arched recess contains the rectangular entrance to Room 2. Each of the two recesses flanking the central one contains a small arched window to this room; the window on the left of the entrance is to the right of centre in its recess, that on the right is to the left of centre.

Hall (2) Room 2 is a flat-ceilinged, rectangular hall with its axis at right angles to that of the vestibule. On each of the long sides of the room are two attached uprights: on the west wall, to the south, is a column, with a simple two-stepped disc capital (Pl. 32a); to the north is a square pier, with a pilaster on its outer face; this has a two-stepped slab capital (Pl. 32b). Opposite, on the east wall, is a member the lower half of which is columnar, the upper half a square pier with pilaster, topped by a two-stepped slab capital (Pl. 32c). At the south end of this wall is another attached column, like that opposite. All four members project strongly and support a heavy rec-

31. Şahinefendi Monastery: Room 1, north wall.

32a. Şahinefendi Monastery: Room 2, west wall, south end.

32c. Şahinefendi Monastery: Room 2, east wall, north end.

32b. Şahinefendi Monastery: Room 2, west wall, north end.

tangular cornice (Pl. 32b). At the far end of the room, in the centre of the north wall, is a deep arched recess, flanked by relief colonnettes which support a moulding outlining the arch. The vault of the recess springs from cornices; these are linked by a moulding across the back wall, cutting off a lunette which is also rimmed by a moulding. In the lunette a kite-shaped recess contains a Latin cross cut in shallow relief. The south wall, containing the entrance from the vestibule, is plain except for a cornice at the ceiling. At each end of the wall the arched windows described above open into the vestibule.

Room 3 The east wall of the barrel-vaulted section of Room 1 contains the remains of an arched recess. This was probably of the same type as the recesses of the north wall, since a moulding rimming the lunette remains. An irregular hole in the back of the niche, probably an enlargement of an original rectangular entrance, opens into Room 3. This is rectangular, with a flat ceiling.

Room 4 At the west end of Room 1 a simple rectangular entrance opens into Room 4, another rectangular room with a flat ceiling. The room contains an accumulation of rock debris which has raised its floor level by about 1 metre at the far (west) wall.

Kitchen (5) To the south of Room 4 are parts of another room (5), of which only the north, west and east walls remain, with a corresponding section of a steep conical vault rising above a deep overhang. The room appears to have been square and was probably the monastery kitchen. Below the vault, rectangular recesses are cut into north and east walls: one in the east wall, two in the north wall; the most easterly of these in the north wall contains a rectangular opening to Room 4. At present this opening is less than 1 metre high, because the ground level in both the kitchen and Room 4 has been raised by the accumulation of debris. There is no entrance in the remaining part of the east wall of the kitchen; possibly its main entrance was in the lost south wall.

Church (6) The church lies to the east of the room complex in an area that has been badly damaged. Boulders falling from the cliff above must have contributed to the destruction, and erosion has produced a heavy accumulation of silt. The entrance is buried and the church is now accessible only through the window above the entrance. The present ground level outside the church is level with the base of this window. (On the plan the window, which is the current means of access, is drawn in thick line, the entrance, now buried, in broken thin line.)

The naos is of inscribed-cross plan, with a central dome carried on four barrel-vaulted cross-arms. Below the dome are rudimentary pendentives decorated with incised triangles. The crossing has two square piers, with chamfered corners, at the east side, and two columns at the west side. Each upright has a simple tapering block capital with square necking and abacus and chamfered edges (Pl. 33). The capitals are coated in white plaster and decorated with an incised leaf-vein pattern picked out in red. The piers stand on square, two-stepped bases, the columns on round, two-stepped bases.

Small arches spring from the crossing capitals to meet wall pilasters framing small corner bays, each of which is covered by a calotte. Above the arches runs a cornice, from which the cross-arm barrel vaults spring. The cornice is decorated with incised triangles, picked out in red. Wall arches, springing from this cornice, define lunettes on the end walls of the cross-arms. Shallow horseshoe-arched niches are cut into each wall, and there is a further niche, flanked by small colonnettes, in the north wall of the northeast bay. The chief plane of the wall is that of the pilaster faces; the niches are cut back beyond this plane.

33. Şahinefendi Monastery: Church, northeast pier.

There are three apses, all slightly horseshoe-shaped in plan: the main apse has a horseshoe-arched entrance with rudimentary pilasters at the springing of the arch; at this level a cornice runs around the apse below the conch. The apse was once closed by low chancel slabs of which only fragments remain. On each of the pilasters flanking the main apse a red and white cross-medallion is painted, level with the tops of the chancel slabs. There is an attached altar at the back of the apse, and a group of three narrow keyhole-shaped blind niches cut into the wall just above it. At the left is a ledge, and at the right a rock-cut seat, which consists of a projecting ledge with a relief upright to the left of it, topped by a disc-shaped finial. The right side of the seat abuts the chancel slab. The north apse has no entrance arch, it opens directly off the east wall. It has a cornice below the conch, fragments of low chancel slabs, a rock-cut altar with three shallow keyhole-shaped niches above it, and a seat at the right. The south apse has an apse arch without pilaster capitals and a painted band in place of a cornice (two horizontal red bands with zig-zag between them). Fragments of low chancel slabs remain, and there is an attached altar with a single wide, shallow, flat-backed, arched niche above it; to the right is a seat with an upright and disc-finial, as in the main apse.

The rectangular entrance to the naos, in the middle bay of the west wall, is blocked with rubble, as already noted. Above it is the small arched window which is the only means of access at present. This window and entrance communicate with what was once a small, domed free-cross narthex, of which only fragments survive. The shallow east arm of this narthex remains above the window, and a similarly shallow west arm, which probably contained the entrance from the outside, is also recognizable among the fragments in the area. The north arm of the narthex is lost; the south, deeper than west and east arms, has its wall pierced by a horseshoe-arched opening which leads into a small, rectangular, flat-ceilinged tomb chamber. This contains two graves in its floor. In its west wall are two horseshoe-arched niches, one at the end of each grave, rimmed by running hood mouldings.

Other rooms A group of cones to the southeast of the monastery contains another series of rooms. (The axis of this room complex is northwest/southeast, but for ease of description, northwest, will be called north.) A roughly arched entrance leads into a small, barrel-vaulted, rectangular room (a); at the back of this is an opening to a large rectangular room (b), also barrel-vaulted. Towards the north end of the vault is a transverse arch

which springs from a pilaster on the west side and tapers into the wall at the east side. In the south wall of (b) is an opening to a rough secondary cavity (d) and in the adjacent west wall is a further secondary opening to (e), a barrel-vaulted room with an original entrance which lies close to the entrance to (a). At the south end of the east wall of (b) are two wide openings (leaving the small area of wall between them as a pier) into (c), a flat-ceilinged, rectangular room.

All of these rooms are roughly cut, their architectural details very casual. The complex does have barrel vaults and a transverse arch, however, which do not normally occur in post-Byzantine cavities made for agricultural purposes. It is therefore probable that these are part of the monastery.

Summary

Şahinefendi Monastery (Fig. 6) was apparently laid out around a courtyard, most of which has fallen away as the hillside upon which it stands has decayed. A vestibule (1) gives access to a hall (2) behind it and two smaller rooms (3 and 4) flanking it. At the west side of the courtyard area is a kitchen (5) and at the east side an inscribed-cross church (6) with narthex and tomb chamber. To the southeast is a further small group of rooms.

Date

The monastery contains no polychrome painting and no inscriptions. Its plan is basically the same as that in Hallaç Monastery and Bezir Hane, with a barrel-vaulted vestibule giving access to other rooms and a church to the east. In detail it differs somewhat: the deep recesses of the vestibule are only distantly related to the shallow blind niches of Hallaç and Bezir Hane vestibules, and the hall is not a basilica. The hall does, however, resemble closely that of Kılıçlar Monastery, described below, which has several affinities with Hallaç Monastery and Bezir Hane. It should probably, therefore, be assigned to the same eleventh-century period as was proposed for these two monasteries. The inscribed-cross church is consistent with such an attribution.

Kılıçlar Monastery

About 50 metres to the north-northwest of Kılıçlar Kilise (Göreme Chapel 29) there is a room complex (Fig. 7) on an area of ground lower than the church.[26] This consists of a vestibule (1), surrounded by rooms, fronted by a

---

26 Jerphanion, *Eglises*, I. i, 45, 48 and 254.

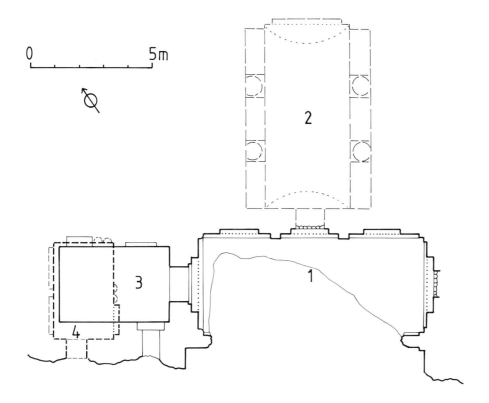

7. Kılıçlar Monastery: plan.

façade. (The vestibule axis runs northwest/southeast, but for ease of description it will be treated as running west/east and other orientations adjusted.) Most of the façade has been lost and in recent years the openings in the north and east walls of the vestibule have been blocked with rough masonry. The most important room of the complex, a barrel-vaulted hall opening off the vestibule (Room 2), is therefore not accessible; it was seen by Jerphanion, who published a photograph of it. The plan given in Fig. 7 records the site as it now appears, except for Room 2, the drawing of which is a conjectural reconstruction based on Jerphanion's photograph.

Façade The façade which once fronted the complex remains only in fragments (Pl. 34): in the upper right-hand corner a piece of two-stepped cornice with zig-zag decoration; below this part of a horseshoe arch, rimmed by a plain moulding; to the right of this a shallow horseshoe-arched blind niche, and, running down the right border of the façade, a square pilaster. At the left

of the façade there remains an area of smooth rock with a square moulding running horizontally at what must have been the level of the springing of the horseshoe arches of the façade. It seems likely that there were originally three arched openings, judging by the relative sizes of the remaining arch and the width of the façade.

The façade is set in a rough recess; at each side roughly finished walls project at right angles to the façade. These may be simply the sides of the recess or are perhaps the remains of courtyard walls, in which case it may be supposed that the complex has suffered considerable losses.

Vestibule (1) The vestibule is rectangular, with a flat ceiling, much of which has been lost. The south wall has, of course, been lost with the façade. The surviving north, west and east walls are decorated with horseshoe-arched blind niches (Pl. 34). On the north wall there are three such niches, separated by pilasters with rudimentary capitals. The west wall contains one blind niche, flanked by attached columns in the corners of the room (Pl. 36).

The east wall also contains a single niche, but in this case L-shaped pilasters occupy the corners of the room (Pl. 35). A horizontal moulding links the niches of all three walls, at the springing of the arches; the flat ceiling is set above a square cornice.

A little carved and painted decoration survives: zig-zag pattern in red paint on protected areas of pilasters and cornices, small incised crosses on the east wall, to the right of the niche, and on the moulding of the right niche of the north wall, and a painted medallion on the back wall of the east wall niche (Pl. 35).

The niches of west and east walls and the central niche of the north wall of the vestibule frame openings into other rooms. As noted above, the east and north openings are now blocked. The east opening is rectangular, its top just below the springing of the niche arch, set off-centre (towards the right) in the niche. The room into which this entrance opened must have been quite small, judging by the size of the area of rock available to contain it.

34. Kılıçlar Monastery: façade and Room 1.

Room 2 The original form of the north opening of the vestibule has been obscured by the masonry blocking; the only opening existing now is a set of pigeon-holes cut into the upper part of the niche. When Jerphanion saw the complex, this entrance was open and his photograph shows that it was originally rectangular, outlined by a plain moulding, with a lintel above it.[27] This entrance led into a large room with a barrel vault springing from a deep overhang.[28] The area beneath the overhang was divided into bays by thick, attached columns with simple tapering slab capitals. Jerphanion gives no description of the room and his photograph shows only one such column; in the plan (Fig. 7) the room is shown in thin broken line: I have assumed two columns on each side of the room, on the basis of an estimate of the size of the visible bay.[29]

35. Kılıçlar Monastery: Room 1, east end.

27 Jerphanion, *Eglises*, pl. 21.1.
28 *Ibid*. pl. 25.1.
29 The dimensions given by Jerphanion for this room are '. . .de dix mètres environ de profondeur sur quatre ou cinq mètres de largeur'. I have drawn the room 7.5 × 5 metres since this seems more in proportion with the rest of the complex. If the room is indeed 10 metres long, then it is perhaps necessary to add a third bay and another pair of attached columns.

36. Kılıçlar Monastery: Room 1, northwest corner.

Rooms 3 and 4 The opening in the west wall of the vestibule is undamaged – it is rectangular, outlined by a recess, and above it a recessed lunette is cut into the back of the blind niche (Pl. 35). The entrance opens into Room 3, which is rectangular with a flat ceiling. At the west end of the north wall is an arcosolium, its base about 0.5 metres above the floor. To the right of this, about 1 metre above the floor, is a shallow rectangular recess. In the east end of the south wall is another recess, housing a window cut through to the exterior. A hole in the floor in the northwest corner of Room 3 opens into a lower room, marked (4) on the plan. This room, accessible through a rectangular opening to the west of the façade, is roughly cut, rectangular, with a flat ceiling. Arcosolia containing grave pits are cut into north, west and east walls, and rough cavities are cut into north and west walls. In 1981 the room was little more than 1 metre high: the floor level may have risen by the accumulation of debris, but it is possible that this was always a low-ceilinged cavity, with a funerary function.

Other cavities Part of the vestibule floor has been cut away and a cavity below it is just visible: beneath the centre niche of the north wall of the vestibule is the top of an arched opening, decorated with red zig-zag orna-

ment. The area was so full of rubble in 1981 that whatever lies behind the arch was inaccessible.

At some point the complex was made into a pigeon house. The pigeon-holes in the blocked entrance to Room 2 have already been noted, and a pigeon-house room with nest-box recesses is visible in the cliff above the vestibule (Pl. 34); there is a further pigeon-house room above Room 3. The removal of some of the vestibule floor is probably also part of the pigeon-house conversion, to give vertical access to the cavity below.

The existence of a cavity below the vestibule raises the question of the original ground level of the complex. There is now a vegetable patch in front of it, at roughly the same level as the vestibule floor. This patch has, however, been created artificially by building a rough retaining wall, about 2 metres high, to the northwest (left) of the complex, thus raising the soil above its natural level. (The field in the courtyard of Hallaç Monastery is similarly contained, see above.) It is not likely, however, that the complex as it now appears is but the upper floor of a much larger one. Several points oppose this: first, the proportions of the façade are such (see Pl. 34) that the addition of a conjectural lower storey would make the complex very tall and narrow. It would also put the vestibule and rooms on the first floor, with no obvious means of access from below. Finally, the raised level cannot account for more than about 2 metres, too little to allow for a lower room or rooms of normal height. Probably, therefore, the area below the vestibule floor is best interpreted as some kind of rock-cut basement or storage area or, as suggested for the cavity below Hallaç Monastery, a cistern.

Refectory Jerphanion mentions a refectory on the Kılıçlar site, but admits to uncertain memory of its location.[30] His photograph shows a room with rock-cut furniture, closely resembling a number of other such refectories in Göreme valley, described below in Chapter 4. This refectory is not part of the complex just described, nor is it to be found behind any of the existing openings in the vicinity of the complex. If it is nearby, then its entrance must have been blocked since Jerphanion's visit; alternatively, it may be elsewhere in the valley and its association with Kılıçlar Kilise the result of an error in Jerphanion's notes. In either case, it is not closely linked to the room complex.

The problem of the church

No church is directly associated with the complex. Given the plans seen already, the expected location of a church would be the area to the east of the vestibule. It may indeed be the case that the blocked east entrance leads into a church, but it would have to be very small indeed, since the rock mass available to contain it is shallow. Further, the opening in the east wall of the vestibule is less elaborate than that to the simple Room 3 on the west side of the complex, and is therefore unlikely to be a church entrance.

There is, of course, a church nearby. Kılıçlar Kilise, one of the most impressive painted churches of Göreme valley, is some 50 metres to the southeast, hence the name given to this complex. The relative positions of the church and room complex are thus not unlike those of the churches and room complexes of Hallaç Monastery and Şahinefendi. However, the distance separating them is much greater on the Kılıçlar site, and the church is at a higher level than the room complex. It is even possible that, several centuries ago, the complex and the church

were not easily accessible to one another, and that their present association is the result of changes in the terrain made by erosion. Nevertheless, given the lack of another church in juxtaposition with the room complex, the possibility of some connection between it and Kılıçlar Kilise must be examined.

Kılıçlar Kilise is an inscribed-cross church fronted by a small, domed narthex. The naos has a full painted decoration of high quality, described in detail by Jerphanion.[31] In brief, the decoration is as follows:

Main apse: (conch) Christ in Majesty; (wall) bishop saints Leontios, Athanasios, Blaisios, Gregory of Nyssa, Gregory (of Nazianzos), (others lost).
North apse: (conch) Virgin and Child; (wall) Divine Liturgy.
South apse: decoration lost.
Cross-arm barrel vaults, lunettes, walls: narrative cycle – Annunciation, Visitation, Proof of the Virgin, Joseph and Mary, Nativity, Adoration of the Magi, Dream of Joseph, Flight into Egypt, Presentation, Angel appearing to John the Baptist, John Meeting Christ, Baptism, Christ and Zaccheus, Healing the Blind, Raising of Lazarus, Entry into Jerusalem, Last Supper, Washing the Feet, Betrayal, Christ before Anaias and Caiaphas, Denial by Peter, Christ before Pilate, Way of the Cross, Crucifixion, Deposition, Entombment, Myrophores, Anastasis, Benediction of Apostles, Pentecost, Dormition.
Dome: Ascension.
Soffits and piers: saints and prophets.

To the south of the church is a side chapel (Pl. 37) which appears to be an addition, rather than an original part of Kılıçlar Kilise, since its floor level is higher than that of the church, and its carving by a different hand. The side chapel is painted, but in a very different style from that of the naos decoration. The paintings of Kılıçlar Kilise naos are generally dated to the early tenth century, on stylistic grounds.[32] The weathered and fragmentary paintings of the side chapel are the work of the painter who decorated the nearby Mereyemana Kilise (Göreme Chapel 33), and are attributable to the eleventh century.[33] The programme is as follows:

30 Jerphanion, *Eglises*, I. i, 254 and pl. 25.3.
31 Jerphanion, *Eglises*, I. ii, 199–242.
32 Restle, *Wall Painting*, I, 21, draws a stylistic parallel with the illuminated manuscript of 905, known as the *Marciana Job* (Venice, Biblioteca Marciana Cod.graecus 538) and this is the date generally given for Kılıçlar Kilise. The church is something of a curiosity in that it has a very long narrative cycle, stylistically and iconographically compatible with Jerphanion's 'archaic' group churches, but placed in an inscribed-cross church instead of in barrel-vault registers as is usual in churches of this group. A tenth-

century date seems highly probable, although not certainly as early as 905.
33 For Göreme Chapel 33 see Jerphanion, *Eglises*, I. i, 243–53. The opinion that the paintings in Kılıçlar Side Chapel and Göreme Chapel 33 are the work of the same painter is my own; the attribution to the eleventh century is based on Jerphanion's association of the paintings of Göreme Chapel 33, on iconographical and palaeographic grounds, with those of the Column churches: Karanlık Kilise, Çarıklı Kilise, Elmalı Kilise, for which see below.

37. Kılıçlar Kilise: entrance and side chapel.

Apse: standing figures of the Virgin and John the Baptist flank Christ enthroned; on each side of the throne is a medallion containing the bust of an (unidentified) saint.

Apse arch: standing figures of St Akakios and St Sisinnios.

East arch: standing figures of St Ephraim and St Alypios.

Southeast pendentive: bust (Evangelist?).

South arch: (east side) St Leontios.

South wall: Nativity.

Donor images: on each of the piers of the apse arch is a rectangular panel showing a standing figure. Both are so badly damaged that they survive only as fragmentary silhouettes, but the outline of the head is present in each case and it is certain that they are without haloes. Traces of lettering in white paint survive on each panel but are now illegible. Jerphanion, however, was able to record the inscription 'Lord help . . .' on the north panel.[34]

It seems, therefore, that Kılıçlar Kilise is a tenth-century church that, in the eleventh century, received the addition of a side chapel, a history that might have a bear-ing on the relationship between Kılıçlar Kilise and the room complex. The possibility that church and complex were carved at the same time, and that Kılıçlar Kilise is thus the monastery church must, I think, be dismissed. As noted above, there is no formal connection between the two, they are at different levels and quite far apart. Another hypothesis is available: Kılıçlar Kilise, as a monument of some importance, might have been the reason for the excavation of a monastery on the site. Separation of church and rooms may be explained by the absence, around Kılıçlar Kilise, of a rock mass large enough to contain the rooms. Such a development might also have been the occasion for the addition of the side chapel, and the donors portrayed in it responsible for the excavation of the monastery. Kılıçlar Kilise would thus be the monastery church in a sense, but would pre-date the complex.

This hypothesis recalls the sequence of events at the monastery of Hosios Loukas of Phokis, in Greece, where in the eleventh century an important monastery grew up on the site of a tenth-century hermitage.[35] The only build-ing remaining from the saint's lifetime is the church of St Barbara (now of the Theotokos), begun before his

34 *Ibid.* I. ii, 201, Inscription no. 26.

35 E. G. Stikas, *To oikodomikon chronikon tes mones Osiou Louka Phokidos* (Athens, 1970), 7ff. & 34–6.

death in 953. Whatever other tenth-century structures once existed must have been removed in the subsequent alterations. It may be conjectured that a similar sequence occurred in Göreme – that Kılıçlar Kilise was hewn on a hermitage site of growing importance and that the original hermitage structures were eclipsed by the later development.

Summary

Kılıçlar Monastery (Fig. 7) consists of a room complex with a vestibule (1) giving access to a hall (2) and two side rooms (Room 3 and a room behind the blocked entrance at the east side of the vestibule); the entrance to Room 2 is also blocked at present. One lower room (4), below (3), is accessible and there are traces of another cavity below the vestibule. The complex has no church but is not far from Kılıçlar Kilise; it was probably cut later than this church and may be contemporary with its side chapel.

Date

For the moment the complete form of Kılıçlar Monastery remains uncertain; unblocking of closed entrances and the excavation of the rubble-filled lower area would doubtless reveal much. If the complex and Kılıçlar Kilise side chapel are part of the same phase, then the monastery should be dated to the eleventh century, with the side chapel paintings. The blind arcading of the façade and vestibule and the columns and capitals of Room 2 are consistent with the architectural context provided by the monasteries considered so far: the vestibule resembles those of Bezir Hane and Hallaç Monastery, while Room 2 appears to be very similar to the hall at Şahinefendi Monastery.

Soğanlı Han

Soğanlı valley, about 35 km south of Ürgüp, is an area rich in painted cave churches. Also found here is a cave monument known as Soğanlı Han, which is cut into a steep hillside (Pl. 38). Now in use as a pigeon house, all its entrances have been sealed with masonry and the interior is inaccessible to all but pigeons. A sketch plan drawn by Smirnov, who visited the site in 1895, and published by Strzygowski, shows a rectangular courtyard with a north façade of blind niches, behind which are two barrel-vaulted rooms. At the east side of the complex is an inscribed-cross church.[36] The complex is clearly not

a *han* (caravanserai), but a monastery. The plan given here (Fig. 8) uses Smirnov's sketch plan for those parts no longer surviving or not at present visible (these are indicated by thin broken line).

Façade, courtyard and rooms The north façade has a decoration of seven tall narrow blind niches with horse-shoe arches springing from rudimentary pilaster capitals (Pls. 38 & 39). It is probable that the niches now appear taller than they originally were, because erosion has lowered the ground level in front of the façade by about two metres. Above the arcade of niches is a plain cornice, and above that about three metres of rock to the top of the outcrop of rock into which the complex is cut. Faint outlines suggest that this area was decorated with a frieze of small arched blind niches (see Pl. 39, above the second niche from the left). In the niches second from the right and second from the left there are double-recessed arched openings which have been blocked with rough masonry (Pls. 38 & 39). These were doubtless originally blind niches, housing the entrances to the rooms shown on Smirnov's plan. These rooms are barrel-vaulted, each divided into three bays by transverse arches springing from pilasters. The westernmost of the two rooms also has a rectangular-plan recess at its north end. Pigeon-holes cut into several of the façade niches probably open into these two rooms.

There are more pigeon-holes in the upper frieze area, and since it is unlikely that the rooms are as tall as this, there must be secondary cavities here, linked by tunnels within the rock. The upper part of the northwest corner of the courtyard has been closed off by a rough masonry wall of large blocks (Pl. 39). The cavity into which three pigeon-holes in this area open is probably also secondary.

The west wall of the courtyard is undecorated, but the rock has been cut back to form a smooth wall (Pl. 39). At the north end of this façade is an arched opening, blocked with masonry, and above it a small arched window, now divided by two stone slabs to make three pigeon-holes (Pl. 39). There is, therefore, a cavity not noted in Smirnov's plan, behind the west façade. The arched window suggests that this cavity is an original part of the monastery, not a pigeon-house room. The entrance below it is roughly cut and too wide to be consistent with the rest of the monastery architecture, but it may be an enlargement of an original rectangular entrance.

Higher up the west wall the left side of an arched groove is visible, its apex at the same height as the cornice above the niches of the north façade (Pl. 39 – the right side of the grooved arch disappears behind the masonry wall

---

36 Strzygowski, *Kleinasien*, 149–50.

38. Soğanlı Han: site.

39. Soğanlı Han: façade, view northwest.

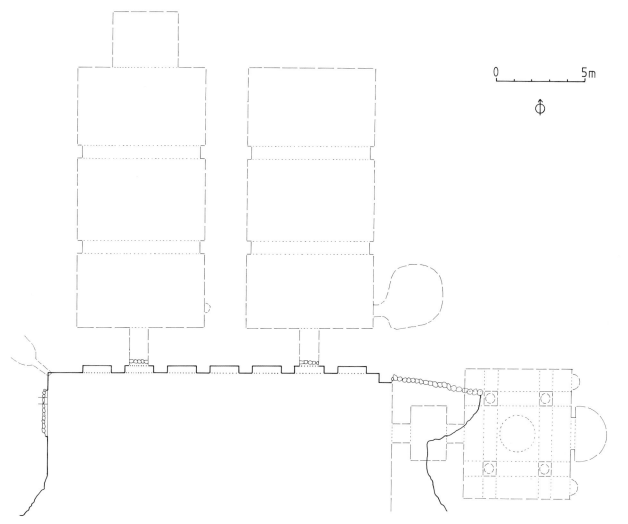

8. Soğanlı Han: plan.

which crosses the corner). A similar feature appears on both east and west walls of the courtyard at Eski Gümüş Monastery (see below), where it may have supported the timbers of a wooden vault covering the area in front of the north façade, probably part of a post-Byzantine phase. The east wall of the courtyard at Soğanlı Han is lost, so it is uncertain whether or not it had a corresponding groove.

Church Smirnov's plan shows an east face to the courtyard with an inscribed-cross church behind it. Little is left of this area: large masses of rock have split off from the steep hillside in which the monastery is situated and fallen into the valley – this was doubtless the fate of the

church. Some of the boulders at the east side of the complex have curved, worked surfaces, which may be the remains of church vaulting (Pl. 38). Jerphanion saw Soğanlı Han in the early years of this century and described it very briefly. Since he makes no mention of the church, it is probable that the collapse occurred before his visit.[37]

The plan shows a small rectangular narthex and an inscribed-cross naos. This had a single central dome carried on columns with square bases; arches sprang from the columns to the walls, framing small corner bays; arches also sprang between the columns. The large main apse had a rock-cut altar, low chancel slabs and a seat at its left side; it was flanked by small lateral apses. A fragment of vaulting and part of an arch rising from a

37 Jerphanion, *Eglises*, I. i, 45.

40. Soğanlı Han: façade, view northeast.

Summary and date

Soğanlı Han appears to have had a courtyard with a decorated façade fronting two large barrel-vaulted rooms (Fig. 8). At the east side there was an inscribed-cross church with a small narthex, both now certainly lost; the large rooms are inaccessible, but probably intact. The plan of the monastery is similar to that employed in the other monasteries described so far, and Soğanlı Han may therefore be roughly contemporary with them. Its inscribed-cross church puts it into the Middle Byzantine period, and the east end formula, with very small lateral apses, resembles the scheme at Hallaç Monastery church.

In some respects Soğanlı Han resembles a small complex not far away in Soğanlı valley, linked with the church of St Barbara (see below, Chapter 5). Here a large barrel-vaulted room, with transverse ribs dividing it into two bays, opens off a façade which was decorated with blind

simple capital are visible beyond a large boulder at the east end of the courtyard (Pl. 40). These may be part of the northwest corner bay of the naos.

niching (Fig. 42). These elements seem to have been added to the site after the church had been in existence for some time. Conceivably Soğanlı Han was the model for the additions made to the St Barbara site, or the similarity may be evidence of the approximate contemporaneity of Soğanlı Han and the expansion of St Barbara. This expansion post-dates the painting of the church in 1006 or 1021, so may be attributed to the mid eleventh century. This date is possibly to be extended to Soğanlı Han.

Karanlık Kilise Monastery

Karanlık Kilise Monastery is in the head of Göreme valley, an area dense with some of the best known of the cave churches and a series of 'monastic units' which will be discussed below, in Chapter 4. This area is now supervised by the Turkish authorities and is known as Göreme Park.

Karanlık Kilise is well known for its elaborate painted programme: it is one of three churches painted by the same workshop and known as the Column group.[38] Just

38 Jerphanion, *Eglises*, I. ii, 393–430; Restle, *Wall Painting*, Cat. no. XXII; Rott, *Denkmäler*, 212–16; Kostof, *Caves of God*, 64; Epstein, 'Fresco Decoration', 27–45.

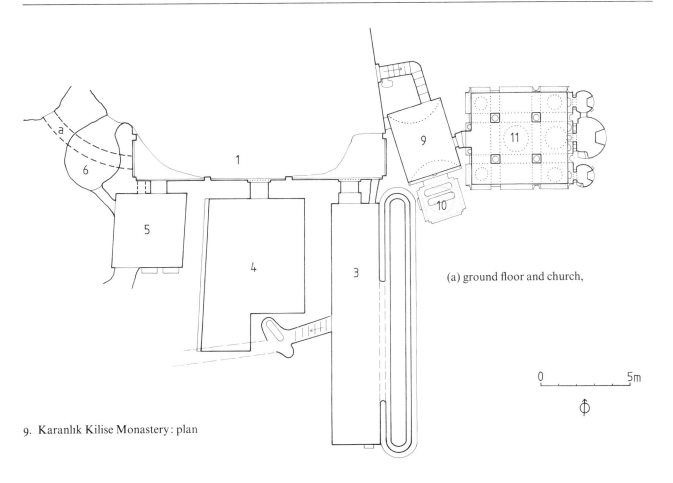

(a) ground floor and church,

9. Karanlık Kilise Monastery: plan

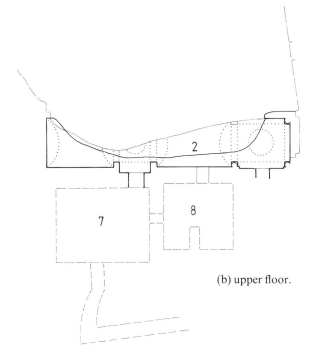

(b) upper floor.

41. Karanlık Kilise Monastery: vestibule, east end.

south of the church is a courtyard and a series of rooms usually called 'the monastery near to Karanlık Kilise'.[39] In fact the church and the room-complex belong together: the entrance to the church is in the east wall of the monastery courtyard (Figs. 9a & 9b and Pl. 41). Further evidence for their association is a painting of the Virgin and Child with Archangels which appears on the east wall of the ground floor unit of the room complex (Pl. 41) and which is the work of the painter(s) who decorated the church. A similar panel appears in Çarıklı Kilise, another of the Column group, where it is certainly part of the church programme, since it is in the naos.[40] Thus, in Karanlık Kilise too, the painting belongs with the church programme and indicates a close relationship between the church and the room complex next to it. Together they form a further member of the 'courtyard' group of monasteries. Like most of the others, it has been used as a pigeon house.

Vestibule (1) The monastery has its rooms and church grouped around a small, slightly irregular courtyard which is open to the north and has lost most of its west side. At the south side of the courtyard there is an elaborate two-storey structure, the ground floor of which is a long, narrow, open-fronted vestibule (Fig. 9a, Pls. 41, 42, 43). This had a flat ceiling above a square cornice. Most of the ceiling is now lost, but fragments remain at both ends (Pl. 41). The long south wall is divided into three sections by pilasters. A frieze of small horseshoe-arched blind niches in groups of two, three or four, separated by pilasters, occupies the upper quarter of each wall; below the frieze is a horizontal moulding which links the rudimentary capitals of the main pilasters. The area was always open-fronted, since forward ends of west and east walls are finished with pilasters. The pilaster at the east side is topped by a small corbel (Pl. 41).

Each bay of the south wall of the vestibule contains an opening: to the left of centre in the eastern bay is a rectangular entrance framed by a horseshoe-arched moulding, the whole set in a shallow rectangular recess; in the centre bay, also left of centre, is a rectangular entrance with a recessed lunette above it, outlined by a moulding, again set in a rectangular recess; in the west bay, to the right of centre is a plain rectangular opening (Pls. 43 & 42).

The vestibule is decorated with red-paint ornament: the cornices bear a chequer pattern and each of the blind

niches of the frieze contains a cross-medallion. The arch of each niche is rimmed by a row of triangles and has a painted gable above it. This decoration has faded from weathering in some places: it is best preserved on the east wall, where part of the ceiling shelters it (see Pl. 41). The painting of Virgin and Child between angels is on this east wall, below the frieze of blind niches.

Room 2 Room 2, directly above the vestibule, is of similar proportions (Fig. 9b). Most of its floor has fallen, as has the front (north) wall. A fragment of the east end of this north wall remains, however, showing a façade decoration of two registers: an upper row of horseshoe-arched blind niches, decorated with ornament in red paint, below a shallow, two-stepped cornice; below them there is another register of double-recessed blind niches (Pl. 43).

The room is divided into four bays which have alternating domed and barrel vaults. The easternmost bay has a truncated dome rising above four arches carried on attached columns with tapering block capitals (the northwest column is lost with the north wall but its capital remains). The dome is cut into a flat area above the four arches, leaving rudimentary triangular pendentives between them (Pl. 41). Red-paint decoration is well preserved in this sheltered area: triangle, chequer and other simple line patterns decorate the vaulting.

The next bay has a barrel vault running west/east and rising above a cornice level with the capitals of Bay 1. The vault is decorated with painted masonry lines and two horizontal bands of hatching and twisted-rope pattern. Just above the cornice is a series of curious patterns and a small figure (Pl. 43).

The third bay has a dome carried on square piers instead of columns (the north pair is lost); a cornice which runs the length of the room at the springing of the arches and barrel vaults continues across these piers. Red-paint decoration here includes a medallion with cross, on the lunette, flanked by tree-like motifs and, to the right, an animal of uncertain species; inscribed above the cross-medallion are the letters A. XN (?), and the lunette is outlined by three rows of hatching (Pl. 42). Masonry lines, triangle patterns and more hatching decorate the arch above the lunette and the remains of dome and pendentives; the southeast pendentives is decorated with a bird, wings spread, and the dome appears to have been decorated with a single large splayed-arm cross. The final bay has a barrel vault which is decorated with masonry

39 Jerphanion, *Eglises*, I. i, 50 and pl. 27.
40 *Ibid*. I. ii, 457.

pattern. A zig-zag border outlines the western lunette.

Three openings are cut into the south wall of Room 2: a rough cavity in Bay 1, a trapezoidal window in Bay 2 and a well-carved rectangular entrance in Bay 3 (this is probably the only original entrance to Room 2, the other openings belong with the pigeon-house phase). The cavities behind Room 2 will be dealt with below.

Refectory (3) Returning to the ground floor, the easternmost opening of the vestibule leads into a large refectory (3); there is a secondary opening to this room, to the east of the original entrance. The refectory is a long room with a flat ceiling. A rock-cut table and benches run the whole length of the east wall, and apses are cut at each end of the table, accommodating the curved ends of the seating bench. The western (free-standing) bench is damaged: it survives complete at each end and the pieces are linked by a scar left by removal of the rest. An opening in the west wall leads to the upper floor.

Rooms 4–6 The entrance in the centre bay of the vestibule leads into Room 4, next to the refectory. This is a slightly trapezoidal room with a projection to the south. It has a flat ceiling and a low ledge runs along the west wall. The decorated entrance to this room indicates that, in spite of its humble appearance, it is an original part of the monastery. There is less certainty about the next room (5), whose rectangular entrance from the third (west) bay of the vestibule is unadorned. Room 5 is rhomboidal in plan and has a flat ceiling. There are two rectangular-plan arched recesses in the south wall of this room, and below them a trough runs the length of the wall and opens into Room 4. Possibly this carried water (perhaps from a spring in the cliff above) but it may be an entirely secondary feature. A rough opening in the west wall of Room 5 leads into an irregular cavity (6), which is at the same level as Rooms 3, 4 and 5 and opens just in front of the vestibule, at the west side of the courtyard; this cavity is probably secondary.

42. Karanlık Kilise Monastery: vestibule, view southwest.

43. Karanlık Kilise Monastery: vestibule, south wall, east end.

Access At present access to the courtyard is by means of a short tunnel (a) which runs under cavity (6) and opens into the west side of the vestibule, below floor level. A flight of steep steps leads up to the vestibule floor (Pl. 42). A secondary entrance to Room 5 opens from the south side of this stairway. The tunnel may have been the original entrance to the monastery, but it is also possible that it is a secondary feature, supplied to give access to the monastery in its pigeon-house phase, after much of the forward part of the courtyard had fallen, leaving the monastery on a steep ledge.

Upper floor (Rooms 7–8) The opening in the centre of the west wall of the refectory (3) leads to a flight of steps. At the top of these the disc and cavity of a 'millstone' closure are visible. This device consists of a large disc of rock, some 2 metres in diameter and resembling a millstone, lodged vertically in a deep recess in the north wall of the passage; there is a recess in the opposite wall, so that the disc may be rolled across to block the passage. It is placed so that it could block off the whole upper floor.

The upward passage containing the millstone leads to the upper floor, but on each of my visits it has been blocked by an immovable metal grille. The following description of the upper floor is therefore based on Jerphanion's plan and the evidence of openings in the south wall of Room 2; the area is shown in thin broken line on the plan. The passage curves to the north beyond the millstone and enters a rectangular room (7) which in turn opens, by means of the well-cut rectangular entrance noted above, into the third bay of Room 2. According to Jerphanion's plan, Room 7 has an opening in its east wall to another room (8) also rectangular, apparently with two deep recesses in its south wall. The trapezoidal 'window' (once a set of pigeon-holes, fragments of which remain at its top) in the second bay of Room 2 presumably opens into this room. A cavity behind Bay 1 of Room 2 is implied by the rough holes in the south wall of this bay: there must either be a further room here, omitted from Jerphanion's plan, or Room 8 must extend further east, above the refectory.

Church The east wall of the courtyard, which meets the south side at a slightly acute angle, is an area of undecorated smooth rock. This façade contains the church entrance, which is of the same form as that of the refectory: a rectangular opening set in a moulded horseshoe arch, the whole set in a shallow rectangular recess (Pl. 41). A cross-medallion is painted on the lunette and the horseshoe arch is decorated with chequer pattern. This

entrance leads into a short stairway which makes a right-angle turn and then opens into the narthex. Just beyond the entrance from the courtyard a secondary cavity is cut into the wall of the passage, to the right of the stairway.

The narthex (9) has a barrel vault on a roughly north/south axis, rising above a rudimentary cornice. The northern lunette is decorated with three horseshoe-arched blind niches. Just to the left of the lunette, an arched window opens to the façade (Pl. 41). The south lunette also has a decoration of three blind niches. A low bench runs across the south wall, and above it a horseshoe-arched opening leads into a small tomb chamber (10) (Pl. 44). This is roughly square and is covered by a dome cut into a flat ceiling carried on four arches (three wall arches and the entrance arch). The floor, which is at the level of the ledge across the south wall, and therefore higher than the narthex floor, contains two grave pits, leaving space for a further pit at the south side. There is also a small arcosolium cut into the west wall of the tomb chamber, with a grave pit of infant size, but this is roughly cut and is probably secondary.

A rectangular entrance in the east wall of the narthex, enlarged to the south by the loss of part of the wall, opens into the naos. This is of inscribed-cross plan. The central dome was originally carried by four slender columns with tapering block capitals. Only one column (the southwest) remains intact. Arches spring between the columns to frame the central bay. The eastern cross-arm is also domed; the other three are barrel-vaulted. Small arches spring from the columns to wall pilasters framing small domed corner bays. The pilasters are of two forms: square-cut to the west and columnar to the east; there are also attached columns in each corner of the naos. A low bench circuits the naos, extending slightly forward of the pilasters. Four seats are cut into this bench, two flanking the naos entrance in the west wall and two more flanking the entrance to the main apse.

The church has three apses. The main apse is larger than the lateral ones and was originally closed by a tall, rock-cut screen, fragments of which remain at each side. The screen had a central mushroom-shaped entrance below an open lunette, flanked by horseshoe-arched lateral openings.[41] There is a rounded rock-cut altar and a seat in the southwest corner. The lateral apses have mushroom-shaped openings. Each apse has an attached, rounded, rock-cut altar with a small arched blind niche above it (to the right of the altar in the north apse, to the left in the south apse). In the south apse there is also a small seat in the southwest corner. An arched opening links the north and central apses.

41 For a reconstruction, see Epstein, 'Rock-cut Chapels', fig. 11.

44. Karanlık Kilise Monastery: Church, narthex tomb chamber.

Painting The church, including its narthex, is plastered and painted throughout. The painted programme is described in detail by Jerphanion[42] and will therefore be described only briefly here:

Narthex and naos

A New Testament cycle begins on the east wall of the narthex, with the Annunciation flanking the entrance to the naos. The cycle continues in the naos, in the barrel vaults of north, south and west cross-arms, and adjacent wall lunettes: Journey to Bethlehem, Nativity, Adoration of the Magi, Baptism, Raising of Lazarus, Transfiguration, Entry into Jerusalem, Last Supper, Betrayal, Crucifixion, Anastasis, Myrophores; the cycle finishes in the narthex vault, with a combined Ascension and Benediction of Apostles.

Main apse: (conch) Deesis; (in an arcade on the wall) group of bishop saints.

North apse: (conch) Virgin and Child; (wall) bishop saints.

South apse: (conch) Abraham; (below) Mandylion; (wall) bishop saints.

Soffits of arches carrying central dome: prophets.

Other soffits, remaining wall space and minor vaults: busts or full figures of saints.

North and south walls: (centre bays) north – Archangel Gabriel; south – Michael.

Narthex west wall: the hospitality of Abraham (the only Old Testament subject in the church).

Outside the church, on the north wall of the vestibule is the panel mentioned above, showing the Virgin and Child, standing beneath a triple arcade, flanked by archangels.

Donor images The painted programme outlined above also includes several donor images, drawn in Fig. 10:

(a) In the Benediction of Apostles on the west side of the narthex vault, a bearded figure kneels at the feet of Christ. He wears a long belted brocade gown, with a scarf at the neck, and a large hat with a tassel; his hands reach forward to Christ's feet. Kneeling at the right of Christ, making a similar gesture, is another figure, wearing a similar robe. He has a slighter beard than the first figure and is either bareheaded or wears a small hat (most of the

42 Jerphanion, *Eglises,* I. ii, 393ff.

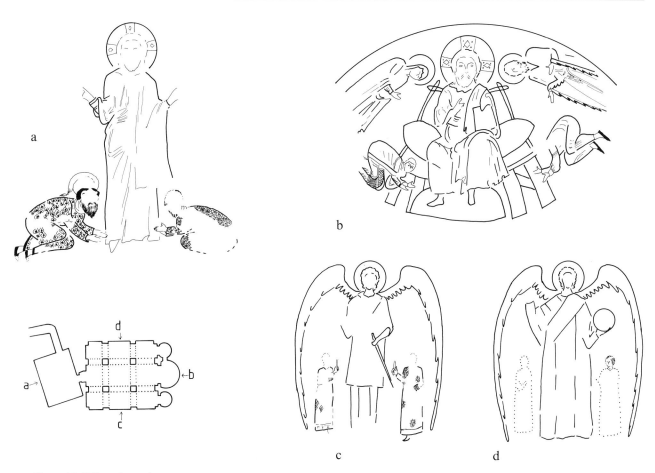

10. Karanlık Kilise: donor images.

head is missing) (Fig. 10a). Inscriptions above the figures were recorded by Jerphanion:

(left)   Δέησις τοῦ δούλου τοῦ Θ(εο)ῦ
         Ἰω(άννου) Ἐνταλματικου
(right) Δέ[ησι]ς
         Γε [νεθ] λήου[43]

Translation: (left) 'Entreaty of the servant of God, John, *Entalmatikos'*,
            (right) 'Entreaty of the servant of God, Ge[neth]lios.'

(b) In the Deesis of the main apse two more donor figures kneel, with arms stretched forward, at the feet of Christ enthroned. To the left is a bareheaded, beardless man wearing priestly vestments: a *phelonion* over a long robe, with an *epitrachelion* falling in front and a smaller vest-

ment around the neck. To the right, the other kneeling figure wears a long robe with sleeves gathered into cuffs, and ornamental bands at upper-arm level, but with no priestly insignia. His face is destroyed, but the small size of the damaged area suggests that this figure too was bareheaded and beardless (Fig. 10b). Inscriptions above the figures read:

(left)   Δέησης τοῦ δούλου τοῦ Θ(εο)ῦ Νηκη
         φόρου πρεσ(βυτέρου)
(right) Δέησης τοῦ δούλου τοῦ Θ(εο)ῦ
         Βασ[ηα]νοῦ[44]

Translation: (left) 'Entreaty of the servant of God, Nikephoros, priest',
            (right) 'Entreaty of the servant of God, Bassianos.'[45]

43 Jerphanion, *Eglises*, I. ii, 396, Inscription nos. 37 and 38.
44 *Ibid.* I. ii, 398, Inscription nos. 39 & 40.
45 Jerphanion reads the name in Inscription no. 40 as BAC[HA]N[OY]; Epstein, 'Fresco Decoration', 37, reads

BAC[I]Λ(E)IOY; the inscription is badly damaged and barely legible, but the evidence of Jerphanion's photograph supports his reading.

At least three more donors, hitherto unrecorded, are represented in the naos:

(c) In a large panel on the south wall, centre bay, the image of the Archangel Michael of Chonae is flanked by two small standing figures. Each wears a long brocade robe of brownish purple, with a brown border beneath which feet shod in slippers are visible. Each turns towards the angel with hands lifted, holding a short cylindrical object (a candle?). Neither figure has a headdress or halo; they are both beardless and have short brown hair (Fig. 10c). Jerphanion recorded an inscription in the panel:

Ἀρχ(άγγελε) βοή[θ]ι τ/ō [σο] δο[υ]λ[ō . . ./— — — [46]

Translation: 'Archangel help thy servant . . .'

This inscription is just above the head of the figure on the right. Doubtless a similar invocation accompanied the figure on the left, but has not survived.

(d) Opposite, on the north wall, a similar large panel contains an image of the Archangel Gabriel. To the right of the angel, below his hand holding an orb, is the head and neck of a small figure. The head is youthful, beardless and without a halo. The wall is very badly damaged and the body of this figure is lost, as is the adjacent area, which might have carried an inscription. A complementary figure probably existed to the left of the angel, but this area, too, is lost (Fig. 10d).

Altogether, therefore, there are seven donor images in the church (almost certainly eight originally). The four figures shown in the apse and narthex would appear to have higher status than the tiny figures in the archangel panels, and John, *Entalmatikos*, appears to be the most senior of all: he is heavily bearded, wears a headdress and has a title. Genethlios, with him in the narthex, is apparently a younger man. Of the other two, one is a priest and the other lacks a title; both appear to be youthful. The small figures in the archangel panels may be children.

It seems probable that there is a link between the donor images and the tomb chamber in the narthex. This chamber is certainly an original element of the monastery, for the painting of the narthex south wall acknowledges the

tomb entrance. The tomb chamber contains only two adult grave pits; there is space for one more adult grave, but no pit is cut. The tomb could not, therefore have accommodated all eight persons depicted on the church walls. Nikephoros the Priest and Bassianos seem the most likely candidates for occupation of the two graves since the Deesis in which they appear is appropriate to a funerary context. If so, then perhaps the monastery was commissioned by John, *Entalmatikos* – with the others as secondary donors, perhaps – as a memorial for these two. Possibly all were members of one family: John, *Entalmatikos*, with three adult sons (the youthful figures in apse and narthex) and four younger sons (or grandsons) in the archangel panels. The hypothesis of family patronage is not without problems, however, since no provision was made for further family burials (at least, not for more than one) and also there is no sign of any female members of the family. Alternatively, the donors may have had some other relationship, as members of a confraternity, perhaps.[47]

The title *Entalmatikos* does not appear in any of the published lists of Byzantine titles.[48] Thierry identifies it as the title of one empowered to execute the mandate of the Patriarchate,[49] but this is uncertain, since the title does not occur in the Patriarchal Acts cited in evidence; there appears only *entalma*, as a term used for certain letters of Patriarchal authority. Even if John's employment is correctly identified, it is not clear whether such a person was sent from the Patriarchate, and would therefore have been a visitor to Göreme or, conversely, was a local resident entrusted with supervising the directives of the Patriarchate in his own area.

Narthex inscription An inscription that might have clarified the relationship of the donors and the nature of their patronage was painted in the narthex, above the entrance to the naos. This is now in such poor condition that it is illegible – not one letter survives complete (Pl. 45). The inscription fragments are on a rectangular field, divided horizontally by a slight change of plane (the upper field overhangs the lower by about 1 cm). The lettering is in white paint on a dark ground, and the inscription seems to be arranged in six lines, judging by the size and placing of the surviving letter fragments. A painting of the Annunciation flanks the naos entrance, with the Angel to the left and Virgin to the right. It is possible, therefore,

46 Jerphanion, *Eglises*, I. ii, 400, Inscription no. 41. Jerphanion did not note the figures.
47 For such societies: J. Nesbitt and J. Wiita, 'A Confraternity of the Comnenian Era', *BZ* 68 (1975) 360–84.
48 N. Oikonomedes, *Les listes de préséance byzantines des 9e et 10e siècles* (Paris, 1972); J. B. Bury, *The Imperial Administrative System in the 9th Century* (London, 1911); Grégoire, 'Rapport', 86, regards

the title as synonymous with *entolikarios*, but this, too, is absent from the lists.
49 N. Thierry, 'L'art monumental byzantin en Asie Mineure du XIe siècle au XIVe', *DOP* 29 (1975) 75–111, at 89, citing J. Darrouzès, *Le régistre synodal du patriarcat byzantin au XIVe siècle* (Paris, 1971), 189–92, and V. Grumel, *Les régestres des Actes du patriarcat de Constantinople* (Paris/Istanbul, 1932), I, 85 and 265.

45. Karanlık Kilise Monastery: Church, narthex inscription.

that the inscription belongs to this scene, but its length and the fact that it is isolated from the figural panels by a border suggest otherwise. More probably, this was a dedicatory inscription, the loss of which would doubtless have irritated the donors as much as it does the historian.

Summary

Karanlık Kilise Monastery (Figs. 9a and 9b) has a small courtyard with an open-fronted vestibule (1) along one side. Behind this is a refectory with rock-cut furniture (3) and two simple rooms (4 and 5). Above the vestibule is a room with four vaulted bays (2) and behind this two more simple rooms (7 and 8). The church is at an upper level at the east side of the courtyard, reached by a stairway. It has an inscribed-cross naos (11), a narthex (9) and tomb chamber (10). Karanlık Kilise is fully painted with a high-quality programme that includes several donor images.

Date

There is no doubt that the church and monastery rooms are part of a single phase of excavation. The church is

an integral a part of the monastery plan, and its entrance from the courtyard is identical in form to that of the refectory. Since there is no layer of polychrome painting in Karanlık Kilise earlier than the one described above, it is reasonable to suppose that this decoration was applied soon after the excavation of the complex. The date of the monastery therefore depends upon the date assigned to the Column group of churches, of which Karanlık Kilise is a member. A date in the mid eleventh century is generally accepted for this group, based on the style of the paintings, the content of the programme and its relationship to other datable programmes in Göreme valley.[50]

Aynalı Kilise Monastery

Aynalı Kilise (Göreme Chapel 14) forms part of a monastery complex about 1 km southeast of Göreme valley.[51] Several rooms and the church surround a small courtyard cut into a low cliff just visible from the beginning of the road which runs to Avcılar from the main Nevşehir–Ürgüp road (Fig. 11a and Pl. 46).

Façade The south wall of the courtyard has a façade of

50 Epstein, 'Fresco Decoration', 27 n. 1, and *idem*, 'Rock-cut Chapels', 115–16.

51 Jerphanion, *Eglises*, I. i, 49; Strzygowski, *Kleinasien*, 151; Kostof, *Caves of God*, 60.

46. Aynalı Kilise Monastery: site.

46a. Aynalı Kilise Monastery: façade, detail.

three bays separated by heavy pilasters and divided horizontally into three registers (Pl. 46). The ground-level register has a tall, double-recessed, slightly horseshoe-arched blind niche in each bay; each niche arch springs from a rudimentary pilaster capital and a simple moulding links the outer arches of each niche to the adjacent pier (Pl. 46a). All three niches house openings into the monastery: at the left an arched entrance to the church narthex, in the centre and to the right, rectangular entrances to Room 1. Above the niches a heavy flat cornice crosses each bay between the piers. The second register originally had a decoration of two double-recessed arched blind niches in each bay, but the right niche of the left bay has been lost by erosion. The left niche of the centre bay is wider than the rest and contains a tall rectangular opening into an upper room (b) (Fig. 11b). There are two more openings into this room: small rectangular windows in the left niches of left and right bays. Above the niches is another set of cornices running between the piers. Very little remains of the upper register: traces of piers indicate that it followed the three-bay division of the lower registers, and in the left part of the left bay one small arched niche is intact. Its size suggests that each of the bays contained four such niches, and a drawing by Smirnov, who saw the site in the late nineteenth century, shows two and a half niches in the right

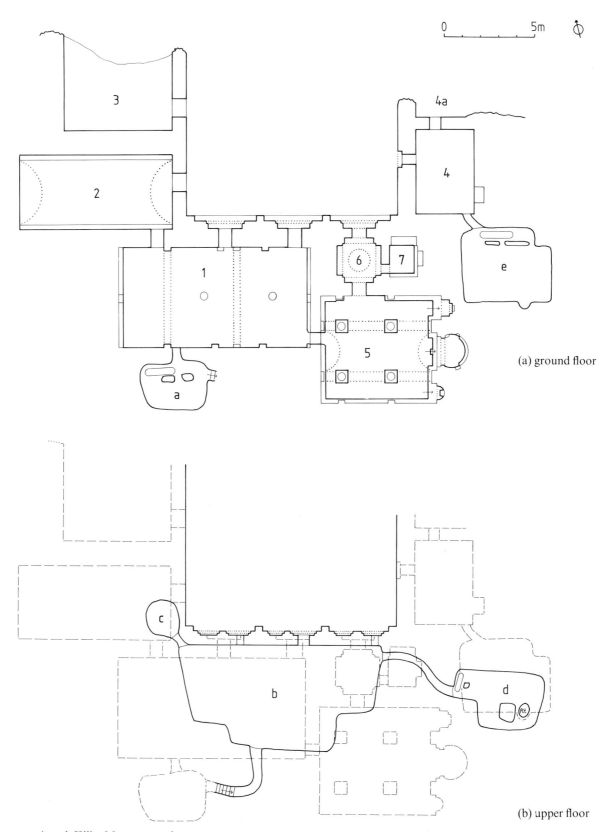

0   5m

(a) ground floor

(b) upper floor

11. Aynalı Kilise Monastery: plan

47. Aynalı Kilise Monastery: Room 1, southeast corner.

bay, with space for one more.[52] The largest room of the complex (1) and the church (5) lie behind this south façade. Other rooms open off the plain side walls of the courtyard.

Room 1   Room 1 is a large hall with a barrel vault running east/west. The vault rises above a cornice and is divided into three bays by transverse arches (Pl. 47). The walls are articulated by pilasters: three on each of the long walls, and one on each short wall. The westernmost transverse arch meets wall pilasters and the easternmost arch springs from corbels above the cornice. A narrow bench runs along east and west walls.

The original entrance to the room is from the central bay of the façade. The opening from the westernmost façade bay is probably secondary, since it cuts through the central pilaster of the north wall of Room 1. Also secondary is a rough opening at the south end of the east wall, which leads into the church (Pl. 47). There is a similar secondary opening in the north wall, west end, into Room 2. An upper floor, described below, lies above Room 1 and is reached through a rough opening in the south wall.

Painted decoration consists of bands of red geometric ornament painted directly onto the rock. Triangle and chequer patterns in bands decorate the cornice, transverse arches and pilaster capitals. Bands of similar ornament run the length of the vault, at the crest and halfway down each side, thus dividing it into two registers on each side. A Latin cross with splayed arms, enclosed in a kite-shaped field, is painted on the east lunette, and a similar painted cross, without a border, fills the second bay from the east of the south wall; the cross has the inscription IC XC painted above its lateral arms. In the first bay of this wall is a curious painting, of very crude execution, showing a helmeted archer aiming his arrow at a bird to the right (Fig. 12a). Another curiosity is the animal of uncertain species (resembling a ladybird beetle) painted on the corbel above the entrance to the hall (Fig. 12b).

Room 2   A simple rectangular opening at the south side of the west wall of the courtyard leads into Room 2. This is a barrel-vaulted room with an overhang on north and south walls from which the vault springs (this room may also be reached from a secondary opening in Room 1).

---

52 Reproduced in Strzygowski, *Kleinasien*, 151.

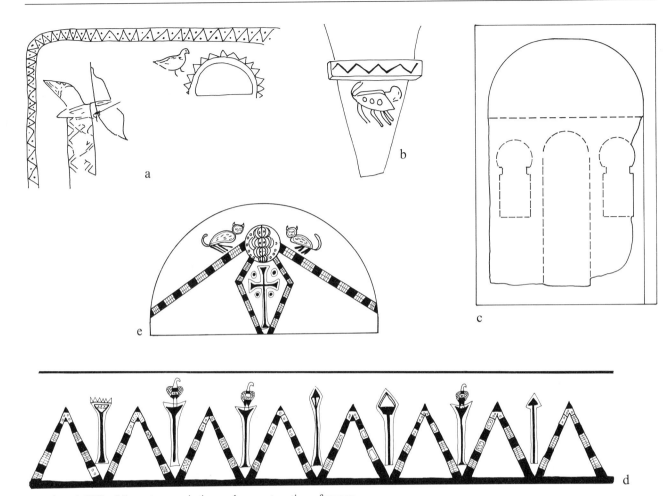

12. Aynalı Kilise Monastery: painting and reconstruction of screen.

A painted chequer-pattern border decorates the cornices and crosses the west wall to link them.

Room 3 Room 3, next to Room 2, is also entered from the west wall of the courtyard through a rectangular entrance with a window of similar form above it. This has a flat ceiling above a rudimentary cornice. The whole of its north wall is lost where the cliff has fallen away.

Rooms 4 and 4a The northern end of the east face of the courtyard is similarly damaged by erosion. A rectangular opening in the courtyard east wall, set in a shallow arched recess, leads into Room 4, a rectangular room with a flat ceiling. An opening in the north wall of this room leads into a fragment of another flat-ceilinged room (4a). This entrance may be secondary, so Room 4a probably had an original entrance on the east façade.

Upper floor Several irregular and roughly cut rooms, linked by tunnels, form an upper storey to the complex (Fig. 11b). A hole in the south wall of Room 1 leads into a smaller irregular cavity (a). This cavity contains a millstone closing device: a heavy disc of rock lodged against two pillars, which may be rolled in front of them to close the entrance. At the west side of cavity (a) a flight of rough steps leads upwards in a curving tunnel to open into a large irregular room (b). This has a large rectangular opening and two rectangular windows in its north wall, piercing the second register of the façade.

A short tunnel in the northwest corner of (b) leads into a small cavity (c), which lies above the southeast corner of Room 2. Another tunnel, opening off the northeast corner of (b), curves to the right and then opens into cavity (d) which is entirely unlit. Just inside the entrance to (d) is another millstone closure. Cavity (d) contains a rough pier, placed towards the south. Beyond this is a pit in the floor which is the top of a vertical tunnel with footholds cut into it. The tunnel links (d) with a roughly rectangular cavity (e) at ground level. In the north wall of (d) there is the entrance to a tunnel leading to Room

4, with a third millstone closure at the entrance.

Area (b) of the upper floor has clearly been used for housing pigeons at some point, since its walls are pitted with nesting recesses. However, the presence of three millstone closures, which make it possible to close off all or part of the upper floor and cavity (e), make it unlikely that the rooms were originally cut for this purpose since pigeon-house entrances are usually closed with rough masonry. Two possibilities therefore exist: either the upper rooms and (e) were an original part of the monastery, designed to be an area of security in case of attack, or a safe place in which to keep valuables, or they resulted from modification of the complex in the post-Byzantine period. The latter is the more likely, since the various rough openings cut to join the rooms of the complex establish the existence of a secondary phase and had the upper rooms been part of the monastery, one would expect them to be finished with the same degree of competence as the rest. A sequence of at least three phases is therefore likely: first the monastery, without an upper floor; next, the use of the monastery rooms as a dwelling, a phase during which securable storage areas were supplied by the excavation of the upper floor and the millstone closures; finally, conversion into a pigeon house.

Church: naos (5), narthex (6), tomb chamber (7) An arched entrance in the easternmost bay of the south façade leads into the church narthex (6). Smirnov's drawing (see above, under *Façade*) shows this entrance framed by mouldings, but these are now lost. The narthex has a free-cross plan with short cross-arms. It is covered by a dome which is cut into a flat ceiling. There are rudimentary pendentives in the four corners below the dome (Pl. 48). The dome is decorated with simple ornament in red paint: four chequered bands running from rim to crown, where there is an equal-armed cross in a medallion; small red medallions encircle the dome at its springing, between the four bands; the vestigial pendentives are also decorated with red ornament, and the northeast one with a stylized bird.

A small square flat-ceilinged tomb chamber (7) is reached through an arched entrance in the east arm of the narthex. This room has benches along east and south sides and a niche in its east wall. There is an arcosolium in the north wall, but this has no grave pit: the area of rock below the arch is solid.

The naos is reached through an arched opening in the south wall of the narthex. It is a squat basilica, with colonnades of three arches each side making the division into nave and aisles (Pl. 49). The nave is barrel-vaulted, the aisles have flat ceilings. At the east end the arcades begin conventionally, with the first arches springing from

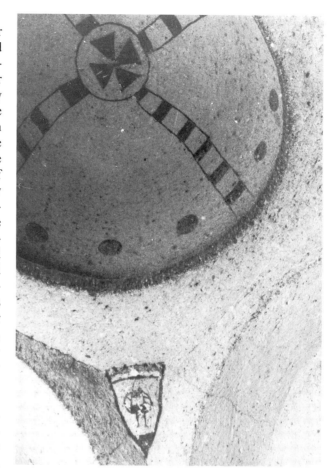

48. Aynalı Kilise Monastery: Church, narthex dome.

attached piers, but at the west end they end abruptly, with sliced-off half-arches running into short pilasters on the walls. These pilasters rise above a carved and painted cornice which circuits the walls (Pls. 49 & 50). The arcades are supported on slender columns with square bases and simple slab capitals. On each aisle wall, pilasters stand opposite the columns of the arcades, but stop short of the aisle ceilings.

A large central apse of horseshoe-shaped plan opens from a rectangular recess in the east wall of the nave (Pl. 49). A scar at the back of the apse shows that it once had an attached rock-cut altar. A ledge runs behind the altar and extends beyond it about halfway around the apse wall. Two niches, an apsidal niche to the left and a blind niche to the right, are cut into the wall above the ledge at its extremities. In the north corner of the apse is a rock-cut bowl, slightly above ground level. At the south side of the apse entrance the right side of a keyhole-shaped opening is visible about three quarters of the way up the wall. Above and below this are small rough areas.

49. Aynalı Kilise Monastery: Church, main apse and southeast corner.

50. Aynalı Kilise Monastery: Church, northwest corner.

These features are probably the remains of a tall screen, with a central opening, lateral windows and open lunette, like that in Karanlık Kilise and in several Göreme churches of the Yılanlı group (Fig. 12c).[53] In the east wall opposite the south aisle there is a shallow absidiole with no screen; it contains an attached altar (Pl. 49). Opposite the north aisle there is a square-plan recess with an arched blind niche cut into its back wall.

A low bench circuits the church, forming a base for the pilasters on the side walls and jutting forward around the attached piers of the arcades on the east wall. The ledge is broken at the north wall entrance to the narthex, and at the secondary entrance to Room 1. The apses are raised above the level of the nave and aisles, the bench forming a step up to them.

Painting (The painting in Room 1 has already been described.) The church is extensively decorated with orna-

ment in red, painted directly onto the rock. The arches of the arcades are rimmed with red, and their soffits painted with alternating panels of plain red and rectangles of 'domino' patterns (Pl. 49). A line of ten medallions containing various motifs, including crosses, runs along the crest of the barrel vault (Pl. 50). The vault is divided into two registers each side by red bands, below which are broad zig-zag bands of red and white chequer pattern. Between the points of the zig-zag are painted pillars topped by devices of various forms: flame, arrow, lantern and kite shapes, but most of all stylized birds: three on the north side (Fig. 12d & Pl. 50) and five on the south side. The spandrels of the arcades have still more of these pillars, each carrying a bird, and on the west wall another pillar carrying a Latin cross enclosed in a kite-shaped border, is enclosed in a further kite-shaped field. It has been suggested that pillar motifs of this type represent military standards: the pillars carrying birds, in particu-

---

53 Epstein, 'Rock-cut Chapels', 130–2, 132–4.

lar, may be seen as distant country cousins of Roman Eagles.[54] In the lunette above the apse another cross, enclosed in a kite-shaped border, is surmounted by a medallion containing a vertical eight-lobed pattern, flanked by two quadrupeds, dimly identifiable, perhaps, as lions (Fig. 12e). A chequer pattern rims the recess in the east wall and the soffit of the apse arch is similarly decorated. In each spandrel flanking the arch is an equal-armed cross. The apse has a cross in a kite-shaped border in the conch, and a chequered 'cornice' below the conch. North and south walls of the naos have a chequered band painted at the level of the arcade capitals and another at the tops of the walls, decorated with a zig-zag pattern. Above the painted band of the north aisle is a painted keyhole shape with a gable above it (Pl. 50); there is a further keyhole shape in the equivalent position on the south aisle wall. A red band runs along the ceilings of both aisles and the ceiling of the north aisle also has two medallions in square frames at the east end. The naos entrance in the north wall is flanked by carved pilasters, painted with the domino pattern, which end about 1 metre above the entrance; a painted gable links them (Pl. 50). The painted band rises above the entrance to form three sides of a square. A similar arrangement is found in the opposite space on the south wall where, however, there is no entrance.

Summary

Aynalı Kilise Monastery (Figs. 11a and 11b) has its rooms grouped around a courtyard with an elaborate decorated main façade. Behind the façade is a large hall (1), a basilical church (5) approached through a narthex (6) with a tomb chamber (7). At the west side of the courtyard is another large room (2) and next to it a simpler room (3). Another simple room (4) opens off the east side of the courtyard, with a fragment of a further room (4a) next to it. A roughly finished but extensive upper floor (Fig. 11b) was probably cut in one or two post-Byzantine phases of excavation. The church and hall have extensive red-paint decoration.

Date

Simple decoration in red paint is ubiquitous in Cappadocian cave churches, either as a primary decoration or as

the only decoration of a church. It is applied even in churches where a developed polychrome painting is later placed over it. Probably the simple geometric ornament was the finishing touch, after the masons had finished work. Its object was evidently to make the interior look as much like a built structure as possible, since it is generally used to emphasize architectural features, such as the rims of domes and arches, and occasionally includes lines imitating the joins in masonry. Usually this red-paint decoration is of little use for dating purposes, since its chronological span is probably very wide. However, elaborate versions of this kind of decoration, such as that described above, are not common and may give some indication of date. Extensive red-paint decoration of this type is found chiefly in Göreme valley: the best parallels are with Chapel 20 (St Barbara), Chapel 21 and Chapel 25.[55] In Chapel 20 there are parallels for the pillar ornament, the domino decoration for soffits, the kite-shaped fields containing crosses and also for the strange animals.[56] Chapels 20 and 21 belong to the Yılanlı group of churches in Göreme valley. The tall chancel screen of Aynalı Kilise forms another link with this group. The Yılanlı group, mentioned above in connection with Hallaç Monastery and Bezir Hane, and discussed in Chapter 4, is probably datable to the mid to late eleventh century. Tentatively, therefore, Aynalı Kilise may be given a similar date. Since there is no reason to suppose a chronological separation between the church and the rest of the complex, this date may be offered for the monastery as a whole.

Selime Kalesi

The Melendiz river valley lies some 25 km to the southeast of Aksaray and its south part, running from Belisırma to İhlara, is a chasm known as the Peristrema valley (Fig. 1). Here steep cliffs either side of the river contain a number of cave monuments.[57] At the north end the sides of the valley are less steep, formed by clusters of large cones. In this area, near the village of Selime, is a cave monastery known locally as Selime Kalesi. The church of this monastery has received some attention, and photographs of some of the rooms have been published.[58]

The monastery is located in a large group of cones above the village and has its rooms grouped around two

---

54 D. Wood, 'Byzantine Military Standards in a Cappadocian Church', *Archaeology* 12 (1959), 38–46, deals with similar standards in St Barbara (Göreme Chapel 20).
55 Jerphanion, *Eglises*, I. ii, 474–8, 484–6, 479; Wood, 'Byzantine Military Standards' (see note 54).
56 For illustrations see Giovannini, *Arts of Cappadocia*, pls. 45, 46, 100, 103, 104.
57 Thierry, *Nouvelles églises*.
58 Thierry, *Nouvelles églises*, 31; N. Thierry, 'Etudes cappadociennes,

Région du Hasan Dağı, compléments pour 1974', *CahArch* 24 (1975), 183–90, at 184–5; J. Lafontaine-Dosogne, 'Nouvelles notes cappadociennes', *Byzantion* 33 (1963), 121–83, at 174–6; *idem*, 'La Kale Kilisesi de Selime et sa représentation des donateurs', *Zetesis (Album Amicorum E. de Strijcker)* (Antwerp/Utrecht, 1973), 741–53; M. Yanagi, *Kappadokya. Höhlenkloster in der Türkei* (Tokyo, 1966), pls. 32–9; Kostof, *Caves of God*, 59; Rott, *Denkmäler*, 263–4.

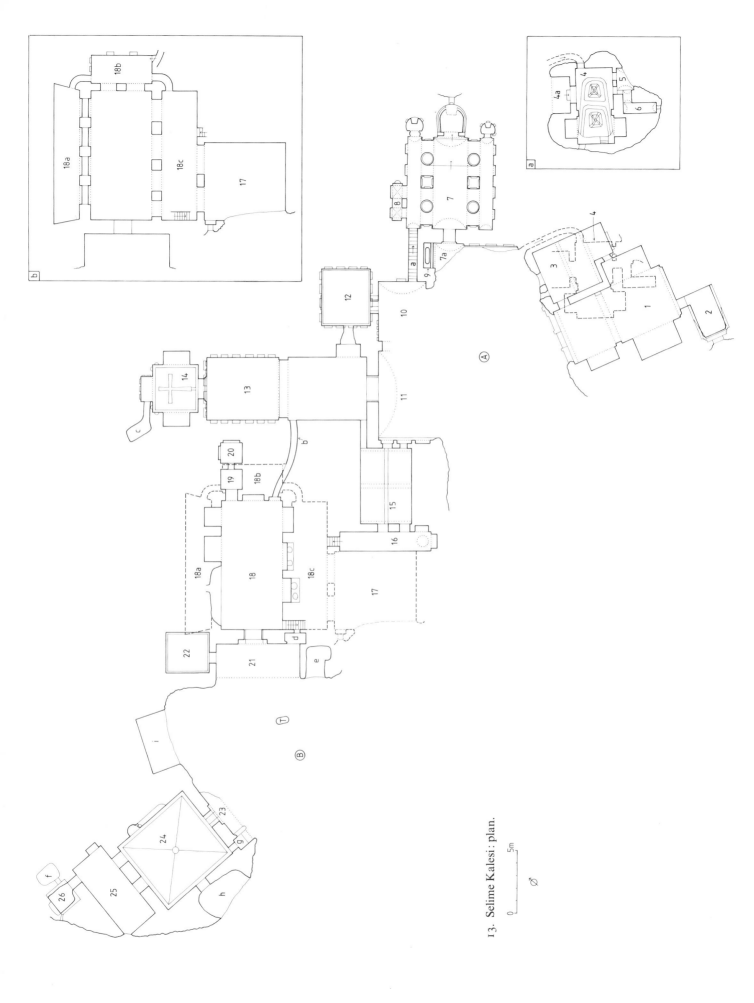

13. **Selime Kalesi**: plan.

0   5m

courtyard areas (A and B), connected by a path which follows the serpentine contour of the site (Fig. 13). This path is quite narrow at present, but may well have been much wider when the monastery was in use. Access was once by means of a wide tunnel that must have begun somewhere near the modern road (which runs along the valley bottom) and opens into the northeast end of Court-yard B at point (T) on the plan. This tunnel is still com-plete in places and the present pathway to the monastery uses parts of it, but most of it is caved in and weathered, and the lower part is entirely lost.

Selime Kalesi is the largest and most elaborate of the cave monasteries. For the sake of clarity and ease of read-ing the plan, the rooms will be described in peram-bulatory order, rather than in order of importance, starting at the east side of Area A, which is the eastern extremity of the complex, and moving westwards.

Room 1 At the east side of Area A is the remains of a façade (Pl. 51), consisting of a rectangular recess cut into the rock and decorated with three blind niches: a tall, double-recessed niche containing a rectangular opening flanked by two slightly wider and shorter lateral niches. The façade runs roughly north/south.

The opening in this small façade leads into Room 1,

which is rectangular, with a barrel vault on a west/east axis (Pl. 52). The vault rises above a two-step cornice and is divided into two bays by a median transverse arch; there are wall arches at each end. In the far (east) corners of this room are two attached columns. The transverse arch of the vault is met by pilasters, each decorated with a relief-carved motif: a pillar on a stepped base, carrying a disc decorated with an inscribed splayed-armed cross (Pl. 53). The lower part of the pilaster on the north wall has been cut away.

The north and south walls of the eastern bay contain deep rectangular-plan arched recesses. In each recess the arch springs from cornices on the lateral walls which are linked across the back wall, marking off the lunette. In the north niche a wall arch outlines the lunette, which is decorated with a low relief carving of two birds facing one another across a central pilaster with stepped base and stylized capital (Pl. 54). A rough secondary opening in the back wall, below the lunette, links the recess with Room 3. In the opposite recess, in the south wall, the lunette is too much damaged for it to be certain whether or not it was similarly decorated. A third, shallower arched recess is cut into the south wall of the west bay. The lunette here is decorated with a relief carved 'disc on pillar' motif, like those on the wall pilasters. In the

51. Selime Kalesi: façade of Rooms 1–3 and porch (4a).

52. Selime Kalesi: Room 1, north wall.

53. Selime Kalesi: Room 1, detail of ornament on south wall.

north wall of the west bay a rectangular opening, outlined by a flat moulding, leads into Room 3.

Room 2 At the south side of the east wall of Room 1 a small rectangular opening leads into Room 2, a narrow rectangular room with a bench along west, east and south walls. The room is roughly barrel-vaulted at its north end and has a flat ceiling at the south end, carried above a cornice. West, east and south walls at this end of the room have a decoration of arched blind niches; those on the west and east walls taper off at their north sides. The niche of the south wall contains a large rectangular window, overlooking the valley (Pl. 55).

Fragments of plaster remain in several areas of Rooms 1 and 2 (Pl. 52). The plastering was clearly done after the Room 1 north wall pilaster was cut away, since the plaster is continuous on the wall at this point, covering the scar (Pl. 52). The problem of phases will be resumed below.

Room 3 The opening in the north wall of Room 1 gives access to Room 3. On the Room 3 side this rectangular entrance has a short arched blind niche above it. Room 3 has a stubby L-shaped plan. The main area is rectangular, with a barrel vault springing from a cornice. A transverse arch divides the vault into two bays and there is a wall arch at the east end (Pl. 56). A rectangular projec-

54. Selime Kalesi: Room 1, detail of north wall recess.

55. Selime Kalesi: Room 2, southeast corner.

56. Selime Kalesi: Room 3, east end.

tion of the east wall forms the upright of the L-shape. This area is covered by a half-barrel vault, continuous with the vault of the main part of the room. The back (east) wall of the projection is decorated with a shallow arched blind niche, its base about 1 metre up from the floor. The main entrance to this room must have been in its west wall, most of which is lost. This entrance seems to have been set in a façade, adjacent to that in front of Room 1, since traces of an arched blind niche to the right (south) of the entrance area remain (Pl. 51).

Room 4 and its porch (4a) Room 4 is in the upper part of the cone which houses Rooms 1–3, and overlies parts of Rooms 1 and 3. On the main plan Rooms 4–6 are indicated in broken line; they are drawn fully in box (a). The long axis of this group of rooms runs northeast/ southwest, but for ease of description this axis will be treated as if running east/west. The same adjustment will be made for the rest of the complex up to and including Room 22.

The floor of Room 4 is rectangular, but the walls slope inwards, following the shape of the cone, so that the ceiling is trapezoidal. Its axis is also different, by about 15 degrees. The ceiling is flat where it meets the walls, and is divided into two bays by heavy two-step cornices. Each bay has a squarish calotte cut into it, with four raised ribs (Pl. 57). The room is very tall, with an upper area somewhat overhanging the lower part, as if two rooms, one above another, once existed. There is, however, no sign of a floor separating upper and lower areas (but this may still have been the original plan, abandoned during excavation).

The walls of the upper area are variously decorated: the long (north and south) walls have an upper register of four shallow blind-arched niches set above a slight overhang (Pls. 57–8). Level with this register on the south part of the west wall there is a rectangular-plan recess which is flanked by rudimentary pilasters and has at its back a section of two-step cornice like that on the long walls (Pl. 57). To the right of the recess is a rough hole to the outside – once, perhaps, a window. The area of east wall level with this upper register is lost. A second register of blind niches lies below the upper register on the long walls. Here the niches are larger and there are only three to each wall. The west wall opposite this register is blank, the east wall lost. The row of niches on the south wall is set above a slight overhang and the upper part of the west wall also overhangs. (The shallow niches in the upper part of this room have not been shown on the plan, since they occur in two registers on sloping walls, and defeat draughtsmanship.)

The lower area is less irregular: pilasters on north and

57. Selime Kalesi: Room 4, ceiling and southwest corner.

south walls divide the room into two bays of unequal size. The smaller (western) bay has deep rectangular-plan arched recesses cut into its north and south walls. These have cornices at the springing of the arch, like the niches of Room 1, but are otherwise undecorated.

The north wall of the eastern bay contains the original entrance to this room: a rectangular opening placed off-centre (towards the west), which leads into a porch (4a) (Pl. 51). The porch is barrel-vaulted, with cornice at the springing of the vault. Its floor level is lower than that of Room 4 and part of a step in front of the entrance remains. Above the entrance there is a relief decoration of uncertain form – perhaps a disc above a horizontal base. The porch overlooks the courtyard area, some five metres below it, and must originally have been reached from the courtyard by steps or a ramp. At present access is by means of a narrow, steep path on the east side of the cone, which meets a rough secondary opening in the east wall of Room 4. It is possible, of course, that the porch was once a room, now lacking its front wall, but the 'porch' formula occurs elsewhere on this site and is

58. Selime Kalesi: Room 4, ceiling and north wall.

therefore probably the original form here.

The south wall of the east bay of Room 4 has two rectangular openings into a rectangular room (5) with a barrel vault running west/east. The vault does not cover the whole of the room, but stops short of its west end. Most of the east and south sides of this room are lost. A barrel-vaulted passage leads from its west side to a further narrow barrel-vaulted area (6), at right angles to (5). At the end of this a rough opening, possibly once a window, opens to the outside.

Church (7) The monastery church (7) is to the north of the cones containing Rooms 1–6. (It lies on a northeast/southwest axis, but orientations will follow the adjustment of compass made above.)

The entrance to the church, opening into the west end of the nave, is a tall, narrow rectangle, cut into a tall keyhole-shaped blind niche which is set in the back of a barrel-vaulted porch (7a) (Pl. 59). The barrel vault rises above a simple cornice on the north side, which meets a wall arch outlining the lunette above the church entrance. To the right of the porch the rock face is cut back to form a façade, with three shallow blind niches of the type seen in Room 4. This area was once sheltered by an overhang, of which only fragments remain. The porch has no south wall, so the south side of its barrel vault must have descended to the level of the overhang. Cut into the north wall of the porch is a deep arched recess (9) which contains a single grave pit behind a low wall.

The church is a three-aisled basilica with the division into nave and aisles made by four-arch arcades. Each arcade is carried on two large columns and a central pier which has columnar projections on each corner; this formula is repeated on the attached piers at each end of the arcades, so there is an alternation of piers and columns. These have two-stepped bases (round for the columns, square for the piers), and stand on a rudimentary stylobate. The floor level rises at the east end, at a point just west of the last column of each arcade (Pl. 60). (On the plan, this change of floor level is shown in thin line.) Slab capitals follow the form of their supports: round on the columns, square on the piers, and have projecting neckings and abaci. There is a deep apsidal niche in the west face of the central pier of the north arcade. This seems to be original, since it is plastered, like the rest of the church. The arches of the arcade are outlined by broad flat running hood mouldings. A cornice runs above the arcade and continues across the west wall, and the barrel vault springs above the cornice. The side aisles are also barrel-vaulted, the vaults springing above cornices placed

59. Selime Kalesi: Church, entrance.

60. Selime Kalesi: Church, north arcade and main apse.

higher than those of the nave, although the vaults themselves are lower than the nave vault.

North and south walls of the church are decorated with arched blind niches, four on each wall. On the north wall the two westernmost niches are cut through to form entrances to a small rectangular area (8). This is divided into two bays covered by cross vaults separated by an arch. There are arched blind niches in the walls of each bay and the east wall niche contains a further, apsidal, niche opening about 1 metre above ground level. At the back of this niche is a small, slab-like projection, perhaps an altar, in which case Area 8 may have been a small side chapel. From the west end of the north aisle a tunnel leads down into Area 10 of the complex

The church has three apses. The main apse is slightly horseshoe-shaped in plan and rather deep, with a cornice at the springing of the conch. It is screened by low chancel slabs. The apse arch springs above attached piers with columnar projections at their corners (the formula used for the piers of the arcade). These rise above the chancel slabs and have rudimentary capitals like the arcade piers. At the back of the apse, is a horseshoe-shaped window, just above the cornice and framed by a recess. Below this is a blind niche. The apse has a two-tier synthronon running around it. The back of the apse is much crumbled, probably because a rock-cut altar has been hacked away – its probable position is marked in thin broken line on the plan.

The north apse is also horseshoe-shaped, but much smaller. It is framed by piers with columnar projections like those of the arcade, and there are no chancel slabs. The apse has an attached altar and two blind niches, one to the north, the other opposite it. The south apse has a rough, low rectangular entrance set in a shallow arched niche. The space thus entered, although it has a horseshoe-shaped ground plan, is not really an apse, but a chamber with a conical vault rising above a cornice. At the back is an attached altar with a blind niche above it. Other niches, flanking this, and also in the southwest corner, may be secondary. The lack of moulded piers at the entrance to this apse, the rough form of that entrance and the lack of consistency with the architectural pattern of the rest of the church in general, suggest that the entire south apse is secondary.

Painting The church is plastered throughout with smooth white plaster and has an extensive painted programme. The paintings are in such poor condition, however, that little more than the outlines of figures can be made out. Some details appear as raised, slightly shiny black areas, others as red stains. This condition is probably the result of burning: the black areas remain where several thicknesses of paint were applied, possibly with an animal glue medium; the red areas are stains left by thinner pigment which soaked into the plaster, which may have been damp at the time of painting.[59]

The only decoration on the columns and piers of the arcades is a series of small panels, on the east-facing and nave-facing sides of each upright. These contain red crosses or other simple motifs (one has a green tree). Busts in medallions decorate the nave-facing spandrels of the arcades. All figures are too much damaged for identification, but the central bust on the south side depicts a monk saint with pointed hood. Each figure has its hands at waist level, in a supplicant gesture (Pls. 61a & b). The soffits of the arcade are also decorated with similar busts in medallions, three to each soffit. Mouldings around the arches of the arcade are decorated with a fine chevron pattern, and the cornice above with a 'spade' pattern (Pls. 61a & b).

The main apse contains a painting of the Ascension: Christ in a mandorla, a pointing angel and a group of figures appear in the upper part of the conch. Below this, above the cornice, there is a second register, divided into two by the window. To the left of the window are seven standing figures, to the right the painting is indecipher-

able. There are no figures visible on the wall below the cornice, but this area is very blackened.

The best preserved, but still much deteriorated, painting is on the south side of the nave barrel vault. Here, in irregularly placed registers, are narrative cycles representing the Infancy of Christ and Life of the Virgin (Pls. 61a & b). Few scenes may be identified with confidence. At the west end of the south side of the vault the Life of Christ is depicted in three registers:

Upper register: Annunciation(?), two or three more episodes, Nativity(?).
Middle register: Adoration of the Magi, Massacre of the Innocents, Pursuit of Elizabeth, Flight into Egypt (Pl. 61a).
Bottom register: one or two episodes (including the Calling of John the Baptist?), Baptism, one or two more episodes (healing scenes?).

At the east end there are two registers, apparently containing a life of the Virgin sequence:

Upper register: lost, except for a series of feet.
Lower register: First Steps of the Virgin, the Virgin Blessed by Priests(?), Presentation of the Virgin in the Temple, the Virgin Fed by an Angel, one more episode(?) (Pl. 61b).

The painting on the north side of the vault is illegible. There seems to be a division into three registers at the west end, as on the south side, and a cross-nimbed figure visible in the bottom register suggests that this is another part of the Life of Christ cycle. Lafontaine-Dosogne, who first described these paintings, identifies a scene in the west lunette as the Dormition.[60]

Donor panel Below the west lunette is a donor panel (Fig. 14 & Pl. 62). The panel is difficult to see since it must be viewed against the bright light which enters through the church entrance, and at a steep angle because it is high on the west wall. In addition, the paint has been damaged by burning, as noted above, and augmented by streaks of white supplied by pigeons perching on the moulding above it. The basic details may, however, be made out. A large nimbed figure (probably of the Virgin) stands in the centre, with hands outstretched towards the heads of two smaller figures: on the left a figure wearing a long brocade gown, possibly presenting a model of a church to the Virgin, and to the right a similar figure in a longer, dark green brocade coat open at the front. Flanking this central group are two groups of three smaller figures: to the left the three wear red brocade robes

59 I am grateful to Mr Stavros Mihalarias, who visited the site with me in 1982, for this analysis; it seems to account well for the curious condition of these paintings.

60 Lafontaine-Dosogne, 'La Kale Kilisesi' 747–8; *idem*, 'Nouvelles notes', 175–6.

61a. Selime Kalesi: Church, south side of barrel vault, east end.

61b. Selime Kalesi: Church, south side of barrel vault, west end.

14. Selime Kalesi: donor panel.

like the figure to the left of the Virgin, and the dress of the three to the right echoes that of the right figure. The figures on the left, with the shorter robes, are probably male, those on the right, female, so this is probably a family group, with father and sons to the left and mother and daughters to the right. There may be another figure, to the extreme left, roughly the same size as the large donor figures.

No inscriptions have been recorded in the donor panel, and probably none has survived the burning, so the family cannot be thus identified. This kind of image, with the Virgin (or sometimes Christ) touching the heads of two figures, is usually found in depictions of imperial groups, where the iconography is that of a symbolic coronation. A parallel for the Selime image is found in the Sacra Parallela (Paris, Bib. Nat. Ms. Gr. 922), of 1059–67, which contains an image of the Virgin crowning Constantine X with Eudokia, and their children flanking the group.[61] The Selime painting is in such poor condition that it is not possible to tell whether the two principal donor figures are wearing crowns, but certainly they do not wear the *loros* or any other obviously imperial insignia. In this case, therefore, the iconography may imply divine protection, rather than coronation, as is the case in an image of Michael VII and his empress in the Homilies of John Chrysostom, probably made 1074–8 (Paris, Bib. Nat. Coislin 79).[62] This appears to be the case also in the only other similar donor image in a Cappadocian cave church: that in Karşı Kilise, where a divine figure touches the heads of two small donors.[63] A looser parallel for this kind of donor image is to be found in the eleventh-century church of St Sophia, Kiev, where members of the family of Yaroslav the Wise flank the seated figure of Christ.[64]

The condition of the painting makes it difficult to use the costume of the figures as a guide to the identity of the donors or their date. Nevertheless, it is clear that although the figures do not wear imperial dress, they are luxuriously clad. The costume of the principal male figure, on the left, resembles that of the *Proedros kai Protovestarios* shown in a group of courtiers flanking Michael VII in another miniature in the Homilies of John Chrysostom mentioned above.[65] That this is an aristocratic family can, in any case, hardly be doubted, given the iconography of the panel, the high quality of the painted programme and the fact that the monastery is the largest and most elaborate of the cave monuments.

Porch inscription The porch, like the church, was plastered, but most of the plaster has fallen away. Fragments remain on the east wall, around the church entrance, and on the easternmost edges of north and south walls (Pl. 59). Just below the cornice on each side is a painted inscription of seven lines on the north side (Pl. 63a) and three lines on the south (Pl. 63b). The lines of the inscription appear to be complete and since they occupy the whole width of the plastered area of the porch it is possible that the plaster did not extend right across the porch wall, but was confined to a narrow vertical band the width of the inscription. Unlikely though this may seem, the alternative is to assume that by chance the area of plaster with the inscription has been preserved while the rest is lost. The text, a dodecasyllabic poem, is as follows:

North side: Μιδὶς τυφ(λ)ούστο τῇ ὀρέξη τοῦ πλ[ούτου]
πωλούς γὰρ ἀπέλεσεν ἰ φιλαργυρήα
ἰ σάρξ γὰρ ταύτη χοῦς, πηλὸς καὶ Γ[.]ΔΝ|. .
[. . . Traces of four more lines.

61 I. Spatharakis, *The Portrait in Byzantine Illuminated Manuscripts* (Leiden, 1976), 104 and fig. 68; for other 'coronation' images, see 40, 109 and figs. 14, 11.
62 *Ibid.* 118 and fig. 70. See 83 and fig. 46 for another example.
63 Jerphanion, *Eglises*, II, 8–10; Lafontaine-Dosogne, 'Nouvelles notes', 124–6; Restle, *Wall Painting*, Cat. no. LI; Karşı Kilise is dated by inscription to 1212.
64 V. Lazarev, *Old Russian Murals and Mosaics from the XI to the XIV Century* (London, 1966), 236.
65 Spatharakis, *Portrait*, 107–18 and pl. 71.

62. Selime Kalesi: Church, donor images on west wall.

South side: . . . .] ΦΕΔΡΟΛΑΝΠΙΝΥΚ [. . . .]ΤΙ
          . . .] ΕΚΟΙΙΤΤΟΘΕΝΤΑΚ [. . . .
          . . .] ΚΑΙΝΟÇΙΟΙ ποθου [. . . .
          No more lines visible

[66]

Translation: 'Let no one be misled by the desire for
          wealth
          for the love of money has destroyed many.
          For this flesh is earth, clay and . . .'

The poem appears to refer to the tomb chamber below
it, but clearly does not supply any information on the
inhabitants of the chamber.

Areas 10 and 11 Moving around to the north side of
Courtyard area A (the adjusted orientation continues),
the first unit encountered is Area 10, which appears to
have been a room, the south wall of which is lost (Pl. 64).
The room also lacks a west wall, and was probably
separated from the adjacent Area 11 by an arcade, since
part of a wall pilaster and the springing of an arch remain

on the north wall. Enough of the arch remains for estima-
tion of its span, on the basis of which a three-arch arcade
may be reconstructed. It is also possible, of course, that
Areas 10 and 11 were separated by a wall with an arched
entrance at its north side, rather than an arcade. Area
10 is barrel-vaulted on an east/west axis, the vault springing from a cornice which continues across the east wall
to underline the lunette. The lunette is rimmed by a
moulding and decorated with a relief-carved column on
a square base, carrying a schematized volute capital with
narrow neck and wide top (Pl. 64). The wall is pitted with
secondary cavities (including one in the base of the relief
motif) which are probably nest boxes from a pigeon-
house phase of the monastery. Below the lunette, slightly
to right of centre in the wall, there is a deep arched blind
niche with its base about 1 metre above floor level; this
is plastered. Further to the right, at the south end of the
wall is the entrance to tunnel (a), which houses a much
deteriorated flight of steps up to the north aisle of the
church. Unlike many other tunnels in the complex, which
are roughly carved, secondary structures, this one is well

66 The first part of the inscription (north side) was published by
   Lafontaine-Dosogne, 'La Kale Kilisesi', 742; also by Rott, *Denkmäler*, 264. A. M. Levadis, *Ai en monolithois monai tes Kappadokias
   kai Lykaonias* (Constantinople, 1899), 118, supplies inaccurate

transcriptions of both parts. The version given here is a reading
from photographs by C. Roueché. Another copy of the poem
appears in Eğri Taş Kilise, also in Peristrema valley (Thierry,
Nouvelles églises, 68–9).

63a. Selime Kalesi: Church, porch inscription, north side.

63b. Selime Kalesi: Church, porch inscription, south side.

finished and may well have been part of the original plan.

At the west (left) side of the north wall of Area 10, a row of four arched blind niches is placed at the springing of the barrel vault (Pl. 65). To the right of the niches the vault is cut back to form a square recess containing two narrow, keyhole-shaped windows into the room behind Area 10 (Room 12). Below the windows the entrance to Room 12 has been roughly enlarged upwards and eastwards (Pl. 65). The loss of both west and south sides of Area 10 makes it impossible to locate its main entrance; it could have been in either wall.

Area 11, alongside Area 10, is barrel-vaulted on a

64. Selime Kalesi: Areas 11 and 10, view northeast.

65. Selime Kalesi: Areas 11 and 10, view north.

north/south axis (Pl. 66). It probably never had a south wall, but was always a large porch, like those occurring elsewhere in the complex. The barrel vault springs from cornices on the west and east walls and a cornice on the north wall at the same level cuts off a lunette. The north side of the vault is set above an overhang. In the north wall there is a large rectangular entrance into Room 13, with a 'lintel' decorated with a stylized foliage pattern in relief. Directly above this entrance, resting on the cornice, there is an arched window almost as wide as the entrance; this is flanked by a pair of attached colonnettes with rudimentary slab capitals – these carry a double moulding which rims the arch and turns, at the springing, to lie parallel with the capitals (Pl. 66).

The whole of the west wall of Area 11 is taken up by three blind niches, set in a rectangular recess (Pl. 67). Each arch is outlined by a simple moulding and in the spandrels are relief-carved columns and capitals with volutes like those on the lunette of Area 10. The northernmost of the niches contains an original rectangular entrance to Room 15 and the centre niche contains a secondary opening to the same room. The three-niche

66. Selime Kalesi: Area 11.

pattern makes it likely that the wall between Areas 10 and 11 was indeed a three-arched arcade, or a three-niche decoration, with an opening at the north end, since it would then match the west wall. A large patch of plaster remains on the west side of the barrel vault of Area 11 and there are other fragments elsewhere.

Room 12   Room 12, behind Area 10, is almost square with a flat ceiling above a simple cornice. A horizontal moulding divides each wall into two registers of roughly equal height (Pl. 68). The upper register is decorated with four blind niches along each wall. L-shaped pilasters fill each corner of this upper register, so that with the cornice below the ceiling and the horizontal moulding they form rectangular frames for each set of blind niches. The niches are similar to those in Room 4, but with square mouldings lining each arch. On the north wall a rectangular panel below the cornice is bordered by a simple roll moulding (Pl. 68). The purpose of this panel, which does not bear an inscription, is not evident.

A secondary opening in the west wall of Room 12 leads into Room 13, described below. The only original opening is the rectangular entrance from Area 10, described above, which opens into the south wall of Room 12 (Pl. 65). In the southeast corner of the room a chimney has been cut through the ceiling, and the room is much blackened by smoke. This blackening is, however, confined to the ceiling and the upper two-thirds of the walls. A clear 'tide mark' runs around the room separating the blackened area from the clean rock of the lower level (Pl. 68). It seems therefore, that at some point, after the abandonment of the monastery, the floor level of the room was raised by the accumulation of rock debris, and when this had reached a depth of about 1 metre, the room was put to secondary use, perhaps as a dwelling, and fires were lit in it. This would also explain the enlargement of the entrance from Area 10: the original opening must have been largely blocked by the accumulated rock debris, and its top was enlarged upwards and eastwards to make an entrance at the new floor level (Pl. 65). At some later time the debris was cleared out.

Room 13   The opening in the north wall of Area 11, with an ornamented lintel and a window above it, opens into Room 13, one of two large elaborate rooms in the monastery (Pl. 69). Room 13 is rectangular, with a barrel vault springing from a cornice which continues across north and south walls. The room is divided into two bays by a transverse arch carried on pilasters. A square moulding circuits the room, two-thirds of the way up the wall, interrupted only by the large pilasters. The front (south) bay of this room has no ornament, other than the mould-

67. Selime Kalesi: Area 11, west wall.

ing, but the back (north) bay has a decoration of blind arcading in the upper register on all three sides. This is carved in deep relief and is not a series of blind niches, as seen in several other rooms, but a true blind arcade: attached columns, on square bases and with slab capitals, carry arches which are outlined by running hood mouldings (Pl. 69).

At the south end of the east wall there is a deep arched recess of the type seen in Room 4 and elsewhere. At the north end of the room two pairs of blind niches high on the wall, just below the horizontal moulding, flank the wide rectangular entrance to Room 14; the entrance is outlined by a double recess (Pl. 69). A narrow rectangular entrance in the west wall, to the left of the pilaster, is the start of a secondary tunnel (b) which runs west to Room 12.

Room 13 has two layers of plaster, both probably belonging to a single phase: a coarse layer with a fine finishing layer on top. The whole of the north bay of the room was plastered, as were the pilasters and the lower register of the south bay, but there do not seem to be any remains of plaster in the barrel vault and upper register of the south bay.

Room 14 Room 14, entered from the north wall of Room 13, is square, with a flat ceiling above a cornice. The ceiling is decorated with a Latin cross on a short stem, carved in relief. North, west and east walls contain large rectangular-plan arched recesses and small apsidal niches are cut into the wall flanking the northwest and northeast corners of the rooms (these may be secondary, but appear more regular than is usual for secondary pits). The east and north walls of the north recess are decorated with shallow arched blind niches: three on the north wall, two on the east. A tunnel leading off the west side of this recess leads into a small, irregular chamber (c) with a pit in its floor.[67]

Room 15 Both entrances from the west wall of Area 11 lead into Room 15. This is a barrel-vaulted rectangular

67 In 'Etudes cappadociennes. Région du Hasan Dağı, compléments pour 1974', *CahArch* 24 (1975), 183–90, at 184, N. Thierry calls this a well, but there was no sign of water on any of my visits.

room, with cornices on north and south walls at the springing of the vault. The lunettes overhang the west and east walls slightly, and are rimmed by wall arches. A transverse arch and a rib running along the axis of the vault make a relief cross on the barrel vault. Fragments of plaster remain in several places. Two rectangular openings in the west wall lead into the next room (16).

Area 16 Area 16 is a long narrow corridor with a low ceiling. At the south end is a small, domed projection, with arched, rectangular-plan recesses in its east and south walls. Two deep round pits, with traces of plaster linings, are cut into the floor, each filling the floor space of a recess and extending into the main chamber. At the north end of Room 16, rough steps lead up to the south gallery (18c) of Room 18. The west wall of Room 16 is only about 1.5 metres high. Above this level the room is open to the adjacent Area 17.

Area 17 (On the main plan, Area 17 and the galleries of Room 18 are indicated in broken line; this area is drawn fully in box (b).) Area 17 is roughly square, with a flat ceiling. Its floor is level with the top of the low west wall of 16. In the north wall of this area two wide arched openings lead into the south gallery (18c) of Room 18. Much of the west wall is lost, leaving the area open to the outside, but the north part of the wall remains and contains a rectangular recess housing a square window.

68. Selime Kalesi: Room 12, northwest corner.

69. Selime Kalesi: Room 13, view northwest.

70. Selime Kalesi: Room 18, southeast corner.

Rooms 18–20 Room 18 is the most elaborate of all the rooms of the complex, with true galleries, a feature very rare in Cappadocian cave architecture.[68] The main area (18) is a large, flat-ceilinged rectangle with its main entrance in the west wall. A slightly overhanging cornice circuits the room dividing the walls into two registers of approximately equal height (Pl. 70). Below the cornice the walls are cut by deep rectangular-plan arched recesses, three in the south wall and at least two on the north wall (the western part of the north wall has been damaged by secondary excavation, but there is enough space for two niches). These recesses are not symmetrically placed, nor are they all of the same dimensions: the first niche of the south wall (moving west to east) has its back blocked by a massive ledge of rock, with two basins cut into it. The second niche is similar, but wider and less deep than the first, with a ledge and two basins. The third niche, of similar size to the last, is without 'fittings', as are the two remaining niches of the north wall. All the 'basins' may be secondary, since such cavities are often cut to make mangers when rooms are turned into animal houses.

In the centre of the east wall there is a wide arched recess, shallower than those of north and south walls.

This is flanked by two narrower arched niches. An opening in the left niche leads into a small, roughly square room (19) which in turn has an opening in its back (east) wall into another small, roughly square room (20) with recesses in north and east walls. An opening in the right niche of the east wall of Room 18 is the entrance to a long tunnel (b), which leads to Room 13 and is almost certainly secondary.

Above the cornice, Room 18 has a series of wide arched openings on north, south and east sides, which form an arcade fronting a gallery in three sections; there are four openings each in the north and south walls and two in the east wall. Each opening has a semicircular arch which overhangs the uprights supporting it, and the uprights of the two openings of the east wall have two-stepped bases applied to their inner faces (Pl. 70). On east and south sides the arcade arches are open down to the gallery floors, but on the north side they are partially closed by parapet slabs about 1 metre high.

The galleries (18a, b, c) have flat ceilings and are undecorated, but carefully carved. The north gallery (18a) is trapezoidal. A barrel-vaulted passage opens from its east wall, makes a right-angle turn and opens into the

68 The only other example is a more modest gallery at the Triconch Church, Tağar (Jerphanion, *Eglises*, II, 187–8).

north end of the east gallery (18b) just behind the arcade. On the north wall of the east gallery (18b), to the right of the tunnel opening, are two small arched blind niches, and on the east wall two deep rectangular recesses. There are two openings in the south wall of the east gallery: to the west, the entrance to another elbow-shaped passage leading to the east end of the south gallery (18c) and to the east an opening into the long tunnel (b) which links the east wall of Room 18 with Room 13. The south gallery (18c) has three openings on its south side – one to the narrow corridor (16) and two to Area 17, through wide arches. At the west end of the gallery a narrow stairway leads down to the ground floor of Room 18.

Area 21, Room 22 and nearby cavities The main entrance to Room 18 is a wide rectangular opening in its west wall. This is set in the back wall of a wide, barrel-vaulted porch (Area 21) which faces Courtyard area B (Pl. 71). The entrance to 18 is set in an arched blind niche, with a recess framing its arch; above is an arched window (the arrangement is similar to that in the entrance porch (11) of Room 13).

A rectangular opening in the north wall of Area 21 leads into a simple rectangular room (22) with a flat ceiling above a cornice. An irregular hole in the back wall of the porch, to the right of the entrance to Room 18,

opens into a small rectangular flat-ceilinged cavity (d) which in turn communicates with the stairway from Room 18 to the south gallery. This cavity may be secondary, but fragments of an archway, rimmed by a moulding, remain above the hole in the porch wall, so there may have been an arched entrance here, or possibly a window, in which case cavity (d) may be original.

The ground level of the porch has been lowered by erosion and the entrances to Room 18 and cavity (d) are now above its floor level. To the right of the porch is an irregular cavity (e) which is probably secondary. A few paces in front of the porch is the top of the long tunnel that winds up from the valley bottom (T). A few steps remain at the top part of the tunnel.

Area 23 and the kitchen (24) The final part of the complex is on the west side of Courtyard area B (compass directions given are now accurate). A large, barrel-vaulted porch, Area 23, forms an entrance bay to Room 24 (Pl. 72). As in Area 21 (the porch in front of Room 18), the back wall contains a rectangular opening set into a wide arched niche, with a recess outlining its arch, and a window directly above it; in this case the window is small and rectangular. Both sides of this porch have fallen, leaving a fragment of the barrel vault overhanging the entrances. Room 24 is square and has a pyramidical

71. Selime Kalesi: Area 21.

72. Selime Kalesi: Area 23.

vault rising above a deep overhanging cornice; at the apex of the pyramid is a smoke hole, so this room is almost certainly the monastery kitchen (Pl. 73). The north wall contains the remains of what may be an oven: an apsidal recess with a long cavity in the wall above it. (On the other hand, this may be secondary: there is no chimney in the wall cavity and it would appear more efficient to have the cooking fire in the centre of the room, below the smoke hole.) A hole in the south wall opens into an irregular cavity (h) open to the outside. Above the cornice is a series of irregular niches, probably pigeon nesting boxes and therefore secondary.

Rooms 25 and 26 A rectangular entrance in the centre of the west wall of Room 24 opens into Room 25; this entrance has a recessed lunette above it. To the right of this is a further rectangular entrance, also opening into Room 25. Room 25 is rectangular in plan, with a shallow concave vault. At the east end of the north wall there is a rectangular recess. A rectangular opening in the north end of the west wall leads into a small room (26), which has a flat ceiling, benches along north and south walls, and a recess in the west wall. A hole in the southwest corner leads down to the outside, like a drain, and a hole in the north wall opens into a further irregular cavity (f).

The whole of this 'kitchen wing' is undecorated.

To the left (south) of porch area (23) is a fragment of a small barrel vault above a cavity (g) containing a rectangular entrance into Room 24. To the right is a series of pigeon-house rooms, identifiable as such by their irregular shapes, low ceilings and profusion of pigeon nesting niches and perch-holes. Only one of these rooms is at ground level; its approximate form is marked (i) on the plan.

Rooms 27 and 28 About halfway up the path from the village, and possibly close to the lower end of the access tunnel, there are several rough cavities which are probably secondary. Also in this area are two rooms that appear to belong to the monastery: Room 27 (not shown on the plan) is a rectangular stable, barrel-vaulted and furnished with rock-cut mangers (Pl. 74). Room 28 (also not shown) is a small barrel-vaulted room with cornices, a transverse arch and wall arches, like so many others of the monastery.[69] One lunette is decorated with a relief carving of a horned animal (Pl. 75). The location of the stable suggests that the tunnel was once the only entrance to the monastery, and that horses and pack animals had

69 This room is called Ambar Oda by Thierry, in 'Etudes cappadociennes', 184–5.

73. Selime Kalesi: kitchen, with entrance to Room 25.

74. Selime Kalesi: stable.

75. Selime Kalesi: Room 28, lunette decoration.

to be left at the foot of the hill and the tunnel entered on foot. The room with the horned animal may conceivably have been a gatehouse of sorts.

Summary

Selime Kalesi is the largest of the cave monasteries, with rooms grouped around two courtyard areas (Fig. 13). At one side of Courtyard area A is a basilical church (7) with tomb chamber (9). The church is fully painted with a programme that includes a family donor image. To the southeast of the church there is a group of rooms on two floors (1, 2, 3 at ground level, 4, 5, 6 at an upper level). At the other side of the courtyard is a porch (11) which fronts a large hall (13). The hall is decorated with blind arcading; at its far end there is a further room (14) with a relief cross on its ceiling. To the right of the porch is the remains of another room (10) and behind this another (12); both have decorations of blind niching. To the west of porch 11 there is a room with a relief cross in its barrel vault (15). Beyond this a narrow corridor (16) and a rough room (17) connect with the south gallery of Room 18. This is the largest room of the monastery and has galleries on three sides (18a, b, c). It is entered via a porch (21) to one side of Courtyard area B. To the west of this area another porch (23) leads to the kitchen (24) and subsidiary rooms (25, 26). Access to the monastery was originally by means of a tunnel, opening at point (T) in Courtyard B. Below the monastery, probably near the tunnel entrance, are a stable and another room.

Date

Although Selime Kalesi is much larger than any of the other cave monasteries, its elements and their arrangement conform to the basic pattern seen in other complexes: a single church (7), with a prominent tomb chamber (9); a kitchen (24), two large halls (13 and 18) and several other well-finished rooms. Many of its architectural details may be paralleled in the other complexes: the barrel-vaulted room with cornices, framed lunettes, division into bays by transverse arches and pilasters, are found at Soğanlı Han and Aynalı Kilise Monastery, already described, and at Direkli Kilise Monastery and Eski Gümüş, described below; the running hood mouldings of Room 13 occur also at Bezir Hane and Karanlık Kale (see below); the deep arched recess and the decorative shallow blind niches are found in most of the complexes. The church type, a basilica, is unusual for the monastery group, but not unique, since it occurs also at Aynalı Kilise Monastery.

Like most of the monasteries, Selime Kalesi offers no

secure evidence of its date. Lafontaine-Dosogne suggested an eighth-ninth century date for the excavation of the monastery, on the basis of the architecture of the basilical church, and tenth century for the paintings in the church and the inscription in the porch.[70] Certainly the narrative cycles in the vault, made up of densely packed, unframed episodes, are consistent with the 'archaic' group decorations of the early tenth century and the mid tenth-century decorations of Tokalı Kilise in Göreme and the Pigeon House Church, Çavuşin (the latter datable to 963–969).[71] Further, although stylistic assessment must be tentative, given the condition of the paintings, a parallel may be drawn between the tall, rather slender figures of the barrel vault narrative and those of the Pigeon House Church. As noted above, however, the costume of the donors and the iconography of their panel is best paralleled in eleventh-century imagery, so perhaps a late tenth- or early eleventh-cenutury date is appropriate.

There is some difficulty in separating the excavation of the monastery and the painting of the church by a century or more, as Lafontaine-Dosogne suggests. There is no evidence of an earlier painted scheme in the church (this may be said with confidence, since so much of the painting has been burned away that an earlier layer should certainly be visible had it existed). So if excavation and painting are to be widely separated then it must be supposed that an aristocratic family of the tenth or eleventh century decorated the church of a very large, very elaborate monastery established a century or more earlier, and that this had no painted decoration in its church, nor any other evidence of its founders. It is more likely that the aristocratic family in the donor panel commissioned the whole monastery, not just the decoration of the church. If the painting is to be placed in the tenth or eleventh century, then so should the monastery. This also avoids the historical difficulty of attributing what seems from its size to have been the most important of the cave monasteries to a date when the volcanic valley area was an uneasy frontier zone.

The secondary pits and tunnels noted above show that after it had ceased to function as a monastery the complex was put to other uses. Parts of it housed pigeons; other parts, such as Room 12, probably housed people. The plastering remaining in many rooms is not likely to belong to this secondary phase. Although the new inhabitants might have plastered the rooms they took for dwellings, they would surely not have thus embellished areas such as the porch barrel vaults or the blind arcade

of Room 13.

In Room 1 the plaster was applied after the north wall pilaster had been cut away. This suggests that before it was plastered the room was used in its naked state long enough for minor alterations to be made. While it is not valid to assume pre- and post-plastering phases for the whole monastery on the basis of this minor detail, it does appear to offer evidence of an alteration made to the monastery while it was in use as such, rather than as part of the post-Byzantine occupation. This being so, Selime Kalesi was probably in use for longer than most of the other courtyard monasteries, which perhaps supports a tenth-century foundation date.

Direkli Kilise Monastery

In the cliff forming the south side of Peristrema valley, opposite the village of Belisırma, is the church known as Direkli Kilise.[72] This church is part of a monastery complex so far unrecorded.

There is no courtyard here, the church and rooms are fronted by a façade whose planes are governed by the natural line of the cliff (Fig. 15 & Pl. 76). The façade is divided into four bays of unequal width by large projecting piers. The westernmost bay, which is decorated with an upper register of blind niches, houses the entrance to Room 1 and a window to Room 1a (Pl. 76). The next bay is much smaller and undecorated, containing the tall arched entrance to the church narthex. To the left of this is a third bay, containing a shallow horseshoe-arched blind niche set in a two-stepped rectangular recess. The niche contains a two-light window into the central north bay of the church. Most of the fourth bay has been smoothed by erosion.

Rooms 1 and 1a Behind the western part of the façade is a two-floor unit: Rooms 1 (ground floor) and 1a (upper floor) (Pls. 77 & 78). An arched entrance, now enlarged by erosion, leads into Room 1 from the façade. A wide, irregular (and probably secondary) opening to the east of this original entrance opens into the east end of the room. Room 1 is rectangular, its main axis parallel to the façade. It is without carved ornament, except for a simple moulding outlining the arch of the entrance. Deep arched recesses are cut into the south end of the west wall and the east end of the south wall. A rough tunnel, probably secondary, leads from the north end of the west wall to the outside.

The upper room (1a) is very slightly larger than the

70 Lafontaine-Dosogne, 'La Kale Kilisesi', 746.
71 Jerphanion, *Eglises*, I. i, 67–94; II, 414–18; I. ii, 297–376, 520–50.
72 Thierry, *Nouvelles églises*, 183–92; J. Lafontaine, 'Note sur un

voyage en Cappadoce (été 1959)', *Byzantion* 28 (1958), 465–77, at 473–5; Lafontaine-Dosogne, 'Nouvelles notes', 144–7; *idem*, Review of Thierry, *Nouvelles églises*, in *BZ* 58 (1965), 135.

15. Direkli Kilise Monastery: plan.

76. Direkli Kilise Monastery: site.

77. Direkli Kilise Monastery: Room 1, west end.

78. Direkli Kilise Monastery: Room 1, east end.

ground floor room and is indicated on the plan in thin line. A timber floor apparently once separated the two rooms (this is lost, but there remains a row of holes along the south wall which must have been cut to take joists which were supported on a ledge at the north side).[73] The remains of a flight of rock-cut stairs are visible on the east wall of Room 1, running up from north to south, to meet a landing in a rectangular recess at the east end of the south wall of the upper room (Pl. 78). Room 1a is barrel-vaulted with a simple cornice circuiting it at the level of the springing of the vault and cutting off lunettes on the end walls. Square mouldings outline the curves of the lunettes. There are deep arched recesses in the centre of the west wall and at the north end of the east wall. Above the latter, in the right half of the east lunette, a large irregular mass projects from the wall, above and to

the west of the entrance to Room 1. This may simply be a nodule of hard rock that was not removed when the room was cut. The arched recesses of the two rooms are all of the same form: a wide arch, slightly incurved, with a cornice at the springing and a moulding rimming the lunette.

Rooms 2 and 3 An opening in the centre of the south wall of Room 1 leads into Room 2. This opening has been enlarged and then partly blocked with rough masonry, so its original form is unclear. Room 2 is rectangular, on a north/south axis, covered by a barrel vault. The room has a deep arched niche in the centre of its east wall, of the same type as those in Rooms 1 and 1a. What appears to be a bench circuiting the room is not an original feature: it has been made by the erosion of parts of the walls. Room 3 is a small undecorated room with a shallow barrel vault, accessible from the south end of Room 2 by means of a rectangular entrance.

---

73 Timber floors in cave monuments are rare; another example occurs in Eğri Taş Kilise, also in Peristrema valley (Thierry, *Nouvelles églises*, 39).

79. Direkli Kilise Monastery: Church, narthex east wall.

Church: narthex (4), naos (6) and side chapel (7) The church lies to the east of the rooms just described. The arched entrance from the façade opens into a rectangular narthex (4), which has a barrel vault on a north/south axis, rising above a two-stepped cornice (Pl. 79). The west wall is decorated with four tall, narrow, horseshoe-arched

blind niches. The east wall has two such niches, which flank the church entrance, which is rectangular, with a recessed lunette above it. Traces of plaster and paint remain on this east wall. Much of the south wall has been demolished, forming a wide opening into Room 5, described below. A secondary opening links the south end of the narthex west wall with Room 1. Four grave pits are cut into the narthex floor.

The naos (6) is of inscribed-cross plan, with a small truncated central dome carried on massive square piers with chamfered corners (Pl. 80). The cross-arms have barrel vaults springing from cornices on the piers. Similar cornices circuit the naos walls. Wide arches spring from the crossing piers to meet wall pilasters. The small corner bays have flat ceilings. Shallow horseshoe-arched blind niches decorate the walls of the southwest corner bay and the west wall of the northwest corner bay. In the centre bay of the north wall a two-light window opens above the cornice (a rough secondary hole now makes this a three-light window). The main entrance to the naos is the opening from the narthex, which enters the centre bay of the naos west wall.

80. Direkli Kilise Monastery: Church, view towards main apse.

81. Direkli Kilise Monastery: Church, entrance to side chapel.

82. Direkli Kilise Monastery: side chapel, view east.

The church has three tall narrow apses, all slightly horseshoe-shaped in plan and each with an attached altar surmounted by a small blind niche (Pl. 80 shows the main apse, Pl. 84b the north apse). All three apses are raised above the naos floor and are reached by steps; they are closed by low chancel slabs of which only fragments remain.

In its central and south bays the south wall of the naos is pierced by two arched openings into a side chapel (7), which has a barrel vault springing from cornices (Pl. 81). The single apse is raised above the chapel floor and reached by a step. It has a rock-cut altar with a niche above it, and is closed by low chancel slabs (Pl. 82). In the south wall of the chapel there is a large arcosolium containing two grave pits. Flanking this are tall narrow horseshoe-arched blind niches, one to the right and two to the left. A further, very shallow, niche is cut into the section of north wall remaining between the two openings into the church. In addition to the two graves in the arcosolium there are three adult and two infant grave pits cut into the floor.

Room 5/5a An arched entrance in the west wall of the side chapel leads into Room 5, which is rectangular in plan and has a barrel vault springing from cornices on its long walls (Pl. 83). The south wall contains a deep arched recess which takes up most of the wall and contains two grave pits. There are blind niches in the east wall, one on each side of the entrance to the side chapel, and the west wall is divided into three bays by shallow pilasters. To the north of Room 5 is a trapezoidal area (5a), barrel-vaulted at a slightly lower level than Room 5. East and west walls of this area each contain an arched niche. The north side of Room 5a is taken up by a roughly arched opening into the narthex. There are several grave pits cut into the floor of Room 5/5a.

The proliferation of grave pits in the floors of the narthex, side chapel and Room 5 is unusual, since most of the monasteries contain only a few such pits. It is probable that the pits were cut after the monastery was abandoned, by people from the nearby village of Belisırma. The infant graves, in particular, seem more appropriate to a non-monastic context.

Painting The church is plastered throughout and parts of it are decorated with polychrome painting. The north apse and main apse are fully painted and there are 22 panels bearing figures of saints, on piers and walls and in the arch joining the north wall with the northeast pier. Most of this programme has been described by Thierry and will only be summarized here; subjects marked * are additions to the record:

83. Direkli Kilise Monastery: Room 5.

Main apse (conch): Deesis – Christ seated on a lyre-shaped throne, the Virgin to the left, John the Baptist to the right, Archangels in imperial dress flanking them; between the figures of the Virgin and John and the throne are two medallions containing busts of Peter (left) and Paul (right) (Pl. 80).

Main apse (wall): Virgin orant flanked by four bishops to the left, including Epiphanios, Gregorios Thaumaturgos and Basil, and five to the right, including John Chrysostom (the others are not identifiable).

Soffit of apse arch: six medallions containing busts of prophets, including Isaiah.

East wall: (above the main apse) Christ Pantocrator in a medallion held by archangels in imperial dress.

North apse (conch): Virgin and Child seated on a lyre-shaped throne between small angels in antique dress; flanking them to the right, Zacharias, in pearl-bordered cloak, holding a book and a censer*[74] and to the left an unidentified male figure in dark robe and light mantle (Pl. 84a).

North apse (wall): bishop saint (in the niche) flanked by two more bishops carrying books. Further to the right one more figure, a martyr, is just visible in an area

where most of the painting is lost (Pl. 84b).

There are inscriptions on the cornices of the north and main apses, which will be considered below. The south apse is unpainted, and was always so, its white plaster bears no trace of paint.

The panels of saints are as follows:

Arch between north wall and northeast pier: four monk saints (busts – no inscriptions are legible).

Northwest pier: (north face) Prokopios; (east) Merkourios; (south) Eustathios; (west) Anna with infant Virgin.

Northeast pier: (north) upper – Pegasios and Elpidios, lower – George; (east) upper – Akindynos and Aphthonios, lower – Sergios and Bakchos (Pl. 85); (south) Panteleemon; (west) John.

Southwest pier: (north) Marina (Pl. 86); (east) George (Pl. 87); (west) Virgin and Child.

Southeast pier: (north) Kosmas and Damianos, below them an unframed image of an orant figure on horseback, the horse facing left, towards a lion*; (west) bishop saint*.

North wall: (west bay) equestrian saint (probably

---

74 Thierry, *Nouvelles églises*, 190, says of these figures: 'évangéliste ou apôtre?, peut-être Jean et Pierre'. In fact they are not dressed

alike and the figure at the right has an inscription: ZAX(αριας).

84a. Direkli Kilise Monastery: Church, north apse, conch.

84b. Direkli Kilise Monastery: Church, north apse, wall.

85. Direkli Kilise Monastery: Church, St Sergios and St Bakchos.

86. Direkli Kilise Monastery: Church, St Marina.

87. Direkli Kilise Monastery: Church, St George.

George) with three-headed dragon* (Pl. 88); (pilaster) military saint*; (next pilaster) upper – two martyrs, lower – Catherine; (east bay) deacon.

South wall: (pier) Euphemia.

West entrance to side chapel: (west) Theodoros; (east) Basil.

Piers flanking main apse: an archangel on each side*; above them, busts (of saints?)*. Each of the niches in these piers contains a painted cross*.

On the west and south walls are several examples of painted interlace patterns which must be artists' graffiti or practice drawings (Pl. 89).

The narthex retains only small areas of plaster, most of them bearing traces of polychrome painting. On the east wall, to the left of the naos entrance, the upper part of a wing is discernible, so probably a pair of angels flanked the naos entrance.

There is no polychrome painting in the side chapel, but it does have some very simple decoration in red and white, painted directly onto the rock: in the conch of the apse, three hanging lamps on chains; on the east wall a painted border with lozenge pattern level with the cornices of the north and south walls; a similar pattern outlines the apse

88. Direkli Kilise Monastery: Church, equestrian saint.

89. Direkli Kilise Monastery: Church, artist's graffiti.

arch and there are white medallions on the chancel slabs. There is also a rough white panel to the left of the north chancel slab (Pl. 82).

Thierry has demonstrated that the painting of the naos may be divided between two hands: one painter did the apse painting, the monks of the northeast soffit and all the saints of the northeast pier except Panteleemon; the second did the rest.[75] The main difference in style between the two hands is that the apse painter worked with less harsh lines than the second painter. The paintings are, however, clearly part of a single phase of work: a close similarity between apse and pier figures is evident when the unidentified martyr of the north apse is compared with Saints Sergios and Bakchos of the northeast pier (cf. Pls. 84a & 85). Also, the panels of the northeast pier, most of which were done by the apse painter, form a uniform part of the programme. The harder, less fluid lines of the second painter suggest that the decoration was carried out by a workshop consisting of (at least) master and assistant, with the master (apse painter) doing the more important work at the east end and a less able assistant doing the rest.

As for the programme of the decoration, a scheme to the placing of panels is apparent: two angels guard the main apse; two more flank the entrance to the naos from the narthex; complementary images of Virgin and Child and Anna with the infant Virgin occupy the west faces of the southwest and northwest piers, and are thus the first images encountered when entering the naos; the deacon saint is placed next to the sanctuary; a guard of military saints occupies much of the space on the lower parts of piers and walls. Reasons for the placing of other saints (and, of course, for the selection of the whole group) were probably personal to the patrons. Such an explanation must be supposed for the appearance of St George three times, in different iconographical forms: on the southwest pier he is a plump figure with thick, curly hair; his armour is held by a pair of jewelled straps across the chest and a spear is held vertically in the right hand (Pl. 87). On the northeast pier the figure of George survives only as head and shoulders – this is a slimmer figure, with shorter hair; a cape masks the armour of the left shoulder and is clasped over the right shoulder; the spear is held sloping across the body. The third images shows George on horseback, dealing with the dragon.

Inscriptions in the apses Direkli Kilise is rare among cave monuments in having a datable inscription, painted in the north and main apses. This was recorded by Thierry:

Along the cornice of the north apse:

c. 18. . .]κὲ ἀφέσεος τὸν ἁμαρτη[ῶν] τοῦ δούλο[υ . . . c. 20.

In the main apse:

c. 25. . .] τοῦτος ὑπὸ Βασηλέος Βασήλου κὲ Κοσταντήνου EC[. . . c. 20.[76]

Translation: '. . . and (for the) forgiveness of the sins of [your] servant . . .' and '. . . in the time of emperors Basil and Constantine . . .'

This inscription may probably be reconstructed thus: '[For deliverance] and forgiveness of sins of your servant [donor name], this [church was built/decorated] in the time of the emperors Basil and Constantine [details of date].'

About 20 letters are missing from the end of the first part of the inscription, so there is room for a single name and perhaps a title. The end of the second part of the inscription, in the main apse, probably gave the day of the month, year and indiction number. The painting was done 'in the reign of Basil and Constantine', probably Basil II and Constantine VIII, who were co-rulers from 976–1025.[77] Indeed, the wording of the inscription is very similar to that of the inscription in the church of St Barbara, Soğanlı, where the assumption that Basil II and Constantine VIII are referred to is supported by two letters of an inscribed date.[78]

Summary

Direkli Kilise Monastery (Fig. 15) has no courtyard; it is cut into a steep cliff and fronted by a decorated façade. Behind this a vestibule (1) gives access to a hall (2); behind the hall there is a small room (3). The vestibule once had an upper floor (1a). To the east of these rooms is the church: an inscribed-cross naos (6), side chapel (7), narthex (4) and funerary room (5). The church is decorated with polychrome painting of high quality, in north and main apses and in panels on piers and walls. An inscription in the apses indicates a date bracket 976–1025.

Date

It is reasonable to suppose that the painted programme in the church was executed shortly after the monastery was hewn, since there is no earlier layer of painting. The inscription in the apses therefore refers to a patron who founded the monastery, which may thus be dated as a whole to the period of the co-emperors, 976–1025. The

75 Thierry, *Nouvelles églises*, 192.
76 *Ibid.* 184.
77 Thierry, *Nouvelles églises*, 184–6.

78 Jerphanion, *Eglises*, II, 309, Inscription no. 182; and see below, Chapter 5.

non-narrative programme, made up of a series of panels, is of the type seen in the eleventh-century Yılanlı group of churches in Göreme, which argues for a date at the latter end of this bracket.[79]

One more aspect of the painted decoration may be of help in dating Direkli Kilise and that is that the programme appears incomplete. The whole church is plastered, but the panels cover only part of the available space. The south apse is entirely unpainted, and there are several blank areas on piers and walls, especially at the west end of the naos. This condition need not imply that the decoration was halted abruptly and left unfinished, but may result from the nature of the scheme employed for the decoration. It would seem that when the images demanded by the patron had been installed, the programme was regarded as complete. The same scheme is found in the Yılanlı group churches, where formal panels, rather than narrative cycles, seldom fill all available space. The full plastering of Direkli Kilise does, however, suggest that there was an intention to provide for augmentation of the programme with more panels. It is significant, therefore, that no further panels were added. The implication is that the church was not in use for long. Several generations of inhabitants would surely have filled the blank spaces. If the Seljuk threat of the mid to late eleventh century be seen as a likely reason for abandonment of the monastery, then a date towards the end of the date bracket provided by the inscription is consistent with relatively brief use.

Local context

Unlike the other monastery complexes described so far, Direkli Kilise Monastery has no courtyard. This is probably a condition dictated by the cliff-side site: excavation of a courtyard would have involved a major task of rock removal. Otherwise, the complex has basic elements in common with the other monasteries: the decorated façade; a room complex organized around a vestibule (Room 1); two halls (1a) and (2); a single church with side chapel and prominent tomb (the arcosolium in the side chapel). Details paralleled elsewhere include the deep arched recess with wall arch seen in Rooms 1 and 1a, found also on Selime Kalesi, Karanlık Kale and Eski Gümüş Monastery, both described below.

Karanlık Kale

Karanlık Kale is a monastery cut into the north cliff of the Peristrema valley, near the village of İhlara (Fig 1).[80]

It is without a courtyard and has no unified façade, but areas of rock are cut back to make flat panels framing its entrances (Fig. 16 and Pl. 90). The principal entrance into the complex is a barrel-vaulted passage opening from one such recessed panel: its entrance arch is decorated with modillions. Above the entrance is an incised, splayed-armed cross on a stem. To the right of the entrance are two small arched blind niches, about 2 metres above ground level. Still further to the right there is a large rectangular recess, descending to ground level, with a small blind niche cut into its east wall. To the right of the recess, past an area of rough rock, is an arched entrance leading to the church and side chapel.

Vestibule (1) The short passage noted above leads into a long rectangular vestibule (1), from which other rooms of the complex are accessible (Pls. 91 & 92). The room is barrel-vaulted with a cornice circuiting it at the springing of the vault. Wall arches outline the lunettes, each of which is divided into two by a vertical bar. At the west end of the north wall there is a horseshoe-arched opening to Room 4, with a cornice at the springing and a modillion frieze on the arch (Pl. 91). In the centre of the wall is a similar opening to Room 2, set in a rectangular recess (Pl. 92); a third arched opening of this type, at the east end of the wall, is not an entrance: it is a deep rectangular-plan recess, with a small arched blind niche cut into its back wall (Pl. 92). Rubble has accumulated in the vestibule and raised the floor level by about 1 metre.

In the east wall another arched recess, undecorated, houses a rectangular entrance to the church (Pl. 92). A wider arched recess, again undecorated and with the summit of its arch just below the cornice, is cut to the north of the west wall (Pl. 91).

Hall (2) Room 2 is a rectangular hall, with a flat ceiling above wide rectangular-section cornices which run along the west and east sides of the room only. These are decorated on their upright faces with a frieze of shallow relief triangles. The ceiling is also decorated with shallow relief carving: a series of splayed-armed crosses in kite-shaped recesses (Pl. 93). Each long wall has three deep blind niches with horseshoe arches linked by running hood mouldings. Below this a simple cornice circuits the room, following the planes of the niches. A similar, but larger niche occupies much of the north wall, its hood moulding linked with the cornice; the arch is rimmed by modillions. Above the arch there is a small relief cross with splayed arms and stem. Cornices and mouldings have, in places,

79 See note 4 above.
80 Thierry, *Nouvelles églises*, 35–7; Kostof, *Caves of God*, 53; Yanagi, *Höhlenkloster*, 40–7.

16. Karanlık Kale: plan.

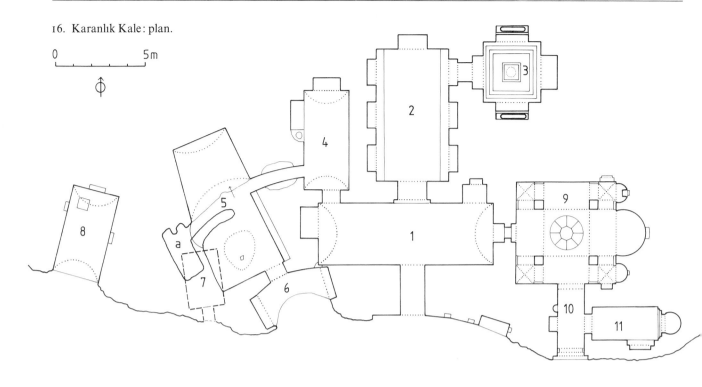

90. Karanlık Kale: site.

91. Karanlık Kale: Room 1, west end.

92. Karanlık Kale: Room 1, east end.

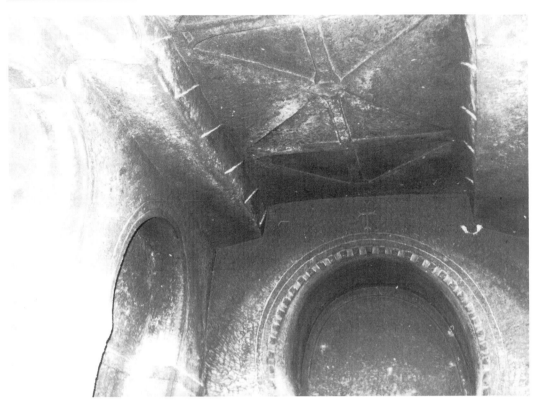

93. Karanlık Kale: Room 2, northwest corner.

a covering of whitewash or thin plaster, onto which simple geometric ornament has been painted in red.

Room 3 The northernmost niche in the east wall of Room 2 frames the entrance to Room 3. This entrance is an arched opening rising to the level of the Room 2 cornice. Room 3 is square, with arched recesses symmetrically placed, one in each wall. These, like the niches in Room 2, have horseshoe arches bordered with running hood mouldings. Shallow L-shaped pilasters fill each corner from cornice to ceiling (Pl. 94). A triple-stepped cornice carries a flat ceiling, broken by a square cavity which in turn has a calotte cut into it. Each of the two lateral recesses (north and south) contains a grave pit set behind a low wall that bisects the recess floor. The east recess has no grave, nor has the west, which forms an entrance bay to the room, shallower than the other three recesses. The room is entirely unlit.

Room 4 The westernmost opening from the north wall of Room 1 leads into Room 4, a rectangular, barrel-vaulted room, less well carved than those so far described (Pl. 95). The room has a wide arched recess in its north wall and a rectangular recess in the north end of the west wall. To the south of this is an irregular, slightly arched recess containing a basin. This resembles the pits often

carved in rooms put to secondary use as animal houses, and may therefore be secondary. However, a tunnel opens off the south end of the west wall and leads into Room 5, the kitchen, so perhaps this room is to be associated with the kitchen in function, and the basin is original.

Kitchen (5) and its ante-room (6) The tunnel noted above opens into the monastery kitchen, an irregular, trapezoidal room, the north end of which is raised about 30 cm above the rest of the floor. This north end has a shallow barrel vault and the south end a roughly conical vault, with a chimney opening in its south side. A bench runs along the east wall of the southern area and on the west side a low spur projects from an apsidal niche in the west wall. This spur curves round into the room and may have been the back part of a cooking range. Behind the spur a small tunnel leads into a roughly rectangular low-roofed cave (5a), probably a storage area. An arched opening in the south wall leads to a well-carved but irregular room (6). This has a concave north wall and arched recesses at west and east ends. The south wall, which must originally have contained an entrance to the outside, is lost.

Room 7 There is a small rectangular room (7) above the southwest part of the kitchen (drawn in broken line on

94. Karanlık Kale: Room 3, northwest corner.

96. Karanlık Kale: Church, view west.

95. Karanlık Kale: Room 4, northwest corner.

the plan). This is roughly cut, with a simple rectangular entrance and a flat ceiling; it is possibly not an original part of the monastery. The northern part of its floor has collapsed into the kitchen, leaving a rough opening into the niche in the west wall of the kitchen.

Room 8 To the west, beyond the rooms so far described, is a further room (8) cut into the cliff face. This is a well-carved, barrel-vaulted room with a cornice on the long walls at the springing of the vault and a moulding rimming the lunette of the north wall. The south wall of the room is lost. There are three small arched blind niches, one in each of the three remaining walls, their bases about 1 metre above ground level. A square hole is cut into the vault at the north end of this room, slightly to the left (west) of the crest of the barrel vault. This appears to lead up to a tunnel above the room, but there is no obvious means of access to it. The cliff above the monastery contains several rectangular openings high up the sheer rock face which must be linked by tunnels inside the cliff. Honeycombing of cliffs in this manner is a familiar local method of making pigeon houses, and it is therefore possible that the tunnel visible through the hole in the barrel vault of Room 8 is part of such a structure. In one of the openings in the cliff, however, a millstone closing

device is visible, and this is not likely to be pigeon-house furniture. Probably, therefore, as in the case of Aynalı Kilise Monastery (see above), Karanlık Kale had a post-Byzantine phase, during which the complex was used to house people and the cliff cavities were cut for storage and occasional refuge.

Church (9) The church is of inscribed-cross plan, with a central dome carried on four square piers with tapering block capitals (Pl. 96); barrel vaults cover the cross-arms. The dome rises above a rim and is faceted, having eight steep sides ending in a flat, octagonal top. Arches spring from the piers of the crossing to meet simple corbels on the walls (Pl. 97). The four small corner bays are covered by shallow cross vaults. A double-recessed arched blind niche is cut into the north wall of the northeast corner bay and there is a deep arched niche in the south wall of the southeast corner bay.

The church has three apses, each of slightly horseshoe-shaped plan, with a cornice below the conch. The main apse is much taller and wider than the lateral apses (Pl. 97). The north apse has an attached rock-cut altar with a shallow round-headed niche above it; similar niches occur in the main and south apses. No chancel screens are visible, but accumulated debris has raised the

97. Karanlık Kale: Church, view east.

98. Karanlık Kale: corridor to Church.

ground level by at least 1 metre and there may be low chancel slabs buried in the rubble. The centre bay of the west wall contains a rectangular opening to the vestibule; this is set in a horseshoe-arched blind niche. The church has its main entrance from the façade, through a corridor which enters the centre bay of the naos south wall (Pl. 98).

Corridor (10) and side chapel (11) The corridor running between the church and façade (10) has arches at each end and, between them, a flat ceiling decorated with splayed-armed crosses in kite-shaped recesses (Pl. 99). The arch at the façade end (south) is set into a horseshoe-arched recess, in turn framed by a rectangular recess (Pl. 90). The walls of the corridor are plain up to the level of the springing of the entrance arches, where there is a horizontal moulding and above this a decoration of blind niches in three double-recessed panels: there is a single horseshoe-arched blind niche in each panel except for the two to the north of the east wall, where there are two niches to each panel (Pl. 99). In the centre of the north wall there is a small rectangular-plan arched niche, and to the right of this is a smaller, apsidal niche, with a rock-cut basin in its floor.

Opposite the first niche of the corridor is the arched entrance to the Side Chapel (11). This is a single-naved chapel with a single apse (Pl. 100). The upper parts of the walls have double-recessed panel decoration similar to that in the corridor: on the north wall, from left to right there is a horseshoe-arched niche, a diagonal cross, another niche and a plain recess; each panel faces an identical one on the south wall. The ceiling is flat, decorated with carved and painted splayed-armed crosses in kite-shaped fields. The single apse is horseshoe-shaped in plan, and has a cornice below the conch with a central round-headed niche above it. The apse is rimmed by a plain moulding and the east wall in which it is set is framed by two more such mouldings. No chancel slabs are visible but, as in the church, an accumulation of rubble has raised the floor level and the remains of low closing slabs may be thus obscured. In the south wall, near to the apse, there is a deep rectangular recess with an arcosolium cut into its back wall – only the top of this is visible above the rubble.

Painting Simple geometric ornament in red and white paint decorates several parts of the monastery. In Room 1 there are vestiges of white paint on the niche framing the church entrance and on the modillions around the arches of the north wall. In Room 2 the cornice and hood mouldings are painted white, with a decoration of

99. Karanlık Kale: corridor, detail of east wall.

100. Karanlık Kale: side chapel.

triangles and chequer patterns superimposed in red. Details of the carved ornament in the side chapel are picked out in red and there is a chequered border rimming the apse arch, a lozenge pattern on the uprights. The mouldings of the east wall are decorated with triangle and 'barber's pole' patterns, and cross medallions decorate the spandrels (Pl. 100). This decoration was once obscured by plaster, fragments of which remain on the east wall.

The church is also plastered throughout, with a fine smooth finish that is still evident, although much damaged by damp. The plastering would seem to be preparation for polychrome painting, but no traces of such a decoration are visible. In the church, as in the side chapel, the plaster has fallen away in places to reveal simple red decoration on the rock surface. This is particularly evident on the capitals, which have triangle patterns on neckings and abaci and medallions containing equal-armed crosses on some faces (Pls. 96 & 97).

Summary

Karanlık Kale (Fig. 16) has no courtyard; it is cut into a steep cliff. The main entrance opens into a vestibule (1) which gives access to a hall (2). A free-cross room (3), which contains two graves, opens from its east wall. Next to the hall is an undecorated room (4) which communicates with the kitchen (5) to the west. An inscribed-cross church (9) lies to the east of the vestibule and is accessible from it, but its main entrance is via a corridor (10) which passes a side chapel (11). The church and side chapel are plastered but not painted. Parts of an aniconic decoration in red paint are visible where the plaster is lost.

Date

The monastery contains no inscriptions and no painting beyond the simple ornament described above, and is therefore very difficult to date. There is no courtyard, but, as in the case of Direkli Kilise Monastery, this is probably a modification imposed by the cliff-side site. In other respects Karanlık Kale is basically similar in layout to complexes already examined, having a vestibule (1), from which the other rooms are reached, a hall (2), a kitchen (5) and several other rooms, and a single church, with side chapel. Although separate from the church Room 3, which contains two prominent graves, and receives no natural light, may be the equivalent of the tomb chamber in the other monasteries. Several decorative details can

be matched in other monasteries described above: the cross in a kite-shaped field is an ornament that occurs at Aynalı Kilise Monastery; the linked hood mouldings of Rooms 2 and 3 are found in the hall of Bezir Hane. The inscribed-cross church, with wide cross-arms and tiny corner bays, large main apse and small lateral apses, resembles the churches of Bezir Hane and Soğanlı Han. Thus its affinities with the other cave monasteries make it unlikely that Karanlık Kale is substantially different in date from them.

Further, as with Direkli Kilise Monastery and Hallaç Monastery, an argument may be made that the monastery was in use for a short period only: there is no sign of phases of alteration, other than those clearly linked to post-Byzantine agricultural phases, and the fine plastering of the church suggests that painting was planned but never undertaken. Once again, if abandonment be associated with the arrival of the Seljuks, then a mid to late eleventh-century date is indicated.

Eski Gümüş Monastery

Eski Gümüş is a village near Niğde (Fig. 1), now linked by modern development with another village (together they are known as Gümüşler). The monastery, in the village itself, is therefore some 70 km away from the main concentrations of cave churches around Ürgüp.[81] This complex is unique among the cave monasteries in having a completely enclosed courtyard: its rooms are grouped around a square well, which is cut into a large mass of rock, and has a tunnel entrance at the south side (Fig. 17).

Courtyard The north façade of the courtyard is decorated with a blind arcade of nine tall, narrow arches, standing out from the wall in high relief. Volutes, some single and some in pairs, are set on the inner faces of each arch, at the springing; above them a plain moulding rims each arch (Pls. 101, 102 & 102a). The lower parts of the pilasters have been hacked away, but fragments of them, and scars on the wall, indicate that they once descended to ground level. The upper parts of the arcade pilasters have crude incised and relief decoration in scroll patterns. Below the second niche from the right is a recessed medallion containing an equal-armed cross in relief (Pl. 102). The arcade is sheltered by an overhang, above which the rock is cut back to form a smooth wall to the top of the rock mass.

The north façade has several openings: below the

---

81 M. Gough, 'The Monastery of Eski Gümüş. A Preliminary Report', *AnatSt* 14 (1964), 147–61; *idem*, 'Second Preliminary Report', *AnatSt* 15 (1965), 157–64; *idem*, 'The Monastery of Eski Gümüş, *Archaeology* 18 (1965), 254–63; H. Grégoire, 'Rapport', 132–4; Restle, *Wall Painting*, Cat. no. LXIV.

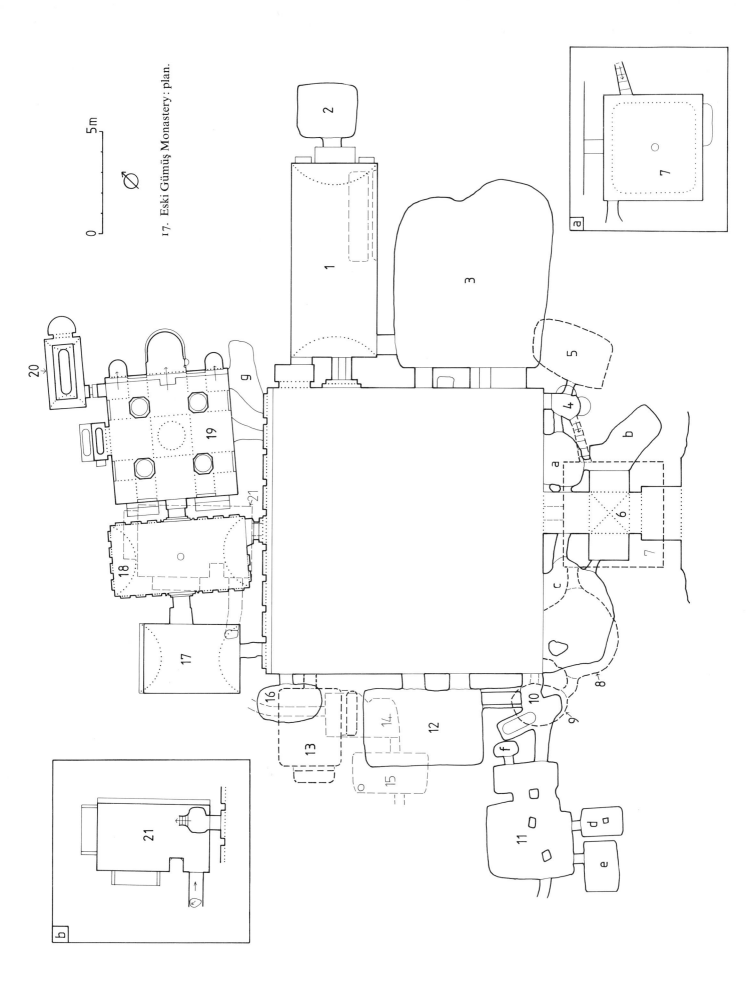

17. Eski Gümüş Monastery : plan.

0   5m

101. Eski Gümüş Monastery: north façade, west end.

102. Eski Gümüş Monastery: north façade, east end.

central arch of the arcade, at ground level, is the entrance to the church narthex (Pl. 101); to the right of this, below the penultimate arch, there is a tall rectangular window into the church and to the right of this a rough opening into a cavity connected with the southeast corner bay of the church (Pl. 102). Above the entrance to the narthex there is an irregular opening into an upper room (21). At the left side of the façade, below the first arch of the arcade, there is an opening to Room 17 (Pl. 101). About one third of the way up the smooth area above the arcade is a regular series of recesses making a horizontal line across the façade. These and other rows of recesses were probably cut to hold the joists of a timber structure built against the façade, probably in the post-Byzantine period.

The other three sides of the courtyard have smooth, undecorated walls, pierced by entrances and windows to the rooms of the complex, and by many secondary pits and recesses (Pls. 103b–105). Entrances and windows will be described below, in connection with the rooms they front. At their north ends the west and east walls of the courtyard each have an arched recess cut into them, its apex slightly higher than the north façade overhang (Pls. 103a & 104). Above this a horizontal recess on each side is aligned with that of the north wall. These recesses were probably cut to take roofing timbers belonging to the post-Byzantine phase noted above.

There are fragments of plaster on the north façade, particularly evident in the first niche from the left. This plastering may have covered the whole façade, since there

102a. Eski Gümüş Monastery: north façade, detail.

103a. Eski Gümüş Monastery: east façade, north end.

are also fragments of it around the entrance to the narthex, where there are also traces of paint on the plaster.

The rooms of the monastery will be described in perambulatory fashion, starting at the north end of the east façade of the courtyard and moving clockwise. This starting point has been chosen in order to end with the church and other important structures on the north side.

Rooms 1 and 2 At the north end of the east wall of the courtyard is a deep horseshoe-arched rectangular-plan recess, set in a shallow arched recess; its arch is carried on simple pilasters with capitals (Pl. 103a). Fragments of white plaster remain inside the recess. Part of the back wall of this recess is cut through to form a secondary, rectangular entrance to Room 1, which lies behind it. The original entrance to Room 1 is to the right of the recess: a rectangular opening in a shallow arched recess, in turn framed by a square recess (Pls. 103a & b). There is a roughly rectangular window to Room 1 directly above this entrance. The room has a barrel vault springing from a cornice which continues across the end walls (Pl. 106). A Latin cross, with splayed arms and a stem, is carved in high relief on the east lunette. Below the lunette a large arched, rectangular-plan recess occupies the centre of the wall, its arch springing above cornices. The floor of this recess is about 20 cm above the floor of the room. Two smaller niches of the same form flank the central recess; these are set into the wall about 1 metre above ground level. A rough rectangular opening towards the left of the

103b. Eski Gümüş Monastery: east façade.

104. Eski Gümüş Monastery: west façade.

105. Eski Gümüş Monastery: south façade.

106. Eski Gümüş Monastery: Room 1, east end.

back wall of the centre recess leads into an ill-carved, roughly square room with a flat ceiling (2).

There are many irregularities in the floor of this room, including a slightly raised area about 4 metres long and 1 metre wide, running parallel to the south wall at the east end (shown in broken line on the plan). There are traces of a bench on the south wall parallel to this mass and together the two features may be the remains of a rock-cut refectory table and benches, such as are found in one other courtyard monastery (Karanlık Kilise Monastery) and in the Refectory monasteries of Göreme valley (see below, Chapter 4). A rectangular opening, probably secondary, runs from the east end of the south wall to Room 3.

Room 3 To the right of the entrance to Room 1 in the east façade is an area of bare rock, and then a small irregular rectangular opening to Room 3 (Pl. 103b). To the right of this is a deep, slightly arched recess and further along is the original entrance to Room 3, larger than the first and bearing the remains of an arch (the entrance has been enlarged and its original side walls cut away); above this entrance is a rectangular window. Room 3 is a large, irregular, roughly cut cavity.

South façade, Rooms 4 and 5 Much of the original form of the lower part of the south side of the courtyard has been destroyed by secondary excavation. The passage (6), which is the only entrance to the courtyard, is in the centre of this façade; above it there is a tall rectangular window to the kitchen. To left and right of the passage the rock is cut back to form very irregular cavities (a) and (c) (Pl. 105).

At the east end of the south façade a rectangular entrance, of which only the top remains intact, leads into a small chamber, Room 4. This has deep, rounded niches cut into its east and south walls about 40 cm above ground level. Each of these contains a deep pit, probably for the storage of food of some kind (Pl. 107). A rough tunnel cuts through part of the easternmost niche and leads upwards into an ill-cut, roughly rectangular room (5), which has a low flat ceiling. This room is well above the ground level of the courtyard and a small part of its north side overhangs Room 3. Since its entrance destroys part of the niche with the storage pit in Room 4, this room is probably secondary. Another rough tunnel, from the west side of Room 4, leads into cavity (a) which lies between Room 4 and the entrance passage (6). To the left of this tunnel is a flight of six steps leading up to Room 7 (Pl. 108).

Kitchen (7) and cavities (8) and (9) Cavities (7) to (9) are all on an upper level and are marked on the plan with a broken line; details of Room 7, the kitchen, are shown

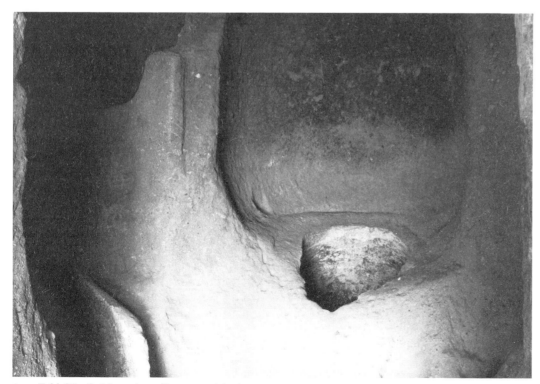

107. Eski Gümüş Monastery: Room 4, with pit.

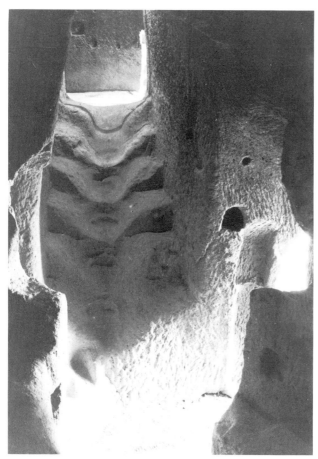

108. Eski Gümüş Monastery: steps to kitchen (7) from Room 4.

Entrance passage (6) The entrance passage into the courtyard (6) opens from a small area of smoothed rock on the outside of the rock mass which houses the monastery. Above the opening are two horizontal rows of pits, perhaps cut to take the timbers of a porch, but probably not part of the original plan.

The first unit of the passage is a barrel-vaulted bay. Beyond this the vault level drops and an archway leads into a square bay with a shallow cross vault. The sides of this bay are extended into arched recesses with cornices at the springing of their arches. The back wall of the eastern recess is cut away, giving access to a rough secondary cavity (b) which also communicates with cavity (a) to the north. The third bay of the passage is a barrel-vaulted unit opening into the monastery courtyard. A rough opening in its west side leads to cavity (c) and much of its east wall is lost, giving access to cavity (a).

Areas 10 and 11 At the left side of the west face of the courtyard there is an irregular opening to a short tunnel (10). A few paces into the tunnel is a rough opening to the next room (12), partly blocked by a mass of rock; beyond this is a millstone closing device: a stone disc housed in a cavity in the north wall of the tunnel, which may be rolled across the tunnel to lodge in a recess in the opposite wall. (The 'mass of rock' referred to may be the result of an attempt to cut a millstone closure close to the tunnel entrance, abandoned in favour of placing the device further in.) The tunnel leads west into an unlit, very irregular cavity (11), which has a low flat ceiling supported on three rough piers. Two openings lead off the south side of this room, to further rough cavities (d) and (e). Cavity (d) contains a rough pier. A tunnel, now blocked, opens off the west wall and a further cavity (f) opens off the east wall. This is clearly a storage area.

Room 12 To the right of the tunnel entrance three more openings from the façade lead into a rough rectangular room (12) with flat ceiling. The first two entrances are rectangular openings; the third is a tall cavity opening slightly above ground level (Pl. 104). At the top of this cavity is an opening to an upper room (14); further up still there is a window into this room.

Rooms 13–16 At the right of the west façade an upper room (13 – drawn in broken line on the plan) is reached through a hole in its south side by means of a modern ladder (Pl. 104). This room is also roughly cut and contains two deep recesses, closed off by low walls, in its west

in box (a). Room 7 is reached by the flight of steps from Room 4 (Pl. 108). It is square and has a conical vault rising above an overhang, with a smoke hole at its apex. It is curious, perhaps, to find the kitchen at an upper level and it may have been thus located to minimize the difficulty of cutting a smoke hole to the top of the rock mass. In the south wall there is a roughly arched recess with holes in its floor opening into the entrance passage below. Both features are probably secondary.[82] A tall rectangular window from the kitchen opens to the courtyard above the arched entrance to the passage in the south façade.

From the north end of the west wall of the kitchen a short passage leads into an irregular chamber (8) which is open to the courtyard on its north side. A hole in the west wall of cavity (8) gives access to a further irregular chamber (9), which has an opening to the south end of the west façade.

---

82 Local guides will explain that this is a machicoulis, for pouring boiling oil on assailants in the passage below. Such an auxiliary

function for a monastery kitchen is appealing, but probably fanciful.

and south walls: these may have been wine presses. A hole in the ceiling above the south recess opens to an upper room (14), from which the window noted above is cut through to the façade. Narrow tunnels lead off the west and north walls of this room: the west tunnel goes straight back into the rock, into a rough room (15) in the back (west) wall of which is the entrance to a further tunnel; in the northwest corner there is a vertical tunnel to the top of the cliff. The tunnel in the north wall of Room 14 leads towards the north façade, and probably joins other tunnels visible from Room 21 (see below); this area was inaccessible in 1978/80. This upper series of cavities (14, 15 and tunnels) is drawn in thin broken line on the plan. Below Rooms 13 and 14 another rough room (16) is accessible through a rough hole in the façade at ground level.

Room 17   At the west end of the north façade there is a rough rectangular opening which is almost certainly secondary, since it cuts across the first pilaster of the arcade. This opens into a rectangular room (17) which has a steep barrel vault on a north/south axis, rising from a rudimentary cornice. There is a bench along the north side of the room and three storage pits in the floor; these are probably secondary. A cavity cut in the southeast corner of the upper part of the barrel vault communicates with a tunnel leading to an upper room (21), described below.

The rest of the length of the north façade at ground level is taken up by the church. Before turning to this, however, it is convenient to move to the last of the monastery rooms, Room 21, which is on an upper level.

Room 21   Room 21 lies above the church narthex (18). It is a rectangular room with a flat ceiling. Unlike the upper-level rooms of the west side of the courtyard (13–15), which are roughly cut, this is carefully finished and is clearly an original part of the monastery. It has a deep arched recess cut into its north wall and another at the north end of the west wall, their bases about 40 cm above floor level (Pl. 109). The arch of each recess is rimmed by a shallow groove and there are shallow steps where the side walls meet the base. A bench runs along the east wall, its top level with the bases of the recesses. An attached pier with chamfered corners projects from the west wall, to the left of the arched recess. To the left of the pier there is an opening to a tunnel which slopes downwards towards the west and opens into the east side of

109. Eski Gümüş Monastery: Room 21, northwest corner.

the barrel vault of Room 17. A few paces into the tunnel from Room 21 an opening in the ceiling communicates with another tunnel, running upwards and probably leading to the top of the rock mass in which the monastery is situated. This upper tunnel may connect with the tunnel from cavity (14), noted above.

Room 21 is now entered through an irregular opening above the narthex entrance, accessible by a modern stairway. The bottom of this opening is about 1 metre below the floor level of the room and it leads into a small stairwell of four steps cut in the floor just inside the room. Viewed from outside, the upper left part of the entrance to Room 21 is seen to be an arched window, with a recess around it.[83] It seems therefore that the entrance and the small stairwell are secondary and the only original opening to the façade from Room 21 was the window. Further, there is no trace on the façade of a rock-cut ramp or steps up to this level, and the area of rock immediately below Room 21 contains the narthex entrance, which would have been obscured even by a wooden staircase. Various pits and recesses form a broken horizontal line across the façade, just below the entrance to Room 21. It is likely that these, together with the recesses on the wall above the overhang and those on the west and east facades, were cut to take the horizontal timbers of a two-floor structure added to the north end of the courtyard when the monastery was modified for other use. At this point the window to Room 21 would have been enlarged to give access to the room, the opening extended downwards to meet the floor level of the upper part of the timber structure. This would have necessitated the cutting of the small stairwell to give access to the room.

A problem obviously now arises as to the original means of access to Room 21. It has no entrances other than the two described, and if the façade entrance is discounted as secondary, then the original entrance must have been the tunnel opening into the west wall. This, as noted, leads into the side of the barrel vault of Room 17. Improbable though it may seem, therefore, it is necessary to conclude that the room was reached by means of a ladder up to the opening of the vault of Room 17.

Room 21 has a polychrome painted decoration of poor quality. A fighting man is depicted on the west face of the pier and all along the east wall, above the bench, there is a series of images identified by Gough as scenes from Aesop's fables.[84] This painting is very crude in style and bears no relationship to the painting of the church. Yet it is not to be classed as graffiti (which is seldom poly-

chrome), since it forms a considered if incompetently executed, programme of decoration, complete with inscriptions to identify the scenes. It is nevertheless of such rusticity that it defies efforts to date it.

The careful carving of the room, and its niches, which resemble those in the west wall of the church, mark it as an original part of the monastery. It must, however, have been used to some extent as a secret room, accessible only with special arrangements in Room 17. Possibly it was a treasury, or a library, but the significance of its secular decoration is far from clear.

Church: narthex (18) Below Room 21, the church narthex is rectangular, barrel-vaulted on a north/south axis and decorated with relief carving. This consists of a broad plain cornice running along east and west walls at the springing of the vault; north and south lunettes are outlined by wall arches (Pl. 110) and the south lunette is decorated with an equal-armed cross on a pedestal, cut in high relief. In the centre of the barrel vault there is a carved boss, surrounded by four painted bosses in a cross formation. The walls are decorated with blind arcades of tall narrow arches, cut in high relief. The arches are horseshoe-shaped, rising above pilasters with rudimentary capitals, set in recessed panels containing three arches each. The proportions of the arcade are similar to those of the arcade on the north façade.

Entrances to Room 17 and to the naos are set in the centre of west and east walls respectively. These are rectangular openings, each framed by two roll mouldings set in a rectangular recess (Pl. 110). Main access to the narthex is from the north façade: a rectangular entrance set in a horseshoe-arched recess which opens to the east side of the narthex south wall.

To the right of the entrance to the naos, in the east wall of the narthex, two of the pilasters of the blind arcade, and parts of their arches, have been cut away to make a flat panel. The panel is decorated with a polychrome painting, on plaster ground, of the Virgin and Child between Angels (Pl. 111). Other painting in the narthex, directly onto the rock, consists of black and red triangle patterns on cornices and arcades, panels of lozenges above the entrances, and imitation masonry pattern on the barrel vault.

Church: naos (19) The naos is of inscribed-cross plan, with a small, truncated central dome carried on very thick columns with slab capitals and octagonal bases (essen-

83 An early photograph shows the façade area in less mutilated condition that it is today: the arched window into Room 21 is almost

complete, although blocked by stones, Grégoire, 'Rapport', 133, fig. 22.
84 Gough, 'Preliminary Report', 162–4.

110. Eski Gümüş Monastery: Church, northeast corner of narthex.

111. Eski Gümüş Monastery: narthex, painting on east wall.

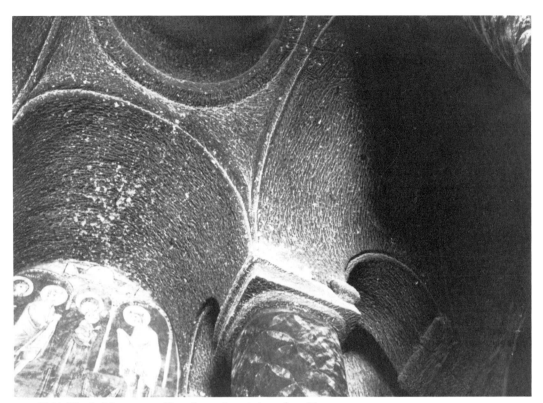

112. Eski Gümüş Monastery: Church, northeast view of vaulting.

tially square bases with chamfered corners; above these are short drums only slightly wider than the columns themselves). The arms of the cross have barrel vaults. Small arches spring between the columns to meet shallow corbels on the walls, framing tiny corner bays with concave vaults (Pl. 112).

The deep main apse, two steps above the nave floor, is oval in plan, with a bench running around it. A rock-cut seat in the right side of the apse wall is formed by a shallow niche framed by two uprights cut in relief and connected by a curved moulding. The apse has no screen and there is no sign that a rock-cut screen was ever in place. The main apse is flanked by small absidioles, also without furniture.

In the west wall, at each side of the entrance from the narthex, there are deep arched recesses, their bases about 1 metre above ground level. Each recess is partly blocked by a ledge running along its back wall. In the south wall a tall rectangular window, opening to the courtyard, is no doubt an enlargement of a much smaller original one; a set of rough steps cut into the area of rock between naos and façade now lead up to it. Early photographs of the site show that this enlarged window was at one point in

use as a doorway, and the ground level of the complex at that time was at its base.[85] To the left of the window a rough opening in the south wall of the southeast corner bay leads into an irregular cavity (g) which occupies the thickness of the rock between the church wall and façade. The façade has crumbled, so this area is visible from the courtyard, but Grégoire's photograph shows that there was not originally a courtyard entrance to it; it is probably secondary.

Tomb recess A tomb recess containing two graves opens from the central bay of the naos (Pl. 113). (The ground level at the entrance to the recess is worn down, leaving a 'step' up to the chamber; since this feature is the result of erosion, it is omitted from the plan.) The recess is framed by a horseshoe arch springing from pilasters and tapering block capitals. Behind this the forward part of the cavity is an arched recess, rectangular in plan, with a grave pit in its floor. In the west wall of this recess, just below the springing of its arch, there is an arched blind niche. About two-thirds of the way up the back wall of the recess is a further cavity, with a grave pit at its base. The plastering of the recess has been damaged: there is

85 Grégoire, 'Rapport', 133, fig. 22.

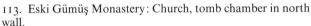

113. Eski Gümüş Monastery: Church, tomb chamber in north wall.

114. Eski Gümüş Monastery: Church, entrance to side chapel.

plaster on the back wall of the forward part of the recess and on the side walls flanking it, including the niche at the west side, but none lower down, around the grave pit; nor any in the cavity containing the upper grave. This condition is doubtless the result of disturbance of the graves – nearly every grave pit in the Cappadocian cave monuments has been emptied, probably by treasure seekers. This adds to the difficulty of establishing the original form of the tomb recess. There are two main possibilities: one that both graves are original, and that, once filled, the upper cavity was walled up and plastered over; the other that only the floor grave is an original part of the plan, and the upper cavity is secondary. The latter seems the more likely since the upper cavity is very roughly cut. Even if designed to be plastered over after the burial it would, if original, surely have had the same careful finish seen in other areas of original excavation.

Side chapel (20) A small, single-naved, barrel-vaulted side chapel (20) is reached through the northeast corner bay of the church. The chapel has a single apse closed by low chancel chancel slabs which have been cut back. Most of the floor space is taken up by a large, rectangular pit, with a grave pit at its base.

The chapel is reached through an opening above a step about 25 cm above floor level, in a recess in the north wall of the northeast corner bay (Pl. 114). The low rectangular entrance is framed by two uprights linked by an upper curve, exactly like the moulding of the seat-back in the main apse. It seems, therefore, that the chapel is secondary, made by cutting through the back of what was once a carved seat: the 'step' is therefore the lower part of the seat.

Painting The rustic painting in Room 21 has been described above. The church of Eski Gümüş Monastery also contains some fine paintings which were cleaned and restored in 1962–5 and have been described in detail by Gough.[86] In addition to the narthex panel already mentioned, there is polychrome figure painting in the main

86 Gough, 'Preliminary Report', 152–60, and 'Second Preliminary Report', 158–62.

apse, absidioles and the centre bay of the north wall, above and flanking the tomb chamber. The columns have a non-figural decoration, a network of simple leaf shapes. The programme, briefly, is as follows:

Narthex: Virgin and Child between archangels (Pl. 111).
Main apse (conch): Deesis (Christ enthroned flanked by the Virgin and John the Baptist).
Main apse (wall): upper register – apostles (busts), lower register – Virgin orant flanked by bishop saints (to the left, George, Blaisios, Amphilochios, Gregory of Nazianzos and Basil; to the right, (?), Nikolaos, Epiphanios, Jason and Athenogenes).
Absidioles: (north) Virgin; (south) John the Baptist.
North wall: (lunette) Presentation; (below) Nativity; (flanking tomb entrance) Annunciation; (soffit) west – Stephanos, east – John the Baptist (Pl. 115).

The programme just outlined is that of the visible painting. This is not, however, the first decoration of the church: the paintings of the apse apparently cover an earlier figural layer, and a layer of aniconic decoration underlies at least part of the north-wall painting.[87]

Summary

The monastery of Eski Gümüş (Fig. 17) has an enclosed courtyard, entered through a passage (6) at its south side; the north wall of the courtyard has a decorated façade. Behind the east wall is a large hall, possibly a refectory (1) with a rough room (2) opening off it. Next to it, to the south, is a large rough room (3). Behind the south wall of the courtyard there is a storage room (4) at ground level, a kitchen (7) on an upper level, and a series of rough rooms and cavities (5, 8, 9, a, b, c) on both levels. At the west side of the courtyard a tunnel (10) leads to a large storage area (11). To the north of this is a series of rough rooms (12–16) at various levels. Behind the decorated north façade is an inscribed-cross church (19) with the side chapel (20), tomb recess (19a) and narthex (18). To the west of the narthex is a barrel-vaulted room (17), a hole in the vault of which is the only original means of access to an upper room (21). There is painted decoration of high quality in the church (apse, north wall and narthex) and of poor quality in Room 21.

Post-Byzantine use

Until quite recently the monastery was used for storage by local farmers and its village site makes it very likely

115. Eski Gümüş Monastery: Church, north wall.

that it has a long history of such use.[88] Many of the irregular cavities and roughly-cut rooms may thus belong to post-Byzantine phases and some (such as Rooms 3 and 12) may be enlargements of more carefully finished monastery rooms. It is likely, however, that the monastery, too, needed storage areas. Cavities that do not damage the monastery architecture, such as Room 11, behind the millstone, may therefore be original. The north façade shows several signs of having had a two-storey timber structure built against it: the arched grooves in the walls flanking the façade, the various rows of beam-holes along the façade and end walls, and the enlargement of the window to Room 21 to make an upper level doorway.

Date

As with most of the cave monasteries, dating depends largely on the attribution of dates to the architecture and

---

87 Gough, 'Preliminary Report', 150, 154. Gough also mentions in passing a still earlier layer in the apse (161) but does not elaborate.

This may have been underpainting.
88 Gough, 'Preliminary Report', 150.

painted decoration of the church. Once again, the inscribed-cross formula can offer little besides a broad 'Middle Byzantine' date, but consideration of the painting makes it possible to narrow this bracket.

Gough divides the paintings of the church among three hands: A, the painter of the apse and narthex panel; B, the painter of the north wall; and C, the painter of the Baptist and Virgin in the absidioles.[89] This distinction of hands seems valid, but does not necessarily imply great chronological disparity between the three sets of paintings. The most striking difference between the Virgin of the apsidiole (hand C) and that of the apse (hand A) is one of quality rather than style, and the paintings of the main apse and the north wall (hands A and B) use the same basic stylistic formulae, the latter rather more harshly than the former.[90] It is possible, therefore, that the painting of all three hands was completed within a relatively short time.

The dating evidence for the work of hands A, B and C has been examined by Thierry, whose conclusions may be summarized as follows: a good stylistic comparison may be made between the apse painting (A) at Eski Gümüş and the painting of another cave church, St Michael, İhlara (in Peristrema valley). The two churches also use the same very elaborate style of lettering in their inscriptions. A fragmentary inscription in St Michael suggests that its paintings were done during the reign of Constantine VIII (1025–8). This is not beyond doubt, since the inscription may refer to Theodora (1055–6) but the earlier date seems more likely, in view of confirmation provided by another stylistic comparison.[91]

The painting of the north wall (by hand B) finds a fairly close stylistic parallel at Karabaş Kilise, in Soğanlı valley, dated by inscription to 1060/61.[92] Inscriptions in the two churches also have letter forms in common.[93] An iconographic parallel also exists with the paintings of Direkli Kilise, for which an eleventh-century date was proposed: Symeon in the Presentation at Eski Gümüş (Pl. 115) may be compared with Zacharias in the north apse of Direkli (Pl. 84a), and the Virgin of Eski Gümüş north absidiole (by hand C) is of the same iconographic type as the figure on the southwest pier of Direkli.[94]

An eleventh-century date therefore seems appropriate for all the top-layer paintings in the apse, north wall and narthex. Possibly the paintings of the north wall are to be placed in the third quarter of the eleventh century (with Karabaş Kilise) and those of the apse and narthex in the second quarter (with St Michael, İhlara). While certainly by a different hand, the painting of the absidioles is stylistically close enough to that of the other paintings for it, too, to be placed in the eleventh century. The gap between the three sets of paintings could be much shorter than the outer limits proposed by the stylistic comparisons (1020s to 1060s) might suggest. It is even possible that the stylistic differences are a matter of hands, not of years: the stylistic range may be compared to that seen in Direkli Kilise, for example, or in Ayvalı Kilise in Güllü Dere, where there is no doubt that the whole programme is of one phase, but executed by more than one painter.[95]

The paintings discussed do not, however, give a date for the excavation of the monastery, since an earlier layer of painting exists both in the apse and on the north wall of the church. The white ground and red borders of panels of this decoration are still visible in places where the later painting has fallen away (at the base of the apse wall, for example). In addition, part of the arcading of the narthex was cut back to accommodate the panel showing Virgin and Child with Angels, implying that the painting belongs to a secondary phase.

Other evidence of phases in excavation concerns the tomb recess in the north wall and the side chapel. First, as noted above, it is probable that the tomb chamber originally contained only one grave and that the upper part of its back wall was later cut back to give space for a second one. There seems no doubt that the tomb recess itself is an original feature, since its opening, a horseshoe arch on simple pilasters and pilaster capitals, outlined by a shallow recess, is identical to the arched recess of the east façade. Also, since an earlier layer of paint existed on the north wall while the other walls were unpainted, it is clear that there was always a special feature in the north wall and the top layer of paint replaced an earlier programme there. The side chapel was clearly an addition to the original plan, since it was made by cutting through the back of a seat in the naos north wall. The following hypothetical sequence combines this evidence:

89 *Ibid.* 158–60.
90 A series of plates in Gough, 'Preliminary Report', makes this clear: for the 'stylistic formulae' compare pls. 34a and 40b, also 34c and 37b.
91 N. Thierry, 'Un style schématique de Cappadoce daté du XIe siècle d'après une inscription', *JSav* (1968), 45–61, at 47–8; Gough's discussion of date is to be found in 'The Monastery of Eski Gümüş', *Archaeology* 18 (1965), 260–3, and 'Preliminary Report', 158–61.
92 See below, Chapter 5 for Karabaş: an apostle in the Divine Liturgy at Karabaş (illustrated in Jerphanion, *Eglises* pl. 197.2) may be

compared with Symeon in the Presentation at Eski Gümüş (illustrated in Gough, 'Preliminary Report', pl. 41a).
93 Gough, 'Preliminary Report', 160.
94 For illustrations, see Gough, 'Preliminary Report', pls. 36a & b, and Thierry, *Nouvelles églises*, pls. 86a & b.
95 N. and M. Thierry, 'Ayvalı Kilise ou pigeonnier de Gülli Dere, église inédite de Cappadoce', *CahArch* 15 (1965), 97–154. The work was executed by at least two hands, their work overlapping in several areas of each nave. See also Chapter 5.

I. The monastery was excavated for a founder who required that an important tomb chamber be placed in the church. The apse and the north wall, around the tomb, were decorated with painting.

II. The painting of Phase I was covered, in the eleventh century, with the present top layer of high-quality work. This may have been done in two phases spanning as much as forty years (with the apse and narthex decorated first, the north wall later), or perhaps just by separate hands operating within a shorter period. Since it includes the painting of the tomb recess, this refurbishing must have been the commission of someone aware of and respectful of the concerns of the monastery founder.

III. The side chapel was cut by digging through the seat in the north wall of the naos. This may have been part of Phase II, or later, but presumably falls into a period when the complex was still in use as a monastery. The deep pit in its floor suggests that another important burial place was required.

IV. A second grave was crudely cut in the tomb recess. This probably happened long after its original significance had been lost, perhaps when the monastery was no longer inhabited by a religious community.

V. After its abandonment, the monastery became the dwelling of a peasant family or community; timber structures were erected in the courtyard and secondary cavities were dug.

The paintings of Phase II may be dated to the eleventh century (probably the second or third quarter of the century). Phase I, the excavation of the monastery, is probably not a great deal earlier. The inscribed-cross church plan gives a general Middle Byzantine date bracket and Eski Gümüş Church shares with those of Hallaç Monastery and Soğanlı Han the east end formula of large central apse and much reduced lateral apses. Other comparisons with eleventh-century churches are also available: a similarity of form and proportion exists between the vaulting of Eski Gümüş Church and that of Göreme Chapel 17 (Pl. 20) where a tiny dome is carried on very wide barrel-vaulted arms and heavy columns. Also, the tomb recess is similar to that in the narthex of Karanlık Kilise (Pl. 44).

Further, it is likely that the repainting of the north wall in Phase II was undertaken at a time when the original purposes of the founder were still of concern. Probably, therefore, no very great length of time should separate Phases I and II.

Appendix: Other complexes

The present survey of Cappadocian cave monasteries is not exhaustive; it is hoped that other complexes will be discovered and recorded. A few that are known to me were, on my brief field-work trips, inaccessible for various reasons. The following notes offer a guide to explorers.

Complex opposite Kılıçlar Kilise

High in the cliff opposite Kılıçlar Kilise (and monastery), on the other side of the valley, is a carved façade (Pl. 116). This was inaccessible in 1980 and the following brief description is based on photographs taken from a distance. This area of cliff contains many pigeon-holes and the complex has obviously been used as a pigeon house: the cavities behind the façade were presumably supplemented by pigeon-house rooms, some of which, their front walls lost, are visible in Pl. 116:

The façade is set in a rectangular recess cut into the cliff. Conceivably this 'recess' was once a room, of which the front wall has been lost: to the left a portion of flat ceiling with a square cornice below it remains. The back wall of the recess is divided into four unequal bays by pilasters with capitals. In each bay a plain moulding divides an upper register from a taller lower one. Each bay of the upper register contains two small blind niches, each lower bay a single niche. The side wall at the left of this recess (or room) is similarly decorated.

Some painted decoration is visible on the façade: red-paint triangle patterns on the cornice and zig-zag patterns outlining the niche arches of both registers. There is also a painted bird, of the same type exactly as those which decorate Aynalı Kilise. The style of carving of this façade, and the red-paint decoration, including the bird motif, suggest that this complex is roughly contemporaneous with Aynalı Kilise Monastery.

The Ürgüp façade

A drawing published by Texier and Popplewell-Pullan shows a façade purportedly in Ürgüp.[96] The drawing cor-

---

96 C. Texier and R. Popplewell-Pullan, *Byzantine Architecture* (London, 1864), pl. 4 facing p. 40.

116. Façade opposite Kılıçlar Kilise, Göreme valley.

responds closely to the written description of a façade given by Texier in an earlier publication and it seems possible that a single monument is the source for both.[97] I know of no such façade in Ürgüp and none is recorded by Rott or Jerphanion. Texier's written description locates the façade in Ürgüp itself, but in other parts of the same text 'Ürgüb' is used as the general name for the region. Possibly, therefore, the placing of the façade in Ürgüp proper is an error. The written description, which lacks the embellishments of the drawing, could apply to the façade of Aynalı Kilise Monastery, which may be the source of the error. Nevertheless, perhaps Ürgüp itself is still to be explored for this elusive façade.

Ala Kilise

Ala Kilise is at the edge of the village of Belisırma, overlooking the Peristrema valley.[98] The façade of this church consists of three bays, articulated by pilasters linked by an architrave decorated with a frieze of small horseshoe-arched blind niches. The bay to the left is about twice as wide as the other two and contains the entrance to the

church. Each bay is divided into three registers by plain mouldings. The topmost register is decorated with horseshoe-arched blind niches, four to each bay. The next register has, in each of the two bays to the right, a pair of large double-recessed horseshoe-arched blind niches. In the large bay to the left the arch of the church entrance occupies part of this register, the rest is undecorated. The bottom register contains the lower part of the entrance to the church in its left bay; the centre bay contains a pair of horseshoe-arched blind niches, each framed with a gable moulding; in the right bay there is a single large horseshoe-arched entrance, now filled with masonry, framed by sloping mouldings.

Ala Kilise is a large inscribed-cross church, which is well finished and decorated with an extensive painted programme of high quality. Thierry notes the affinity of this painted decoration with those of the Column churches of Göreme and proposes an eleventh-century date for it.[99]

On both my visits the entrance to the right of the church was sealed with masonry and whatever lies behind it could not be explored. If this is a monastery, rather than simply a church with an elaborate façade, then it is to be

97 C. Texier, *Description de l'Asie Mineure . . . etc.* (Paris, 1849), II, 76.

98 Thierry, *Nouvelles églises*, 193–200 and pl. 17b.

99 *Ibid.* 200.

supposed that the existing façade was originally at the back of a courtyard, and that flanking walls, with further rooms behind them, have been lost. This is not improbable, for the modern road goes right past the façade and its construction may have been the occasion for clearance of the area.

Yaprakhisar

In Yaprakhisar, on the Selime–İhlara road, is a façade similar to that fronting Ala Kilise. I have not seen this and the following description depends upon Thierry's photograph.[100] The façade appears to have five bays, articulated by pilasters, each bay with three registers. The top register has three horseshoe-arched blind niches per bay and the next register four such niches per bay. The bottom register is obscured by rough modern masonry or timber structures. In the centre is a large horseshoe-arched opening. Thierry notes that large rooms in the area are in use as dwellings by the local people.

Sümbüllü Kilise

Also in Peristrema valley, not far from İhlara, is a two-floor unit associated with the chapel known as Sümbüllü Kilise.[101] A rough wall of rock contains a shallow horseshoe-arched blind niche containing a rectangular entrance with an arched window to the left of it. The entrance leads to a barrel-vaulted room, from the left side of which a small and somewhat irregular chapel (Süm-büllü Kilise) is accessible. A flight of steps leads to an upper level, where there is a narrow terrace; at the back of this is a decorated façade, parallel to the rough wall described below. The façade consists of five deep bays separated by pilasters which are linked by an architrave decorated with small horseshoe-arched blind niches. The second and fourth bays have arched openings in them, the other three have horseshoe-arched blind niches, opening about one metre above ground level. The entrances lead into a barrel-vaulted room with its long axis parallel to that of the façade.

When I saw the site in 1982, recent excavation to the right of the lower part of the complex had begun to uncover the remains of a large church. On previous visits it was perplexing to find that a complex of this type should have no church other than Sümbüllü Kilise, which seems more like a minor chapel than a monastery church. The discovery of the large church is an important one, and it is hoped that the whole complex will soon be revealed.

Çeltek

A rock-cut monastery near Çeltek, to the southeast of Aksaray, has been reported by Rott, Bell and Thierry.[102] The site is near the important built church known as Çanlı Kilise (see Chapter 6). Thierry mentions a complex with a courtyard and several rooms decorated with blind niches and other ornament. One room has a cross cut in relief on its ceiling and a wall decorated with a row of blind niches and gable mouldings. Bell also notes the existence of an inscribed-cross church.

---

100 Thierry, *Nouvelles églises*, 33 and pl. 17a. The façade is also mentioned briefly by Rott (*Denkmäler*, 264, where he refers to Yaprakhisar as 'Ibrasa').

101 Thierry, *Nouvelles églises*, 175–81, pl. 20a & b, 78–81.

102 Rott, *Denkmäler*, 257–8; Ramsay & Bell, *1001 Churches*, 418; N. Thierry, 'Etudes cappadociennes. Région du Hasan Dağı, compléments pour 1975', *CahArch* 24 (1975), 183–90, at 189.

3

Açık Saray

To the west of the Nevşehir–Gülşehir road, about 28 km from Göreme, is a site known as Açık Saray, the 'Open Palace'.[1] Here, carved into a series of large, squat cone groups, are several courtyard complexes which have been described as monasteries.[2] This is almost certainly an error and discussion of their function will be found at the end of this chapter. They are nevertheless included in this study because no details of the complexes have so far been published and it is relevant to examine the form and function of all the large cave complexes in order to isolate those that are monastic. Further, since an element of doubt as to their function remains, it is necessary that the evidence be laid out for scrutiny.

The site covers an area of about one square kilometre, and no plan of it has been published. The sketch included here (Fig. 18) is very approximate indeed. Since earlier nomenclature for the complexes is incomplete and sometimes confused, I have abandoned it and re-numbered the complexes 1–7.[3] As in the descriptions of courtyard monasteries, the term 'vestibule' will be used below to describe a large room at the front of a complex from which other rooms are accessible and 'hall' will be used for other large rooms.

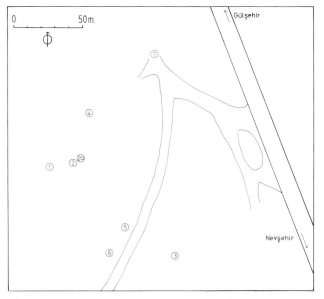

18. Açık Saray: site (approximate locations of complexes).

1 On some maps (including that supplied in Hild & Restle, *TIB*, 11) Açık Saray is shown just south of the Kızılırmak, on what is marked as 'the probable Byzantine road'. In fact, the site is to the west of the modern Nevşehir–Gülşehir road, some 6 km to the southwest of the point shown.

2 Rott, *Denkmäler*, 242–5; Jerphanion, *Eglises* I. i, 27; F. Verzone, 'Gli monasteri de Acık Serai in Cappadocia', *CahArch* 13 (1962), 119–36; Kostof, *Caves of God*, 65.

3 Rott, in *Denkmäler*, 242–5, records three façades: I, II and III, which correspond to my numbers 3, 1 and 7 respectively. Verzone's account ('Gli monasteri . . .'), although a useful first publication of the site, was apparently based on a brief examination of the site and consequently contains some ambiguities. Verzone labels several façades and rooms as 'Monastero A,B,C' etc. Açık Saray 1 is called both Monastero C (123, figs. 5 & 6) and Monastero E (fig. 10) and the former is wrongly equated with Rott façade I; Room 1 of Açık Saray 2 is also called Monastero C (123, fig. 7); the façade of Açık Saray 4 is called both Monastero D (123, fig. 8) and E (126, fig. 9) and the former wrongly identified wth Rott façade II; Açık Saray 5 is called Monastero B; Açık Saray 6 Monastero A; Açık Saray 7 Monastero E.

19. Açık Saray No. 1: plan.

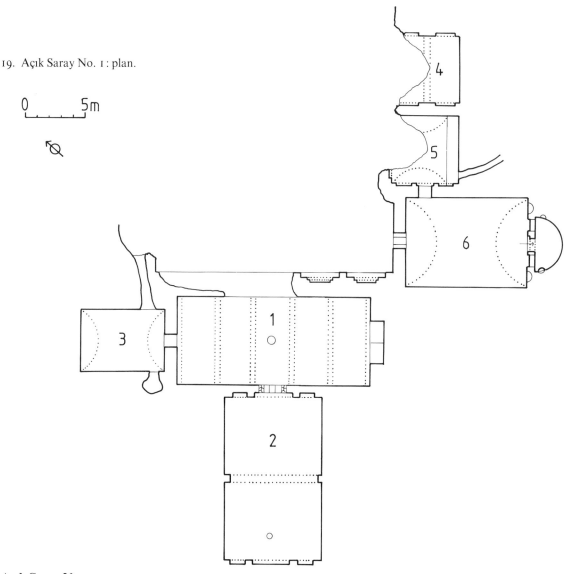

0 _____ 5m

Açık Saray No. 1

The rooms of Açık Saray No. 1 opens off two sides of what was probably once a square courtyard. (The façade runs northwest/southeast, but will be treated as running north/south for ease of description.) East and south sides remain and there may have been a west side, but the courtyard was probably always open to the north, where the hillside slopes down (Fig. 19). As one approaches the complex the most conspicuous feature is an elaborately decorated façade (Pl. 117). This is divided into three registers by horizontal square mouldings. The top register consists of ten bays articulated by vertical pilasters. Each bay contains a pair of double-recessed horseshoe-arched blind niches. Below this the second register has blind niches of the same form, but about half the size of those above. This area is much weathered, but appears to con-

sist of a continuous row of niches without division into bays. The ground-level register is very badly eroded, but an arrangement of five bays formed by projecting pilasters, each bay containing a double-recessed blind niche, may be supposed from the two surviving bays at the left of the façade and other fragments further along.

Vestibule (1) In the centre of the façade there is an irregular opening which is doubtless an enlargement of the original entrance (Pl. 117). This opens into Room 1, a rectangular vestibule with a longitudinal barrel vault (Pl. 118). The vault is divided into five bays by seven transverse arches (the outer two are wall arches, the rest are evenly spaced along it). At the crest of the vault in the middle bay is a circular boss. Below the vault a heavy

117. Açık Saray No. 1 : façade.

plain cornice circuits the room. A deep recess, rectangular in plan and with a gable top, is cut into the east wall. Most of the north wall below the three central bays of the vault has been lost, but from inside the room fragments of arched recesses cut into each of the three bays are visible : these were probably windows.

Hall (2) An entrance in the centre of the south wall of the vestibule opens into a hall (2). The original form of this entrance is uncertain, for it appears to have been enlarged at some point and then lined with masonry (Pl. 118). Above the entrance there is a horseshoe-arched window. A longitudinal barrel vault springs from plain cornices. The room is divided into two bays by a transverse arch which is met by wall pilasters. In the crest of the vault, at its south end, there is a circular boss. There may have been other such bosses (in a cross formation, perhaps), but the vault surface has been eroded everywhere except at the south end. The south wall contains a tall central horseshoe-arched blind niche flanked by smaller lateral niches. There is a similar arrangement on the north wall, where the wide niche encloses the entrance and window, and narrow niches flank it.

Room 3 At the west end of the vestibule (1) a rectangular entrance opens to Room 3. This is a small barrel-vaulted room with a cornice at the springing of the vault, but no transverse arches. A secondary tunnel leads from the north side of this room to the outside.

Church (6) The east side of the courtyard is badly damaged, but an area of plain façade remains. This contains a rectangular entrance, with a window above it which opens into a church (6). This is single naved, with a longitudinal barrel vault springing from cornices. There is a single apse, raised slightly above the nave ground level (Pl. 119). A small niche is cut into the apse wall at the north side, and what may have been a seat is cut at the south side : a niche above a slight projection. The apse is closed by a rock-cut chancel screen which has a single arched entrance flanked by arched lateral openings of unequal size : the opening to the south is larger than that to the north. A cornice projects at the top of the screen, forming an entablature of sorts, and above this is an open lunette. Flanking the lateral openings of the screen and roughly level with them are two apsidal niches cut into the east wall.

Room 5 A rough opening in the north wall of the church leads into Room 5, which is square and barrel-vaulted on a north/south axis (Pl. 120). Most of the west wall of this room is lost. The vault is irregularly placed, springing

118. Açık Saray No. 1: Room 1, east end.

119. Açık Saray No. 1: Church, east end.

120. Açık Saray No. 1: Room 5, southeast corner.

directly above the wall on the west side, but from a deep overhang on the east side. A hole in the east side of the vault shows a cavity above the overhang: probably the eccentricity of the vault was dictated by the existence of this cavity.

The south wall has a decoration of three very shallow horseshoe-arched blind niches, the central one housing the rough opening to the church. The remaining fragment of the west wall shows another shallow niche and probably also had the three-niche decoration. The entrance to Room 5 from the courtyard was probably in the centre of this lost west wall. A low tunnel, probably secondary, runs from the south end of the east wall through the rock mass containing the complex.

Room 4 To the north of Room 5 is another square room (4), also lacking its west wall. The room has a barrel vault on an east/west axis, divided into two bays by a single transverse arch. North and south walls have a decoration of shallow blind niches, one in each bay. The east wall may have had such a decoration, but it is badly eroded. A fragment among the boulders in front of this room shows a lunette outlined by a moulding, and below its base the top of an arch. This was presumably part of the lost west wall, which must have contained the entrance to the room from the courtyard.

Upper area Openings in some of the niches in the upper register of the decorated façade indicate that a cavity or cavities lie behind it, above the vestibule (Pl. 117). These openings are irregular and randomly placed and since there is no access from the existing ground floor rooms of the complex to the upper cavity it is probably secondary.

The next two complexes to be described are cut into opposite sides of a large cone mass. They are thus very close together and, on site, not immediately distinguishable one from the other, so I have called them Açık Saray No. 2 and No. 2a (Fig. 20).

Açık Saray No. 2

This is a group of rooms arranged around an open space (A), probably once a three-sided courtyard only two sides of which remain, both very much eroded. Most of the main façade, running north/south, has fallen, so that the first room behind it now has an open front. A fragment of the façade remains at the north side: a corner pilaster and, to the south of it, what is probably the right side of a double-recessed blind niche.

Vestibule (1) The vestibule (1), behind the façade, has a barrel vault springing from cornices (Pl. 121). Three transverse arches, asymmetrically placed, divide the vault into four bays (three narrow and one wide) and complementary wall arches rim the lunettes. Traces of chequer ornament in red paint survive on the transverse arches and cornices, and a splayed-armed cross is carved and painted on the north lunette. An opening in the west wall leads into Room 2. This is a rectangular entrance, with a recessed lunette above it, set in a double-recessed arched niche. The side walls of the entrance have been replaced by rough masonry. An arched opening above the entrance and similar openings in the flanking bays open into a gallery, described below.

Hall (2) Behind the vestibule there is a large free-cross hall (2). Four columns with short tapering block capitals and square bases are linked by arches to form a central bay. This has a flat ceiling, containing a rectangular recess lined by a roll moulding; the recess is cut by a small flat-topped calotte, also rimmed by a roll moulding. Small arches spring between the columns and the walls of the west and east arms of the cross, meeting pilasters; similar small arches spring north and south of the four columns, meeting corbels on the north and south walls of west and east cross-arms (Pl. 122). The arms of the cross are barrel-vaulted. In the northwest corner of the west arm there is a carved basin, in a block about 1 metre high, and in the floor of this west arm, near to the basin, there is a large pit, which is probably secondary. The entrance from the hall into the vestibule is set in an arched recess, with a moulding outlining the arch.

Gallery (B) Above the entrance from the hall (2) to the vestibule (1) a rectangular window opens into a gallery (B) which is lit by the three openings noted above, in the west side of the barrel vault of Room 1. There are also secondary openings between the hall and the gallery, one at each end of the east wall of the hall. The gallery itself was inaccessible in 1980, but appeared to extend slightly

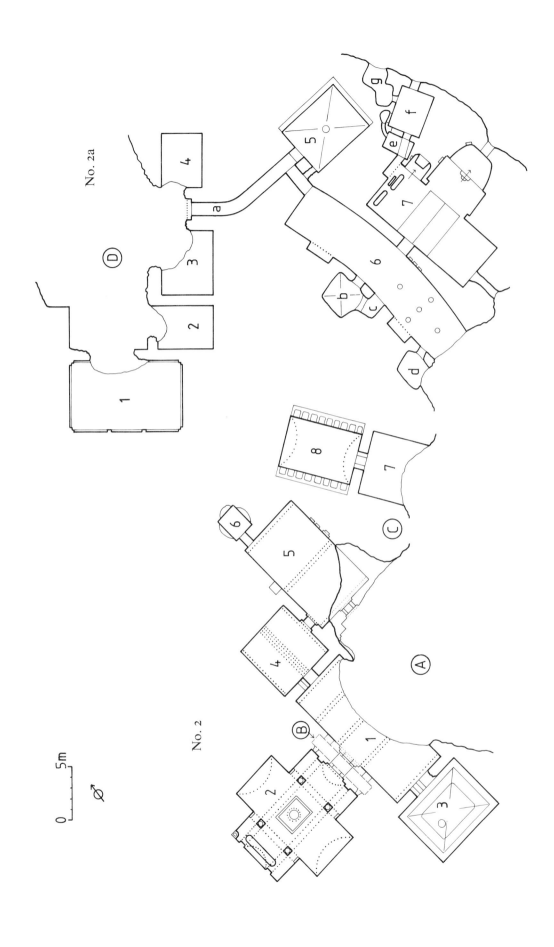

No. 2a

No. 2

0 5m

20. Açık Saray Nos. 2 and 2a: plan.

121. Açık Saray No. 2: Room 1, northwest corner.

122. Açık Saray No. 2: Room 2, west arm.

beyond the limits of the east wall of the hall. It is barrel-vaulted, with a cornice below the vault, and has pilasters at intervals along its west wall (the east wall was not visible from the ground). There is no access to the gallery from the vestibule or the hall; presumably it is reached from a tunnel running through the top of the rock mass in which the complex is situated.

Kitchen (3) Fragments of a rectangular entrance remain in the south wall of the vestibule. Above this entrance is a small arched window, set into an arched recess. Window and entrance open into the kitchen (3), which is square, and has a pyramidical vault rising from a cornice. There is a moulding about halfway up the vault and a smoke hole to the southwest of its apex.

Room 4 To the left of centre in the north wall of the vestibule is a rectangular entrance framed by a round moulding and covered by a lintel made of two rows of similar round moulding. To the left of the entrance, in the north wall lunette, there is a small arched window, outlined by a recess. Entrance and window open into Room 4, a square room with a barrel vault runnning east/west above a cornice and divided into two bays by a two-stepped transverse arch. Wall arches outline the lunettes of west and east walls and each lunette is decorated with

an incised splayed-armed cross of the type seen on the north wall of the vestibule.

Rooms 5 and 6 Returning to the courtyard, what must once have been a north façade is now badly eroded, but still forms a front wall for Room 5 and contains the top part of the rectangular entrance to this room. The entrance has an arched recess above it on both the courtyard and room sides; above it is an arched window. Room 5 is rectangular, barrel-vaulted on a north/south axis, with a cornice below the vault and a transverse arch dividing it into two bays; as usual, wall arches outline the lunettes (Pl. 123). In the north bay of the west wall there is a deep rectangular recess, its base halfway up the wall, framed by a round moulding. Opposite, on the east wall, are two small keyhole-shaped blind niches and a similar niche set in a rectangular recess. Rooms 4 and 5 are linked by a rectangular opening which is in the centre of the east wall of Room 4 and enters the south end of the west wall of Room 5. On each side an arched recess houses the opening.

At the west end of the north wall of Room 5 a narrow rectangular opening, with a recessed lunette lined by a roll moulding above it, opens into a small flat-ceilinged room (6), which has rough recesses cut into its north, west and east walls.

123. Açık Saray No. 2: Room 5, northwest corner.

124. Açık Saray No. 2: stable entrance.

Stable (8) and Area 7 The south side of the floor of Room 5 has fallen in, revealing a rough cavity below it. This is one of a series of very irregular cavities to the north of the complex, their walls so broken down that they form a small labyrinth of interconnecting spaces; most of them are probably secondary. Following this area (C) round to the east, the ground slopes downward sharply and at a level below that of the main complex there is a further cavity (7) which seems once to have been a rectangular room with a flat ceiling. This area is open-fronted; it may have lost its south wall, or may always have been an open porch area, sheltering the entrance to the stable that lies behind it. In the centre of its north wall there is a wide rectangular entrance with a square window above it. To the left and right are roughly arched windows, each with rough masonry blocking (Pl. 124). This north wall has suffered from extensive secondary cutting – it contains several pits and irregularities, notably a deep recess, possibly a tunnel opening, above the entrance.

The stable (8), has a very shallow longitudinal barrel vault. The long (east and west) walls are lined by deep recesses, their bases about 1 metre from the floor, into which mangers are cut: eight along the west wall and nine along the east.

Açık Saray No. 2a

Beyond the stable of Açık Saray No. 2, further to the northeast, begins the series of rooms which forms Açık Saray No. 2a, a complex with its courtyard on the other side of the spur of rock containing Açık Saray No. 2 (Fig. 20). The description will begin with the rooms that surround the courtyard (D) and then proceed to the rooms further back in the rock, ending in the area to the northeast of Açık Saray No. 2, just described.

The courtyard is roughly rectangular, with rooms along east and south sides (in fact, the axis of the court-yard lies northeast/southwest, but for ease of description will be called north/south). The walls of this courtyard are very ruined, leaving the rooms open-fronted. Part of a plain west wall remains, as does the southeast corner, between Rooms 1 and 2.

Hall (1) To the south of the courtyard there is a large hall (1) with a flat ceiling very much damaged by erosion (Pl. 125). The walls are divided horizontally by a broad plain moulding placed about a quarter of the way down from the ceiling. Two floor-to-ceiling pilasters cut across this moulding, dividing the long wall into three bays;

125. Açık Saray No. 2a: Room 1.

there are complementary L-shaped pilasters in the corners. Below the horizontal moulding the walls are plain, but above it is a series of paired horseshoe-arched blind niches, each pair separated from the next by a broad pilaster. There are three such pairs on each short wall and six, two per bay, on the single remaining long wall. The room must once have had an opening through its north wall to the courtyard.

Rooms 2–4 Rooms 2 and 3 have flat ceilings; they are carefully cut and finished, but without decoration. They must once have opened onto the east side of the courtyard. Further to the north, Room 4 is a small, roughly cut room, which must have had an entrance in its south wall, most of which is now lost.

Passage (a) and the kitchen (5) Between Rooms 3 and 4 is the entrance to a long passage (a) leading back into the rock. Most passages found in cave complexes are low-ceilinged secondary tunnels, associated with the post-Byzantine use of the complexes as pigeon houses or storage areas, but this one is well carved, about 3.5 metres high and has its entrance set below an arched recess. It is certainly an original part of the complex.

The passage runs straight back into the rock for a short distance and then curves to the left, leading to the rectangular entrance to the kitchen (5). This has a pyramidical vault rising above a cornice, with a smoke hole at its apex. A low bench runs along north and east walls. (Here, and for the rest of the complex, the orientations given are undistorted.)

Room 6 Shortly before the passage reaches the kitchen (5) it makes a right-angled turn to the south and continues a short distance to Room 6. A secondary opening links this part of the passage with the kitchen (5). Room 6 is a long, roughly rectangular room with a slight curve to its west and east walls (Pl. 126). The ceiling is flat, and at its south end has a decoration of five circular bosses, arranged as a Latin cross. This area is more carefully finished than the north end of the room, and a cornice runs below the flat ceiling. On the west wall of Room 6 are, starting at the north end and moving south: first, an arched, rectangular-plan recess; next a rectangular opening into a small, slightly trapezoidal chamber (b) which has a roughly pyramidical vault; next, a rough, and probably secondary cavity (c) that opens, through a rough hole, into (b); then another arched recess and finally a rough secondary cavity (d). The south wall of Room 6 is lost.

126. Açık Saray No. 2a: Room 6, view north.

The east wall of Room 6 has only one opening, the centrally placed rectangular entrance to the church (7). To the right of this is a panel of carved ornament: two shallow keyhole-shaped blind niches and a deeper rectangular niche. To the right of this carved panel, very crudely painted in red directly onto the rock are, from left to right: a horned animal, an equestrian saint and another horned animal. The horned animals resemble the carved bulls in Açık Saray No. 7, Room 1 (see below and Fig. 26).

Church (7) The church (7), entered from the east wall of Room 6, is of eccentric form (Pl. 127). It is T-shaped in plan, with its entrance from Room 6 in the centre of the west wall (the top bar of the 'T'). A small secondary opening to the area northeast of complex No. 2 pierces the south wall. The ceiling is flat, except for an area running from above the church entrance to the end of the bars of the 'T', which is cut back in two planes to form a pitched roof. At the base of the 'T' stem is an irregular apse, which is raised about half a metre above the level of the nave, and is reached by two small, centrally placed steps (Pl. 127). The apse has an arched entrance and a flat back, which contains a rectangular window. The bay in front of the apse has pilasters at each side of its entrance from the main part of the nave, and its only decoration, on the north wall, near the apse, is a shallow rectangular recess containing an incised cross outlined in red paint.

A side apse is cut in the arm of the 'T' to the north of the main apse. This is an arched recess of roughly rectangular plan, raised about half a metre above the nave floor, and containing an attached rock-cut altar. A small arched blind niche is cut into the north wall, just above the level of the altar top.

In the north wall, to the left of the side apse, there is an arcosolium, which probably has a grave pit in its floor, now filled with debris. The arcosolium has been damaged by secondary cutting to give access to other cavities, described below. In the floor in front of the north wall are three grave pits, two adult and one infant.

It is possible that the whole of this church was once plastered and painted: small areas of painted plaster remain on the arcosolium arch and in the lateral apse and there are other, blackened areas of crumbling plaster on most walls. It is difficult to assess the quality of this decoration from the tiny fragments remaining, but it appears to have been poor: the arcosolium arch retains part of a simple border in thin, reddish-brown paint, executed with a rough brush-stroke.

The crude form of this church is most unusual among the cave monuments, where attention to detail and concern with close imitation of built church architecture is usually the case, even in the humblest chapels.

127. Açık Saray No. 2a: Church, view northeast.

Other cavities The demolition of the right side of the arcosolium in the church has opened the way to a series of cavities which form a rock-cut wine press. A small rectangular room (e) is separated from another (f), by a low wall with an open lunette above it; (f) has a roughly concave ceiling, rudimentary cornice at one side and an opening to the outside in its east wall. A channel runs from the north wall of (e) to a pit in the north wall of (f). At present the low wall dividing (e) from (f) is cut through, making it possible to walk through from the church to the outside. The press is probably not an original part of the complex, since its connection with the church is certainly secondary and it has no other link with the complex. To the north of (f), accessible from its north wall, is a further rough cavity (g), with a wide irregular opening to the outside.

Açık Saray No. 3

Açık Saray No. 3 is about 200 metres from Nos. 2 and 2a, and has a three-sided courtyard (Fig. 21). North and south walls of this have crumbled, but the east façade is intact, although badly damaged; the west side is open. The east façade (Pl. 128) has two registers, the upper register about one-third the height of the lower. The upper register is divided into bays by vertical pilasters, some of which may have continued down into the lower register (the extensive weathering here makes it difficult to be sure of the original form). The arrangement in the upper register is as follows, from left to right: a square pilaster defining the northern limit of the façade; two double-recessed horseshoe-arched blind niches; a pilaster; three more bays, framed by pilasters, each containing a large horseshoe-arched window framed by a recess; two more bays with paired horseshoe-arched niches; an area of flat rock. At the top of this flat area, below a fragment of an overhang that probably once ran the length of the façade, is the remains of a wide projecting mass, the lower part of which has been cut away. A little further to the right is a rectangular opening set in a crudely arched recess.

The form of the lower register is obscured by erosion: depressions in the weathered surface suggest that this, too, had a decoration of blind niching, articulated by pilasters, but the damage is too great for even tentative reconstruction. In the centre of this lower register is an opening, originally rectangular (its flat top remains) but now enlarged to an irregular form. Above this entrance the remains of a recessed lunette contain a small arched window, rimmed by a moulding, so the entrance was probably set in an arched niche.

Rooms 1 and 2 The entrance just described leads into Room 1, which is a roughly carved rectangular room with a flat ceiling. It contains a single rough pier placed in the northeast quarter of the room. An arched recess in the south side of the east wall contains a rectangular opening to Room 2, another roughly cut, flat-ceilinged room, rectangular in plan, with a projection at the east end. A tunnel leads northeast from this eastern projection to an unlit rough cavity (a); a further tunnel opens from the north side of (a).

Room 3 Another, flat-ceilinged room (3) is accessible through a rectangular opening in the north wall of Room 1. This room also had an entrance from the façade, again a rectangular opening set in a recessed niche: a fragment of the top of this is visible on the façade. A secondary tunnel links Room 3, through its north wall, with Room 7.

Room 4 One more room (4) opens off the façade, to the right of the entrance to Room 1. Again, the original form of the entrance has been obscured by erosion, but it was probably rectangular, beneath the recessed lunette containing a small arched window, which survives. Room 4 is barrel-vaulted and the remains of a cornice below the vault and wall arches outlining the lunettes are present.

Room 5 and the kitchen (6) On the south side the courtyard wall is lost, exposing two more rooms. Room 5 is roughly cut, with a flat ceiling. It has straight west and south walls and an irregular east side; the north wall is lost. Next to it is a square kitchen (6), with a domed vault rising above an overhang. The dome is pierced by a central smoke hole.

Room 7 The north side of the courtyard has also fallen in, revealing in longitudinal section a church (see below) and another room (7). A rough secondary opening links its west wall with the apse of the church and a rough tunnel runs from the south end of its east wall to Room 3. The only primary feature of the room is an opening in the east wall, to a stairway which leads to the upper floor of the complex.

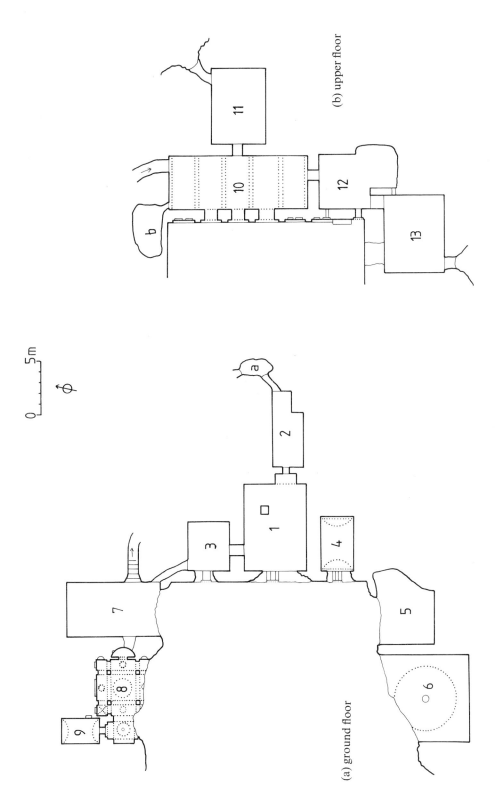

(b) upper floor

(a) ground floor

21. Açık Saray No. 3: plan.

128. Açık Saray No. 3: façade.

Church (8) and Room 9 The church (8), to the west of
Room 7, lies parallel to the courtyard wall. It must have
had a lateral entrance, in its south side, but this area is
now lost. The church is of inscribed-cross plan, and has
a domed narthex. In the naos a shallow central dome was
once carried on four columns or piers (these are gone,
but the size of the suspended capitals suggests that the
supports were slender) (Pl. 129). Only two capitals
remain, at the north side. These are tapering blocks, the
northwest one plain, the northeast with leaf-like projections at its upper corners (Pl. 130). The four arms of the
cross have slightly concave vaults with calottes cut into
them, very like the arrangement at Hallaç Monastery
church. Horseshoe arches spring between the piers and
the walls, where they meet pilasters with simple capitals.
The western corner bays have cross vaults and the eastern
ones flat ceilings. The north wall has keyhole-shaped
blind niches cut into each bay.

The church has a single apse originally closed by a tall
screen, of which only the upper part remains. A large
central opening is flanked by two arched lateral openings:
all three arches are rimmed with borders of scroll-like
foliage ornament carved in relief. Slender pilasters with
palm-like capitals flank the central opening, carrying an
entablature decorated with a row of small keyhole-shaped
blind niches, interrupted by a pair of medallions containing quatrefoils over the crest of the arched entrance

(Pl. 130). Above the entablature the lunette is closed, decorated with a horseshoe-arched recess. Flanking the apse,
each lateral bay of the east wall contains an apsidal niche,
set about 1 metre up from the floor. The back wall of
the apse is broken through to form a secondary entrance
to Room 7.

The centre bay of the west wall of the naos contains
an arched entrance into the narthex; in the lunette above
is a decoration of two horseshoe-arched blind niches. The
narthex is of free-cross plan, its eastern arm formed by
the entrance to the naos (Pl. 131). The dome, with a
circular boss at its summit, rises above rudimentary
pendentives. A rectangular entrance in the north arm
opens into a small barrel-vaulted room (9), which is badly
eroded because most of its vault has fallen in: a fragment
of cornice running below the vault remains. A small,
roughly cut secondary room below the narthex is visible
through a hole in the west side of the narthex floor; this
is one of a series of rough cavities excavated to the north
of the complex.

Upper floor: hall (10) The upper floor of the complex
is accessible via the flight of steps leading from Room 7,
which curves round to the right and opens into the north
end of the hall (10). This lies above Rooms 3 and 1, parallel to the façade, which forms its west wall (Pl. 132). The
room has a barrel vault rising above cornices and is

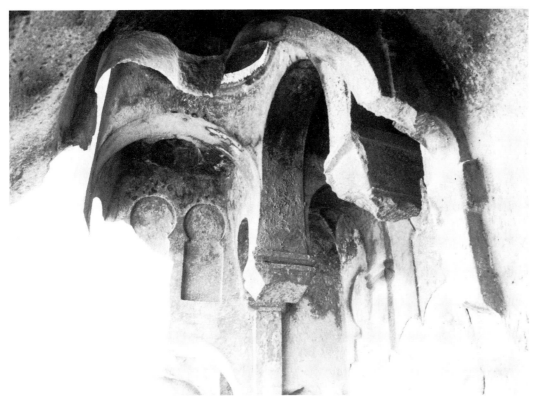

129. Açık Saray No. 3: Church, view northwest.

130. Açık Saray No. 3: Church, view east.

131. Açık Saray No. 3: Church, narthex vault.

132. Açık Saray No. 3: Room 10, view southwest.

133. Açık Saray No. 4: façade.

divided into five equal bays by four transverse arches; complementary wall arches at each end frame the lunettes. A rough, secondary opening in the north wall of the room leads into an irregular cavity (b). In each of the three central bays of the west wall an arched window runs through to the façade.

Rooms 11–13 A rectangular entrance in the centre bay of the east wall of the hall opens to Room 11. This is a rectangular room with a flat ceiling, but is better carved than the rooms of the ground floor. Another rectangular entrance, in the south wall of the hall, leads into Room 12, originally square, but with its southeast corner extended by secondary cutting. Like Room 11, this is well carved, but undecorated. A small (probably secondary) window runs through to the façade from the west wall of Room 12 and a larger rectangular opening, rising from the floor of the room at the south end of the west wall, also opens onto the façade – this, too, may be secondary.

A rectangular opening in the south wall of Room 12 leads into a large flat-ceilinged room (13) which is set behind the south façade, above Room 5. Rough openings break through the walls to Room 12, the courtyard and the south side of the rock mass in which the complex is situated.

Açık Saray No. 4

Açık Saray No. 4 was planned around a small courtyard, its main façade running roughly north/south and the east side open (Fig. 22). The façade is divided horizontally into two registers, the lower one twice the height of the upper. Prominent pilasters originally divided the façade into three bays; all but the northernmost pilaster are very much weathered (Pl. 133). The upper register of each bay consists of groups of double-recessed horseshoe-arched blind niches: in the northern bay there are two such groups, of two and three niches (reading left to right) separated by a pilaster. The niching of the centre bay is too much damaged for its details to be made out, and the south bay repeats, in reverse, the pattern of the north bay. The scheme was probably, therefore, symmetrical about the mid-point of the façade. The niches of this upper register stand on a two-stepped cornice, which seems to have continued around the main pilasters.

Only a small part of the lower register remains undamaged: in the north bay there is a large horseshoe-arched

134. Açık Saray No. 4: Room 1, view northeast.

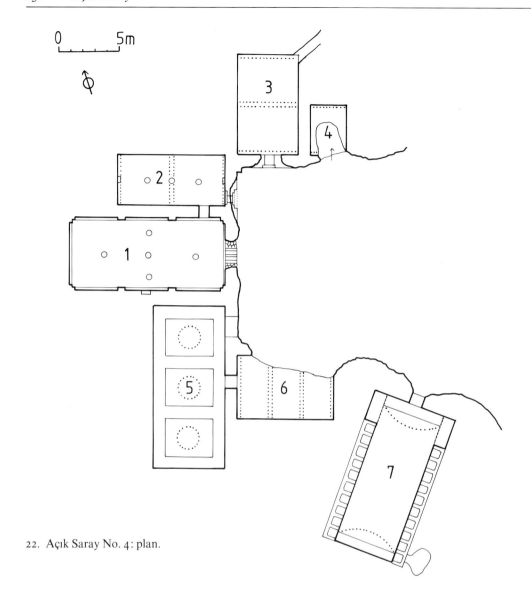

22. Açık Saray No. 4: plan.

blind niche, double-recessed, containing a square window. Small niches of similar form, two on each side, flank the arch of the large niche. This pattern was probably repeated in the centre and south bays to the left, but erosion has obscured most of the detail. The large niche of the central bay has two narrow keyhole-shaped windows in its lunette, and below them a large irregular opening lined by rough masonry is probably the enlargement of an original rectangular entrance into the hall (1).

Hall (1) The opening described above, the only one in the main façade, opens into the hall (1) which has a flat ceiling decorated with five bosses arranged in a cross formation. A square cornice supports the ceiling, and below

this the walls are divided horizontally by a wide square moulding. The upper register is half the height of the lower. Division of the room into three bays is made by vertical pilasters – two on each long wall and L-shaped pilasters in each corner (Pl. 134). The wall areas of the lower register are blank, except for an arched blind niche in the centre bay of the south wall, its base about 1 metre up from the floor. The upper register is decorated with paired horseshoe-arched blind niches: each bay of the long (north and south) walls has two pairs of niches, separated by pilasters, and there are three such units on the west and east walls. Most of the central unit of the east wall is taken up with the two windows above the entrance. The easternmost bay of the north wall of Room

1 contains a rectangular entrance to Room 2, outlined by a roll moulding which is extended above it to form a gable (Pl. 134).

Room 2 Room 2, to the north of Room 1, is barrel-vaulted, with a cornice at the springing; the vault has a transverse arch dividing it into two bays and wall arches at each end (Pl. 135). At the crest of the vault are three circular bosses, one on the transverse arch and the other two central in each bay. On the wall arches at each end of the vault there are square bosses. A secondary cavity is cut in the south part of the east wall lunette and this contains the square window visible in the façade north bay.

Room 3 A smooth wall, its lower part crumbled, forms a north façade to the courtyard. Fragments of a rectangular opening set in an arched recess are all that remains of the entrance to Room 3; above the entrance is a square window set in a recess. Room 3, like Room 2, is barrel-vaulted, divided into two bays by transverse arches and wall arches, and has a cornice. A rough secondary tunnel opens from the northeast corner of this room and doubtless connects with a labyrinth of rough rooms in the spur of rock to the north of the complex.

Room 4 To the right of Room 3, at a higher level, there is a small room (4) which has a barrel vault springing from cornices, and wall arches outlining each lunette. Very little remains of this room, its entrance must have been in its south wall (the north façade) reached by steps or a ramp. Below Room 4 there are two roughly cut cavities with flat ceilings – these are probably secondary and belong with the series of other rough cavities mentioned above.

Rooms 5 and 6 To the south of Room 1, Room 5 is rectangular, with its axis parallel to the west façade. It has a flat ceiling cut by three rectangular recesses with calottes. As in Room 1, a horizontal moulding separates a lower register from an upper one one-third its height. The lower register is undecorated, the upper one is divided into square bays by pilasters. The room has a window to the west façade in the north end of its east wall, but there is no entrance to the room from the façade. Since the window cuts through the façade decoration, it is probably secondary. The room is reached through a rectangular entrance in the west wall of Room 6; this lies to the east of Room 5 and has a barrel vault springing from cornices, and a division into three bays made by two transverse arches and two wall arches. The west lunette,

135. Açık Saray No. 4: Room 2, view northeast.

136. Açık Saray No. 4: stable.

above the entrance to Room 5, is decorated with a shallow rectangular recess flanked by two shallow horseshoe-arched blind niches. The axis of the room lies parallel to the south façade, which is now lost, leaving the room without a north wall. This room must once have had an entrance from the south façade.

Stable (7) A few paces to the east, beyond Room 6, is a large stable (7), of the type seen in Açık Saray 2. A shallow barrel vault covers most of the room, but it meets short areas of flat ceiling at each end. Each long wall has a recess running most of its length, housing ten mangers (Pl. 136). At the north end of the room, after the rows of mangers, each wall contains a deep arched recess. A rough cavity is cut into the east wall at its south end, just above the last manger of the row.

Açık Saray No. 5

The forward part of Açık Saray No. 5 (Fig. 23) has been lost through massive rock-falls and there are several large boulders on the ground in front of it (Pl. 137). The area marked '1' on the plan may therefore be interpreted either as the remains of a courtyard, with vestiges of an over-

hang sheltering it, or as a large, rectangular vestibule, the front of which has fallen away. The latter seems the more likely, since the remaining long west wall of the area lacks the niched decoration of other façades on the site.

Vestibule (1) The west wall noted above has a grooved moulding running across it one-third of the way down the wall, which continues on to the remaining portions of the north and south walls. The only primary features on the west wall are the entrance and windows to the hall (2). This rectangular entrance is set in a double-recessed horseshoe-arched blind niche in the centre of the vestibule wall; above this, and above the moulding, is an arched window, also framed by a recess. Two more windows, rectangular this time, are set below the moulding in arched niches, each equidistant from the entrance and the side wall. At the top of the wall, below the fragment of ceiling, is a simple cornice. There are traces of red paint on the moulding, and around the arched recesses surrounding the windows and entrance to Room 2.

Hall (2) Behind the vestibule there is a basilical hall (2), divided into three aisles by arcades of five arches each. Each arcade was supported on four free-standing col-

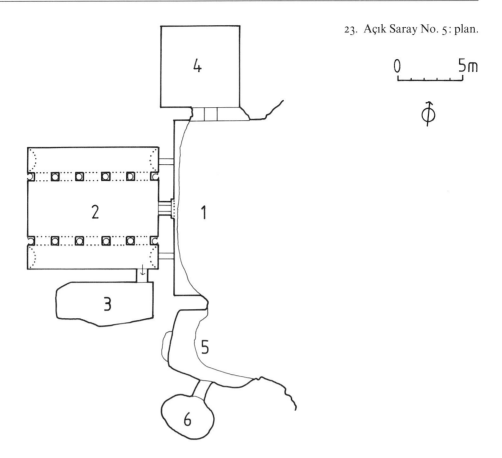

23. Açık Saray No. 5: plan.

0 ____ 5m

umns and three-quarter columns attached to north and south walls. Only the two westernmost columns survive; the rest are lost, but their square bases remain. Running hood mouldings rim the arches of the arcade and bear traces of red hatching. The central aisle has a flat ceiling, the side aisles are barrel-vaulted. Each aisle is lit by a window in the east wall (these are the three windows described above).

Room 3 Towards the east end of the south wall of the hall, a rectangular entrance opens into an irregular, flat-ceilinged room (3), which lies about 1 metre above the floor level of the hall.

Room 4 and cavities 5–6 To the north, Room 4 is square, with a flat ceiling, and has lost most of its south wall. The upper part of a rectangular entrance into this room from the north wall of Room 1 remains. To the south is an irregular cavity (5) open to the weather; an opening in the south side of this leads into a further irregular cavity (6). These may be secondary additions to the complex, as may other irregular rooms cut in the rock above the complex (one of these is visible in Pl. 137, occupying about half the area above Room 1).

137. Açık Saray No. 5: Room 1.

24. Açık Saray No. 6: plan.

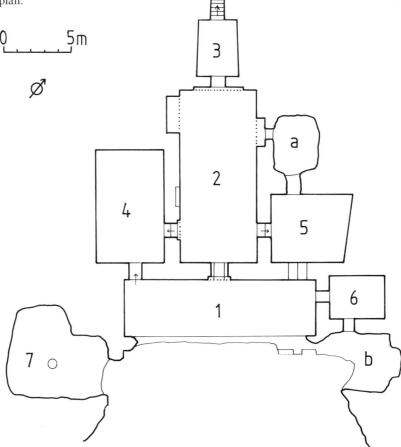

Açık Saray No. 6

Açık Saray No. 6 (Fig. 24) is cut into the same ridge of cones as No. 5. Here too, the front of the complex has fallen away and most of the façade is lost (Pl. 138). (The façade runs northeast/southwest, but for the sake of clarity orientations will be given as if it ran east/west.)

The main decoration of the façade was a row of tall, deeply cut, horseshoe-arched blind niches, their arches rimmed by running hood mouldings. Only two such niches remain, and the back of the easternmost one is cut through to make a rectangular window which is probably secondary. Above the niches is a plain moulding and above this an upper register of blind arcading. The arcade is carved in sharp relief, with horseshoe arches resting on pilasters with rudimentary capitals; these are set in a rectangular ground made by a recess in the rock. Projections of rock on each side of the façade make it probable that there was once a courtyard in front of it, now obliterated.

Vestibule (1) Behind the façade the vestibule (1) has a flat ceiling and no decoration except for a plain cornice

below the ceiling and a moulding about one-third of the way down each wall, making a division into two registers (Pl. 138). An arched recess in the centre of the north wall contains the rectangular entrance to the hall (2); above this is a rectangular window which descends to the top of the arched recess and cuts through the moulding – it may be secondary, or may be an enlargement of an original, smaller window.

Hall (2) Room 2 is a large hall with a flat ceiling. At the north end of the west wall there is a deep arched recess, and at the south end a shallow arched niche housing a rectangular entrance to Room 4; to the right of this is a shallow blind niche. The north wall contains one wide horseshoe-arched niche, in the centre of which a rectangular entrance opens to Room 3. The north end of the east wall contains an arched recess, with a hole cut through its back wall to a rough secondary cavity (a). At the south end of this wall there is a rectangular entrance to Room 5.

138. Açık Saray No. 5: façade and Room 1.

Room 3 Room 3, entered from the north wall of the hall (2), is slightly trapezoidal, tapering towards the north. At the north end a flight of steps leads upwards to a dead end, which suggests that further excavation was planned, but abandoned. (It is possible that the 'dead end' is merely a blockage, but if so, then its filling has been finished to look like solid rock, an unusual refinement.)

Room 4 The entrance in the west wall of the hall (2) leads up two steps to a roughly cut, flat-ceilinged room (4), with no decoration. In its south wall there is a rectangular entrance to the vestibule, its lower part blocked by rough masonry. This 'entrance' may be secondary, perhaps an enlarged window, since it does not descend to the floor level of the vestibule.

Room 5 Opposite the entrance from the hall to Room 4 there is a similar rectangular opening to Room 5, again with two steps up to a higher floor level. Room 5 is an irregular quadrilateral, roughly cut, with a flat ceiling. A rectangular window in the south wall opens into the vestibule, and seems to have been extended downwards from its lower left corner and then partly blocked with rough masonry (Pl. 139).

Room 6 A rectangular opening in the east wall of the vestibule (1) leads into Room 6, a roughly cut rectangular room with low flat ceiling. A rough opening in the south wall leads into a rough cavity (b). Above this is a further rough cavity, probably secondary (visible in Pl. 138).

Room 7 Opposite cavity (b), on the west side of the complex, is a room of irregular plan with a slightly concave ceiling which has a central smoke hole; this was probably a kitchen, although it is of less regular form than the kitchens described for other complexes.

139. Açık Saray No. 6: Room 1.

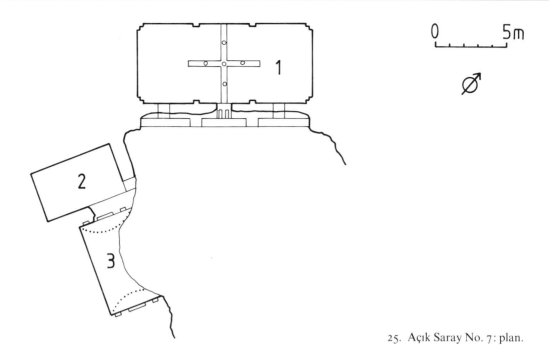

25. Açık Saray No. 7: plan.

Açık Saray No. 7.

Açık Saray No. 7 now consists of a small group of rooms on two sides of an open space, probably the remains of a three-sided courtyard (Fig. 25). It has an elaborate façade on a northwest/southeast axis (Pl. 140). (In the description that follows this façade will be called north.)

Façade The façade is divided into three bays by prominent pilasters; a third pilaster defines the eastern limit of the façade but the corresponding western one is now lost. The centre bay is still intact, but the lateral bays are badly eroded and details of their ornament lost. There is a division into three registers made by heavily projecting cornices. In the centre bay the top register consists of narrow, keyhole-shaped blind niches above a simple cornice that appears to have run the width of the façade, but its extremities are lost. The centre bay of the second register has two double-recessed keyhole-shaped niches on each side of a central motif of recessed rectangle and lunette. Below this is a prominent cornice, decorated with two horizontal grooves, ending at the right side with a cross: this cornice links the vertical pilasters and does not extend right across the façade. There are pairs of weathered niches in the lateral bays also, so the second register once ran across the whole façade. In the bottom (ground-level) register of the centre bay a large horseshoe-arched recess houses a rectangular entrance and, above it in the lunette, two deep keyhole-shaped niches. Mouldings form a gable

over the arched niche and a cornice at the level of its springing runs horizontally across the whole façade, following the planes of the pilasters. A relief cross on a raised square field decorates the right pilaster and a triangular mass, possibly a horned animal head, occupies a similar position on the left pilaster. Each lateral bay of the lower register has a large horseshoe-arched blind niche, cut through to form a window. Small double-recessed keyhole niches flank the left window and the pattern was probably identical in the right lateral bay, where only one small keyhole niche (to the left) remains.

Hall (1) The entrance in the centre bay of the façade opens into the hall (1). This has a flat ceiling carried above a cornice and decorated with a large equal-armed cross carved in relief, with bosses at the centre and on each arm. A horizontal moulding divides the walls into two registers, the upper one half the height of the lower. On north, west and east walls, the upper register contains a frieze of paired keyhole niches, separated by pilasters. Below are two pilasters on each long wall, dividing the room into three bays, and L-shaped pilasters in each corner. On the south wall the frieze of paired niches continues above the two outer bays, but the centre bay, above the entrance, is decorated with a pair of confronted animals, cut in relief. These appear to be bulls, but their heads are lost because a secondary cavity has been cut between them. The two windows cut through the lateral niches of

140. Açık Saray No. 7: façade.

the façade open into this room, but are probably secondary, since they damage the frieze decoration. Fig. 26 is
a schematized drawing of this wall, with the windows
indicated in broken line and the lost niches reconstructed.

Rooms 2 and 3 The west wall of the courtyard has crumbled, leaving two more rooms exposed. Room 3 is barrel-
vaulted, with a cornice below the vault. On the north and
south walls wide central niches are flanked by pairs of
shorter, narrower ones (Pl. 141).

Room 2, to the north of this, is a roughly cut rectangular cavity with a flat ceiling. A rough hole leads from
this room to the west façade and part of the wall between
Rooms 2 and 3 is broken through. A number of large
boulders on the east side of the open space in front of
the façade suggests that there were once other rooms here.

141. Açık Saray No. 7: Room 3.

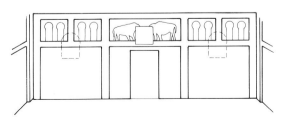

26. Açık Saray No. 7: Room 1, south wall.

(a) No. 1

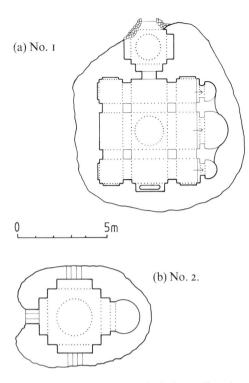

0   5m

(b) No. 2.

27. Açık Saray Churches

Açık Saray Churches Nos. 1 and 2

There are two churches on the Açık Saray site which are not linked to room complexes. Açık Saray Church No. 1 (Fig. 27a) is in a solitary cone about 200 metres from the nearest complex.[4] It is of inscribed-cross plan, with a central dome carried above four arches rising from small square slab capitals (these once topped square piers; all four crossing supports have gone, but a fragment of the northeast pier remains attached to its capital). The arms of the cross are barrel-vaulted and the corner bays have flat ceilings (Pl. 142). The arches which link the piers and the walls spring from pilasters. Each corner bay wall is decorated with a blind horseshoe-arched niche. The church has a slightly raised sanctuary with three apses, each with a horseshoe-arched entrance. The apse piers and the walls separating the apses are lost, together with whatever chancel furniture existed. One rock-cut altar remains, in the south apse. In the centre bay of the south wall there is an arcosolium housing a single grave pit.

To the north of the naos there is a small, domed free-cross narthex. The south arm of the cross houses the opening to the naos; the north arm contained the entrance to the narthex from outside (this is lost and has been replaced by modern masonry).

Naos and narthex were once fully painted, but the paintings are badly weathered because part of the naos vaulting has caved in. What remains of the programme has been described by Schiemenz, and will only be summarized here.[5] Briefly, the programme is as follows:

Narthex
Dome: Christ Pantocrator.
Cross-arm soffits and flanking piers: saints (surviving inscriptions identify Anastasia, Eupraxia, Theodota, Sophia and George). In the lunette of the west niche is an episode from the Martyrdom of St George, with George on a wheel.

Naos
North apse: Christ in Majesty.
Main apse: Ascension (Pl. 142a).
South apse: Transfiguration.
North wall: Raising of Lazarus, Entry into Jerusalem, Christ with Martha.
West wall: Crucifixion, Anastasis, Pentecost (lunette and barrel vault).
A few figures of saints survive with their inscriptions: Constantine and Helena in the niche of the southeast bay; Probos, Tarachos, Gourias in the northeast bay.

The scenes in the naos follow narrative order only if one begins reading in the west end of the north wall and moves around clockwise. In this case the lost paintings of the south wall and south bay of the west wall could have included the earlier scenes of the Passion cycle: Last Supper, Betrayal and so on, and there would not have been room for other cycles.

The painting is in bad condition as a result of both weathering and vandalism, but enough remains to permit some definition of style. The painting is of very poor quality, with details of figures and their draperies drawn in rather clumsy dark lines against areas of solid colour (or, in the case of draperies, against a very simplified

---

4 The church lies to the southwest of Açık Saray No. 3; my field notes do not permit better definition of its location.

5 G. P. Schiemenz, 'Die Kreuzkirche von Açık Saray', *IstMitt* 23/24 (1973–4), 233–62.

142. Açık Saray Church No. 1: northwest corner.

142a. Açık Saray Church No. 1: painting in main apse.

system of light and dark tones) (Pl. 142a). This style appears to have some affinity with that of the painting of Karşı Kilise, which is further along the Nevşehir–Gülşehir road and which is dated by inscription to 1212.[6] A late twelfth- or early thirteenth-century date is therefore a possibility for this programme.

6 Restle, *Wall Painting*, Cat. no. LI, pls. 468–73.

Church No. 2 Açık Saray Church No. 2 is not far from Church No. 1, and is again not linked with a room complex. It is very small, a domed square with deep arched niches in each wall (Fig. 27b). The north, south and west lunettes have two-light windows with central colonnettes, and the east lunette has a complementary decoration of two blind niches. There is a single apse, horseshoe-shaped, without a screen; there is no painted decoration.

Summary

The site contains eight room complexes and two 'solitary' churches. Although no two complexes are identical, all appear to share a basic plan based on the three-sided courtyard with a decorated main façade. This is so for Açık Saray Nos. 1, 2, 3, 4, and 7, and Nos. 2a and 5 also probably had this form (No. 2a has a courtyard, but its walls are lost; the fronts of Nos. 5 and 6 are lost). In several complexes (Nos. 1, 2, 6 and probably 5), the first cavity behind the main façade is a long vestibule from which other rooms are accessible. In Nos. 1 and 2 the vestibule is barrel-vaulted, in Nos. 5 and 6 it has a flat ceiling. In all complexes a large, carefully finished hall lies behind either the vestibule or the main façade. In No. 3, which has two floors (Fig. 21), the large room (10) on the upper floor appears to be the equivalent of the hall in the other complexes, since the large ground-floor room (1) is roughly finished. It is among the halls that the greatest architectural variety is found: in No. 1 the hall is barrel-vaulted; in No. 2 it has a free-cross plan, in No. 5 it is basilical; in Nos. 2a, 4, 6 and 7 it has a flat ceiling. Three complexes (Nos. 1, 2a and 3) have churches, each of a different form; these will be considered below in the discussion of the function of the complexes.

Half the complexes have kitchens (Nos. 2, 2a, 3 and 6); of the others, Nos. 1 and 7 may each have had a kitchen in the lost north areas of their courtyards and in No. 5 the rough room at the south side of the courtyard may have had this function. All complexes have other rooms, usually smaller than the hall and ranging in number from two (No. 7), to nine (No. 3). Two complexes (Nos. 2 and 4) have stables. A single complex (No. 2a) has a wine press, but this is almost certainly a later addition, since it has no connection with the complex other than the clearly secondary opening into the arcosolium in the church.

Function

In many respects the Açık Saray complexes resemble the courtyard monasteries. There are similarities of overall plan in the courtyard with rooms around it and in major elements, such as the halls and vestibules. Further parallels of form exist between other components, such as stables, kitchens and other rooms, especially the barrel-vaulted rooms articulated by transverse arches and wall arches. The two groups also have a decorative vocabulary in common: horseshoe-arched blind niches, often arranged in groups or as a frieze; plain cornices and pilasters. The frieze decoration in Room 1 of Açık Saray No. 2a and Room 7 of Açık Saray No. 7 resembles that

in the vestibule of Karanlık Kilise Monastery. The ceiling-with-calotte-and-recess seen in Room 2 of Açık Saray No. 2 and Room 5 of Açık Saray No. 4 appears also in Karanlık Kale Room 3 and Selime Kalesi Room 4. Even the low-relief animals in Açık Saray No. 7 have their counterparts in the lunette decoration in Room 28 at Selime Kalesi.

One important feature which sets the Açık Saray complexes apart from the courtyard monastery group, however, is the paucity and apparent lowly status of churches on the site. Açık Saray No. 1 has a small, single-naved church, poorly finished and without painted decoration; Açık Saray No. 2 has no church; Açık Saray No. 2a has a church barely recognizable as such, of irregular form and roughly finished (with fragments of a painted decoration, it is to be admitted, but of poor quality); Açık Saray No. 3 is alone in having a well-carved church of some refinement; Açık Saray Nos. 2, 4, 5, 6 and 7 are all without churches. In the case of Açık Saray No. 7 it may be argued that a church once existed on the lost right-hand side of the courtyard, but no fragments compatible even with simple church architecture are to be found among the boulders there. None of the other complexes without churches has an area of damage sufficient to account for a lost structure. A church might be provided for Açık Saray No. 2 by assuming that it should not be separated from complex No. 2a, but that both belong to a single complex. Although close to one another, however, Açık Saray Nos. 2 and 2a have no formal link; indeed, they originally had none at all, since the present connection between them is by means of secondary openings in the south part of Açık Saray No. 2 (see Fig. 20). Such a coalescence would in any case make the crude church of Açık Saray No. 2a a minor part of a large complex.

Thus, five of the Açık Saray complexes lack churches altogether and in two more the church is a rather humble affair. In the courtyard monasteries, however, the church is always a prominent feature of the complex, carefully carved and often decorated with paintings; it usually also has a prominent tomb chamber, another feature lacking in the Açık Saray complexes. The Açık Saray complex most resembling a courtyard monastery, in that it has a well-carved inscribed cross church, is Açık Saray No. 3. Even here, however, the parallel is limited, because the church is a rather small element in one of the largest complexes on the site.

This lack of churches in most of the Açık Saray complexes and their relative insignificance in the others argues strongly that these complexes are not monasteries. It remains to be considered, of course, whether the complexes are not to be separated, but should instead be seen as parts of a single establishment, which would include the two isolated churches (Açık Saray Churches Nos. 1 and 2). Such an interpretation still does not support identification of the site as a monastery, however, since it must then be supposed that a very large monastery had only four small chapels (in Açık Saray Nos. 1, 2a and 3, and Church No. 2) and one church (Açık Saray Church No. 1) which is quite separate from any rooms, crudely decorated and surely not acceptable as the *katholikon*. Treating the complexes as a single unit seems in any case implausible, since their dispersal is too great to be explained by physical limitations of the site: a large assembly of rooms could have been more compactly placed in this area of large cone-clusters.

It seems reasonable to conclude that the Açık Saray complexes are not monasteries, but determining what they are is more difficult. They are evidently Christian: the churches in Açık Saray Nos. 1, 2a and 3 and carved crosses of various forms in Açık Saray Nos. 2, 4 and 7 establish this; they may therefore be seen as secular complexes provided with a few churches to meet the needs of those using them. Beyond this the way is obscure, since no obvious secular function suggests itself. Uniformity of architectural form and style argues against the possibility that the complexes accumulated on the site over a long period; they are surely chronologically close to one another, if not virtually contemporaneous. In addition, such complexes are not known anywhere else in the volcanic valley area. It is necessary, therefore, to look for a function that requires a group of complexes on a single site.

The name, Açık Saray (open palace) raises one possibility, although the name alone has little worth as evidence: it doubtless derives from the Turkish habit of calling any impressive ruin of unknown function *saray* (palace) (or, if on a hill, *kale*, castle). Further, since so little is known of Byzantine domestic architecture, particularly in the depths of Anatolia, assessment of Açık Saray along these lines must be conjectural.[7] The complexes do not appear to be organized along domestic lines: if a semi-public function be assigned to the large halls and vestibules (making of them reception rooms of some kind), then what is left for dwelling in each complex is a few small rooms – hardly adequate, it would seem, to accommodate a household grand enough to require the large reception areas. An alternative is to suppose that

the large halls were the dwelling areas (as in the western medieval hall which accommodated a whole household) and the small rooms were for various aspects of domestic maintenance. In this case, however, given the severity of the Anatolian winter, the large rooms should surely have some provision for heating and yet none of them even has a smoke hole. Further, were the complexes palaces, it would be reasonable to expect similar structures to be found elsewhere in the volcanic valley region, which is not the case. Scant information is available on Anatolians of the palace-owning class, but since their wealth usually depended upon ownership of land they are not likely to have huddled gregariously on one site.[8] Nor, perhaps, are they likely to have chosen to live in caves, however well appointed. Some of these problems may be overcome by supposing that the complexes were summer palaces, used during a few months of hot weather by families with permanent residences on scattered estates. But what might have attracted them? Was there hunting? I have never seen greater prey than rabbits in the area and in any case such activity could surely not be agreeable in the fierce heat of summer. Might they have come for the mineral water common in the valleys?[9] There is a good spring on the Açık Saray site, but I have not tested it. Might the churches and monasteries of the area have been an attraction? Could the placing of several complexes on one site have had a social purpose, or been a matter of security? I conclude that while the complexes are unlikely to have been palaces in the sense of permanent residences, the possibility that they were temporary residences should be retained.

A second explanation might be that the complexes are the Byzantine equivalent of the Turkish *hans*, stopping places for travellers, especially merchants with trains carrying goods. The complexes do not, however, much resemble the Seljuk *hans* of the area, with which parallels might be sought, if only as the product of similar function. These *hans* have completely enclosed square plans, with rooms placed in two or more rows around the inside perimeter. In some cases a core of rooms, often on two floors, surrounds a narrow corridor, providing accommodation for people; around this there is a ring of stables and between the stables and the outer wall a corridor giving access to the stables. Occasionally the stables are placed in an extension of the basic square plan,

---

7 R. Krautheimer, *Early Christian and Byzantine Architecture* (3rd edn;, Harmondsworth, 1979), 363 and 366. L. M. E. de Beylie, *L'habitation byzantine* (Grenoble/Paris, 1902–3), which is still the major compilation of data for Byzantine domestic architecture, has no material for inland central Anatolia.

8 G. Ostrogorsky, *History of the Byzantine State* (2nd English edn, Oxford, 1980), 272ff., 320f., 329f.

9 I know of mineral water wells (made simply by scooping away the ground in suitable areas) in Balkan Deresi (near Ortahisar) and in the valley to the north of Sinasos, near the Church of Holy Apostles (no. 7 on Plan 2 in Giovannini, *Arts of Cappadocia*, 198). Doubtless there are many more: damp areas in several locations have the rust-coloured stains typically produced by mineral water.

leaving the main square as a courtyard area, lined by rooms for human habitation. In all cases provision for animals is greater, in terms of ground area, than for people.[10] The Açık Saray complexes, on the contrary, have open courtyards, far fewer rooms and limited space for animals. However, some of these differences may perhaps be accounted for by the restrictions on design implicit in rock-cut architecture and in any case a *han* of the Byzantine period need not have had the same pattern as a Seljuk one, so this approach deserves further consideration. Only two complexes (Nos. 2 and 4) have stables, with 37 mangers between them, which seems inadequate provision for the animals of travellers sufficiently numerous to require the accommodation offered by the other rooms. Perhaps, though, a seasonal factor might operate here, as proposed for palaces: the complexes may have catered for warm-weather travellers who could reasonably be expected to tether their animals in the courtyards; the rock-cut stables might then have provided shelter only for the animals of a permanent staff living on the spot all year round. The problem of distribution mentioned above is also relevant to this interpretation since *hans*, like permanent palaces, should surely be scattered over a wide area, not concentrated on one site. It is the case, of course, that rock-cut complexes cannot be found in areas where the rock is unsuitable, so this may account for the lack of similar complexes elsewhere and other *hans*, of standard, built architecture, may have existed, forming a chain that included Açık Saray as a unique, rock-cut example. The placing of eight *hans* on a single site may perhaps be explained by resort to several different proprietors. The case remains shaky but possible. If the Açık Saray complexes are *hans*, then a Byzantine road south from Zoropassos (Gülşehir) to Malakopea (Derinkuyu) probably followed the modern Gülşehir–Nevşehir road for its first part, and a substantial traffic must be assumed to account for the number of complexes.[11]

One more group of candidates for the tenancy of Açık Saray remains. For soldiers, security makes a good argument for gregariousness and it is possible that the Açık Saray complexes were military staging posts of some kind, each one serving some army sub-division. The small provision for the stabling of horses need not hinder this interpretation, if it be assumed, as for *hans*, that the stables existed to shelter the animals of a small number of people permanently based on the site, and that others came and went, leaving their animals outside. A major route to the southeast, which passes the volcanic valley area, had on it a series of *aplekta*, which were the points at which provincial divisions of the Byzantine army would meet the emperor on his way to campaigns in the east.[12] Açık Saray cannot be identified with any of the *aplekta* known from documentary sources, but is placed roughly mid-way between two of these: Koloneia (Aksaray) and Kaisareia (Kayseri) and so might be construed as a minor station on a major military route.[13]

While none of the above explanations for the Açık Saray complexes is compelling, it seems that better cases can be made for princes, merchants and soldiers as users than for monks, and the complexes may thus be dismissed from the list of rock-cut monasteries. Whatever the solution to the problem of function, detailed parallels between the Açık Saray complexes and the courtyard monastery complexes suggest that they are of the same tenth- or eleventh-century period; the inscribed-cross church of Açık Saray 3 is consistent with this. The possibility of a thirteenth century date for Açık Saray Church No. 1 does not hinder such an attribution, since the church is not connected with any of the complexes and may be a later addition to the site.

A final speculation: it will be argued below, in the concluding chapter, that the rock-cut monasteries represent an increase of activity in the volcanic valley region in the eleventh century; perhaps the Açık Saray complexes, whatever their function, are a secular manifestation of this expansion.

10 A. Tükel, 'Alara Han'ın Tanıtılması ve Değerlendirilmesi', *Belleten* 33 (1969), 429–91 (English summary, 462–91, see 488); K. Erdmann, 'Berichte über den Stand der Arbeiten über das Anatolische Karavansaray', *Atti del Secondo Congresso Internazionale di Arte Turca, Venezia 26–29 Settembre 1963* (Naples, 1965), 73–81 and plates.

11 In Hild & Restle, *TIB*, 11, the map shows the Byzantine road in this area arching towards the east and passing through Sulusaray. As noted above, it wrongly places Açık Saray to the west of this road.

If the Açık Saray complexes are indeed *hans*, then they perhaps provide an argument for making the proposed Gülşehir–Nevşehir route the more important in the Middle Byzantine period.

12 W. M. Ramsay, *The Historical Geography of Asia Minor* (London, 1882), 202–3.

13 Ramsay (see previous note) argues that the *aplekton* preceding Kaisareia was Saniana, not Koloneia, but it is certainly Koloneia that appears in the list; see G. Huxley, 'A List of *Aplekta*', *GRBS* 16 (1975), 87–93, at 88.

4

The refectory monasteries

In addition to the courtyard monasteries described above, the volcanic valleys of Cappadocia contain a second group of monasteries which lack the formal architecture of that group. A monastery in this second group has a church, a refectory with rock-cut table and benches and a few randomly grouped undecorated rooms. I have called these establishments 'refectory' monasteries, after their most conspicuous feature. Most examples of the type are in Göreme valley, densely grouped in the area at the head of the valley which now forms Göreme Park (Fig. 30). Two more, Yusuf Koç Kilisesi Monastery and the Archangel Monastery, are found on other sites. These will be described first, since they occupy discrete sites and the extent and components of each monastery may be more easily determined than in the case of the crowded complexes of Göreme.

Yusuf Koç Kilisesi Monastery

In a valley near the village of Avcılar[1] there is a monastery linked with the church known as Yusuf Koç Kilisesi. The rooms of this monastery are grouped around the edges of a large cone (Fig. 28 and Pl. 143) and may extend into two more cones to the south. Much of the rock in this area is riddled with cavities, some of them pigeon-house rooms, others of less certain origin, so the extent of the monastery is unclear. The cavities described below are all carefully cut rooms with flat ceilings and no decoration.

Refectory (2) The front of the refectory has been lost entirely. There remain three sides of a rectangular room with rock-cut furniture. One table-and-bench runs along part of the back (west) wall and there is another at right-angles to it, along the south wall (Pl. 144). Each table has a basin cut into it at one end, but these may be secondary.

Shallow blind niches are cut into the north and west walls, opposite the ends of the tables. To the right of the refectory is a rough secondary cavity (a).

Room 3 and its porch To the south of the refectory there is a plain, double-recessed façade (Pl. 143). A rough secondary cavity (b) has been cut at the lower right of this façade but the main feature is a deep recess to the left. This forms a porch fronting Room 3. It has two-stepped cornices at the springing of its barrel vault and a relief ornament above the rectangular entrance to Room 3, which is in its back wall. Exactly what is represented by the ornament (Pl. 145) is unclear: it seems to be a tall stemmed cross with short lateral arms and a long vertical extension from its top. A rectangular recess is cut into the left (south) wall of the porch.

Room 3 is a small undecorated room for which the frontage provided by the porch and façade seems rather elaborate. Since its entrance is very simple, without mouldings or other ornament, it may be that Room 3 is secondary and the 'porch' was originally just an arched recess. However, the entrance to the church (Pl. 148) is also a simple rectangle, so this form is not necessarily diagnostic of secondary work. Alternatively, Room 3 may have had an importance not associated with size: as a treasury, perhaps, or a repository for relics.

Rooms 4 and 5 Further to the south, beyond another irregular cavity, there is a larger room (4) with deep recesses in north and west walls. Still further south, at a higher level, are the remains of a small room (5) with two arched recesses in its back wall. The recess to the left has its base at floor level and seems to be an arcosolium. The arch is rimmed with red-paint ornament and there are painted crosses above it and on the back wall of the recess. The

1 Anciently Matiana, then Maçan, later still Avcılar, now Göreme. See Chapter 1, note 14, and Hild & Restle, *TIB*, ii, 231.

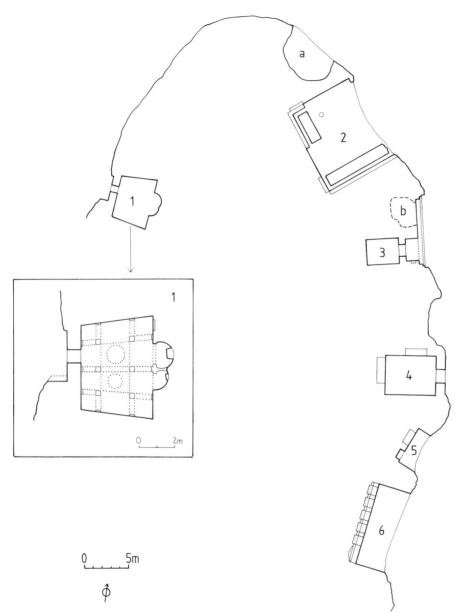

28. Yusuf Koç Kilisesi Monastery: plan.

arched opening to the right, also rimmed with geometric ornament, lies above a low wall, now partly cut away (Pl. 146). The function of this recess is unclear. It resembles the rock-cut wine presses often found among the cave monuments, but its situation (next to a tomb) makes such an interpretation implausible; possibly it is another grave.

Stable (6) The next room to the south, again with its front wall lost, is a stable: a rectangular room with a series of rock-cut mangers in the remaining back wall (Pl. 147).

Church: Yusuf Koç Kilisesi (1) Yusuf Koç Kilisesi lies on the west side of the cone containing the rooms described above. It is fronted by a recessed façade originally decorated with three horseshoe-arched blind niches, of which only traces remain (Pl. 148). The rock at the front of the church has been eroded considerably so that the church entrance is about 2 metres above the present ground level. An arcosolium is cut into the rock at the right of the entrance.

The church has an irregular form: a doubled inscribed-cross plan with two domes at the centre, surrounded by

143. Yusuf Koç Kilisesi Monastery: site, view southwest.

144. Yusuf Koç Kilisesi Monastery: refectory.

145. Yusuf Koç Kilisesi Monastery: porch leading to Room 3.

146. Yusuf Koç Kilisesi Monastery: site, view northwest.

147. Yusuf Koç Kilisesi Monastery: stable.

148. Yusuf Koç Kilisesi Monastery: Church, entrance.

149. Yusuf Koç Kilisesi Monastery: Church, St Demetrios and donor.

ten bays (Fig. 28). Its six cross-arms are barrel-vaulted and the corner bays have flat ceilings. The arches to the twin centre bays spring abruptly from the walls (there are no pilasters). Apses open from each of the two eastern bays opposite the domes, but coalesce to form a single irregular recess. There are no chancel screens, but the apse walls are damaged and there may originally have been low slabs. A horseshoe-arched blind niche is cut in the east wall of the northeast bay but the walls are otherwise undecorated. The church is fully painted with a programme that has been described by Thierry.[2] The following summary incorporates corrections and additions to that original account (these are marked*):

South apse (conch): Deesis.
North apse (conch): Virgin and Child.
Beneath the image there is a fragmentary inscription:

...]ǪIǪ[.] TONṆ [.] Ṛ [.] ǪNǪ [.] ǪC [...]
ỊṬỊNOTONAPA [.] ỊΛIOY +

The text is doubtless an epithet or prayer referring to the image in the conch of the apse, but I cannot decipher it.
North Apse (wall): arcade with bishop saints (Gregory the Theologian, Basil, John Chrysostom* and Nikolaos*).
Domes: the four Archangels, two in each dome.

Barrel vaults and dependent lunettes
South part of church: (east vault) Luke and Matthew; (lunette) Peter and Paul; (south vault) Mark and Andrew; (lunette) John; (west vault) Simon and Bartholomew; (lunette) Jacob.
North part of church: (west vault) Bakchos and Sergios; (lunette) Christopher; (north vault) Kyriakos and Tryphon; (lunette) ornament; (east vault) Phloros and Lauros; (lunette) Christ Pantocrator.
Ceilings of corner bays: (southeast) Ananias (one of the Three Hebrews); (southwest) Azarios (one of the Three Hebrews); (northwest) male saint, unidentified (bust); (northeast) male saint, unidentified (bust).

Walls (reading left to right)
East (niche): Mishael (one of the Three Hebrews), deacon, male saint, Prokopios (with donor).
South: Demetrios (Pl. 148a), George and Theodoros (both equestrian), military saint.
West: military saint, Constantine and Helena, Daniel, female saint (bust) above two standing female saints*.

North: as previous panel – three female saints*, Annunciation (with donor), military saint.

The programme thus consists of apostles in the vaults of the south part of the church, martyrs in the barrel vaults of the north part, a number of military saints on the walls and a group of female saints in the northwest corner bay. The Annunciation, on the north wall, is the only narrative image, and the Three Hebrews the only Old Testament subject.

The programme also includes three donor figures, as follows:
(a) In the Annunciation panel, a small male figure kneels at the Virgin's feet. He has a short beard and wears a brocade robe, a large turban-like headdress and pointed slippers (Fig. 29a). Above his head is the inscription:

Δέισις τοῦ δ – – –

Translation: 'Entreaty of the servant ...'

(b) In the Prokopios panel a small figure to the left of the saint kneels and grips the saint's foot. The outline of the head is smooth and this may be a woman wearing a veil. No inscription is legible (Fig. 29b).

(c) In the Demetrios panel a small figure stands next to the saint and gestures towards him (Fig. 29c & Pl. 149); the donor is inscribed:

Δέισις τοῦ δούλου τοῦ θ(εο)ῦ Θεοδόρου[3]

Translation: 'Entreaty of the servant of God, Theodoros.'

Date

Thierry attributes the church to the mid eleventh century, on grounds of style, iconography, epigraphy and programme.[4] However, a close iconographical correspondence between the military saints of Yusuf Koç Kilisesi and those of St Barbara, Soğanlı (cf. Pls. 149 & 178), which is dated 1006 or 1021 (see below, Chapter 5), suggests that the period of attribution might be widened: the first half of the eleventh century, perhaps, rather than the middle. Since there is no earlier painting in the church, it appears reasonable to date the church by its painting, and the monastery by its church; a date in the first half of the eleventh century is therefore proposed for the monastery as a whole.

---

2 N. Thierry, 'Yusuf Koç Kilisesi. Eglise rupestre de Cappadoce', *Mansel'e Armağan* (Ankara, 1974), I, 193–206; N. Thierry, 'Quelques églises inédites en Cappadoce', *JSav* (1965), 625–35, at 630–2.

3 Thierry, in 'Yusuf Koç Kilisesi', 198, records the inscription with Γ substituted for Y; this is an error.

4 *Ibid.* 195–6, 199, 201–3.

29. Yusuf Koç Kilisesi: donor images.

Other cavities in the vicinity The cones near Yusuf Koç Kilisesi are riddled with cavities, many of them cut as pigeon-house rooms. Some, however, have arched entrances that suggest other origins. To the south, two arched openings lead into a flat-ceilinged, roughly cut room (Pl. 143), and to the north there is a façade decorated with blind niches (Pl. 146). The cavities behind this façade are in use as a pigeon house and the entrances are blocked except for pigeon-holes, so they cannot at present be explored. Possibly, therefore, the rooms described above are only part of a larger establishment. Those elements described do, however, form a compact group, and may probably be regarded as the core of the monastery.

The Archangel Monastery, Cemil

The Archangel Monastery is to the south of Cemil, a village on the way to Soğanlı from Ürgüp (Fig. 1). The monastery consists of a church, chapel, refectory, hall and other cavities, scattered in a group of broad-based cones at the west side of the modern road. Jerphanion visited the site in 1912, when its church was still in use by the local Greek population. A decade later it was derelict.[5] I have visited this site only briefly and can offer only a cursory description.

Refectory The refectory is a long narrow room (Jerphanion gives its dimensions as 19.5 × 4.5 metres). It is divided longitudinally into two aisles by an arcade formed of plain arched openings. The sections of wall between the openings form nine rough piers. In the middle of the arcade a pier wider than the rest contains a shallow apsidal niche in the side facing the right aisle. Both aisles have flat ceilings. The left aisle is narrower than the right and contains a rock-cut table and a bench which runs along the left wall, into a shallow apse at the far end, and along the arcade on the right side. In the right aisle there are parts of a bench along the wall and the outline of a table in front of it (debris has filled the space between benches and tables and raised the ground level). There was probably never a bench on the arcade side of this aisle, since the area must have been an access passage. Jerphanion describes each table as being divided into three sections; this division is no longer clear since large parts of the tables have been broken up.

The entrance to the refectory is a rough opening the width of the room, doubtless a crude enlargement of the original entrance. Flanking the refectory are two very roughly cut rooms.

Hall and the lower room Across a clearing, not far from the refectory, the side of a large cone is cut back to form a façade on an east/west axis (Pl. 150). The façade is rectangular, framed by a square moulding and divided into two registers by a further moulding. The top register consisted originally of two recessed panels of double-recessed horseshoe-arched blind niches (five in the left panel, four in the right), with a pilaster separating them; most of the

5 Jerphanion, *Eglises*, I. i, 32, 598; II, 128–55.

150. Archangel Monastery: façade.

left panel has been cut away. The lower register is plain: it was once divided into two by a pilaster meeting that of the upper register, but this has been cut away. The left bay contains a rectangular entrance, framed by a moulding and a relief arch which forms a lunette above the opening.

This entrance leads into the north side of a rectangular hall, eight or nine metres long and five or six metres wide, its long axis parallel with the façade. A barrel vault springs from cornices on the long walls and a transverse arch divides the vault into two bays. At the west end a deep arched recess occupies about two-thirds of the wall.

Much of the floor of the hall has fallen in, to reveal another room below. This is on the same axis as the upper room, but is slightly wider and longer (its east wall is level with that of the upper room, but to the west it extends a further three or four metres). The south wall is broken by three recesses separated by pilasters. Each recess is fronted by a low wall, forming a series of troughs in the wall. The entrance to this lower room is in its west end, through two roughly cut cavities, which may be reached by walking around the cone containing the hall, towards the west. Possibly the lower room was a storage area of some kind.

The Archangel Church As noted above, the church of the

Archangel is one of the few cave churches that was in use until relatively recent times. Consequently, the architectural form of the church is the result of several phases of alteration, some of which may be as late as the twentieth century. In its present form the church has two naves, each with a single apse. The naves communicate via an irregular opening in the middle of their common wall, above which a dome has been cut, damaging both vaults. A narthex runs across the west ends of the two naves and has openings to them in its south wall. The front part of the narthex is built of masonry, probably a nineteenth- or twentieth-century repair necessitated by erosion of the original rock wall.[6] To the west of the narthex there is an irregular room containing a pier and, at the far end, an opening closed by a millstone.

Jerphanion proposes the following sequence of phases for the church:

I. A single-naved chapel (the present south nave) with a small narthex.

II. The addition of a second nave and extension of the narthex.

6 Jerphanion, *Eglises*, pl. 23.1 shows the masonry wall in a better condition than it is at present.

III. Cutting of the domed passage between the two naves and enlargement of the openings from narthex to naves.[7]

The painting with which the church is decorated also shows several phases of work, some of them recent. It consists of the following:

Narthex
North wall: large figure of Archangel Michael.
Vault: (south side) Annunciation, Visitation, Presentation, Virgin Fed by an Angel; (north side) Adoration of the Magi?, Flight into Egypt, Dream of Joseph, Dormition, Joshua Stopping the Sun.
East wall: Joshua and the Angel; naked figures (part of a Last Judgement?).
Irregular arch (between narthex and south nave): St Nikephoros, The Paralytic at Bethesda.

South nave
Vault: Ascension, Anastasis, Transfiguration, Baptism, Crucifixion.
Tympanum: Entry into Jerusalem.
West wall: Nativity.
South wall: saints, including Eustathios, Theopiste and their children.
Apse: Christ.

North nave
Vault: Last Supper, Transfiguration, Washing the Feet, Raising of the daughter of Jairus?, Women at the Tomb, Betrayal, Entombment.
North wall: military saints.
Apse: Christ in Majesty (with kneeling donors?); (niche) Hetoimasia; (wall) saints, including John the Baptist.

Jerphanion attributes the Presentation and Dormition of the narthex and the Ascension and Transfiguration of the south nave to Phase I, and the rest to various subsequent phases. The record of recent use, and the apparently eccentric ordering of scenes, suggest that there have been several phases of restoration or repainting. The painting is so blackened that much of it is barely legible and these phases cannot be established until the surface has been cleaned. The large Archangel of the narthex north wall is, however, almost certainly nineteenth-century work.

St Stephen A short distance from the Archangel church is the small, single-naved chapel of St Stephen.[8] This has a single apse, closed by low chancel slabs, and a free-standing rock-cut altar; the apse wall contains three niches. The flat ceiling is carried above a simple cornice. The north wall is decorated with four shallow arched blind niches. The south wall, which contains the entrance to the chapel (towards the west end, now blocked with masonry) seems to have been plain. The eastern part of this wall has been cut away to form the present wide entrance to the chapel. The west wall has a single blind niche like those on the north wall. Two secondary arcosolia are cut into the east end of the north wall. At the west end part of the floor of the chapel has been cut away revealing a large water-filled cistern below.[9]

The chapel, like the Archangel Church, has several layers of painting. Jerphanion identifies the following phases:

I. A figural decoration, of which a few fragments are visible where later paint layers have fallen away:
North wall: (easternmost blind niche) standing male saint; (next niche) equestrian saint with dragon.
South wall: Communion of Apostles?

II. A largely ornamental layer, with some figural elements:
Ceiling: three ornamental panels – (west), interlaced circles; (centre), a coffer pattern; (east), a jewelled cross on a ground of vine scroll. The three panels are enclosed by a knotted-circle border.
North wall: (first two niches) floral pattern; (third niche) large cross with an inscription invoking the Holy Cross;[10] (spandrels) bust in medallion, cross (with inscription: 'The cross of St Euphemia'), a second cross.
Apse: (conch) cross, two busts of saints in medallions; (wall) standing figures.
Walls: floral and other ornament. (This layer is the main surface layer, occupying much of the wall space and all of the ceiling and apse.)

III. Scattered additions:
North wall: (third niche) Annunciation?
East wall: (left of apse) orant saint and an inscription invoking the Virgin.[11]

To Phase III should be added a panel on the west end of the south wall, showing a figure of Christ between a pair of tetramorphs, with a lion at his feet; also a small panel to the left of this, above the blocked entrance, with an equestrian figure and two quadrupeds.

---

7 *Ibid.* II, 128–9.
8 Jerphanion, *Eglises*, II, 146–55.
9 This is, perhaps, the 'hagiasma' mentioned by Jerphanion, *Eglises*, I. i, 32, but he refers to 'three sanctuaries', the 'hagiasma', the Archangel Church and St Stephen, which suggests that the 'hagiasma' and St Stephen must be separate.
10 Jerphanion, *Eglises*, II, 153, Inscription no. 155.
11 *Ibid.* 151, Inscription no. 154.

This sequence is challenged by Restle and further field work is needed to establish the sequence of decoration.[12] Nothing now visible in the decoration endorses the dedication of the chapel to St Stephen, the name by which it was known in the early years of this century.

Date

The façade fronting the hall uses a decorative vocabulary familiar from the courtyard monasteries and the room complexes of Açık Saray. The hall itself also fits easily into this context. The refectory with rock-cut table and benches resembles in concept, if not in detail, the refectories of Göreme valley (see below). An eleventh-century date, based on these comparisons, is therefore a possibility for these elements.

As noted above, the paintings in the Church of the Archangel and St Stephen are in poor condition and exist in several layers whose sequences have not been established with certainty. At present, therefore, they cannot be used to date the monastery. Cleaning may elucidate much in the Archangel Church, but with the chapel of St Stephen the problem is of a different sort. The chapel is not blackened and careful observation will surely one day sort out the phases, but all the decoration is of very poor quality and much of it is non-figural. It is therefore very difficult to date by stylistic comparison with other painting. The non-figural aspect of the main layer of painting in it has given rise to speculation that it should be dated to a time close to the period of Iconoclasm (mid eighth to mid ninth centuries), when the depiction of figures in religious art was the subject of an imperial ban. This main layer is not, however, aniconic, for it includes the figures in the apse.[13] It is in any case not valid to assume that aniconic decoration must necessarily be associated with Iconoclasm. It can as well be a matter of taste, rusticity, or even the lack of a good painter to hand, since ornament is much easier to produce than figure painting.[14]

For the moment, therefore, the monastery rooms suggest approximate contemporaneity with the other cave monasteries and the paintings of church and chapel neither confirm nor deny this.

The fact that the site was in use when Jerphanion saw it does not, of course, establish that it had been in continuous use since the Byzantine period. Indeed, it seems not to have been functioning as a monastery in Jerphanion's time, since he makes no mention of a monastic community. As noted above, there is no reference to St Stephen in the decoration of the chapel, and the dedication of the church to the Archangel is reflected only in the large nineteenth-century painting on the north wall of the narthex. These dedications are, therefore, likely to be recent and suggest a break in continuity during which the original dedications were lost. Many shifts of population in central Anatolia took place before the removal of the Cappadocian Greeks in the 1920s and it is quite possible that the Archangel Monastery was abandoned, perhaps for centuries, and then restored to parochial, rather than monastic, use.[15]

Göreme monasteries

At the head of Göreme valley, in the area which is now enclosed to form Göreme Park, there are eleven refectories with rock-cut tables and benches. One of these is part of Karanlık Kilise Monastery, one of the courtyard monasteries described above. The others are found together with a number of churches and rooms. The rooms are generally small, roughly cut, with flat ceilings and no decoration. Many of these cavities may, of course, owe their existence to the requirements of the Turkish peasantry rather than to those of Byzantine contemplatives, but it is reasonable to suppose that some are contemporaneous with the refectories and churches.

Two possible interpretations of this dense grouping of cavities are available: either there was here one large monastery, with many churches and a series of refectories, or there was a number of small monasteries, each with a single refectory and single church. The latter seems most likely to be the case, first, because in spite of the crowding, some refectories do appear to be closely associated with specific churches, and also because no single church is of a size or quality to give it more importance than the others. Tokalı Kilise, the most elaborate of all the cave churches, is of course nearby, but probably

---

12 Restle, *Wall Painting*, I, 157.

13 Jerphanion, *Eglises*, II, 146–51 and 413, notes the problem of an 'Iconoclast' decoration containing figures (especially St Euphemia, used by the Iconodule faction to endorse its case) and settles for a ninth-century date, just after the end of Iconoclasm, when caution might have been the rule. A date as early as this, or earlier, is also accepted by N. Thierry, 'Les peintures murales de six églises du Haut Moyen Age en Cappadoce', *CRAI* (1970), 444–79, at 444–8.

14 For an aniconic decoration with no Iconoclast implications, see I. Pallas, 'Eine anikonische lineare Wanddekoration auf der Insel

Ikaria', *JÖB* 23 (1974), 271–314; *idem*, 'Une note sur la décoration de la chapelle de Haghios Basileios de Sinasos', *Byzantina* 48 (1978), 208–25.

15 For a summary of population movements, see S. Vryonis, *The Decline of Medieval Hellenism in Asia Minor* (Los Angeles/London, 1971), 444–52. Jerphanion found most of the churches of Sinasos (not far from Cemil and a Greek centre of local importance in the nineteenth century) to be eighteenth century or later (*Eglises*, II, 118–20). This may indicate a relatively recent recolonization of the region by Greeks.

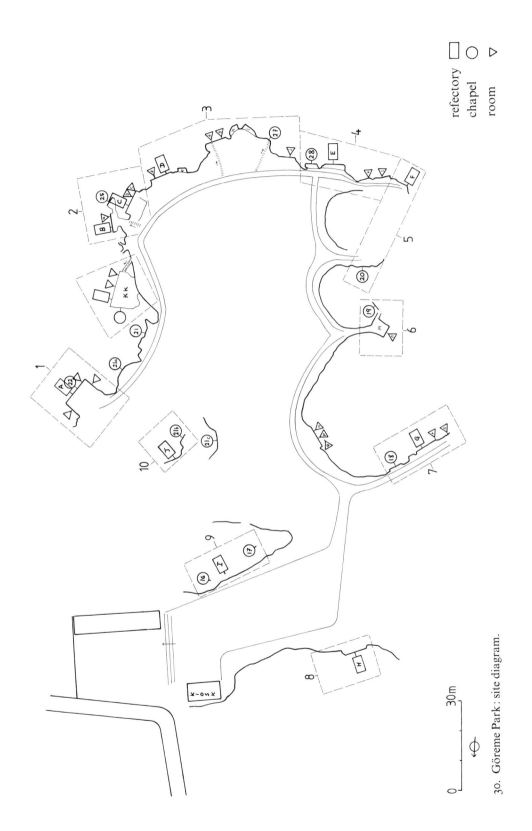

refectory ▢
chapel ◯
room ▽

30. Göreme Park: site diagram.

30m

pre-dates the Göreme Park churches and refectories by at least a century; its relationship with the Göreme monasteries will be considered below, in Chapter 6. Further, the structures of Göreme Park may be read as a collection of units like that seen in Yusuf Koç Kilisesi Monastery: a church, a refectory with rock-cut furniture and a few roughly cut rooms. On the plan (Fig. 30) the monuments are therefore divided into *monastery units*, with broken lines drawn to isolate them.

The monuments of Göreme Park are cut into a series of large cones which form a rough crescent shape (Fig. 30).[16] The description below does not follow the crescent from one tip to the other, but is arranged in a manner that may be more useful to visitors to the site: it begins at the far end of the modern path and proceeds back along the path towards the Park entrance, thus covering about two-thirds of the crescent. The first third, which is less easy of access, is then approached from the Park entrance.

A note on nomenclature: the churches of Göreme were labelled by Jerphanion as 'Chapelle' 1, 2, 3 and so on; some also have local names (Chapel 19 is Elmalı Kilise, for example). Although the distinction between the terms 'church' and 'chapel' is often blurred, the latter is usually applied to a minor place of worship attached to a larger establishment. Although it would therefore probably be more appropriate to call most of the Göreme monuments churches, not chapels, Jerphanion's nomenclature is firmly established and will be followed here. In the descriptions that follow, 'room' denotes a rectangular or square cavity with a flat ceiling and plain walls; a 'cavity' is less regular. I have not measured the rooms and cavities of Göreme. Most of them are about 5 × 6 metres in size; 'large' means about 8–10 × 6–7 metres, and 'small' means about 4–5 × 3–4 metres.

The churches of Göreme Park are among the best known of the Cappadocian cave monuments. Full descriptions of their wall paintings have been provided by Jerphanion and to repeat them at length would be redundant. Summary descriptions are provided, however, so that an overall picture of the Göreme monasteries and their churches may be had without frequent recourse to other volumes.

Unit 1 The first of the Göreme units is not typical, in that its organization is more formal than is the case for the other units; it is something of a hybrid between the courtyard and refectory types (Fig. 31). The monastery is fron-

ted by a two-storey façade (Pl. 151). The upper storey is formed by a rectangular recess in the rock, its back wall framed by simple corner pilasters and a square cornice. A single rectangular opening, placed off-centre in the façade, leads into the church (Çarıklı Kilise). This entrance has a recessed horseshoe-arched lunette above it and flanking mushroom-shaped niches.

The lower storey is wider, cut back to about the same plane as the upper register. Here the decoration consists of an upper frieze of small keyhole-shaped blind niches. There are four such niches in each of two compartments, separated by a pilaster. The frieze occupies the top quarter of the wall; the remaining three-quarters is plain and contains two rectangular openings into Rooms 2 and 3, described below. Short side walls to the lower part of the façade each contain rectangular entrances and frame a small courtyard area, marked (a) on the plan. There was once a floor of sorts separating upper and lower parts of the façade; traces of this remain at each side, partly roofing area (a). It seems unlikely that this floor extended very far forward, because the side walls of area (a) are short, but it probably formed a wide ledge which gave access to the church, the entrance to which now hangs several metres above ground level and is reached by a modern metal ladder (Pl. 151).[17]

The short west wall of the upper part of the façade is plain. An opening to a secondary tunnel cuts through the southwest corner. The east wall of the upper façade contains part of an arched opening into a shallow recess which has a flight of rock-cut steps leading up to it. Several pits are cut into this recess and to the left of it a tunnel leads up into a labyrinth of roughly cut cavities higher in the rock. Pl. 151 shows a 'chimney' with footholds in this area, which suggests that these cavities belong to a secondary, pigeon-house phase. The recess itself, however, may be part of the original means of access to the church.

Traces of red paint remain on the façade: niche arches on both levels are rimmed with triangle or chequer patterns and the cornice of the upper register has a chequer pattern on its outer face, triangle patterns on the lower face. Each niche of the lower register frieze contains a splayed-armed Greek cross within a medallion (the same formula exactly as that seen in the ground floor area in Karanlık Kilise Monastery). A single further cross-medallion is placed above and to the left of the church entrance in the upper register.

16 See Giovannini, *Arts of Cappadocia*, 79, figs. 28 and 29 for a plan and lateral view of the area. My Fig. 30 is based on his fig. 28, incorporating a few corrections.

17 Jerphanion (*Eglises*, I. ii, 455) suggests that there was a narthex in front of the church, but the front area, with its cornice and moulding, is definitely a façade, not the back wall of a lost chamber (Pl. 151).

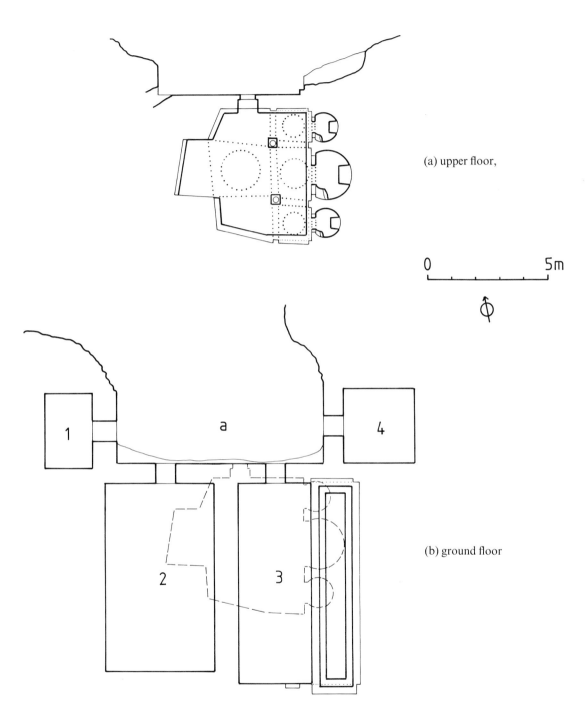

(a) upper floor,

0   5m

(b) ground floor

31. Çarıklı Kilise and complex (Göreme Unit 1): plan

151. Çarıklı Kilise Monastery: exterior.

Four rooms surround area (a): *Room 1*, entered from the short west wall is a small room with a low ceiling; *Room 4* opposite, behind the east wall of area (a), is similar, but with a higher ceiling. Entrances in the façade lead into *Room 2* (to the right) and the *Refectory* (3), to the left (Pl. 152 and Fig. 32, A). This is large and carefully finished. A rock-cut table and benches run the length of the east wall and at each end of this area an arched recess is cut into the wall. A small arched niche is cut to the right of the south recess. The arch of this recess is decorated with a chequer pattern; its back wall contains a painting of the Last Supper, above a band of painted marbling. This painting forms part of a narrative cycle, the rest of which is in the church above. The association of church and refectory is thus confirmed.

The church which lies above the refectory and Room 2 is Çarıklı Kilise (Göreme Chapel 22), one of the Column churches.[18] It has a modified inscribed-cross form, with only two columns, instead of four. Barrel-vaulted arms support the central dome on north, south and west sides; the east arm of the cross has a dome cut into a flat ceiling. The eastern corner bays are also domed, the domes rising above rudimentary pendentives. The existing slender columns with slab capitals are modern replacements: Jerphanion's photographs show suspended arches with

neither capitals nor supports.[19] The church has three apses, all horseshoe-shaped in plan and each with a rock-cut altar and a seat at the south side. The main apse was once closed by a tall screen with an open semicircular lunette and a single arched entrance, only fragments of which remain.[20] The side apses have narrow chancel slabs which are substantially complete. A low bench runs around the naos, along all walls except those of the west bay and where broken by the church entrance in the north wall.

The eccentric form of the church is probably the result of an accident (or error of judgement) during excavation, which eliminated the area of rock that should have been left for the western pair of columns.[21] The entrance is in the north cross-arm. This is a requirement of the site: the church was placed parallel to the façade in order to give the apse an eastern orientation.

'Çarıklı Kilise' means 'the church of (or with) the sandal(s)'. The name refers to two depressions in the floor of the south cross-arm, and visitors are told that these 'holy footprints' are the *raison d'être* for the church. This obviously cannot be the case. The church is a cave monument, and was excavated rather than built, so it follows that the marks in the floor must have been a product of excavation. They are depressions left by the mason's

18 Jerphanion, *Eglises*, I. ii, 455–73; Restle, *Wall Painting*, Cat. no. XXI.
19 Jerphanion, *Eglises*, pl. 125.1.
20 For a reconstruction: Epstein, 'Rock-cut Chapels', 132, fig. 8.
21 *Ibid.* 122. See also Chapter 6, note 14.

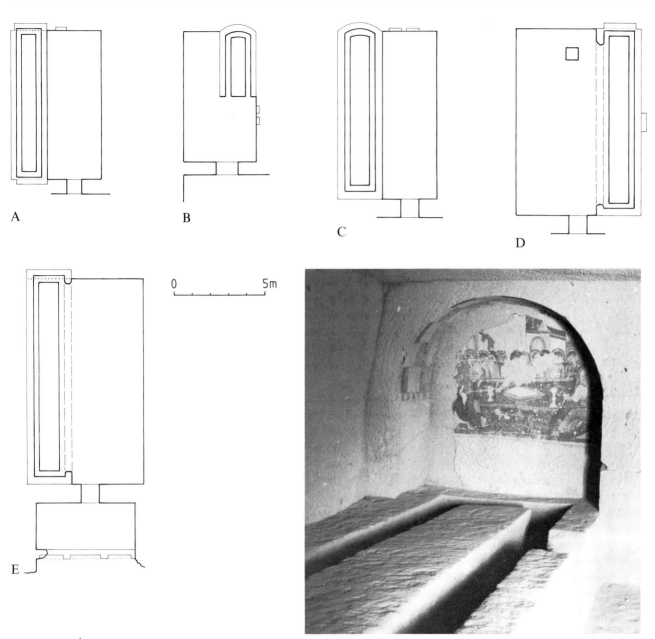

32. Göreme Refectories A to E.

152. Çarıklı Kilise Monastery: Refectory A.

chisel; dozens of similar, but rather smaller marks cover the floor. Further, since the 'holy footprint' is a feature of Islamic tradition, it is probable that the marks on the floor gathered their significance in the post-Byzantine period, from an interpretation supplied by the local Muslim population.[22]

22 For example, the Dome of the Rock in Jerusalem is still popularly believed to shelter the place where Mohammed set his foot as he ascended to heaven (O. Grabar, *The Formation of Islamic Art* (Newhaven, 1973), 51).

The church has an extensive painted decoration which has been fully described by Jerphanion, and so a summary only will be given here:

Central dome: Christ Pantocrator in the summit; below this, six medallions containing busts of Archangels Michael, Uriel, Mishael, Raphael, Gabriel, and of Christ Emmanuel.

Pendentives: figures of the four Evangelists, seated and writing their gospels.

153. Çarıklı Kilise: donor panel.

Subsidiary domes: Archangels Michael, Gabriel, Uriel.

A narrative cycle in thirteen scenes begins with the Annunciation on the *chancel screen* of the main apse[23] and continues on the *barrel vaults and adjacent lunettes*: Nativity, Adoration of the Magi, Baptism, Transfiguration, Raising of Lazarus, Entry into Jerusalem, Betrayal, Way of the Cross, Crucifixion, Anastasis, Myrophores, Ascension. One episode of the narrative cycle, the Last Supper, is painted in the refectory. A single Old Testament scene, the Hospitality of Abraham, occupies the lunette above the north apse.

Main apse: (conch) Deesis; (wall) six bishop saints in an arcade (Blaisios, Gregory the Theologian, Basil, John Chrysostom, Nikolaos, Hypatios).
North apse: Virgin and Child (bust).
South apse: Archangel Michael (bust).
Soffits of the arches forming the northeast corner bay: standing figures of Andronikos, Tarachos and Probos (the three martyrs of Cilicia).

North wall: female orant; Paraskeve; Kosmas and Damianos.
South wall: Theodoros (equestrian); Virgin and Child between Archangels in an arcade.
West wall: Constantine and Helena; Eudokia and Barbara; Theodoros and George; Prokopios.

On the west wall of the west bay there is a donor panel containing a standing nimbed figure carrying a long cross-staff, inscribed ὁ τήμιος σταβρός (the Holy Cross) flanked by three donors (Pl. 153). This nimbed figure is sometimes described as Christ[24] but, unlike other images of Christ in the church, has white hair and beard and is not cross-nimbed. The figure also lacks the usual identifying $\overline{\text{IC}}$ $\overline{\text{XC}}$ inscription. More probably the image represents Simon of Cyrene.[25] To the left of this figure is a standing male donor with head bowed and hands stretched forward in a gesture of supplication. He has black hair and beard and wears a white turban and a long reddish-brown coat over an ankle-length cream tunic, at the neck there is a

23 Epstein, 'Rock-cut Chapels', 123 n. 69.
24 Jerphanion, *Eglises*, I. ii, 457; Rott, *Denkmäler*, 217; J. Lafontaine-Dosogne, 'La Kale Kilisesi de Selime et sa représentation des donateurs', *Zetesis* (Antwerp/Utrecht, 1973), 741–53 at 750.

25 He is thus identified by C. Jolivet, in 'La peinture en Cappadoce de la fin de l'iconoclasme à la conquête Turque', in *Le Aree omogenee della civiltà rupestre nell'ambito dell'Impero bizantino: La Cappadocia* (Galatina, 1981), 159–97, at 192.

white scarf. Next to the figure an inscription reads:

Δέησης τοῦ δούλου/τοῦ θ(εο)ῦ Θεογνόστου [26]

Translation: 'Entreaty of the servant of God, Theognostos.'

To the right of the nimbed figure stand two more male figures. The first has short black hair and is either beardless or has a very short beard (the area of the face is badly damaged). He wears a long blue robe with a girdle at the waist and a gold border at the neck; he has the same stance as Theognostos: head bowed, hands towards the nimbed figure. An inscription reads:

Δέησης τοῦ δού/[λου] τοῦ θ(εο)ῦ Λέοντος [27]

Translation: 'Entreaty of the servant of God, Leon.'

The third figure is largely obliterated by damage to the wall. Only the head and shoulders remain, and resemble those of Leon: short dark hair and beard, a dark brown robe with a white scarf at the neck. Next to him is the inscription:

Δέησης τοῦ δού/λου τοῦ θ(εο)ῦ Μιχαή[λ] [28]

Translation: 'Entreaty of the servant of God, Michael.'

The status of these three donors and their relationship to each other is unclear, for they lack titles. Since Theognostos is placed alone at the right hand of Simon and the Cross, and since he wears a turban and heavy beard, it is likely that he is the senior member of the group, possibly the father of Leon and Michael. The church would appear to be dedicated to the Holy Cross.

Unit 2 Moving southwest from Unit 1, the path curves left around an outcrop of rock, past two small chapels (Nos. 21a and 21, see below), and shortly reaches Karanlık Kilise Monastery (Marked KK in Fig. 30). Beyond this, moving towards the south, Unit 2 consists of a group of cavities placed vertically in the rock. At the top of this area there is a small recessed façade decorated with an upper frieze of seven small horseshoe-arched blind niches. Below this, the arched entrance to Chapel 25 (see below) is flanked by large horseshoe-arched niches (Pl. 154a). The carved ornament of the façade is decorated with red paint: borders of triangles above the frieze and around the niche arches, a chequer border outlining the church entrance and flanking bays and cross-medallions in each blind niche.

154a. Göreme Unit 2: site, with entrance to Chapel 25.

Five steps lead down from the chapel, towards the left, to a ledge in front of another small rectangular façade, with a simple cornice at its top. Again there is red-paint decoration: a zig-zag on the cornice and cross-medallions below (Pl. 154b). There are two openings in this façade: on the right a rectangular entrance in a roughly arched recess opens into a small irregular cavity (a); the opening on the left, again rectangular and set in a shallow arched recess, is to *Refectory B*. This has rock-cut table and benches filling the upper right quarter of the floor space (Fig. 32, B). The table is a long slab of rock, framed by a U-shaped bench, the curved part of which fits into a shallow apse cut into the back wall. A pair of small horseshoe-arched niches, their bases about 1.5 metres above floor level, are cut into the right wall, about 0.5 metres forward of the end of the table.

Below and to the right of Refectory B is a further

26 Jerphanion, *Eglises*, I. i, 458, Inscription no. 42.
27 *Ibid.* 458, Inscription no. 43.
28 *Ibid.* 458, Inscription no. 44.

154b. Göreme Unit 2: site, with entrances to Refectory B, cavity (a) and Refectory C.

154c. Göreme Unit 2: site, with entrances to Refectory C, cavities (b) and (c).

155. Göreme Unit 2: Refectory C.

recessed façade, containing two rectangular openings (Pls. 154b & c). The opening to the left is topped by a double-recessed horseshoe-arched lunette containing a red painted cross-medallion. This leads down two steps into *Refectory C*, in which the rock-cut table and benches run the whole length of the left wall and are in a good state of preservation (Fig. 32, C, and Pl. 155). The table top is rimmed by a square moulding, which in effect gives it a recessed top and projecting edge. The seating bench curves into an apsidal niche at the head of the table in the far wall. To the right of this are two rectangular recesses, their bases about 1 metre above the floor. A secondary tunnel links the forward end of the left wall with a rough cavity lying below part of the upper façade which contains Refectory B.

The entrance in the lower façade to the right of that to Refectory C (Pl. 154c) opens into room (b) which has an opening in the forward part of its right wall to a flight of steps down to another room (c). The main entrance to this room is set in a small horseshoe-arched porch which is to the right of, and at a lower level than, the façade fronting Refectory C.

The church at the top of Unit 2 is *Göreme Chapel 25*.[29]

It has an inscribed-cross plan. The central dome is carried on four slender columns with tapering block capitals and square bases. Arches framing the corner bays spring from wall pilasters to the columns. The cross-arms are barrel-vaulted and small domes cover each of the corner bays (Pl. 156). A low bench runs right around the naos and across the east end; it has a step cut into it in front of the entrance to the main apse. This main apse is closed by a tall screen with a horseshoe-arched central entrance flanked by a pair of small arched openings with recessed panels below them. Above the screen there is a large horseshoe-arched open lunette (Pl. 157). The apse contains a rock-cut altar, a seat at the right side and a small niche in the back wall, to the left of the altar. There are small side apses, closed by low chancel slabs; the south apse has a rock-cut altar, seat and niche, as the main apse; the north apse has a niche only. The naos is reached through a small square domed narthex, with blind niches cut into each wall. The floor contains one grave pit.

Decoration consists of red-paint geometric ornament: zig-zag, triangle and plain borders rimming the main lines of the vaulting (arches, domes, soffits); imitation masonry lines in the barrel vaults; cross-medallions in subsidiary

29 Jerphanion, *Eglises*, I. ii, 479.

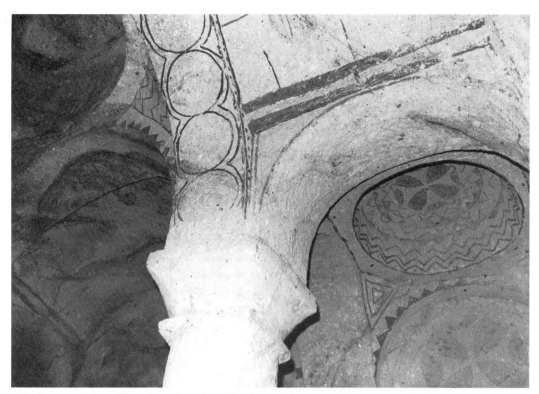

156. Göreme Unit 2: Chapel 25, view of vaulting (central dome, south arm, corner bay).

157. Göreme Unit 2: Chapel 25, apse and chancel screen.

domes and on the walls. On the chancel screen there is a painted entablature of chequer pattern (Pls. 156 & 157).

Unit 3 Beyond the lower room (b) of Unit 2 there are two simple rectangular entrances. The first opens into a room (d), the next into *Refectory D* (Fig. 32, D, and Pl. 158). This has its table running the whole length of the right wall; at the head of the table, in the back wall, is a flat-backed arched recess. The end of the table nearest the recess is lost, as is almost the whole of the free-standing bench. The wall bench is largely complete. About 1 metre from the back wall, equidistant from the long walls, there is a rough square pier.

To the right of Refectory D there is a rough, open-fronted cavity (e), then a further rough cavity with a convex grille over a hole in its wall (f). This cavity has its original entrance at the left side of a recessed façade (Pls. 159 & 160). In the centre of the façade there is a well-cut rectangular opening with a recessed horseshoe-arched lunette above it, which leads only into a small cavity (g). Beyond the façade there are two more open-fronted cavities (h & i), and to the right of these a flight of steps up to Chapel 27. Further to the right, but lower down, at the level of the path, a rectangular entrance, with recessed lunette above it, opens into a shallow cavity (j).

Göreme Chapel 27 is a domed, free-cross church with

158. Göreme Unit 3 : Refectory D.

159. Göreme Unit 3 : site, with entrance to Chapel 27.

160. Göreme Unit 3: site, with entrance to cavity (d) and Refectory D.

three apses, the lateral apses opening off the north and south arms of the cross.[30] The main apse is closed by a tall screen with an arched central entrance, small arched lateral openings and an open lunette above.[31] The church is preceded by a large rectangular narthex, which has been extended at its south end. The floor contains about thirteen grave pits, some of them infant-sized. There are more graves in arcosolia cut into the west and south walls. The entrance to the narthex is an arched opening at the top of steps in the rough rock-face, visible in Pl. 159.[32]

There is a little very simple red-paint decoration in Chapel 27: splayed-armed crosses on the chancel screens and on the piers flanking the east bay; hatching on the rim of the dome and imitation masonry lines in both naos and narthex. Polychrome decoration consists of only two panels: Christ enthroned, in the main apse, and a bishop saint on the wall of the east arm. Two inscriptions are painted directly onto the rock in red.

On the narthex wall, to the right of the entrance to the naos:

Κύ(ριε) βούθη / τὸν δῦλό / συ Θαμαδη +

and on the wall to the right of the north apse:

Κύριε / βούθη / τὸν δῦ/λό συ / Μ/η/χ/α/ύ/λ ? +[33]

Translation: 'Lord help thy servant, Thamades' and 'Lord help thy servant, Michael'.

The rusticity of these inscriptions would seem to identify them as graffiti. They are, however, executed in the same red paint as the church decoration and may refer to patrons. In most of the Göreme Park churches (with the exception of the three Column churches), the quality of decoration is poor and representation of donors (by image or inscription) cursory, a context not inconsistent, therefore, with interpretation of the inscriptions as donor invocations.

Unit 4 Beyond Unit 3, at the foot of the path down from Çarıklı Kilise, are the remains of the small, rectangular, flat-ceilinged narthex to Yılanlı Kilise (Chapel 28); in the

30 Jerphanion, *Eglises*, I. ii, 480–1, pl. 133.2.
31 Jerphanion, *Eglises*, pl. 133.2.
32 Jerphanion's description of the entrance to Chapel 27 as set in a

façade decorated with blind niching is an error: he is describing the entrance to Chapel 25; *ibid.* I. ii, 480, 483, pl. 12.4.
33 *Ibid.* I. ii, 481, Inscriptions nos. 65 & 64.

left wall of this area there is a large arcosolium.

Göreme Chapel 28 (Yılanlı Kilise) has a very irregular form: a transverse barrel-vaulted nave, entered from the north end, with a flat-ceilinged extension at the south end, and a further extension beyond that, through an arcade of two arches, the supports of which are lost.[34] There is a single apse in the long east wall of the nave, closed with low chancel slabs. Polychrome painting is confined to panels as follows:

Apse: Deesis
East side of the vault: saints Onesimos, George and Theodoros (both equestrian, their horses trampling a dragon), Helena and Constantine.
South side of the vault, north end: saints – Onouphrios, Thomas and Basil.
South lunette of the nave: standing figure of Christ, with a small figure of a donor at his side (a beardless male with short hair, wearing a long robe, his hands held at chest level in a gesture of prayer, inscribed simply: Θεόδορος, without an invocation).[35]

To the right of Yılanlı Kilise there is a fragment of a façade, set in a rectangular recess and decorated with horseshoe-arched blind niches (Pl. 161). There were probably originally three niches: a central one containing an entrance , flanked by two slightly smaller niches. Much of this has been cut away, leaving only one niche (to the left) and the top part of the centre niche. Behind the façade is a small room the back wall of which contains a rectangular entrance to *Refectory E* (Fig. 32, E). This has its table running along the left wall. Most of the free-standing bench is gone, but the wall-bench and table are largely intact, although the latter has been damaged by the excavation of several pits in its top. At the head of the table, in the back wall, there is a flat-backed arched recess housing the far end of the bench.

The main path now turns to the right, but a rough footpath continues south. It leads to a rough recessed façade, divided into two by a rudimentary pilaster with a cross painted on it. The façade contains two rectangular openings, both closed by modern metal grilles. The first leads into a room (k) with a bench down its left side and two deep recesses in its back wall; the second leads into a small room (l).

Unit 5 A little further along the footpath, past Unit 4, a rough hole, just above ground level, opens into a rough cavity which is the present means of access to *Refectory*

161. Göreme Unit 4: entrance to Refectory E.

F (Fig. 33, F). This is almost filled with accumulated silt, so that in most of the room there is only about one metre of clearance to the ceiling. In the far right corner, however, the debris has been dug away to form a rectangular pit (marked in broken line on the plan) in front of an arched, flat-backed recess. This, placed at the right of the back wall, suggests that the refectory table and benches ran along the right wall (they may still exist, buried under the silt). The refectory is now entered through the upper part of its forward wall, from the rough cavity noted above which may be part of a small ante-room. The original entrance to the Refectory is doubtless buried below the silt.

Refectory F is close to Chapel 20 (the Church of St Barbara), but separated from it by a cleft in the rock. This break may be a relatively recent development, since this part of the site consists of a curve of high ground above

34 Jerphanion, *Eglises*, I. ii, 481–3. An accurate plan is to be found in Epstein, 'Rock-cut Chapels', 131, fig. 5; that given in Restle, *Wall*

Painting, II, pl. 245, contains errors.
35 Jerphanion, *Eglises*, I. ii, 482, Inscription no. 66.

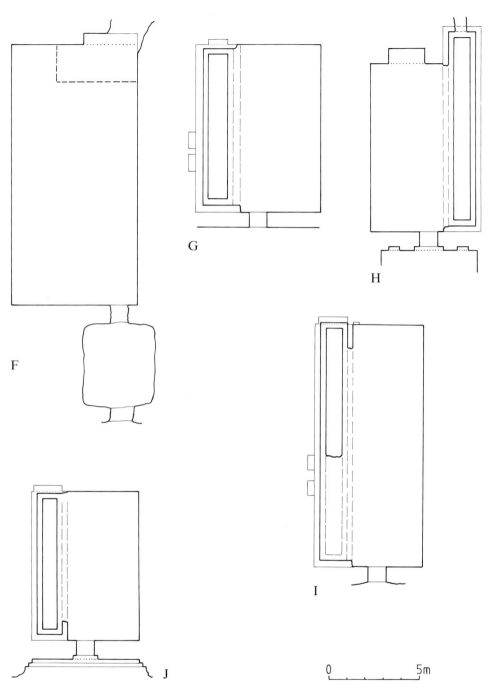

33. Göreme Refectories F to J.

a precipitous descent into the valley. The edges of this area are gradually crumbling and falling away, and the loss of massive areas of rock must have distorted the original relationships of some of the cavities. I have put Chapel 20 and Refectory F together as a unit because it seems possible that they were closely associated before erosion and rock falls created a chasm between them; it is also possible, of course, that they should not be linked, but that each was once associated with another church and refectory respectively, in the lost area. This is a reminder, if one be needed, that the division into 'monastery units' given here is not to be interpreted rigidly.

Chapel 20 (Church of St Barbara) has almost exactly

162. Göreme Unit 5: entrance to Chapel 20.

the same architectural form as Çarıklı Kilise: an abridged inscribed-cross plan, with lateral entrance and three apses.[36] Its lines are more regular than those of Çarıklı Kilise, however, and probably not the result of incomplete cutting. Instead, Chapel 20 was probably a copy of Çarıklı Kilise.[37] The central apse is closed by a tall screen with central arched entrance, small arched lateral openings and an open lunette. The lateral apses have low chancel slabs.[38] The church now has a 'façade' decorated with three blind niches: a central niche, flanked by a pair of small horseshoe-arched blind niches, sheltered by a gable moulding; there may have been a pair of small blind niches each side of the gable (Pl. 162). The naos entrance is in the centre niche. This 'façade' was once the east wall of a narthex of which the stubs of north and south walls survive. The floor of the narthex is filled with grave pits, at least six, and more graves are cut into the floor of an adjacent area to the west.

Primary decoration consists of elaborate red-paint ornament: masonry lines in the barrel vaults; triangle and chequer patterns rimming arches and on soffits; hatching and circles below the dome; on the walls there are medallions, 'pillar' ornaments, stemmed splayed-armed crosses and bizarre animals.[39] The range is very similar to that found in Aynalı Kilise (see Chapter 2).

Several polychrome panels have been painted over this primary scheme:

Apse: Christ enthroned.
West arm: (north wall) St Barbara.
North arm: (west wall) two more female saints (one – on a footstool – probably St Catherine); (north wall) confronted equestrian saints Theodoros and George, trampling on a dragon.

Between these two saints there is an inscription:

Κ(ύρι)ε [β]οίθι τὸ(ν) / δοῦ[λ]όν σου / Φαλ[ι]βονα / ΠΝ[.]ΑΛΟ / ΨΥ[.]ΛΟΝ

and, to the right:

Κ(ύρι)ε βοήθη τ(ὸν) / δοῦλόν σου Λέ/οντα Μαρουλινε [40]

36 Jerphanion, *Eglises*, I. ii, 484–6; Restle, *Wall Painting*, Cat. no. XIX.
37 Epstein, 'Rock-cut Chapels', 122. See also Chapter 6, note 14.
38 *Ibid.* fig. 7, 131, for a drawing of the sanctuary barriers.

39 D. Wood, 'Byzantine Military Standards in a Cappadocian Church', *Archaeology* 12 (1959), 38–46.
40 Jerphanion, *Eglises*, I. ii, 485, Inscriptions nos. 67–8.

Translation: 'Lord help thy servant, Falibon (?), Priest (rest uncertain)' and 'Lord help thy servant, Leon Marulines'. The end of the first inscription is very uncertain. Jerphanion suggested, very tentatively: π[ρ](εσβύτερο)ν [κὲ] ἀλόψυ[χ]ον, 'priest and foreigner'. The traces that remain of the name are also so fragmentary as to make the restoration 'Falibon' uncertain.

These inscriptions are in the same white paint and the same letter style as the names of the saints. They therefore belong with the painting of the panel and Falibon?, priest, and Leon Marulines were probably patrons, not writers of graffiti.

Unit 6 Beyond Chapel 20 the main path curves towards the west, to a narrow passage which sinks below ground level and leads to a narrow recess containing a rectangular opening with a crudely cut recessed lunette above it (Pl. 163). Through this a narrow tunnel leads into a roughly rectangular open area (m). To the right of centre in the back wall of this area is a rectangular opening, with a crude recessed lunette above it. The opening is blocked by a modern metal grille behind which there is a a small cavity (n). A rough opening in the south wall leads to a small tunnel, which in turn opens into the north wall of Elmalı Kilise (Chapel 19) This, at present, is the only means of access to the church, but it is clearly secondary, since it damages the painting of the church wall (the original church entrance is still intact in its west wall). The cavities just described did not, therefore, originally have their present close association with Elmalı Kilise and may be an entirely secondary development.

Chapel 19 (Elmalı Kilise) is an inscribed-cross church.[41] The centre bay is formed by four slender columns with squat tapering block capitals. Arches spring between the columns, framing the centre bay, and between the columns and wall pilasters, framing the corner bays. All eight subsidiary bays are domed. The main apse was closed by a tall screen with open lunette and a single entrance, as at Çarıklı Kilise; the lateral apses have keyhole-shaped entrances formed by low chancel slabs. The naos entrance, in the centre bay of the west wall, now opens to a sheer drop. Minor acrobatics permit the observation of carved blind niches flanking the exterior entrance. These may have been the decoration of a façade or, more probably, of the east wall of a narthex.

The extensive painted programme in Elmalı Kilise consists, briefly, of the following:

163. Göreme Unit 6: entrance to area (m).

Central dome: Christ Pantocrator.
Minor domes: Archangels.
Main apse: (conch) Deesis; (wall) bishop saints.
North apse: Virgin and Child.
South apse: Archangel Michael.
Cross-arm vaults with dependent lunettes and upper wall areas: narrative cycle – Nativity, Adoration of the Magi, Baptism, Transfiguration, Raising of Lazarus, Entry into Jerusalem, Last Supper, Betrayal, Way of the Cross, Crucifixion, Entombment, Myrophores, Anastasis, Ascension.
Wall panels: two Old Testament subjects (the Hospitality of Abraham and the Three Hebrews).

The programme is very similar to that in Çarıklı Kilise and Karanlık Kilise, the other two members of the Column group. It appears to lack the Annunciation, but this may have been on the chancel screen where the paint is

41 Jerphanion, *Eglises*, I. ii, 431–54; Restle, *Wall Painting*, Cat. no. XVIII.

lost. It also lacks the 'Virgin and Child between Arch-angels', present in the other two Column churches, but it is possible that this was in the narthex, since at Karanlık Kilise this scene is outside the church (see Chapter 2). There are a few additional scenes in the narrative cycle: Journey to Bethlehem, Last Supper and Entombment (at Çarıklı Kilise the Last Supper is in the refectory).

The saints depicted on walls, pilasters and soffits include the same group of bishops as at Çarıklı Kilise, six female saints (including Barbara, Kyriaka and Eirene), all the martyrs of Çarıklı Kilise and several in addition: Phloros and Lauros, Sergios and Bakchos, Probos and Tarachos, Aniketos and Photios, Niketas, Demetrios, Mamas, the five martyrs of Armenia (Orestios, Eugenios, Mardarios, Auxentios, Eustratios), Gourias and Abibos.

There is no donor image in Elmalı Kilise. Much paint has been lost, especially from the middle and lower parts of the walls, where a donor panel might be expected, but all areas can be accounted for and there is no space left for a donor image. Such a panel may, however, have existed in the narthex.

As noted above, the cavities through which Elmalı Kilise is now approached have no original connection with it, so the church is not part of a refectory and rooms group. The site here is not complete, however. As noted

above in connection with Unit 5, the area being described is at the edge of a mass of high ground above a steep descent. The area to the west of Elmalı Kilise has been lost and its entrance hangs above a precipice. Whatever structures were originally associated with Elmalı Kilise were either lost in the fall of rock that took away the narthex, or are possibly still in existence on the inaccessible south side of the church. Indeed, it is conceivable that Refectory F, described above, belongs not with Chapel 20 but with Elmalı Kilise, a further reminder that the boundaries given in Fig. 30 are uncertain.

Beyond Elmalı Kilise, continuing towards the Göreme Park entrance, the path curves around an area to the left which contains several more cavities. A recessed façade contains a rectangular opening with a recessed horseshoe-arched lunette above it (Pl. 164). This leads into a room (o) almost filled with silt (a flat ceiling with one carved boss are just visible). Above this room is another flat-ceilinged room (p), entered through a rectangular open-ing in an upper part of the façade. To the left of this is another rectangular entrance, into a small cavity (q). There is no church or refectory close to this group.

Unit 7 Beyond this area, the path makes a sharp turn to the left to a small plain façade containing an arched

164. Göreme: cavities (o) and (p), between Units 6 and 7.

165. Göreme Unit 7: entrances to Chapel 18 and Refectory G.

entrance to the north end of the narthex of *Chapel 18* (Pl. 165).[42] The narthex is a long rectangular room with at least twelve grave pits cut into its floor. Three irregular openings in its east wall lead into the naos, which has a transverse barrel-vaulted nave, with three apses closed by low chancel slabs. Painted decoration consists of isolated panels, as follows:

> *Narthex:* (on the small, pier-like area of wall left between the two southernmost entrances to the nave) St Catherine.
> *North wall of naos:* bishop saint; St Theodoros on horseback, trampling a dragon.[43]
> *Main apse:* bust of Christ holding an open book.
> *South wall:* another equestrian saint, again with a dragon (probably St George); to his left, a standing military saint.
> *East wall:* (to the right of the central apse) standing Virgin and Child, with a small male donor figure kneeling at the Virgin's feet. This figure is wearing a brocade

robe, and has short hair and beard. The inscription above his head reads:

Κύρη[ε] / βοήθι / τὸν δοῦ/λό σου Ἰ[. . .] / ΤΑΤΗ [. .] Q̣/ μου[να]χọ́[44]

Translation: 'Lord help thy servant (?), monk.' Jerphanion reconstructed the name as 'Ignatios'.

A little beyond the church, in a small recessed façade, there is a rectangular entrance with a recessed lunette above it, decorated with a splayed-armed inscribed cross (Pl. 165a). This is the entrance to *Refectory G* (Fig. 33, G), of which only parts of the walls remain; much of the ceiling has also fallen in. The table runs along the left wall and is largely intact, as is the wall bench, but the the free-standing bench is lost. There are two deep recesses in the long wall above the table, and a flat-backed arched niche in the back wall, at the head of the table.

Beyond the refectory there is a room (r) now fronted by a modern door and window, and a large cavity (s)

42 Jerphanion, *Eglises*, I. ii, 486; Restle, *Wall Painting*, Cat. no. XVII.
43 A common error, resulting from confusion with St George; it occurs also in Göreme Chapel 28 (Jerphanion, *Eglises*, I. ii, 482). For discussion of the equestrian saints in Cappadocian painting see G. P. Schiemenz, 'Herr, hilf deinem Knecht. Zur Frage nimbierter Stifter

in den kappadokischen Höhlenkirchen', *RQ* 71 (1976), 133–74, at 155ff.
44 This inscription is no longer legible; Jerphanion, *Eglises*, I. ii, 487, Inscription no. 70.

165a. Göreme Unit 7: entrance to Refectory G.

which in 1982 contained the disc part of a millstone closure.

Unit 8 Opposite Unit 7, to the left of the Göreme Park entrance kiosk, is a recessed façade decorated with three horseshoe-arched blind niches. A large central niche contains a rectangular entrance and is flanked by smaller niches (Pl. 166). The entrance is to *Refectory H*, which is rectangular with a short projection at its far end (Fig. 33, H). The table runs along the right wall and into the projection. The wall bench, which lines the projection, extends down the long wall and across the forward wall; the free-standing bench is lost. A deep arched recess is cut into the back wall to the left of the table and benches. A secondary tunnel leads back from the projection.

In the rock above the refectory, several openings indicate the presence of more cavities, probably pigeon-house rooms. There is no church nearby, but there may well have been one in the area to the right and forward of the refectory, which is very much eroded and contains fragments of several cavities.

Unit 9 The rest of the itinerary proceeds from Göreme Park entrance back towards Çarıklı Kilise. On the left,

just beyond the Park entrance, is a cliff containing a number of cavities, many of them very irregular. A modern metal ladder leads up to *Refectory I*, which is roughly rectangular: the room widens towards the back as its right wall curves outward. The table and benches are set against the straight left wall and probably once ran its whole length (Pl. 167 and Fig. 33, I: the irregularity of the wall is not shown in the plan, which, like the others, is schematized). The wall bench remains, but a stub at the far end is all that remains of the free-standing bench. At the head of the table there is an arched recess. Two more recesses are cut in the left wall, above the table. In the ceiling above the table there are two bosses.

There are four churches or chapels in this area. First, to the left, and slightly higher than the refectory, is the remains of *Chapel 16*, which was once a three-apsed, transverse-barrel-vaulted church.[45] Only the south part remains, consisting of part of the main apse, the south apse and the south end of the barrel vault. The church was once fully painted, apparently with an Infancy cycle. Remaining scenes are: Annunciation, Visitation (south lunette), Proof of the Virgin and Presentation (barrel vault). The transverse vault had a band of medallions along its crest, of which two remain, containing the busts of

45 Jerphanion, *Eglises*, I. ii, 492–5; Restle, *Wall Painting*, Cat. no. XV.

166. Göreme Unit 8: entrance to Refectory H.

167. Göreme Unit 9: Refectory I.

Moses and Elias. On the south wall there are scenes of the life and martyrdom of St George. The fragment of the main apse retains parts of a Deesis, and in the south apse is the badly damaged figure of an an Archangel with staff and globe.

To the right of the refectory, a little further round the cone, is *Chapel 17 (Kızlar Kilise)*.[46] This is an inscribed-cross church with a central dome, carried on four thick columns with tapering block capitals (Pl. 20). The cross-arms are barrel-vaulted and have small calottes cut into their crests. The northeast corner bay has a flat ceiling, the other three are covered by calottes. Blind niches decorate the walls of the four corner bays. There are three apses, the central one closed by a tall screen, with a central horseshoe-arched entrance flanked by small horseshoe-arched openings; above these are two more such openings and above the entrance a small horseshoe-arched lunette; a larger lunette opens above the top of the screen. The lateral apses have narrow chancel slabs.[47] The naos is preceded by a rectangular narthex with a transverse barrel vault, entered by means of a short tunnel from the outside. The only painting is a panel on the north wall of the centre bay, showing a standing figure of Christ.

Schiemenz records two more chapels close to Chapel 17. *Chapel 17a* is a small, single-naved, barrel-vaulted chapel, above Chapel 17, entered through a narthex with five floor graves and one arcosolium. The apse contains a Deesis panel and the east wall a panel showing St Basil. *Chapel 17b*, next to 17a, is a free-cross chapel with a dome and single apse.[48]

Unit 10 Beyond Chapel 17 a steep path leads upwards to *Chapel 21b*, which has a rectangular opening below a recessed lunette, set in a small plain façade with a cornice at its top.[49] This is a free-cross chapel, with barrel-vaulted cross-arms and a central dome carried on rudimentary pendentives. The main apse, opening off the east arm, is closed by tall chancel slabs. The apse contains a rock-cut altar, a seat at the right and a niche at the left, above the level of the altar. Small side apses open off the north and south cross-arms; each contains a rock-cut altar. A bench runs around the church, broken by a step in front of the main apse. The plan closely resembles that of Chapel 27.

Painted decoration consists of red-paint ornament only: four painted ribs made up of triangle patterns in the dome; chequered borders on cornices, apse arches

and chancel slabs. On north and south walls there are 'pillar' ornaments like those seen in Aynalı Kilise (see Chapter 2).

A few paces to the left of Chapel 21b, at a lower level, is a rectangular entrance below a recessed lunette, set in a small plain façade. This is the entrance to *Refectory J* (Fig. 33, J), which has its table and benches along the left wall. The free-standing bench is lost and only the back two-thirds of the wall bench remains.

Other churches in Göreme Park Several churches in Göreme Park are not in close proximity to refectories. Given the casual relationship between structures in the Göreme Park area it is uncertain whether or not these churches belong to the refectory development. I must here anticipate my conclusion as to the date of these churches and assert that they are probably contemporary with the churches described above and therefore likely to be associated with the monastic development of the Park region. For this reason, and given the desirability of offering a full picture of the site, they are described briefly below.

Two of these churches lie between Çarıklı Kilise (Unit 1) and Karanlık Kilise Monastery. The first is *Chapel 21*.[50] This has an entrance set in a three-niched façade which leads first into a free-cross narthex, the dome of which is decorated with four ribs and a central boss. The narthex has nine graves cut into its floor and two more in arcosolia. The naos is a domed free-cross, the dome rising above a drum of blind niches and rudimentary pilasters. The single apse is closed by a tall screen with an arched central entrance, small lateral arched openings and an open lunette above, differing slightly from those already seen to the extent that the rock between central and lateral openings is finished as a pair of colonnettes with capitals. The cross-arms are barrel-vaulted. Two corbels are carved in each arm where the springing of the vault meets the end wall.

Painted decoration is confined to panels:
Apse: (conch) Deesis; (wall) medallions with busts of saints (Gregory, Basil, John Chrysostom and one other) and a Mandylion below.
East arm barrel vault: (north side) Constantine and Helena; (opposite) Niketas and Sisinnios; (crest of the vault) Archangel Michael, in a medallion.
East wall of the north arm: St Theodoros, in military dress.

46 Jerphanion, *Eglises*, I. ii, 488–91; Epstein, 'Rock-cut Chapels', 121–2.
47 For a drawing of the screen: Epstein, 'Rock-cut Chapels', fig. 6, 131.
48 G. P. Schiemenz, 'Nachlese in Göreme', *AA* 87 (1972), 307–18, at 307–14.
49 Giovannini, *Arts of Cappadocia*, Plan no. 4, Avcılar and Göreme, for the location of this chapel.
50 Jerphanion, *Eglises*, I. ii, 474–8; Rott, *Denkmaler*, 219; Restle, *Wall Painting*, Cat. no. XX.

South wall of the south arm: St George, on horseback, with an inscription:

Κ(ύρι)ε βοήθη τὸν δοῦ/λόν σου Αρμολοι/κον [51]

Translation: 'Lord help thy servant, [?H] armoloikos.'

The inscription is in the same script and paint as the rest of the lettering in the panels; it is therefore original, not a graffito.

On the south wall of the east arm, below Sisinnios and Niketas, a standing figure of St Catherine has a small donor figure kneeling at her right side, inscribed:

Δέισις ῎Ανη [52]

Translation: 'Entreaty of Anna.'

Chapel 21a is a very small, domed free-cross chapel, with a large single apse.[53] It has a lateral entrance, into its north arm, from a rectangular narthex with four graves in its floor and two more in an arcosolium in its east wall. The chapel has red-paint ornament only.

Chapel 21c is near Chapel 21b, but at a lower level.[54] This is a small, single-naved barrel-vaulted chapel, with a single apse and a rock-cut bench running along the north side of the nave only. It is preceded by a rectangular, barrel-vaulted narthex, the north and south walls of which contain deep arcosolia; the narthex floor contains seven graves.

The top part of a church entrance, partly obscured by a bush growing in front of it, is visible to the left of the path towards Unit 10. The entrance is rectangular, framed by a plain moulding. The church, which I shall call *Chapel 21d*, has a free-cross plan with barrel-vaulted arms. The centre bay is covered by a dome and there is a single apse in the east end. The church is quite large – perhaps six or seven metres square. At present (1978–82) it is almost filled with debris and there is barely room to stand in the west arm entrance bay, so a full description cannot be given.

Chapel 22a, recorded by Schiemenz, is another domed free-cross chapel with a single apse.[55] This contains a fragment of painting in its apse: part of a throne with an archangel in imperial dress at one side.

Finally, it must be noted that there are more rooms and perhaps even a few more chapels in Göreme Park that await exploration. The development of the Park as a tourist attraction has led to the closing off of some cavities with fixed metal grilles and the use of others as utility rooms for the Park staff.

Conclusion

Most of the churches associated with the monastery units described above fall into one of two groups: the Column group and the Yılanlı group. The Column group consists of Elmalı Kilise, Çarıklı Kilise, and Karanlık Kilise (this last is part of a courtyard monastery, see Chapter 2). These were recognized as close relatives by Jerphanion and I believe them to have been painted by the same workshop (workshop rather than painter, since more than one hand was at work in each church).[56] They are therefore roughly contemporaneous. The mid eleventh-century date proposed for the Column churches by Jerphanion has been convincingly supported by Epstein, on the basis of an analysis of the painting style and its relationship to other programmes in Göreme valley.[57]

As for sequence of production of these three churches, Epstein places Karanlık Kilise first, and the other two after it, on the basis of the complexity of the programme, quality of painting and the use, in Karanlık Kilise, of expensive blue pigment.[58] All these points are valid, and to them may be added the fact that Karanlık Kilise is clearly the most important of the three churches, associated as it is with a courtyard monastery. A plausible history for the Column churches, therefore, is that the workshop was brought to Göreme to decorate Karanlık Kilise and stayed to execute two less important, but still impressive, commissions. This is an important point for the dating of the cave monasteries, for it establishes the approximate contemporaneity, or, at least, chronological overlap, of members of the courtyard and refectory groups.

The Yılanlı group is named after Yılanlı Kilise (Göreme Chapel 28); other members of the group are: Chapels 17, 17a, 18, 20, 21, 22a, 27, which have been described above, and 10 and 11a which are outside the Göreme Park area.[59] The group is defined principally by the style, content and organization of the painted decoration in the churches. This consists of isolated panels of painting rather than a continuous scheme. The panels usually contain figures of saints, or formal compositions,

---

51 Jerphanion, *Eglises*, I. ii, 475, Inscription no. 58 (and n. 6 for other readings of the donor name).
52 *Ibid.* I. ii, 475, Inscription no. 57. This inscription is no longer legible.
53 Giovannini, *Arts of Cappadocia*, 202–3, Plan no. 4, Avcılar and Göreme, for the location of this chapel.
54 *Ibid.* 202–3, Plan no. 4 and 79, fig. 29.
55 Schiemenz, 'Nachlese in Göreme', 314–16.
56 Jerphanion, *Eglises*, I. ii, Ch. 11. The opinion that a single workshop

executed all three programmes is endorsed by Epstein, 'Fresco Decoration', 36.
57 Jerphanion, *Eglises*, II, 421–2; Epstein, 'Fresco Decoration', 27; *idem*, 'Rock-cut Chapels', 115.
58 Epstein, 'Fresco Decoration', 36, 38.
59 Schiemenz, 'Nachlese in Göreme', 310; *idem*, 'Zur Chronologie der Kappadokischen Felsmalereien', *AA* 85 (1970), 253–73.

such as the Deesis. The quality of painting is generally mediocre. The churches are of several different architectural types, but there is considerable uniformity of carving style and architectural detail in the group: the tall screens noted in the descriptions given above are the most conspicuous example of this. There is also a uniformity of overall arrangement to the extent that most of the churches have narthexes with large numbers of graves. It cannot be said with certainty that all the graves belong to the period in which the monasteries were functioning, but it is reasonable to suppose that the narthexes did have a funerary function, given that the narthexes are nearly always very large in proportion to the size of the naos.

Seven of the churches described above do not belong to either the Yılanlı or Column groups as currently defined. These are: Chapels 25, 21b, 17b, 16, 21a, 21c and 21d. Some of these do, however, have close affinities with one, sometimes with both, groups: Chapel 25 is an inscribed-cross church with proportions and details very similar to those of the Column churches, and may therefore be linked with them. Chapels 17b and 21d are both domed, free-cross chapels and therefore similar to Yılanlı group Chapels 21 and 27. Chapel 21b has an elaborate red-paint decoration resembling that of Chapel 20 (St Barbara) and so should also be aligned with the Yılanlı group. Chapels 21a and 21c are undecorated chapels and therefore difficult to place, but since they are small chapels with large funerary narthexes they too should perhaps be included with the Yılanlı group. There remains Chapel 16, the decoration of which Jerphanion attributed to the period of the Column churches. The style of the painting in Chapel 16 has indeed much in common with that of this group, most conspicuously the use of 'comb' highlighting on draperies and of a harsh dark outline for hair and faces.[60]

None of the churches is firmly dated by inscription. As noted above, Jerphanion's attribution of the Column churches to the mid eleventh century has been confirmed by recent work. As for the Yılanlı group, basing her analysis on stylistic comparison with painting outside Cappadocia, and the evidence of dated graffiti in the churches, Epstein has convincingly dated the Yılanlı

group to the second half of the eleventh century.[61] All the churches of Göreme Park may therefore be dated from the mid to the late eleventh century, since all of them either belong to the Yılanlı or Column groups, or may be associated with one or other of those groups on stylistic grounds.

Göreme Park is, of course, a modern enclosure of just part of the valley. There are many other churches in the valley outside the Park area, on both sides of the modern road to Avçılar. Some of these belong to the Yılanlı group (Chapels 10, 11a and 12, for example) and many others to the 'archaic' group of the early tenth century (Chapels 6, 8, 9, 11, 13, for example).[62] The separation of Göreme Park from the rest of the valley, implied in the above description, is not merely an arbitrary one, however. The park area also forms a coherent geographical entity in that it encompasses the crescent of large cones containing the monastery units, set on a high bluff of rock which overlooks the valley. It must always have been difficult of access except by the path into the curve of the crescent which forms the present Park entrance. Thus, the crescent is separated from the rest of the valley by its geography, not just by the Park gates. This separation is reflected in the dates of the monuments of Göreme valley: the earlier painted churches of the 'archaic' group are outside the Park crescent. It would appear, therefore, that the monastery units of the crescent were an eleventh-century development of the church-excavating tradition in Göreme valley. This development was not confined to the crescent, since eleventh-century churches are scattered elsewhere in the valley, but the monastery units may perhaps be regarded as its core.

Of the two refectory monasteries outside Göreme, Yusuf Koç Kilisesi Monastery is datable to the first half of the eleventh century and may therefore be slightly earlier than the Göreme development. The Monastery of the Archangel, the façade and hall of which find parallels in the courtyard monasteries, may have a similar foundation date. No conclusion in this respect is possible, however, until more is understood of the history of the Church of the Archangel and the chapel of St Stephen.

60 Jerphanion, *Eglises*, I. ii, 495. The similarity may be seen by comparing photographs published in Restle, *Wall Painting*, II, 155–9 & 160–244; for example: Simeon of the Presentation in Chapel 16 and the Prophet Elias in Elmalı Kilise (pls. 155 & 169); Joseph of the Presen-

tation in Chapel 16 and Matthew in Elmalı Kilise (pls. 155 & 199).
61 Epstein, 'Rock-cut Chapels', 119–20 and 124.
62 See Giovannini, *Arts of Cappadocia*, 202–3, Plan no. 4, for the distribution of churches in Göreme valley.

5

Hermitages

Introduction

The material remains of hermitages are obviously less recognizable than those of monasteries.[1] A small dwelling cave, with simple rock-cut furniture, is not easily distinguished from a cave cut by the local peasantry for agricultural use. This, in any case, is likely to be the fate of a hermit cave once the anchorite has left, and a few centuries of use as a stable or pigeon house is likely to obliterate most signs of its original purpose. Further, the anchoritic habit itself is inconvenient for the archaeologist, for the hermit who succeeds best at removing himself from the world leaves no trace.

Nevertheless, there are a few chapels in the volcanic valleys which appear to be associated with hermitages. The evidence for this is of various kinds. Some churches have dwelling caves attached to them, or nearby, and some have inscriptions identifying hermits. In other instances evidence of long occupation of a site suggests that it was a particularly venerated place and therefore likely to have been the location of a hermitage. The six sites described below are unlikely to account for the total hermit population of the volcanic valleys. There may well have been many more, their dwellings no longer identifiable for the reasons given above. Further, very little attention has been given to undecorated caves found in the vicinity of painted churches, and closer study of these may lead to the identification of more hermitage sites.

Hermitage of Niketas the Stylite

A tiny chapel in an eastern branch of Güllü Dere contains an inscription in its painted programme referring to 'Niketas the Stylite'.[2] Güllü Dere (the rose-pink valley) is among the most enchanting of the volcanic valleys, lined by banks of undulating cones of dusty pink rock.[3] The valley floor contains a series of small vegetable patches, orchards and vineyards and the hermitage is in such a clearing (Pl. 168).

Chapel of Niketas the Stylite The chapel is cut into the base of a solitary cone (in Pl. 168 the cone in the middle distance, not the one in the foreground). Its arched entrance, set in a small recessed rectangular façade, opens into a narthex with a longitudinal barrel vault (Fig. 34a). Most of the north wall is taken up by a large arcosolium which has been damaged by considerable enlargement. Much of the east wall, between narthex and naos, has also been destroyed and only the top part remains (Pl. 170). Beyond it, the naos is also barrel-vaulted and has much of its north wall cut away to make a large secondary cavity.

The apse is wide and rather shallow. It is damaged by another large cavity at the north side and by an opening in the south side. Fragments remain of three niches in the apse wall, one small one at the back, at the base of the conch, two more flanking it, but lower down. The apse is lit by a square window at the extreme right of the wall. Whatever chancel furniture once existed is now lost, since the apse entrance has been demolished and a small part of the arch is all that remains. The chapel is well cut, but with very little carved detail; there are no cornices or pilasters.

At the south side of the cone containing the chapel, the rock is hollowed out to form a shallow cavity with

---

1 In the present context, a hermit is understood to be a monk who lives either in solitude or with a small group of followers, rather than in a formal monastic community.

2 G. P. Schiemenz, 'Die Kapelle des Styliten Niketas in den Weinbergen von Ortahisar', *JÖB* 18 (1969), 239–58; N. Thierry, 'Art byzantin du Haut Moyen Age en Cappadoce: L'église peinte de Nicétas Stylite et d'Eustrate Clisurarque, ou fils de Clisurarque en

Cappadoce', *Communications, 14e Congrès international des études byzantines, Bucharest, 1971* (pub. 1976), 451–5.

3 The eastern extension of Güllü Dere is sometimes called Kızıl Çükür (the red hollow). Local opinions on the name of the area containing the hermitage of Niketas appear to differ; since this area is geographically part of Güllü Dere, this name is used here.

168. Hermitage of Niketas the Stylite: site.

(a) plan of chapel

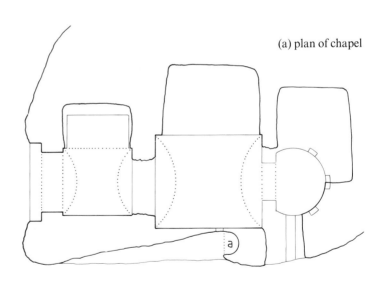

(b) plan of nearby chapel.
     (no scale)

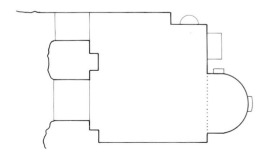

34. Hermitage of Niketas the Stylite

169. Hermitage of Niketas the Stylite: Chapel entrance and niche.

a floor level about two metres lower than that of the chapel. At the east end of this cavity there is a small apsidal niche (Pl. 169 and (a) on the plan, Fig. 34a). The wall of the niche is so thin that it is broken through to the nave at one point. It is likely that the original ground level of the cavity and niche was only slightly below that of the chapel floor, since the lower parts are very much eroded. The niche would then have been just above ground level.

Painting The church is painted throughout, with a single layer of painting. The programme, first described by Schiemenz, is as follows:

Narthex
Barrel vault: single field containing a large jewelled cross, from the base of which springs stylized foliage which fills the field (Pl. 170).
Walls: plastered and discoloured in places – there may have been painting here, but this is not certain.
East lunette: fragment of a medallion with haloed bust, inscribed ПѲ/ΥΜ/ΗΟϹ (perhaps Euthymios?) (Pl. 170).[4]

Nave
Barrel vault: jewelled cross with stylized cornucopia scroll filling a rectangular field framed by interlaced circles containing crosses in medallions; below, on each side, a row of Apostles in arcades – (north) Simon, Thomas, Mark, John, Jacob, Paul; (south) six figures, their names lost.
South wall: five crosses in an arcade (this decoration continued on the west wall and probably on the north also, which has been cut away); the lower part of the wall is unpainted.
West wall lunette: standing figures of saints (Damianos, Kosmas, Panteleemon, Anna).
East wall lunette: (centre) Crucifixion; (left) St Symeon on his pillar; (right) John the Baptist (Pl. 171); John holds a scroll bearing a line from John 1.29, 'Behold the Lamb of God which taketh away the sins of the world'.
Apse: (conch) Virgin and Child enthroned, flanked by Archangels Michael and Gabriel; (summit) a cross on a ground of concentric circles, the rest of the field filled with peacock feather pattern; (arch) medallions, at the crest a hand; flanking it, David, Daniel(?), two others.

4 Schiemenz, 'Die Kapelle', 242.

170. Hermitage of Niketas the Stylite: Chapel (narthex, nave, apse).

In addition to inscriptions identifying the saints and the figures in the Crucifixion, the east lunette bears two other inscriptions. These were first published by Schiemenz and also copied by Thierry. The text given here for the second inscription follows that established and interpreted for Thierry by I. Ševčenko and C. Mango.[5]

To the left of the column of Symeon the Stylite:

+ Ὑπὲρ εὔχης κ(αὶ) σοτι/ρίας κ(αὶ) [ἀ]φέσεος ἁμαρτί/ον Ν[ι]κίτα στυλίτ[ου] / πήστι ἀσχήτου Κ[. .] / ΓΙϹΑΝΤ [. . . ./οι [. . .

Translation: 'For the prayer and salvation and the forgiveness of sins of Niketas, stylite, by the faith of the ascetic. . .'

Although interpretations of this line vary, the inscription does appear to be an invocation for a stylite, Niketas.[6]

The second inscription is below the scroll held by John the Baptist:

+ Ὑπ[ὲρ] ἁγήας ἡεραρχί/α[ς] δόξις τὶν ὑπερεσή/αν ενθέος καρποφορείσαν/τος Εὐστρατίου εὐκλεοῦ[ς] / κλησουριάρχου Ζευγους / [και] Κλαδους. αὐτὸν φύλαξον.
                                                                    Ἀμήν

Translation: 'For the glory of the Holy Hierarchy, Eustratios, divinely inspired, offered this service, the famous *Kleisourarch* of Zeugos and Klados. Protect him. Amen.'[7]

The text is therefore an invocation on behalf of a donor, Eustratios the *Kleisourarch*. Literally the commander of a mountain pass, a *Kleisourarch* was, at least from the ninth century, in charge of a frontier area of military administration, the *Kleisoura*.[8] The locations of Zeugos and Klados are unknown, but Thierry suggests Zygos, in Antitaurus, for the former.[9]

Other cavities In the top of the cone containing the chapel an area of rock has fallen away to reveal the remains of a small rectangular cavity. This has a flat ceiling decorated with a relief cross, the lateral and upper arms of which are linked by an arch. This room is now inaccessible. Its entrance seems to be on the east side of the top of the cone, where there is an irregular hole in one of two surviving spurs of rock (to the left in Pl. 168). Below this opening there is a series of depressions that, with imagination, may be reconstructed as steps. Possibly, therefore, there was once a rock-cut stairway on the outside of the cone.

To the east of the cone containing the painted chapel there is a further small chapel (Fig. 34b). This has a small, flat-ceilinged rectangular nave; a single apse has a niche cut in its back wall. To the left of the apse, in the east wall, there is an apsidal niche with its base about 1 metre above the floor. In the adjacent north wall there is a similar, but smaller niche. Entry is through a rectangular opening in the south end of the west wall. The chapel

5 *Ibid.* 248–9; N. Thierry, 'Les enseignements historiques de l'archéologie cappadocienne', *Travaux et Mémoires* 8 (1981), 501–19, at 507.
6 Thierry, 'Les enseignements', 507, offers 'Pour la prière, le salut et la remission des péchés du stylite Nicétas, le sanctuaire étant décoré grace à la piété de l'ascète'. Schiemenz, 'Die Kapelle', 248, gives 'Für das Gelübde und die Erlösung und die Vergebung der Sünden des

Styliten Niketas im Glauben ein Asket auf der Erde'.
7 This differs substantially from the interpretation given by Schiemenz ('Die Kapelle', 249) and seems to be the more plausible.
8 H. Glykatzi-Ahrweiler, 'Recherches sur l'administration de l'empire byzantin au IXe–XIe siècles', *BCH* 84 (1960), 1–111, at 81–2.
9 Thierry, 'Les enseignements', 508.

171. Hermitage of Niketas the Stylite: Chapel, east wall.

appears to have been plastered throughout, but there is no sign of painting.

A large cone opposite the chapel, towards the west (in the foreground of Pl. 168), contains a rough cavity with various pits and ledges (a window to this is visible in Pl. 168), and a rock-cut wine press. On the west side of the cone there is an arched recess, outlined by crudely cut heavy mouldings which may be a blocked entrance (Pl. 168). It is presently inaccessible, being several metres above ground level, but it is clear from the 'erosion line' on the cone that when this recess was cut the ground level was at its base.

Whether all of these structures should be associated with the painted chapel is uncertain. As noted above, the clearing containing the hermitage is in an area of small orchards and vegetable patches, so the rough cavities and the wine press may well be quite recent, made by local farmers.

Discussion

The two inscriptions of the east lunette of the chapel nave refer to a stylite, Niketas, and a military man, Eustratios the *Kleisourarch*. The probable relationship between these two is that Niketas was a hermit, dwelling in Güllü Dere, and Eustratios a patron who paid either for the decoration of the chapel, of for both its decoration and excavation. The chapel inscription refers to Niketas as a stylite, a term used for those ascetics who spent their days on top of columns. There is no column in Güllü Dere, but since the solitary cone forms a natural pillar, the room at the top was very probably the dwelling cave of Niketas. The niche at the side of the cone may have been the place in which pious visitors left their offerings. The humble chapel nearby (Fig. 34b) may have been the hermit's own creation later supplanted by the more elaborate painted chapel, provided by his patron and sited at the foot of his 'column'.

The arcosolium in the chapel narthex was perhaps the stylite's tomb, but he was probably not ready for it when the church was painted. The recess is plastered but not painted and had the commission for decorating the chapel been occasioned by the death of Niketas then a funerary inscription would surely have been placed on the tomb. It seems to have been common practice among ascetics of the volcanic valleys to prepare their own graves, since there is evidence of this at two more sites considered below – the hermitage of the monk Symeon and Karabaş Kilise complex.

Date

The programme and style of the painting in the chapel have no convincing parallels among dated cave-church decorations. Schiemenz suggests that the saint on the east wall of the narthex might be Euthymios the Younger, a stylite who died in 863, which would then be the earliest date for the painting of the church. This is, however, questionable, since the saint may as well be Euthymios the Great, himself a hermit and therefore a reasonable choice for an important position in the programme.[10] Thierry assigns the painting to the late seventh or early eighth century, on the basis of iconographic details, style of ornament and epigraphy. In particular, the prevalence of crosses in the decoration is linked to the development of the cult of the cross in the period from the late sixth century to the early eighth century.[11] The argument is not conclusive, since pictorial celebrations of the cross need not be contemporary with the rise of the cult. Chronological placing on the basis of style of ornament is also tenuous, given the conservatism of this branch of decoration. The title *Kleisourarch* appears at least as early as the late seventh century, but was still current in the late tenth century.[12] The date of the chapel remains uncertain, therefore, but it is possible that it is among the earliest of the Cappadocian cave churches.

Hermitage of the Monk Symeon

In a valley not far from the (now abandoned) rock-cut village of Zelve there is a number of conspicuous solitary cones, many of them topped with the columnar projections known locally as 'fairy chimneys' (Pl. 172). The site is on the right of the modern road as one approaches Zelve. Several small chapels and other cavities are cut into the rock here, some of which were described by Jerphanion and treated as a group; these are as follows.

Chapel of St Symeon the Stylite In the base of a large solitary cone (Fig. 35b & Pl. 172) there is a small chapel which takes its name from a St Symeon cycle in its painted programme.[13] It is single-naved, with a ceiling divided into four compartments by a relief cross bordered by a cornice (Fig. 35a). A single small arched niche is cut into the eastern end of the north wall. A rock-cut bench runs along north, south and east walls. The single apse is slightly raised and has no chancel slabs. It contains a free-standing rock-cut altar and seats at each side, flanking the entrance. A rough secondary window cuts through

172. Hermitage of the Monk Symeon: site.

the right side of the apse to the outside. The naos is reached through a small rectangular narthex with a barrel vault running north/south. Benches run along east and west walls and most of the north wall is taken up by a large arcosolium. The narthex is entered from its south side through a wide archway (Pl. 172a). To the right of the entrance, on the outside of the cone, there is a large arcosolium containing a single grave pit and a recessed cross in its east wall (Fig. 35b, (c), and Pl. 172a). The arch of the arcosolium bears traces of a shallow moulding like that around the narthex entrance, so the two openings are likely to be contemporary. A further cavity, to the right of the arcosolium, is roughly cut and probably secondary. At present, the narthex and chapel floors are higher than the outside ground level and a modern slab

10 *Synaxarium CP*, 405, 7–33.
11 Thierry, 'Les enseignements', 507; *idem*, 'L'église peinte', 452–5.
12 J. Ferluga, 'Le clisure byzantine in Asia Minore', *Byzantium and the Balkans* (Amsterdam, 1976), 74; N. Oikonomedes, *Les listes de préséance byzantines des 9e et 10e siècles* (Paris, 1972), 271.
13 Jerphanion, *Eglises*, I. ii, 552–80.

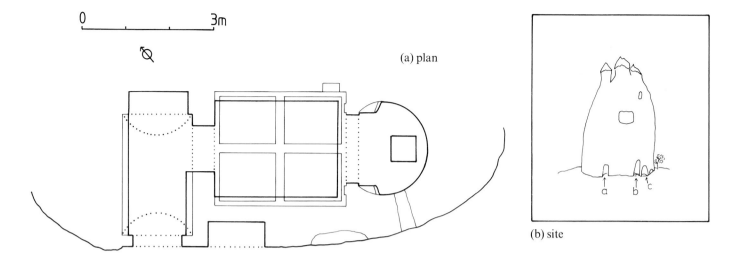

0 _____ 3m

(a) plan

(b) site

35. Chapel of St Symeon

forms a step up to the narthex. The outside ground level has doubtless fallen and was, at the time of excavation, level with the narthex floor. Such a level would put the base of the arcosolium at ground level and its grave pit below ground.

172a. Hermitage of the Monk Symeon: Chapel of St Symeon, entrance.

The chapel is plastered and painted. The painting is now in very poor condition and the following summary of the programme is largely based on Jerphanion's description, since many of the details he noted are no longer legible:

Apse: (conch) Christ enthroned (Prophetic Vision, with Ezekiel and Isaiah); (wall) Virgin and John the Baptist in centre, two groups of Apostles and saints (about 18, including Thomas and Luke); (arch) medallions containing a cross (centre) and busts (flanking).

Nave
Ceiling compartments: Constantine, Helena, Solomon, David.
East wall: (north side) Basil (Pl. 173); (south side) Symeon on his column.
South wall: (west to east) Symeon and his mother, Symeon healing the dragon, Symeon and the woman who swallowed a snake, Symeon and the rope, Vocation of Symeon, Daniel and the lions, Three Hebrews.
West wall: (south to north) Paraskeve, Catherine, Joulitta, (?)(female), Theodota, Barbara, Thekla.
North wall: (west to east) Sozon, Christopher, (?), Leontios, Gregory, (?), Prokopios, (Pl. 173a for the last three), John Chrysostom.
Niche: ornament.

Narthex: unidentified saint (the narthex is plastered but unpainted except for this panel, which is to the right of the nave entrance).

Cell above the Chapel of St Symeon A vertical tunnel with footholds cut into it leads to cavities in the cone above the chapel of St Symeon (see Fig. 35b: the entrance to

173. Hermitage of the Monk Symeon: Chapel of St Symeon, northeast corner.

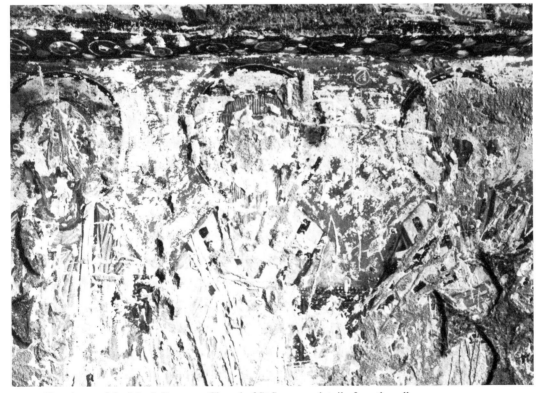

173a. Hermitage of the Monk Symeon: Chapel of St Symeon, detail of north wall.

the tunnel is the opening (a) to the left of the chapel entrance (b)). The first cavity reached is a roughly oval room with a series of benches and niches around its walls.[14] Much of the wall of this cavity is lost, leaving the room open at one side (Pl. 172). The walls of the chamber are decorated with relief crosses and simple pious invocations in red paint.[15] A stairway leads from this cavity to a further small chamber near the top of the cone. This is roughly rectangular, with irregular niches cut into the walls.[16]

Chapel with painted panels A short distance from the Chapel of St Symeon the Stylite, in another solitary cone, there is apparently another small chapel, but I have been unable to find this.[17] The chapel, as recorded by Jerphanion, is single-naved and barrel-vaulted. Each wall has three blind niches. The single apse is closed by low chancel slabs and has a rock-cut altar attached to the back wall and a rock-cut seat to the right. A narthex precedes the nave and has an arcosolium cut into each wall. Painted decoration consists of three panels: Virgin and Child, St George, St Christopher. Jerphanion describes these as being of differing periods and compares the painting of the Virgin and Child panel with that of Kılıçlar side chapel and that of St Christopher and St George with the painting of the Column churches, both probably eleventh-century work.[18]

Tomb chamber Opposite the above chapel is a rough cavity containing rock-cut benches and niches and an arcosolium.[19] On patches of white plaster on the wall there are several red-paint inscriptions of pious slogans and quotations from scripture.

Two of them read:

Κ(ύρι)ε βοήθη τὸν/δοῦλόν σου/Cυμεόν/μοννᾳχόν[20]

Translation: 'Lord help thy servant, Symeon, monk.'

The cavity contains the tomb of Symeon, a large arcosolium with an inscription painted above it. This is a verse epitaph, painted before the death of Symeon, with a gap left for the obituary details which were added by another hand:

[+ βρ] έφος ἐπλάστην ἐν κυλία μητρός μου
μῆνας θ´ τροφῆς οὐκ ἔδον ἤθη
ἐτρεφόμην ἐν ἐκ‖[νά]μᾷ[σ]ε̣[ι] νοτίδος.
ἐξονύστρησα ἐξ ἠδίας μ(ητ)ρ(ό)ς μου
ἴδα το κτίσμα, ἐπέγνοσα τον κτήστην, |
[. .]Δ̣ΟΝ̣‖ ΘΗΝ τε γραφὰς τὰς θεοπνεύστους,
κατενόισα τοὺς πρός με [ἐν]τελμ | ένους
ΙΟΙΛ δὲ ἔλθον Ἄδαμ τοῦ προτοπλᾳστου
ὅτη τέθνηκεν ‖ κὲ πάντες ὑ προφῆτε
ζῶν ηὐτρέπησα τύμβο λελοξευμεν[ον] |
δέξε οὖν, τάφε, κάμε ὅς τὸν [στυ]λ̣[ίτ]ην +

+ Ἀνεπαύσατο ὁ δοῦλο[ς] τοῦ
θ(εο)ῦ Cυμεόν μ(ονα)χ(ὸς) μη(νὶ) Ἰουνίω
θ´ [. . . . .] ἔτ [ους . . .]ϛ´[21]

Translation:

I was formed an infant in my mother's womb.
For nine months ?not consuming normal nourishment,
I was nourished in the flow of liquid.
I ?came out from my own mother
I saw the creation, and recognized the creator
I [?learnt] the divinely-inspired scriptures
? and understood those sent to me
? who came, sons of Adam, the first-created,
that he had died, and all the prophets.
Still living, I prepared an excavated grave;
so, tomb, receive me too, like (my namesake) the Stylite.

The servant of God, Symeon the monk, died on the ninth of June, . . . in the year. . . .[22]

Jerphanion described this cavity as the dwelling cave of Symeon. However, given the choice of a St Symeon the Stylite cycle for the decoration of the chapel, and the reference to the Stylite in the funerary inscription, it seems more probable that Symeon the monk was a stylite who dwelt in the cavities above the chapel. The 'dwelling cave' is therefore a tomb chamber in which Symeon prepared his own grave and wrote his own epitaph.

Date

The very poor condition of the paintings of the Chapel of St Symeon makes stylistic comparison with other painting very difficult indeed. Jerphanion assigned the

---

14 Giovannini, *Arts of Cappadocia*, 91, fig. 40, for a photograph of the room.
15 Jerphanion, *Eglises*, I. ii, 569.
16 *Idem*, *Eglises*, pl. 27, for approximate plans of both chambers.
17 *Idem*, *Eglises* I. ii, 570–80.
18 See above, Chapter 2 for Kılıçlar side chapel and Chapter 4 for the Column churches.
19 Jerphanion, *Eglises*, I. ii, 571–80.

20 Jerphanion, *Eglises*, I. ii, 573, Inscription nos. 105 and 107.
21 *Ibid.* I. ii, 576–7, Inscription no. 111; see also pl. 143.1. The text given here uses Jerphanion's transcription and a reading from photographs by C. Roueché.
22 Many of the readings are uncertain and the sense difficult in some places. See the commentary in Jerphanion, *Eglises*, I. ii, 577–80, incorporating comments by Grégoire and Mariès.

painting to his early tenth-century 'archaic' group.[23] Two points confirm this. First, the decoration of the east wall includes single standing figures in panels to left and right of the apse opening, and chequer-pattern 'spandrels' between the panels and the upper part of the apse arch (the left side of this scheme is visible in Pl. 173). This formula is found also in Ayvalı Kilise in Güllü Dere and in the Church of Holy Apostles, Sinasos, both painted by a single workshop and datable to 913–20 by an inscription in Ayvalı Kilise (see below).[24] Second, the hair of the bishop in the north wall (Pl. 173a) is rendered by using parallel white lines against a dark ground; this formula also occurs in Göreme Chapel 6 and Göreme Chapel 1, both 'archaic' group chapels.[25] The drapery style of the Göreme chapels, using strong white highlights on dark grounds, is also used at the Chapel of St Symeon. An early tenth-century date does, therefore, seem appropriate for the decoration.

Discussion

The site of the chapel of St Symeon and the nearby cavities is very similar to that described for the hermitage of Niketas the Stylite. It is an area of clearings containing vegetable patches and orchards, with a group of conspicuous solitary cones. The arrangement of cavities in the large cone, with a small painted chapel at the base and a cell at the top, is closely paralleled in Güllü Dere. A comparable sequence may therefore be proposed here: the monk Symeon established himself as a stylite in the pillar-like cones of the valley near Zelve. He attracted the attention of a patron who provided the painted chapel. The decoration of the chapel with a St Symeon the Stylite cycle would then reflect the name and habit of the hermit. Since the painting is probably datable to the early tenth century, this is the date for the hermitage. There is no reference to a patron in the surviving programme. The painting is in such poor condition, however, that a dedicatory inscription may have existed and been lost. The chapel may have been the commission of a secular patron or, perhaps, that of a group of followers of Symeon.

The inscription in the tomb chamber (and the burial of the monk there, since the inscription was completed) does, of course, establish that neither the arcosolium of the chapel narthex nor that to the right of the north entrance was the burial place of Symeon. Some other function must therefore be sought for these. The narthex arcosolium may be secondary, but since the wall around

it is unpainted there can be no certainty about this. The other arcosolium, outside the chapel, appears to be original. Possibly, however, its function as a tomb is secondary: it may have begun as a recess (for the reception of gifts, perhaps, as proposed for the exterior niche at the Hermitage of Niketas) and later have been provided with a grave pit. Or, if original, one or both tombs may have been intended for other monks on the site at the time of the excavation of the chapel and its decoration – followers of Symeon, perhaps.

The 'chapel with painted panels' is probably datable to the eleventh century (see above) and was therefore not an original part of the hermitage. It is of interest, however, in that it suggests that the site continued in use well beyond the early tenth-century date of the painting of the Chapel of St Symeon. The secondary arcosolium on the exterior of the cone (and possibly that of the narthex) may perhaps be associated with these later phases.

Karabaş Kilise and its complex

Soğanlı valley, unlike Güllü Dere and Zelve, is a broad, open valley of desolate appearance. Each side is crested by cliffs, below which smooth slopes run down to the valley bottom, interrupted by occasional outcrops of cones. Karabaş Kilise, a painted church, is part of a small complex in one such outcrop.[26]

The church and a series of cavities linked with it lie at the right (roughly east) side of an irregular open space surrounded by rock on three sides (Fig. 36). At the back of this area there is a large rectangular *hall* (1) on a northwest/southeast axis (but for convenience of description the long axis will be called north/south). At present the hall is visible through two rough holes in the west side of its vault (Pl. 174). The floor of the room is about two metres below the outside ground level. The hall has a barrel vault springing from cornices which continue across the end walls. It is divided into three bays by two transverse arches and there are wall arches at each end. Each lunette is decorated with a relief ornament too much crumbled for definition. In the south wall there is a large arched recess and in the north a rectangular opening, now blocked, which appears to be the original entrance to the hall. At the west side of the site there are the remains of an arched *recess* (2), the back of which is filled with rough masonry; presumably there is a cavity behind the blockage. Access to the hall was probably via the arched recess, but neither the current nor the original relationship of

23 Jerphanion, *Eglises*, I. ii, 552–3; II, 414–18.
24 For the east wall of Holy Apostles, see Jerphanion, *Eglises*, pl. 150.2.
25 Jerphanion, *Eglises*, pls. 29–31 for Chapel 6, 39.2 for Chapel 1 (El

Nazar).
26 Jerphanion, *Eglises*, II. 333–60; Restle, *Wall Painting*, Cat. no. XLVIII; Rott, *Denkmäler*, 135–9; Grégoire, 'Rapport', 96.

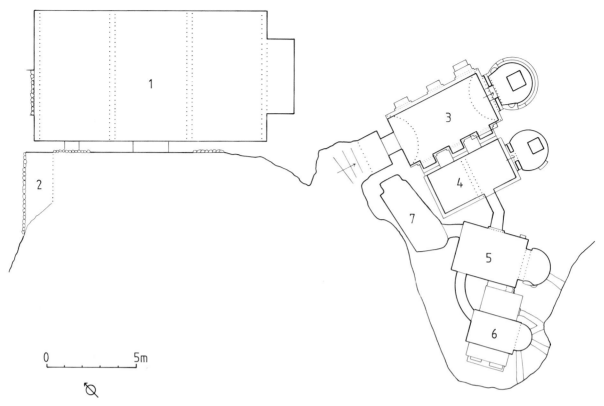

36. Karabaş Kilise and complex: plan.

174. Karabaş Kilise complex: site, with opening to Room 1.

these structures is clear and the masonry blockings make exploration impossible. The issue of sequence of excavation and relationship of structures on the site will be resumed below.

On the east side of the site a rectangular opening in an arched porch is set about two metres above the main ground level (Pl. 175). This is the entrance to *Karabaş Kilise* (3), which is the first of five linked cavities. It is a small, single-naved chapel with a barrel vault springing above a two-stepped cornice. It has a single apse, slightly raised, closed by low chancel slabs. A ledge runs round the apse, meeting a rock-cut seat at each extremity of the apse wall. Above the ledge rises another, smaller ledge which stops short of the lateral seats. There is a free-standing rock-cut altar (Pl. 176).

There are three large blind niches in the north wall of the nave; the easternmost of these has a further niche cut into the upper part of its back wall. The south wall now consists of a three-arched arcade, but this form is the result of secondary excavation. It is evident from details of the painted programme (see below) that the easternmost opening of the arcade was still a niche when the present painted decoration was applied. It is probable that the south wall originally had three niches, like the north wall, and that these were cut through in subsequent phases of excavation. A low bench runs around the nave, in front of the north wall niches and across the east end. The bench originally ran along the south wall also, but has been cut back in front of the niches.

The second cavity, a *side chapel* (4), may be reached through all three south wall openings of Karabaş Kilise. The side chapel is also single-naved and barrel-vaulted, this time with a transverse arch dividing the vault into two bays. It has a single apse with low chancel slabs and a free-standing altar. A bench runs around the walls and into the three openings to Karabaş Kilise. The floor level is about half a metre above that of Karabaş Kilise.

A rough rectangular opening in the south wall of the side chapel leads, up a few steps, to another, still smaller *chapel* (5). This is rectangular, with a flat ceiling and raised apse.

A tunnel from the southwest corner of the chapel (5) leads into an irregular fourth *chamber* (6), which is roughly rectangular, with a flat ceiling. The south wall contains a rectangular recess with further small recesses cut into its back wall at two levels. The north wall has a single large rectangular recess, the back wall of which once contained a small square window to chamber (5). (This was the case until 1980, but by 1982 much of the north wall, including the window, had been knocked away.) Another square window links the east wall of the recess with the outside, via a tunnel. Both these windows

175. Karabaş Kilise: entrance.

176. Karabaş Kilise: east end.

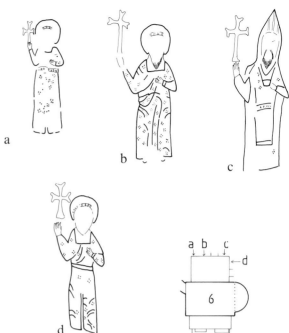

37. Karabaş Kilise: images of monks.

are original: they are framed by recessed borders and painted (see below). The east end is roughly apsidal. Cavity (6) seems to have been a tomb chamber, since four portraits of monks, accompanied by obituary inscriptions, are painted on the wall of the north recess (see below).[27] A further very irregular room (7) lies alongside the west end of the side chapel (4) and is entered from the northwest corner of the third chapel (5).

Painting: in chamber (6), on the walls of the large rectangular recess, there was once a series of four very crudely painted portraits of monks: three on the north wall, one on the east wall (Fig. 37). Two of these are now lost since, as noted above, the area of wall bearing them was recently destroyed. The drawings in Fig. 37 are made from my photographs, taken before the destruction of the

wall, with some details which are now lost supplied by Jerphanion's photographs.[28] Each monk occupies a rectangular panel and is shown standing, holding a splayed-armed cross in his right hand. The background is painted in three broad horizontal bands of strong colour: ochre, green and rust. On the north wall the first monk on the left (Fig. 37a) is inscribed:

Μηνὶ Αὐγούσ/του ἰς τὰς ἐνέ/α ἐτελη/όθιν ὁ/ δοῦλος/τοῦ Θ(εο)ῦ / Φοτις[29]

Translation: 'The servant of God, Photios, died on August 9.'

This monk is smaller than the others, perhaps because he was a juvenile, or perhaps because the rustic artist left too little space at the left side of the wall to paint a figure on the same scale as the others. The next monk, to the right, has an inscription identical except for the month, day and name. This is Bardas, who died on September 10 (Fig. 37b). The panel on the east wall, iconographically identical to these two, commemorates Za(charias?) who died on 3 February (Fig. 37d).[30] These three monks wear ochre habits with square necks and girdles at the waist; the cloth is decorated with a four-dot motif. They also

27 Grégoire, 'Rapport', 98, describes 'trois sarcophages taillés dans le roc. Au-dessus de ces tombeaux, sur le mur, des fresques grossières représentent les défunts.' There is no longer any sign of grave pits in the recess.

28 Jerphanion, *Eglises*, pls. 200.3 and 200.4.

29 *Ibid.* II, 357, Inscription no. 201.

30 *Ibid.* II, 357, Inscription nos. 202–3.

wear dark, bonnet-like headdresses, with the fullness of the bonnet apparently held by a band on the forehead.

The fourth panel, at the right of the north wall of the recess, shows a monk in different dress: he wears a grey/blue *omophorion* over a long rust-coloured tunic and has a striped and pointed hood (Fig. 37c). The inscription next to him reads:

Ἐγο ὁ Βαθύστρο/κος ὁ ἀβᾶς, ὁ πο/λὰ κάμον ἡς τὸ
ναὸν τοῦτον κὲ / με[τ]ὲ ταῦτα ἀπό/θανον, ἔνθα κα/
τάκημε. ἐτελήό/θην μηνή [31]

Translation: 'I, Bathystrokos *Abbas* who worked hard for this church and thereafter died, lie here. I died in the month' (left unfinished – the inscription is not damaged).

Bathystrokos, with his title *abbas* and his costume different from the others, appears to be the senior member of this small group of monks. His obituary inscription is clearly incomplete, since it is without the name of the month and the day.

The palette used for the monk panels is uniform, the figures share the same background and there is no overlap of borders (the 'borders' are simply lines painted on the common background). The panels were not, therefore, painted one at a time, on the death of each monk, but all at the same time. Since the *abbas'* inscription is incomplete, it appears that he survived the others and painted (or had painted) their epitaphs, along with his own. Apparently no one was instructed (or available) to complete the latter when the time for it came. The inscriptions are painted in large, ill-formed letters set in groups separated by vertical rows of two or three dots.

The third chapel (5) is decorated with simple crosses in medallions painted in red on the east wall – two on each side flanking the apse. Jerphanion recorded inscriptions I̅C̅ X̅C̅ NI KA next to them. At the right, the square frame of one of the medallions also contains an inscription, apparently a short homily on the name of Jesus Christ.[32] A panel of crude polychrome painting in the apse is now so deteriorated as to be unreadable, but Jerphanion reported it to contain a female figure (inscribed:

ΑΓΗΑ COФHA) and an inclined male figure to the right with an invocation:

Θ(εο)ς ἐν τὸ ὀνό/ματί σο σõσό/με κὲ ἐν τί δυ/
[ν]αμι σου κρίν/[ον μ]ε / Κ[οσ]μας [33]

Translation: 'God, in your name save me, and in your power judge me. Kosmas.'

The text is based on Psalms 54.1. In this inscription, too, groups of letters are separated by vertical rows of dots. The figure of Kosmas is now lost and Jerphanion does not describe it. Kosmas may have been another monk, or perhaps a patron.

The side chapel (4) has similar simple decoration, including medallions containing crosses on the east wall and an inscription, a homily on the name of Jesus, similar to that in chapel (5).[34]

Karabaş Kilise has two layers of painting on plaster, some of which has fallen away to reveal an earlier layer still. In one such area of loss, on the east face of the west niche of the north wall, there is a fragmentary portrait of a hooded monk. Next to the figure is an inscription:

Κ(ύρι)ε βοί[θι] / τὸν δοῦ/λόν σου / Ῥουστια/κόν [35]

Translation: 'Lord help thy servant, Roustiakos.'

The portrait of the monk, which is very crude, survives only as a silhouette. It is not of the same strong colours as the monk panels in chamber (6), and the lettering of the inscription is of a different type and without the vertical-dot separators.

The first layer of painting on plaster is also visible in places where the second (top) layer is thin or damaged. This first layer included a barrel-vault decoration of narrative scenes in four registers. Nothing of the scenes can be made out, but the lines separating the registers are visible. Parts of a Prophetic Vision may be seen in the apse: the face of Christ and the sun and the moon in medallions. Fragments of this layer are visible on the walls, but none large enough for identification of subjects.

The top layer of painting is a polychrome decoration of fairly high quality which covers the whole interior.[36]

---

31 *Ibid.* 11, 356, Inscription no. 200.
32 *Ibid.* 11, 352–5, Inscription no. 198.
33 *Ibid.* 11, 355, Inscription no. 199.
34 *Ibid.* 11, 351–2, Inscription no. 197.
35 *Ibid.* 11, 338, Inscription no. 192.
36 An apparent colour difference between vault and walls led Restle to suppose that the vault painting belonged to a phase separate from that of the walls (*Wall Painting*, 1, 161–2). He notes four phases: (1) Prophetic Vision (apse) and vault registers; (2) repainting of vault and apse; (3) repainting of niches; (4) a layer of green paint 'covering not only the grey background and the picture inscriptions, but also parts of the figures in layer 2'. I do not accept this analysis: layer 4 is probably underpainting showing through, and 2 and 3 are the same phase. Jerphanion attributed the difference in tone between

vault and walls to the flaking of the paint of the second layer, leaving lighter patches showing through and brightening the whole field (*Eglises*, 11, 335); this does appear to be the case. Another contributing factor may be that the walls were thickly plastered before painting, whereas the vault was not, so differences of ground may account for the differences of tone. Uniformity of the top layer of painting may be demonstrated by comparing figures in the various parts of the church: for example, the draperies of Adam in the Anastasis in the vault and those of the first apostle to the left in the Divine Liturgy in the apse are virtually identical; the same applies to the figure of the Virgin of the Annunciation on the east wall and the Virgin in the Presentation in the vault (for illustrations, see Jerphanion, *Eglises*, pls. 199.2, 197.2, 196.2, 198.2).

A full description of the programme of this second phase of painting is provided by Jerphanion. Briefly, it is as follows:

Main apse
Conch: Divine Liturgy.
Wall: (in the centre) a Deesis (Virgin, Christ, John the Baptist); flanking this, groups of bishop saints – (to the left) Epiphanios, Blaisios, Eleutherios, Gregory the Theologian, Basil; (to the right) John Chrysostom, Kornoutos, Modestos, Athenogenes.

Nave
East wall: (flanking the apse) Annunciation.
Vault: (south side) Nativity, Presentation; (west lunette) Transfiguration; (north side) Crucifixion, Myrophores, Anastasis.
On the other walls there are figures of saints and donors:
South wall: (east to west) Anna; (east niche) bishop saint, donor (Skepides); (wall between niches) George; (centre niche) Pegasios, Akindynos, Aphthonios, Elpidiphoros; (wall) Demetrios; (west niche) Anempodistos, Menas, Vikentios.
West wall: (flanking the door) two orant female saints.
North wall: Merkourios; (west niche) donor (Catherine), St Catherine with two donors (Eirene and Maria), Lauros, Phloros, donor (unidentified male); (wall) Prokopios; (centre niche) Panteleemon, Archangel Michael with two donors (Eudokia and Nyphon), Kyriakos, Kosmas, Damianos; (wall) Theodoros; (east niche) Mardarios, donor (Basileios), Virgin and Child, Orestios, Sergios, Bakchos, Eugenios, Eustratios, Auxentios.

The selection of saints thus includes a series of military saints (placed on the nave walls) and a series of martyr groups (in the niches).

On the cornice of the west wall there is a dedicatory inscription:

+ Ἐκαλιεργήθι ὁ ναὸς οὗτος δηὰ συνδρομῖς Μιχαὴλ πρωτοσπαθαρίου τοῦ Σκεπιδι κὲ Ἐκατερίνις μοναχ(ῆς) κε Νυφονος (μον)αχ(οῦ), ἐπὶ βασιλέος Κων/σταντίνου τοῦ Δοῦκα ἔτος ͵ϛφξθ' ἠνδικτήονος ιδ'. ὑ ἀναγηνόσκωντες εὔχεσθε αὐτους δηὰ τω Κ(ύριο)ν . Ἀμήν.[37]

Translation: 'This church was decorated at the expense of Michael Skepides, *Protospatharios*, and Catherine,

nun, and Nyphon, monk, in the reign of Constantine Ducas, year 6569, indiction 14. You who read (this), pray for them, through the Lord. Amen.'

Three donors were therefore responsible for the redecoration of the church, in 6569 (1060/61). The paint layer bearing the inscription is that of the rest of the programme just described and the inscription is in the same lettering as other inscriptions in that programme, so this layer of painting is securely dated.

Donor images
East arch, south wall: a male figure without halo; to the right of the head and shoulders the inscription:

Δέησις / τοῦ [δού/λου τοῦ θ(εο)ῦ / ᾱσ]παθαρίου / τοῦ Σκεπ/ίδη.[38]

Translation: 'Entreaty of (the servant of God) [*Proto*]-*spatharios* Skepides.'

This is almost certainly the Michael Skepides of the west wall inscription. He is dressed in a long robe with a coat open at the front and slightly shorter than the robe (Fig. 38f). Robe and coat are decorated with elaborate patterns: the robe with stripes of ornament and the coat with medallions containing animals and birds. He carries a long sword with ornamental scabbard, presumably attached to a belt at the waist, since the hand does not grasp the pommel. The left hand gestures towards the left; the right hand and arm are lost, but must be making a similar gesture, since if held across the body or at the side, they would be visible. (This attitude of the figure establishes that the archway he occupies was once a niche; he is gesturing towards a figure or group originally painted on the back wall of the niche.) The head is fairly well preserved and shows a mature man with short black beard, wearing a turban.

West niche, north wall: on the back wall of the niche there was once a large figure of St Catherine, with two small, richly clad figures flanking her. A recess has been dug into this wall and destroyed most of the panel, (Fig. 38b). Jerphanion saw the painting in a better condition and records that the lateral figures were without haloes, bowing towards Catherine and inscribed 'Eirene' and 'Maria'.[39] On the west face of the niche there is a female figure, without a halo (Fig. 38a), wearing a long yellow robe with a dark grey-blue mantle, and a stole or scarf falling in front, with a decorated end. Her hands, at chest level, gesture towards the saint on the back wall of the niche, and her head is swathed in a loosely folded

---

37 Jerphanion, *Eglises*, II, 334, Inscription no, 186.
38 *Ibid.* II, 336, Inscription no. 187.
39 *Ibid.* II, 337–8.

38. Karabaş Kilise: images of donors.

headdress; her sleeves (or cuffs) are grey. Above and to the left of her head is an inscription:

Δέησις τῆς δούλις / τοῦ θ(εο)ῦ / Ἐκατε/ρίνας / μονα/χῆς⁴⁰

Translation: 'Entreaty of the servant of God, Catherine the nun.'

On the east face of the niche there is a male figure (Fig. 38c) without a halo, wearing a long red robe and long open coat of grey-blue with an elegant, stylized foliage pattern in darker blue on it; the cuffs are red; in his right hand he holds a long spear and there is a sword at his waist. The face is lost, but the top of a large turban survives, decorated with 'kufic' ornament. The inscription is lost except for Δέισις. The figure is similar to that of Michael Skepides in the south wall arch, but is not making a gesture of supplication.

Centre niche, north wall: on the back wall the Archangel Michael is flanked by kneeling donors (Fig. 38d). To the left, a woman in a white folded-cloth headdress, kneels with both hands outstretched towards the Angel's feet. The painting is badly damaged, but the costume appears to be of brocade, with ornament on the sleeves. Most of the face is gone, but the right ear and an area of yellow hair above it remain. Above the head an invocation reads:

Δέισις τῇ δού/λις τοῦ θ(εο)ῦ Εὐ/δοκίας⁴¹

Translation: 'Entreaty of the servant of God, Eudokia.'

The figure to the right is that of an elderly man with white hair and beard and a cloth headdress. The face of this figure, and that of Eudokia, are lost, but both appear in Jerphanion's drawing and were presumably intact when he saw them.⁴² The elderly man wears a brown robe with yellow sleeves. He leans forward from his kneeling position and grasps the Angel's left foot. Above him is the inscription:

Δέισις τοῦ δού/λου τοῦ θ(εο)ῦ Νυνφο/νος μοναχοῦ⁴³

Translation: 'Entreaty of the servant of God, Nyphon the monk.'

East niche of north wall: on the west side of the niche-within-the-niche is a youthful figure, beardless, with brown curly hair. He wears a long tunic with a decorated stole in front (Fig. 38e). He gestures towards the Virgin and Child in the back of the niche. An inscription reads:

Δέισις τοῦ δούλου /τοῦ θ(εο)ῦ Βασιλίου / πρ(εσβυτέρου)⁴⁴

Translation: 'Entreaty of the servant of God, Basileios, priest.'

Discussion

The donor images may be summarized as follows:
    South arch: (Michael) Skepides, (*Proto*)*spatharios.*
    North wall: (west niche) Catherine the nun, unidentified male, Eirene and Maria; (centre niche) Eudokia and Nyphon; (east niche) Basileios the priest.
Jerphanion assumed the man opposite Catherine to be Michael Skepides, and the Skepides of the south arch to be another relative. However, it would seem that the important position given to the south arch figure (facing the apse, in a niche to himself with, originally, a divine figure on the back wall to receive his supplication) identifies him as the person named in the dedicatory inscription.

Three of the donor portraits, therefore, each one in a different niche, represent those named in the west wall inscription: Michael Skepides, Catherine and Nyphon. Jerphanion suggests that, since the Archangel Michael and St Catherine are depicted with donors, Michael Skepides and Catherine the nun are husband and wife, and the other donors are their children. The assumption is that Catherine retired to monastic life while her husband remained in the world, and that two of their children, Nyphon and Eudokia, did likewise. The range of ages discernible among the male figures argues against this, however. Nyphon appears to be elderly, with white hair and beard, while Skepides and the other man are merely mature, with black hair and beards. It is improbable that if Nyphon were a child of Michael and Catherine he would be represented as an elderly man while they appear much younger.

An alternative to this interpretation is that the two niches of the north wall represent immediate family groups: Catherine, her husband (the unidentified male) and their children (Maria and Eirene), who are all in the west niche, and Nyphon and his wife Eudokia in the centre niche. Since Nyphon is the only elderly figure in the church, he and Eudokia are probably the parents of Michael, Catherine and perhaps also of Basileios the priest. (The portrait of Eudokia does not show an elderly woman, but age does not apparently wither Byzantine ladies, as is evident from the youthful portrait of the elderly empress Zoe in St Sophia in Constantinople.)⁴⁵ In this hypothetical scheme the parents, Nyphon and Eudokia, have a niche to themselves, and there is a niche

40 *Ibid.* II, 338, Inscription no. 190.
41 *Ibid.* II, 339, Inscription no. 193.
42 *Ibid.* pl. 202.3.
43 *Ibid.* II, 339, Inscription no. 194.
44 *Ibid.* II, 340, Inscription no. 195.
45 T. Whittemore, *The Mosaics of Haghia Sophia at Istanbul. Third Preliminary Report* (Boston/Oxford, 1942), 14–17, pls. 13–15.

for each of the three children: Michael, Catherine and Basileios; Catherine has in her niche her own immediate family: husband and children.

The purpose behind the donation is not explicit. Nyphon, although described as *monachos*, appears to wear elaborate secular costume, rather than monastic dress, and if Eudokia is his wife then he cannot have been a lifetime contemplative. The same applies to Catherine, with husband and children. Doubtless, therefore, these two adopted their monastic titles in retirement or on their deathbeds.[46] Had any members of the family been buried in the church, however, one would expect them to be provided with graves in arcosolia, in the usual fashion of rock-cut Cappadocia. Also, the inscriptions are not funerary. In the event of Catherine and Nyphon being alive, but in retirement, it is hardly to be supposed that they retired to the tiny, dark caves to the south of Karabaş Kilise, nor to any other part of the site. It is probable, therefore, that the Skepides family had a symbolic, rather than direct, connection with the site. They perhaps painted the chapel to mark the occasion of the retirement to monastic life (or the death) of two members of the family.

The next problem is the nature of the establishment thus patronized and its previous history, for which it is necessary to consider the phases of both excavation and decoration. The first layer of painting on plaster in Karabaş Kilise may be attributed to the first quarter of the tenth century, since its programme, with a Prophetic Vision in the apse and a vault decoration in registers, follows the scheme employed in 'archaic' group chapels.[47] The Skepides programme is dated 1060/61. Thus the Skepides family were latecomers to an establishment already over a century old. The painting of the monk Roustiakos is earlier than both of these phases, since it underlies them. The other paintings (the monk panels in chamber (6) and the Kosmas panel in the third chapel (5)) seem to belong to a single phase. Their inscriptions are all in the same large, ill-formed script, with groups of letters separated by vertical lines of dots. This is true also of the theological inscriptions in cavities (4) and (5). There are, therefore, four phases of painting: Roustiakos, the 'archaic' layer, the Skepides layer (in that order) and the 'rustic' phase of uncertain place in the sequence.

The crude portrait of Roustiakos the monk is clearly not part of a formal programme of decoration. It belongs with the 'masons'' decorations found in many cave churches below polychrome layers, and may indeed have been a pious gesture on the part of one of those engaged in the work of excavation. The 'archaic' layer was, therefore, the first formal decoration and was probably executed shortly after the chapel was cut.

The excavation of the complex also took place in phases. The only access to cavities (3)–(7) is through the entrance to Karabaş Kilise (3). The sequence of excavation for these cavities must therefore have been 3, 4, 5, 6, 7 (or possibly 7, 6, but since 7 is a very rough cavity it is likely to be the last addition and perhaps very recent). The cavities were not excavated in a single operation, however. It is evident from the gesture of Michael Skepides in the eastern arch of the south wall that this arch was originally a niche and was intact at the time of the painting of the Skepides programme. Further, the side chapel (4) has a floor level higher than that of Karabaş Kilise. This is not easily accounted for if Karabaş Kilise and the side chapel were cut at the same time. The difference of level may explained, however, as the result of a later phase of excavation which cut through the niches of the south wall of Karabaş Kilise. It is evident, therefore, that Karabaş Kilise existed as a solitary church for some time before the other cavities were cut. Very possibly the 'archaic' decoration was undertaken while the chapel was in its original, intact form.

Cavity (5) is now a chapel and cavity (6) a tomb chamber. They do not, however, have the regular lines of Karabaş Kilise and the side chapel and may have begun with different functions. It may be significant that the recesses which probably formed the tombs of the monks are not arcosolia, the ubiquitous form for tomb cavities in the rock-cut monuments. Further, cavity (6) contains two carefully cut windows, one to cavity (5) and another to the outside, both clearly original since they are framed with recesses and painted decoration. Windows are hardly a necessity in a sepulchre, so perhaps (5) and (6) were originally dwelling caves, wherein windows would suit the needs of the living better than those of the dead. Later, (6) was turned into a tomb chamber and (5) into a chapel.

It is probably impossible to establish at what point cavities (5) and (6) were added to the complex. They are much more crudely cut than the side chapel (4) and so may belong to a later phase still. Alternatively, the drop in quality of excavation may reflect the lesser importance of cavities (5) and (6). Thus possibly the whole series of cavities (4)–(6) belong to a single phase and represent the activity of the *abbas* Bathystrokos and his group, or that of Kosmas were he a patron.

46 Among documented examples of people adopting such a procedure one of the best known, of about this period, is the wife of Eustathios Boilas: S. Vryonis, 'The Will of a Provincial Magistrate, Eustathius Boilas (1059)', *DOP* 11 (1957), 263–77, at 265.

47 Jerphanion, *Eglises*, 1. i, ch. 3, 67–94; 11, 414–18.

It is certain that by the time the Skepides family re-decorated Karabaş Kilise the side chapel, at least, had been excavated, since two of the niches of Karabaş Kilise had been cut through: the lower border of the Skepides' layer of painting follows the line of the steps up to the side chapel. Since the years in which the monks of cavity (6) died are not recorded in their obituary inscriptions it is impossible to know certainly whether the 'rustic' phase preceded or followed the Skepides decoration. It would seem likely, however, that it preceded it, since Michael Skepides and his family must have had a reason for choosing to redecorate a small chapel at least a century old, and the continued occupation of the site by monks might be such a reason.

Next comes the problem of the relationship between this group of cavities and the hall (1). It seems reasonable to conclude that this was not excavated at the same time as Karabaş Kilise. It is at a much lower level than the church and had they been planned together, as a small complex, then a site would have been chosen upon which the two structures could have been more harmoniously grouped. (The two-level arrangement is virtually diagnostic of excavation in stages. It is obvious that in order to make a large room with a high ceiling or vault, the entrance must be cut well down in the cone mass; conversely, the entrance to a small church may be quite near the top of the mass. If it is decided to cut a room next to an existing chapel which is close to the top of the rock containing it, then the room must be cut below the church so that there is sufficient depth of rock to accommodate it.) The difference in level between room and church is therefore evidence that it was excavated after Karabaş Kilise. It was probably an addition undertaken as the importance of the site grew. It is probable, indeed, that the hall belongs with the Skepides phase, since it resembles rooms found in courtyard monasteries and is therefore consistent with the eleventh-century date provided by the painting.

One secure element of the sequence is that cavities (5) and (6) must have been cut after Karabaş Kilise and the side chapel because they are accessible only through these. Cavities (5) and (6) cannot, therefore, have been the dwelling cave of a hermit for whom a patron commissioned a rock-cut church. If Karabaş Kilise were excavated on the site of a hermitage, following the pattern proposed for the Hermitages of Niketas the Stylite and Symeon the monk, then the hermit lived nearby, not in caves (5) and (6). The presence of a monk at the beginning of the sequence, when Karabaş Kilise was intact, is established by the crude portrait of the monk Roustiakos. Possibly, indeed, he was the original anchorite. Closer examination of the site may reveal a dwelling cave, but

this may well have been destroyed when the hall was excavated.

At least a century lies between the tenth-century 'archaic' decoration and the Skepides decoration of 1060/61. Several generations of monks must therefore be conjectured were the site continuously inhabited. There may, of course, have been a break in continuity and subsequent re-occupation of the site by monks before the arrival of Skepides. Such, perhaps is the implication of the uncompleted obituary inscription of *abbas* Bathystrokos.

The following possible sequence may be offered:

I. A hermitage (of the monk Roustiakos?) consisting of a dwelling cave in the vicinity of the present complex.

II. Excavation of Karabaş Kilise and its decoration with the 'archaic' layer of painting, probably in the first quarter of the tenth century. The rustic portrait of Roustiakos was probably painted on the north wall when the church was finished, shortly before the polychrome decoration.

III. Excavation of the side chapel, beginning by cutting through two niches of the south wall of Karabaş Kilise.

IV. The excavation of cavities (5), (6) (and perhaps 7). Cavities (5) and (6) may have been dwelling caves. (This may have been a separate phase or part of Phase III.) Pious inscriptions and simple decoration were added to cavities (4)–(6), including the portrait of Kosmas who may have been a patron.

V. Conversion of cavity (6) into a tomb chamber and the painting of the funerary portraits of *abbas* Bathystrokos and three monks.

VI. Redecoration of Karabaş Kilise in 1060/61 by the Skepides family.

VII. Excavation of the hall (probably part of Phase VI).

Obscurities concerning details of this sequence remain, but it seems certain that Karabaş Kilise complex developed upon the site of a hermitage. This endured for at least a century and a half, and attracted at least two acts of patronage, which supplied the tenth-century 'archaic' painting and the eleventh-century redecoration. There may have been a third, less important, patron, in the person of Kosmas in cavity (5). Michael Skepides probably redecorated the church of the small colony to mark the retirement to monastic life of members of his family, choosing the site because it was occupied by monks who might have been entrusted to undertake prayers and services for the family.

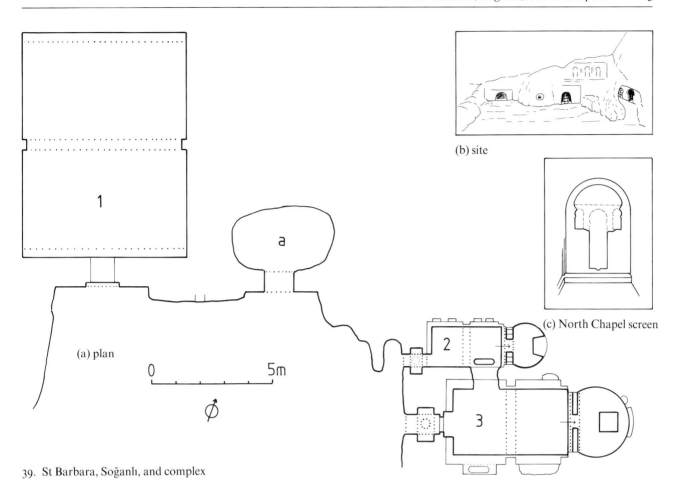

(b) site

(c) North Chapel screen

(a) plan

0   5m

39. St Barbara, Soğanlı, and complex

St Barbara in Soğanlı and its complex

Another site in Soğanlı valley is of interest in the present context because, as at Karabaş Kilise, there is evidence of the development of a small complex around a single original church. The church in question is the Church of St Barbara, which is dated by inscription to 1006 or 1021.[48]

The arrangement of cavities on the site (Fig. 39a) resembles that at Karabaş Kilise complex. An open area in front of the church has been enlarged to form a rough courtyard by cutting back the rock to the north and west. The south side is open and the east side follows the irregular contour of the rock (Fig. 39b). The west wall of the courtyard is plain, but faint traces of blind arcading remain on the upper right part of the north wall.

Two arched openings pierce the north wall. The opening to the right leads into a small, roughly cut *cavity* (a). The other opening, to the left, to a large rectangular *hall* (1). This has a barrel vault springing from cornices and divided into two bays by a transverse arch which meets wall pilasters. Wall arches frame lunettes at each end of the vault.

As at Karabaş Kilise complex, the ground level of the hall is considerably lower than the present ground level outside: the semicircular opening through which the room is visible is a window. The entrance to the room must be below this window, and is now buried: it must have been blocked before the courtyard became filled with debris. Between the two arched openings of the north

48 Jerphanion, *Eglises*, II, 307–32; Restle, *Wall Painting*, Cat. no. XLVI; J. Lafontaine-Dosogne, 'Nouvelles notes cappadociennes', *Byzantion* 33 (1963), 121–83 at 133–4; Rott, *Denkmäler*, 145–8.

177. St Barbara, Soğanlı: entrance to Church and side chapel.

façade there is a further small opening, now blocked and surrounded by whitewash. This appears to be a secondary feature, doubtless associated with a pigeon-house phase of the complex.

A small area of the irregular east side of the courtyard is cut back to form a smooth façade housing two arched entrances (Pl.177). These open into two small single-naved chapels (2 and 3); the painted *Church of St Barbara* is the southernmost of these (3). The church has a barrel vault which springs above a heavy square cornice. The vault is divided into two by a median transverse arch which meets pilasters on the wall to divide the nave into two bays. A rock-cut bench circuits the nave; just above it, in the west bay of the south wall, there is a small arcosolium. The only other primary recess in the nave is a small arched niche, set into the north wall of the east bay, about one metre above the bench. The single apse was once closed by low chancel slabs, only fragments of which survive, and has a free-standing rock-cut altar. At the back of the apse a wide blind niche is set into the wall above the altar; to the north of it there is a narrower, apsidal niche. The church is entered by a rectangular opening in its west wall, through a small free-cross narthex which has a tiny dome; the arched entrance from outside opens to the west wall of the narthex.

The *north chapel* (2) resembles St Barbara, but is smaller. It, too, is barrel-vaulted and is divided into two bays by a transverse arch and pilasters. Its north wall is decorated with narrow, tall keyhole-shaped blind niches, two in each bay. The north pilaster has two similar niches, placed vertically. A bench runs along west, north and east sides of the chapel only. The apse, with attached altar, was once closed by a tall screen. This had an arched central entrance, with small keyhole-shaped openings flanking it and an open lunette above. The lower part of

the entrance and the outer sides of the small lateral openings are all that remains of the screen (Fig. 39c shows a reconstruction). Like the Church of St Barbara, the north chapel has a small, domed free-cross narthex, the entrance to which is now blocked by rough masonry. The two chapels are linked through a rough opening that runs from the east bay of the north chapel to the west bay of St Barbara, where it destroys an area of painting.

A grave is cut into the floor of the north chapel, at the south side of the east bay, just before the opening to the south chapel. The grave is lined with plaster upon which was once a simple funerary inscription in red paint, recorded by Jerphanion: '(Here) lies the servant of God, . . .?, daughter of . . .?'[49] A woman was, apparently, buried here, but the interment is likely to be a later event, not associated with the excavation of the chapel, since a primary grave pit would probably have been placed in an arcosolium let into the wall.

Painting The north chapel is undecorated, but the Church of St Barbara has a full polychrome decoration. This was fully described by Jerphanion, and may be summarized as follows:

Apse
Conch: Christ enthroned with Evangelist symbols, Adam and Eve.
Wall: four Evangelists, in medallions, two each side of the apse niches; below them, a row of Church Fathers in three groups of four – (left) four, unidentifiable; (centre) Kornoutos, Athenogenes, Leontios, Basil; (right) John Chrysostom, Blaisios, Nikolaos and Theophylaktos.
North niche: Daniel the Stylite, on his column, flanked

49 Jerphanion, *Eglises*, II, 308, Inscription no. 181.

by John Kalibites and another; above the niche, Symeon the Stylite.

Centre niche: a hexapterygos, tetramorph and two pairs of flaming wheels (elements of the Prophetic Vision related to the conch scene above).

Arch: prophets in medallions (Elias, David, Solomon, Isaiah).

Piers: deacons – (north) Stephanos; (south) Romanos.

Chancel slabs: (east faces) half-figure angels in imperial dress; (inner faces) unidentifiable figures of saints.

Altar: (east face) Christ Pantocrator.

Nave

Barrel vault: Annunciation, Visitation, Proof of the Virgin, Reproaches of Joseph; (lunette) Journey to Bethlehem, Nativity, Anastasis.

Transverse arch: the Seven Sleepers of Ephesos (busts in rectangular frames – surviving names: Martinos, Diomedes, Iamblichos).

Crest of vault: medallions – (east) Daniel, Ezekiel, Jeremiah; (west) three, unidentifiable.

East wall: (right of apse) St Barbara.

South wall: (east bay) Deesis (most of this has been destroyed by the excavation of a secondary arcosolium); (south pilaster) Theodota (west face), George (south), Theodoros (east) (Pl. 178); (west bay) military saint, Eustathios and two sons, Theopiste, Christopher (Pl. 179).

West wall: George (equestrian), Paraskeve, Catherine, Anastasia.

North wall: (west bay) Panteleemon, Hermolaos, Niketas, Theodoros, Merkourios; (north pilaster) Leontios (east face), Prokopios (north), Theodota, (west); (east bay) Constantine and Helena; (niche) Sabas on the back wall, Kosmas and Damianos on the side walls, Mandylion below.

178. St Barbara: military saints.

179. St Barbara: St Theopiste and St Christopher.

Narthex
North arm: Viktor, Vikentios, Menas, military saint.
South arm: Andronikos, Probos, Tarachos, military saint.
West arm: Nikephoros, Elpidiphoros.
East arm: (vault) angels; (lunette) Virgin and Child.

On the west wall, above the church entrance, there is a dedicatory inscription the right side of which is now much deteriorated. Recorded by Jerphanion, it reads:

+ | 'Εκαλιεργ]ίθ̣ι [ὁ ναὸς οὖτ]ος [τῆς] ἁγίας
Βα[ρβ]άρας . 'Επὴ βασηλήας Κω[στα]ντήνου (καὶ)
[Β]ασ[ι]λείου / ἔ[τ]ους ἐξακας φ[. . κ]ὲ ἠδι[κ]τήονος δ΄ κὲ
μη(νὶ) Μαήου . 'Ης ⟨ἧς⟩ τὰς ε΄, δηὰ συνδρόμης
Βασηλείου διο/μεστι[κ]οῦ κ(αὶ) ἐπὺ ΘΥ [. . . ύ]
ἀναγηνόσκοντες εὔχεστε ὑπὲρ αὐτ[ὸ] δι[α] τὸν Κ(ύριο)ν. [50]

Translation: 'This Church of St Barbara was (decorated) in the reign of the emperors Constantine and Basil, in the year 65 . ., indiction 4, in the month of May, the 5th day, by donation of Basileios the *Domestikos* and in charge of ? You who read (this), pray for him through the Lord.'

The date '65 . .' gives outer limits of 6500 to 6599 (992–1091 in the month of May). Basil II and Constantine VIII reigned 976–1025 and the only fourth indictions in the period 992–1025 were 1006 and 1021. The church painting is therefore datable to one of those years. The inscription is unquestionably part of the painted programme: it is on the same (and only) paint layer, and is in the same script as the inscriptions which identify saints and narrative scenes.

Discussion

In spite of some architectural similarity between the two chapels, it is clear that they are not part of a single phase. The two have quite different sanctuary barriers (St Barbara has low slabs, the north chapel a tall screen) and the shallow pilasters and transverse arch of the north chapel do not resemble the heavy forms in St Barbara. Further, as noted above, the link between the two naves is a rough secondary opening which damages an area of painting in the church of St Barbara.

Several points suggest that the north chapel was a secondary addition. First, the chapel is asymmetrical: it has no ledge running along its south side and there is no south pilaster to meet the transverse arch of the vault.

The narthex is not centrally placed in the west wall, but is at the south side. This asymmetry may be explained as resulting from an error of judgement were the side chapel cut as an addition to the Church of St Barbara. Thus, the core of the new chapel was dug, the north wall was finished first and it was then discovered that the area of rock left between the two chapels was not thick enough to complete a symmetrical structure. The south wall was therefore smoothed off and left without ledge or pilaster and the narthex placed to one side. The exterior confirms that the two chapels are not contemporaneous: the rock surrounding each entrance is cut back to make a smooth façade, but the area around the north chapel entrance is cut with a rougher finish than that around the entrance to the Church of St Barbara.

The floor of the courtyard must originally have been at least two metres below its present level, to allow for an entrance to the hall, and yet the entrances to the chapels are slightly higher than the window in the north façade (Fig. 39b). If the whole courtyard once had the floor level of the hall, then the chapels must have been approached by a steep ramp or a stairway. Possibly there was never a level courtyard floor and the original lines of the hillside were not altered in front of the chapels. The arrangement is very similar to that at Karabaş Kilise complex, described above, and again, the two-level arrangement implies more than one phase of excavation, with the hall excavated later than the church.

The hall resembles many of the rooms in the monastery complexes examined above, for which an eleventh-century date has been proposed, and the shallow blind niches just visible on the façade are also familiar from many of the courtyard monasteries. Similar niches in the north chapel suggest that it belongs with the hall-and-courtyard development, and its tall screen is consistent with the mid to late eleventh-century date.[51]

As noted above, the Church of St Barbara is dated by its inscription to the first quarter of the eleventh century. Probably, therefore, it originally existed alone, and later in the century the site was elaborated by the addition of the courtyard, the hall and the north chapel.

The patron of the church, Basileios, has the title *Domestikos* κ(αι) ἐπὶ θε . . . . The letter following Θ has been recorded as C (and therefore possibly E) and as Y, and the end of the title reconstructed as ἐπὶ θε[μάτων] and ἐπὶ θυ[ρῶν].[52] The first of these gives Basileios a military office and the second makes him a minor cleric of St Sophia, Constantinople, or perhaps of some other

---

50 *Ibid.* II, 309, Inscription no. 182.
51 Epstein, 'Rock-cut Chapels', 121, figs. 6–8.
52 C or E: Grégoire, 'Rapport', 103; Y: Pridik (cited by Jerphanion),

Eglises, II, 310. Grégoire (106) also suggests
ἐπὺ θ[εμάτος Χαρσιανοῦ], but the inscription offers no basis for this.

church. There appears to be no recorded example of the title ending in ἐπὶ θυρῶν , which is Jerphanion's conjecture only, whereas there are precedents for ἐπὶ θεμάτων.[53] Jerphanion favoured the identification of Basileios as a minor cleric on the grounds that a *Domestikos* of the military variety would be a person of too great importance to permit the orthographic errors present in the inscription. In fact, by the eleventh century, '*Domestikos* of the theme' was not a particularly elevated title, and the possibility that a patron of any rank might have had to accept the local epigraphical standard is surely to be considered. Indeed, in the eleventh century, with the eastern borders of the empire threatened, a military officer is perhaps just as likely to be in the area as someone holding a minor clerical office. The predominance of military saints in the programme would also seem more appropriate to a soldier than a cleric.

The chapel may, therefore, have been commissioned as a pious gesture on the part of a military man, perhaps a visitor stationed for a while in the region. It seems, however, that the church also had another function. It contains a single arcosolium in the west bay of the south wall. This was once fully painted, but most of the paint is lost. Very possibly images or inscriptions giving more details of the burial were on the back wall. The painted border survives, however, and this is uniform with other decorated borders in the church (of the St Sabas niche, for example). The church has only one layer of painting, and since this acknowledges the arcosolium, it is probable that excavation and painting of the church constitute a single phase, and that the excavation and decoration of the arcosolium were part of Basileios' commission. The grave pit in the arcosolium is very small, not large enough for an adult. Thus it seems that provision for the burial of a child was one of Basileios' motives for commissioning the church.

Several features of the painted programme endorse this. To the left of the grave, in the east bay of the south wall, is the large Deesis panel, appropriate to a funerary context. (There may have been a donor image or further inscription here, but the lower part of the panel has been destroyed by secondary excavation.) Next, the Seven Sleepers of Ephesos, shown on the transverse arch, are not depicted in any other Cappadocian cave church. They cannot, therefore, be dismissed as a standard element in church decoration, but were specially chosen for this programme. The Seven are, in most sources, seven youths, and are therefore appropriate in a funerary programme

for a child.[54] The most important clue, however, is the narrative cycle of the vault. The selection of scenes appears eccentric, since it includes five episodes of an Infancy cycle and then just one more scene, the Anastasis. This combination becomes rational if the chapel is interpreted as a funerary monument for an infant.

The rest of the programme consists of bishops, military saints, martyrs, female saints and monk saints. The placing of bishops and deacons in the sanctuary is conventional, and most of the martyrs and female saints probably had a personal significance for the donor which cannot be determined. The military saints, as noted above, may reflect Basileios' occupation.

The inclusion of monk saints may also be significant, for they are given special prominence. St Sabas occupies the niche in the north wall of the nave and there are two stylites, Daniel and Symeon, in a niche in the apse. At this point it is necessary to return to consideration of the site as a whole. It was proposed above that the church of St Barbara originally existed alone, and that later, probably about 30 to 50 years later, the north chapel and the hall were added to form a small complex. The additions parallel those made to the Karabaş Kilise site and their architectural forms are consistent with those of much of the monastic architecture described in previous chapters. It is reasonable to suppose, therefore, that a small monastic community grew up around the church of St Barbara. That such a community should be generated by a secular funerary chapel is less probable, however, unless it were the case that Basileios chose for his monument a site which already had pious associations, such as a hermitage. Such an establishment would have had a monk or monks available to say prayers for the deceased. In such circumstances, the special attention given in the painted programme to monk saints finds an explanation. Subsequent development of the site would follow the pattern proposed above for other hermitages: a gradual increase in importance accompanied by the growth of the community.

Ayvalı Kilise

Güllü Dere, the 'rose-pink' valley mentioned above in connection with the Hermitage of Niketas the Stylite, extends northwards as far as the village of Çavuşin. Ayvalı Kilise is in the northern part of the valley, about ten minutes' walk southeast of the village. The church contains a painted decoration and inscriptions, details of

---

53 G. Schlumberger, *Sigillographie de l'empire byzantin* (Paris, 1884), 560; Oikonomedes, *Les listes de préséance byzantines*, 89, and for

Domestikos of the theme: 63, 109, 157.
54 *Synaxarium CP*, October 22, col. 155, 1.9.

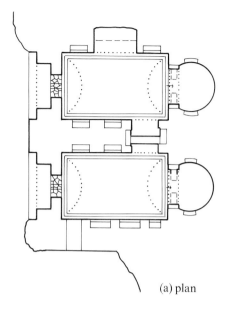

(a) plan

40. Ayvalı Kilise

(b) South Chapel, south wall.

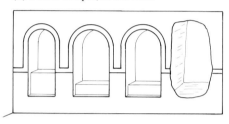

which suggest that it was associated with a hermitage.[55] The church is in an area similar to that around the Hermitage of Niketas the Stylite, with small cultivable patches between large banks of pinkish cones.

Ayvalı Kilise is a twin-naved church cut into a large cone (Fig. 40a & Pl. 180). Each nave originally had, at its west end, a rectangular entrance, with a small rectangular window above it, set into an arched niche. The church is now used as a pigeon house and the entrances are blocked by rough masonry. Small square pigeon-holes, set into rectangular recesses, have been cut above the original entrances (Pl. 181). The only entrance to the church at present is a small secondary opening which cuts into the west end of the south wall of the south nave. The ground level to the south of the cone falls sharply, so this entrance is several metres up a sheer rock face and difficult of access (Pl. 180).

Each nave has a longitudinal barrel vault springing above a two-stepped overhang. Each also has a single apse, slightly horseshoe-shaped in plan and containing a pair of symmetrically placed, lateral arched niches outlined with roll mouldings. The apses once had low chancel slabs: a fragment of the north slab in the south apse is still in place, bearing fragments of a carved medal-lion on its east face (the lost parts of the slabs are indicated on the plan in broken thin line). The two naves communicate by a passage through their common wall, at its east end.

The walls of each nave contain deep arched niches with running hood mouldings. The niches open above ground level and each has a ledge at its base (Fig. 40b). The south wall of the south nave contains three such niches; that at the east end of the wall is taller and narrower than the other two; at the west end of this wall is the rough opening that now forms the only entrance to the church. This was probably cut through a further narrow niche, in which case the niching of the wall would originally have been symmetrical about its mid-point. The north wall has two niches and, at the east end, the arched opening to the passage linking the two naves. In the north nave the form of the south wall mirrors that of the south nave north wall. On the north wall the three-niche scheme is modified, occurring as two small niches flanking a large arcosolium; this has been extended backwards by secondary excavation (Pl. 182). The passage which links the naves is barrel-vaulted and contains two niches, one in each wall; a raised bar in the floor forms a minor obstacle between the two naves. Details of carved decoration such as cornices,

55 N. & M. Thierry, 'Ayvalı Kilise ou pigeonnier de Gülli Dere, église inédite de Cappadoce', *CahArch* 15 (1965), 97–154; the church is mentioned briefly in Jerphanion, *Eglises*, I. ii, 594, and Restle, *Wall Painting*, Cat. no. XXIX. See also N. Thierry and A. Tenenbaum,

'Le cénacle apostolique à Kokar Kilise et Ayvalı Kilise en Cappadoce: Mission des apôtres, pentecôte, jugement dernier', *JSav* (1963), 229–41.

180. Ayvalı Kilise: site.

181. Ayvalı Kilise: exterior.

182. Ayvalı Kilise: North Chapel, north wall.

mouldings and niching, are identical in each nave and there is no reason to suppose other than that the two were carved in a single operation, and that the north nave arcosolium is part of the original scheme.

The only other nearby cave is an irregular cavity immediately to the south of the church which contains a rock-cut wine press of a type common in the region; it is impossible to know whether this is contemporary with the church.

Painting The church has two layers of painting. The surface layer of high quality painting (Phase II) is damaged in places to reveal a much cruder decoration underneath (Phase I). This includes figure painting, visible in the south chapel on the north wall and on the east wall lunette, and ornament in the barrel vault.[56] This Phase I painting is rustic in quality, its figures very clumsy, and can hardly have been the work of professional painters. The programme also includes clumsy inscriptions, frag-

ments of which survive on the rim of the archway to the passage from the south nave and on the rim of the south chapel apse.[57]

The Phase II painting is of high quality, and has been attributed to the workshop that decorated Tokalı Kilise Old Church.[58] The programme, first described by N. and M. Thierry, is as follows:

South chapel

Nave

Vault: (east end) Infancy cycle – Annunciation, Visitation, Proof of the Virgin, Journey to Bethlehem, Nativity, Adoration of the Magi, Dream of Joseph, Flight into Egypt, Massacre of the Innocents, Presentation; (west end) Ascension.

West lunette: Transfiguration.

South wall: (east to west) Baptism; start of Passion cycle – Raising of Lazarus, Entry into Jerusalem, Washing of the Feet.

56 N. & M. Thierry, 'Ayvalı Kilise', 102, refer to a cross on the south nave vault, of the St Stephen type (see above, Chapter 4, the Archangel Monastery) but admit that only the ornamental filling of the cross-arms is visible. I do not think there is such a cross: the lines that are clear in photographs do not fit such a scheme.

57 *Ibid.* 102 for the passage inscription, which is a prayer referring to

the 'celestial armies of God'. The apse arch inscription is not recorded by Thierry and is so high up that it could not easily be read in 1978 when I visited the church. It probably could be deciphered if viewed at close quarters.

58 *Ibid.* 144; N. Thierry, 'Un atelier de peintures du début du Xe siècle en Cappadoce', *BAntFr* (1971), 170–8.

West wall: Last Supper, Betrayal.
North wall: Crucifixion, Deposition, Entombment, Myrophores, Anastasis.
East wall: Virgin and Child between angels.

Apse
Conch: Christ in majesty with Isaiah and Ezekiel, Archangels.
Wall: bishop saints – (left) Amphilochios, Eusebios, Peter; (right) Klemes, Hypatios, Spyridon; (north niche) Joachim, Zacharias, Stephanos; (south niche) Ezekiel with two unidentifiable figures.
Soffit of arch: seven medallions – six busts of prophets including Habakkuk, Zacharias and Jeremiah, flanking a central Lamb with cross-nimbus.
On the cornice of the apse is an inscription:

[᾿Ανισ]τορίστι ὁ ναὸς τοῦ ἀγίου ᾿Ηǫάγνου ἐπὶ βα[σι]λέος Κον[σταντίνου ... c. 25 ...]ΤΟΥ ἐχ πό[θου] κὲ πί[σ]τεος ὑκο[δ]ομõντα τὶ μόνην τῖς Παναγίας κὲ πάντον τõν [ἀγίω]ν. ὁ ἀναγινόσκον εὔχετε / ὑπὲρ ἀὐτοῦ διὰ τὸν Κ(ύριο)ν.[59]

Translation: 'The church of St John was decorated in the reign of Constantine ... from love and faith built the monastery of the Panagia and All [Saints]. May he who reads this, pray for him through the Lord.'

On the walls, below the Passion cycle, in niches and wall spaces between them, there are images of saints:
East wall: Constantine and Helena (flanking the apse arch).
South wall: Kyrillos, Vales, Krispos, ?Eutychios, Aetios, Sisinnios, Xanthios, Smaragdos, Klaudios, ?Eunoikos, Leontios, Philoktemon, (?), (?).
West wall: Thekla, Anastasia, (?)(female), Euphrosyne, Joulitta.
North wall: (?), Sakerdon, (?), (?), Athanasios, (?), Ignatios, Priskos, Theophilos, Eutychios, (?), (?).[60]
Porch: (arch) Constantine and Helena; (flanking entrance) a military saint (left) and a martyr (right).

Passage: (vault) Elijah and the Chariot, Elijah and the Fire, Elisha and the Mantle; (west wall) Damianos, Hesychios, Sacrifice of Abraham, Flavios; (east wall) Nikolaos, Amphilochios, Konon, Paul *ho homologitis*, Nikandros.[61]

North nave
Apse: (conch) Deesis; (wall) Akindynos, Orestios, Thomas, Eustathios, Agapios, (?); (arch) seven prophets in medallions – Joel, Hosea, Jonah, Nahum, Obadiah, one unidentifiable.

Nave
Vault: Second Coming – at the east end, a cross held by flying angels, two groups of standing angels; at the west end, Christ in a mandorla, Apostles enthroned in two flanking rows.
West lunette: Sea and Earth giving up their dead.[62]
East lunette: Deesis.
North wall: (upper part) Dormition (Pl. 182), three male martyrs, including Demetrios, four bishop saints.
West niche: (left wall) female donor (Fig. 41 & Pl. 182); next to her the inscription:

[῾Υ]πὲρ [ἀ]φέσεος [ἁ]μα[ρτί]ον / τῖς δούλις τοῦ θ(εο)ῦ Δεμνις[63]

Translation: 'For the forgiveness of sins of the servant of God, Demna.'

West niche: (back) an equestrian saint with donor inscription:

[Κ(ύρι)]ε βοίθι τὸ σο δοῦλον Θεόδορον[64]

Translation: 'Lord help thy servant Theodoros.'

West niche: (right wall) Justus; (wall between niche and arcosolium) Niketas.

Arcosolium: (right wall) male martyr; (the back wall of the arcosolium is lost); (left wall) orant monk, with a halo – he has a long beard and wears a pointed hood with vertical stripes and rows of small crosses, a stole

---

59 Published by N. & M. Thierry, 'Ayvalı Kilise', 99. My transcription differs slightly.
60 Most of the male saints are members of a single group, the Forty Martyrs of Sebaste; the only exception is Ignatios. The Forty are not complete and errors were made in naming them (Eutychios appears twice, 'Krispos' is probably a confusion of 'Priskos' and therefore another duplicate).
61 The only two bishop saints with this epithet listed in *Synaxarium CP* are Paul of Nicaea (34.5) and Paul of Constantinople (197.5).
62 The painting of the west lunette has been largely destroyed by the excavation of pigeon-holes and only the extremities of the scene remain. At the left a woman without a halo is sitting in front of a small enclosure containing several human heads. Other heads appear above it and behind the woman. The enclosure is of the type

often used to represent a tomb, as in representations of the Women at the Tomb. At the right side of the lunette all that is left are the tails of four fishes. N. and M. Thierry suggest that this scene represents Earth and Ocean in an image pertinent to the Resurrection ('Ayvalı Kilise', 144, note additionelle), but do not mention the inscription above and to the right of the seated woman: ΗΓ. / . . CITOY NEKPO AY .. and what may be a name inscription next to her: Η Γ. (ἡ γῆ – the earth), which indeed suggest that the scene includes 'Earth giving up the Dead' as a pendant to Revelation 20.13: 'And the sea gave up the dead which were in it.'
63 Published by N. & M. Thierry, 'Ayvalı Kilise', 128; my transcription differs slightly.
64 *Ibid.* 128.

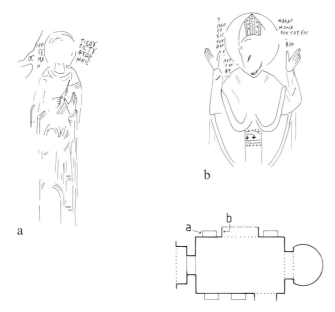

41. Ayvalı Kilise: images in the North Chapel.

shows beneath his cape, which has a pale border (Fig. 41). Next to him is the inscription:

Ὑπὲρ εὔχις του δούλου τοῦ θ(εο)ῦ/Μακαρ μοναχοῦ τοῦ EN [. . . . .] BON [. .]

Translation: 'For the prayer of the servant of God, Makar(ios?), monk of . . .'[65]

On the rim of the arcosolium is a further inscription:

[. . . Ἰω]άννι[ς εὐχα]ριστισάμην αὐτον ἄγιον ἔτος κόσμου , ϛΥ[. . c.15] ἐν μινὴ Νοεμβρίου ἡς τὰς ιδ΄[66]

Translation: 'I, John, gave this holy (place?) as a thank-offering, in the year of the world 64 .., in the month of November, on the fourteenth.'

East niche: Klemes, Karterios, Loukianos.
East wall: (left of apse) Hieron, Phokas; (right of apse) Tryphon, (?).
South wall: (left of passage)? Christopher;[67] (above the passage opening) Antonios and Arsenios; (right of passage) Eustathios and the stag; (upper register) Theopiste, Euphemia, Eupraxia, Olympia, Christina;

(lower register, walls and niches) (?), Aphthonios, Pegasios, (?), Elpidios, (?), (?), Abibos, Helena.
West wall: (left of entrance) Archangel Gabriel; (right of entrance) Archangel Michael of Chonae; (above entrance) a monk saint and Archipas.[68]
Porch: (arch) Proklos, another bishop, Pachomios, another monk; (flanking the entrance) Barbara and another female saint.

Thus the Phase II decoration of the south nave consists of a Christological programme (Infancy, Ministry and Passion cycles, Prophetic Vision), whereas the north nave has a funerary programme: Deesis, Resurrection/Second Coming, Dormition. This and the presence of the arcosolium make it clear that the north nave had a funerary function. The choice of Elijah for the passage may be symbolic: the translation from this world to the next. The programme described is certainly all of one phase, but painted by at least two hands. One painter was responsible for the greater part of the decoration, but another, of lesser ability, painted the Second Coming of the north vault, the wall of the north apse and the north porch.[69]

Discussion

The south apse inscription records that the Church of St John (presumably Ayvalı Kilise) was decorated by a patron who built the Monastery of Panagia and All Saints, in the reign of Constantine. No donor name survives, but the grammar of the text indicates that it refers to a single male donor. It seems reasonable to suppose that 'John' of the arcosolium inscription is the donor. Thus the church is dedicated to his name-saint (probably, but not certainly, John the Baptist).[70] The date given in the arcosolium inscription is 14 November 64 .., thus 891–990, a period during which Constantine VII reigned as sole emperor from 913–20 (and for a few months in 945, but not including November).[71] The Phase II painting of the church may therefore be attributed to 913–20. Demna and Theodoros, in the west niche, were probably related to John, the principal donor. It is unusual, perhaps, that Demna should have a portrait

65 N. & M. Thierry, 'Ayvalı Kilise', 128, give: 'En mémoire du serviteur de Dieu le moine Macaire de . . .'
66 N. & M. Thierry, 'Ayvalı Kilise', 100.
67 No inscription is legible; the figure is very large and has one arm raised, with the hand curled, as if holding a staff; N. & M. Thierry suggest that this is another Constantine.
68 N. & M. Thierry identify the first monk as Antonios; on my visit no inscription survived for this figure.
69 Cf. the figures of Isaiah in the south apse with that of St Andrew

in the north vault. For illustrations see N. & M. Thierry, 'Ayvalı Kilise', 117, 138, (figs. 12 and 28).
70 The painted programme gives little clue as to which of the many saints John was the object of dedication. John the Baptist appears twice, but each time in the context of formal *Deesis* images. John the Evangelist appears in the usual narrative images.
71 N. & M. Thierry, 'Ayvalı Kilise', 101; for fuller discussion of the date, see R. S. Cormack, 'Byzantine Cappadocia. The Archaic Group of Wall Paintings', *JBAA* 30 (1967), 19–36 at 20–1.

when there is none for the chief patron. There may have been such an image, however, on the back wall of the arcosolium which has been destroyed by secondary excavation.

Ambiguity surrounds the image of a monk and the inscriptions next to it on the west face of the arcosolium (Fig. 41). It is not clear whether the image is of Makar, or of a monk saint, with the invocation for Makar placed next to it. It is not uncommon in the cave churches to find invocations inscribed next to images of saints, but in such cases the saint usually has his own name-inscription as well as the invocation. Since there is no such inscription for the arcosolium monk, it would seem that this is a portrait of Makar. Against this, the figure has a halo and is iconographically identical to figures of monk saints elsewhere in the church (Antonios, Arsenios, Archipas and others). However, the workshop that painted Ayvalı Kilise used 'standard' types for figures: old men, young men, bishops, and so on (as perhaps would most workshops of the time). The use of a standard 'monk' type for an image of Makar is therefore entirely plausible and would account for iconographical similarity with the images of monk saints. The retention of the halo from the 'saint' model may also be an indication of the venerable status of Makar.

The image of Makar and references to the patrons appear in the most recent (Phase II) decoration of the church. The existence of the rustic earlier decoration indicates, however, that the church itself was not the commission of John and the other donors. The arcosolium of the north chapel, which is certainly an original feature, establishes that this nave was designed to be a funerary chapel from the start. It is significant, therefore, that the Phase II decoration in this nave has a funerary programme. It establishes that the patron John was aware of the original function of the chapel and sought to maintain it. The Phase II programme includes the invocation for and probably the image of, the monk Makar, in the arcosolium. This monk may have been the occupant of the arcosolium, placed there shortly after the church was excavated and celebrated in the later decoration provided by the patron John. Alternatively, he may have been a monk still living on the site at the time of John's patronage, a follower of an earlier holy man for whom the tomb was cut.

A possible sequence is, therefore, that Ayvalı Kilise was excavated on the site of a hermitage, equipped with a funerary nave for the burial of the hermit, probably Makar. It was decorated with the Phase I painting of

rustic quality. It may then be supposed that the site gained in venerability and later attracted a patron, John, who commissioned the repainting of the naves, fully aware of the earlier history and motivated by it.

John is described as one who 'built the Monastery of Panagia and All Saints'. There are no buildings nor any cave complexes in the immediate vicinity of Ayvalı Kilise that might be identified with this monastery. Further, the existence of the Phase I painting establishes that John was the redecorator, not the founder. The monastery of Panagia and All Saints may therefore be another establishment, and the reference to it serves to identify 'John' and record a previous pious endowment. It is, in effect, a title.

N. and M. Thierry have observed that the painting of Ayvalı Kilise is closely similar in style to that of the mosaic of the dome of St Sophia, Salonica.[72] This was completed in the late ninth century and the workshop responsible for it was probably from Constantinople.[73] It is possible, therefore , that the painters who decorated Ayvalı Kilise were not local, but came either from the capital or from somewhere else where metropolitan influence was strong. The possibility that the painters were imported perhaps supports the hypothesis that the patron, John, was a visitor to the volcanic valleys and the Monastery of Panagia and All Saints elsewhere.

John's benevolence is datable to the first quarter of the tenth century. The rustic Phase I decoration and the excavation of the church are undated but, given the continuity of function discussed above, should perhaps not be placed too far forward of the patronage of John: a foundation date in the second half of the ninth century seems plausible.

Tokalı Kilise

Tokalı Kilise, in Göreme valley, is unusual among cave churches in that several phases of alteration took place to produce the monument as it now appears. Repainting is not unknown, as is evident from the churches discussed above, but major structural changes are rare. It is clear, therefore, that the site was a particularly venerated one, possibly that of an important hermitage.

The church is at the head of Göreme valley, shortly before the entrance to the crescent area (now Göreme Park) which contains the Göreme refectory monasteries (see above, Chapter 4). The modern road runs very close to Tokalı Kilise and its construction may have destroyed valuable evidence as to the original appearance of the church entrance. The church is now fronted by a modern

72 N. & M. Thierry, Ayvalı Kilise', 145–54.
73 R. S. Cormack, 'Ninth-Century Monumental Painting and Mosaic in Thessaloniki' (London University Ph.D thesis, 1968), 211.

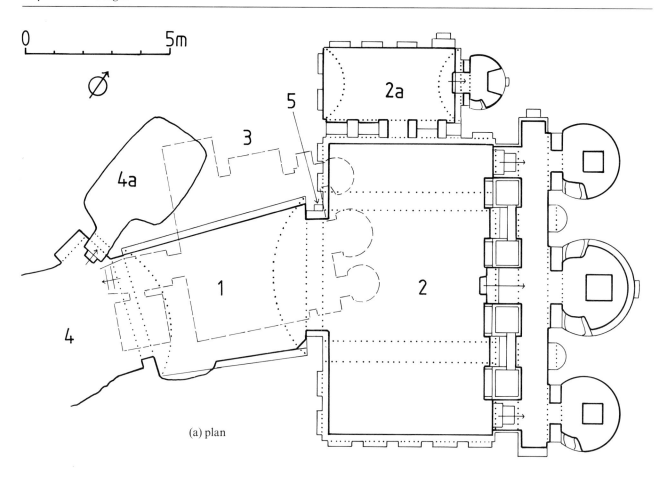

0   5m

3

5

2a

4a

1

2

4

(a) plan

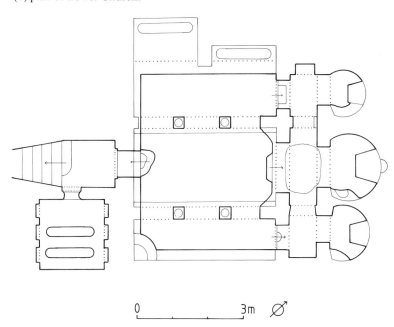

(b) plan of Lower Church.

42. Tokalı Kilise

0   3m

concrete archway, flanked by masonry walls.

Tokalı Kilise consists of four main elements as follows (the numbers refer to Fig. 42a): the small single-naved *Old Church* (1), with the remains of a *vestibule* (4) in front of it; the much larger *New Church* (2), and, below the Old Church, the *Lower Church* (3). Both Old and New Churches are decorated with extensive programmes of polychrome painting, which were described very fully by Jerphanion, and have been the subject of discussion elsewhere.[74]

The Old Church (1) (Pl. 183) now forms an entrance bay to the New Church (2) but was originally a single-naved barrel-vaulted church. Its lines are irregular: the barrel vault is asymmetrical, with its crest to the north of the axis, and a pronounced concavity at the west end of the north wall. At the base of each wall there is evidence of secondary excavation, probably the removal of benches and the lowering of the floor. The sanctuary was destroyed when the New Church was dug out behind the Old Church; the original form of this sanctuary will be discussed below. The entrance to the Old Church is a wide arch which is probably a slight enlargement of the original entrance. This is evident since a painting of the Trans-figuration on the west lunette is slightly truncated, but there are no obvious gaps in the programme that could be accounted for by loss of a large part of the west wall. The entrance was therefore wider than is usual for small, single-naved chapels. This, and the fact that the Old Church is set quite deep into the cone mass that houses it, suggest that the church was originally fronted by a narthex.

The Old Church is painted with a very full narrative cycle placed in two registers on each side of the vault and one on the upper part of each wall. The cycle covers the Infancy, Ministry and Passion of Christ. It begins at the east of the top register of the south side of the vault and spirals around and down to end at the east end of the north wall register. The scenes are: Annunciation, Visitation, Proof of the Virgin, Journey to Bethlehem, Nativity, Adoration of the Magi, Massacre of the Inno-cents, Flight into Egypt, Murder of Zacharias, Flight of Elizabeth, Calling of John the Baptist, Prophecy of John the Baptist, Christ meeting John the Baptist, Baptism, Miracle at Cana, Calling of Apostles, Miracle of the Loaves and Fishes, Healing the Blind, Raising of Lazarus, Entry into Jerusalem, Last Supper, Betrayal, Christ before Pilate, Way of the Cross, Crucifixion,

183. Tokalı Kilise: Old Church, north wall.

Deposition, Entombment, Myrophores, Anastasis.

The Transfiguration is on the west lunette, the Ascension on the east lunette. Also on the east wall, south side, is a fragment of the Presentation in the Temple.

Figures of standing saints decorate the lower part of the wall: on the north wall (west to east) – Agape, Anastasia, Marina, Dometianos, Kattidios, Pan-teleemon, Theodoros, Constantine and Helena, Catherine. (At the east end of the wall a few later panels have been added, including a large figure of Hieron, which is part of the New Church programme.) The saints of the south wall are lost, except for fragments of haloes at the east end.

The workshop responsible for this decoration also painted the Phase II programme of Ayvalı Kilise in Güllü Dere, described above, and the Church of Holy Apostles, Cemil.[75] The painting in Ayvalı Kilise is, as noted above,

74 Rott, *Denkmäler*, 224–9; Jerphanion, *Eglises*, I. i, 262–94 and I. ii, 297–376; *idem*, 'La date des plus récentes peintures de Toqale Kilise, en Cappadoce', in *La voix des monuments, notes et études d'archéolo-gie chrétienne* (Paris/Brussels, 1930), II, 208–36; E. Wiegand, 'Zur Datierung der Kappakokischen Höhlenmalereien', *BZ* 36 (1936),

337–97; Budde, *Göreme* 13; J. Lafontaine-Dosogne, 'Nouvelles notes cappadociennes', *Byzantion* 33 (1963), 23–183, at 130ff.; Cor-mack, 'Byzantine Cappadocia', 22–33.

75 N. & M. Thierry, 'Ayvalı Kilise', 144; Cormack, 'Byzantine Cap-padocia', 23; N. Thierry, 'Un atelier de peintures', 170–8.

datable by one of its inscriptions to the period 913–20; a similar date bracket may therefore be assumed for the painting of Tokalı Old Church. There is no reference to a patron in the surviving decoration, but the two areas most likely to have had a dedicatory inscription – the apse and the west wall above the entrance – are both lost. As noted above, the painting in Ayvalı Kilise was done by two hands, one more accomplished than the other. Most of the painting in the Old Church seems to be the work of the less able of these two painters, but work by the more accomplished hand survives on the south fragment of the east wall. Possibly, therefore, the master painter decorated the east end and an assistant worked on the vault and walls. If, as suggested above, the workshop was not local, then it would seem that it was brought to the volcanic valleys to decorate Ayvalı Kilise and stayed to execute other commissions. (The reverse, that Tokalı Old Church was the initial commission, is unlikely since at Ayvalı Kilise the greater part of the painting was done by the master painter, whereas he painted only the east end of Tokalı Kilise.)[76]

The New Church (2) (Pl. 184) was excavated to the east of the Old Church, by digging back into the rock through the Old Church apse. The New Church has a large transverse nave with a barrel vault divided into three bays by transverse arches. The nave walls are decorated with blind arcading on north, south and west sides. On the north side a true arcade was excavated, but most of its openings were then blocked to provide a continuous surface for painting. The easternmost opening was retained and forms the entrance to a barrel-vaulted, single-apsed side chapel (2a). The east wall of the naos is also an arcade, with five openings to a passage which runs in front of the three apses (Pl. 185). The second and fourth openings are partly blocked by low parapet slabs. There is a small niche in the north wall of the passage and there are two large apsidal niches in its east wall, flanking the main apse and opposite the two bays of the east wall arcade which have parapet slabs. The central apse contains an altar and two seats, the smaller side apses have altars and one seat, on the south side in each case. All three apses are closed by low chancel slabs.

The church is decorated with an extensive programme of high quality painting. In the nave, Infancy, Ministry and Passion cycles start in the north bay of the vault and continue in a wall register above the arcades:

Vault and north lunette: Annunciation, Visitation,

Joseph's Reproaches, Proof of the Virgin, Journey to Bethlehem, Dream of Joseph, Nativity, Adoration of the Magi.

West wall: Flight into Egypt, Presentation, Christ in the Temple, Calling of John the Baptist, Christ and John the Baptist, Baptism, Temptation, Calling of Matthew, Calling of Peter, Andrew, James and John, Miracle at Cana.

East wall: Healing the Blind, Healing the Lepers, Widow's Mite, Healing the Withered Hand, Healing the Possessed.

South wall: Healing of the Nobleman's Son, Raising the Daughter of Jairus, Healing the Paralytic, Raising of Lazarus, Entry into Jerusalem, Last Supper.

West wall: Washing the Feet, Betrayal, Way of the Cross, Christ before Pilate.

Main apse: (conch) Crucifixion; (wall) Entombment, Deposition, Anastasis, Myrophores; (arch) Jeremiah and Ezekiel.

Several important scenes are in the centre and south bays of the barrel vault: Ascension, Benediction of Apostles, Pentecost, Mission of the Apostles.

North apse: (conch) Prophetic Vision; (walls) Angel and Demon, Zosimas and Mary the Egyptian, Hospitality of Abraham, Antonios, Symeon the Stylite, Timotheos, Epiphanios, Arsenios; (arch) Nikandros, Alypios, Euthymios, Blaisios.

South apse: decoration lost.

On the *west wall* of the naos, between the entrance and the north wall, and on the *north wall* itself, are several episodes from the life of St Basil: The Dispute for the Church of Nicaea, Basil and the Emperor Valens, Prayer of the Arians, Prayer of the Orthodox, Meeting of St Ephraim and St Basil, Absolution of the Sinful Woman, Funeral of Basil.

The rest of the decoration consists of figures of saints distributed on walls, soffits and the ceiling of the east end passage: martyrs (including the Forty Martyrs of Sebaste), a large number of bishop saints, monks.

A very fragmentary inscription on the nave cornice was recorded by Jerphanion. It begins:

+ Còν ναòν ίερ[ώτατον . . . c. 40 . . . δι' ὅλου?
ά]νηστόρησεν Κονσταντῆνος ἐκ πόθου
πρòς μον[ὴν ? τῶν οὐρανίων ἀσω]μάτον.
Κοσμῆ νεουργον ίκόστην σεβασμήες
γράφον ἐν ἐαυ[ταῖς . .[77]

---

76 The third church of the group, Holy Apostles in Cemil, is in such poor condition that its relationship to the others is difficult to assess. It appears, however, to be a much less elaborate monument than Ayvalı Kilise, which would therefore seem to be the most important

of the three and the likely context for the introduction of the workshop.

77 Jerphanion, *Eglises*, I. ii, 305–7, Inscription no. 34.

184. Tokalı Kilise: New Church, northeast view.

185. Tokalı Kilise: north wall and niche.

186. Tokalı Kilise: Lower Church, northwest corner.

Translation: 'Your (most holy church) was ?completely decorated by Constantine out of love for the monastery (of the heavenly angels). He adorns his new work with twenty venerable images....' (descriptions of scenes follow).

There is a further inscription, also recorded by Jerphanion, in the north apse:

+ ἐκαλιωρήθη το βῆμ[α ... c. 11 ... Νικ]ιφόρου διὰ συντρομίς τοῦ δούλου τοῦ θ(εο)ῦ Λέοντος Κοσταντήνου κε ὑ ἀναγηνόσκοντες εὔχεσθε ὑπὲρ αὐτους διὰ τὸν Κ(ύριο)ν. Ἀμήν. [78]

Translation: 'The bema was decorated by ... Nikephoros, at the expense of Leon, son of Constantine. You who read [this], pray for them through the Lord. Amen.'

The name of the painter was therefore Nikephoros, and there were two patrons. As Jerphanion suggests, they were probably father and son, each taking a share of the expense of the project. Neither Constantine nor Leon has a title. This may mean that they were persons of little importance or, on the contrary, that they were so well known, locally at least, that it was thought unnecessary to include their titles. Certainly they must have been persons of wealth, since the excavation of an elaborate church, and its decoration with high quality painting, must have been costly. Further, Cormack notes stylistic parallels between the New Church painting and the art of tenth-century Constantinople[79] which suggests, as in the case of Ayvalı Kilise and the Old Church, that the work was not done by local painters, but by a workshop brought in specially for the purpose; this, too, implies patrons of wealth and sophistication.

The paintings of Tokalı New Church may be attributed to the mid tenth century on the following grounds: the painter of the Pigeon House Church, Çavuşin, apparently used the Ascension/Benediction scene from the barrel vault of Tokalı New Church as his model for that scene.[80] The Pigeon House Church was painted between 963 and 969, probably in 963–4, so Tokalı New Church would pre-date this. It is likely that a phase of excavation and painting (the vestibule) intervened between the completion of the Old Church and the excavation of the New

78 *Ibid.* I. ii, 308–9, Inscription no. 36.
79 Cormack, 'Byzantine Cappadocia', 32.
80 G. de Jerphanion, 'La date des peintures de Toqale Kilisse en Cap-
padoce', *RA* 20 (1912), 236–54, at 246–51; L. Rodley, 'The Pigeon House Church, Çavuşin', *JÖB* 33 (1983), 301–39.

Church (see below). Allowing for this intermediate phase and for a reasonable period of use of the Old Church before its apse was demolished, the date of the New Church probably lies close to the end of the available bracket.

The Lower Church (3) (Fig. 42b and (3) in Fig. 42a) is three-aisled with arcades of three arches each. The original supports of the arcades have been lost and replaced by modern columns (Pl. 186). The central aisle is barrel-vaulted and the side aisles have flat ceilings. A bench runs around north, west and south walls. To the east, there is a raised passage reached by steps from each of the three aisles (Pl. 187). The passage is divided into three bays by arches rising from pilasters or corbels; the centre bay has a small calotte covering it, the lateral bays have flat ceilings. Three apses open off the passage, aligned with the three aisles. The entrance to each apse is narrowed by low chancel slabs. Each apse also has an altar, attached to the back wall, and a seat in the south corner. The north wall of the church is cut back to form two deep arcosolia, each containing a single grave pit. The westernmost arcosolium is twice as deep as the other, and its single grave is at the back of the recess, leaving a forward area large enough for the excavation of another grave pit. A further grave, probably secondary, is dug into the floor of the nave, at the west end, north side, parallel to the colonnade.

The Lower Church is reached by steep steps starting slightly forward of the northwest corner of the floor of the Old Church (Pl. 188). The steps descend to a small landing just in front of the entrance to the Lower Church. Opening off this landing, to the south, is a small roughly square chamber with a flat ceiling and a decoration of three blind keyhole niches on west and east walls. The floor has two grave pits cut into it on the south side, leaving enough space for two more.

The Vestibule (4). Just in front of the Old Church are the remains of a barrel-vaulted vestibule. An arch only

187. Tokalı Kilise: Lower Church, corridor in front of apses.

188. Tokalı Kilise: steps to Lower Church.

slightly lower than the Old Church and vestibule barrel vaults, decorated with a painted interlaced circle pattern, separates the two. The top of the stairway down to the Lower Church is just inside the vestibule, close to the north wall. To the west of the steps a blind niche is cut into the north wall. This is a wide rectangular niche, the upper corners rounded off, set an angle of about 45 degrees to the vestibule wall. To the right of the niche there is a roughly arched entrance to a rough cavity (4a). The whole of the west end of the vestibule has been lost and replaced by modern masonry.

The vestibule vault is decorated with a painting of the Pentecost: the apostles are shown seated on lyre-shaped thrones on each side of the vault, with a fragment of the *hetoimasia* above them. The surviving portion of vault includes only three apostles on each side: the vestibule must once, therefore, have been at least twice its present length, if all twelve apostles were accommodated. The niche in the north wall contains images of St Jason and St John the Baptist. A fine chevron ornament decorates the east face of the arch between the vestibule and the Old Church.

The style of the painting in the vestibule is quite different from that of either the Old Church or the New Church. It is very similar, however, to painting in a group of Göreme chapels (Chapels 1, 4a, 6, 8 and 13) which I have called the 'Theotokos group'.[81] None of these is dated, but most belong to Jerphanion's 'archaic' group, attributable to the first half of the tenth century.[82]

The Niche (5). In the north side of the entrance from the Old Church to the New Church there remains one half of a niche, the right side of which was evidently sheared off when the New Church west wall was finished (Pls. 183, 184, 185). It is painted in a rustic style quite unlike that of any other painting in Tokalı Kilise, with the bust of a saint and a peripheral inscription. This was identified by Jerphanion as part of Psalm 22: '. . . in the midst of the congregation, I will praise thee'.[83]

Other painting A few areas of painting are not part of the schemes already described. In the New Church, a panel with the figure of St Theodoros in military dress, carrying shield and spear, has been painted over the right side of the image of the Martyrdom of St Eustathios and his family, on the south parapet slab in the east arcade.[84]

From its style, which is comparable with that of the Column group churches, the Theodoros panel would appear to be an eleventh-century addition. There is another added panel, showing the Virgin and Child, on the north fragment of the east wall of the Old Church.[85]

Discussion

A few points in the sequence of excavation and decoration of Tokalı Kilise are easily established: the Old Church is dated by its painting to 913–20; it obviously precedes the New Church since the latter has no entrance other than that provided by the Old Church. The New Church was finished and painted by 963–4, when part of its barrel-vault programme was copied in the Pigeon House Church.

The vestibule is not an original part of the Old Church since its painted decoration is not uniform with that of the Old Church, and its arch cuts through the paintings of the east wall of the Old Church. Something, however, must have existed in front of the Old Church nave for this to have been placed so far back in the rock. Probably a small narthex preceded the Old Church nave and this was enlarged to make the vestibule. This modification probably preceded the excavation of the New Church, for several reasons: first, that the vestibule painting belongs stylistically with that of churches in the 'archaic' group of the first half of the tenth century and second, that if the modification had not yet been made at the time of the enlargement, the masons of the New Church would probably have carved a new entrance for the whole complex. They did not, and this was probably because they could not, for the area in question had already been cut to form the vestibule. Finally, were the vestibule part of the New Church phase, it would probably have been decorated with New Church painting. The excavation and decoration of the vestibule may therefore be placed between the excavation of the Old and New Churches. The date of the vestibule phase probably lies closer to that of the Old Church than to that of the New Church, since its painting is in a style found in churches of the 'archaic' group. Further, the intervention of this phase between the Old and New Church phases probably places the latter towards the end of the period available for it (that is, towards 963/4).

81 L. Rodley, 'Architecture and Decoration of Cave Churches and Monasteries in Byzantine Cappadocia' (London University Ph.D. thesis, 1980), 46–53. For Chapels 1, 6, 8, 9, 13, see Jerphanion, *Eglises*, I. i, 177–98, 95–112, 112, 121–37 and 138 respectively; for Chapel 4a, Restle, *Wall Painting*, Cat. no. IV (and for Chapels 1, 6, 9, Cat. nos. I, VIII, XII).

82 Jerphanion, *Eglises*, I. i, 67–94; II, 414–18.

83 *Ibid.* I. ii, 303, Inscription no. 33.

84 Jerphanion's account of the painting of the parapet slab is in error on several points. It has been cleaned recently and is now legible: it shows Eustathios and Theopiste, with two small figures of their sons Theopistos and Agapios, all four lodged in a brazen bull amidst flames. This seems to be part of the original New Church programme. The head of the bull which is to the right, has been covered by the later St Theodoros panel.

85 Jerphanion, *Eglises*, I. i, 268–9.

It is reasonably certain that the Lower Church does not precede the Old Church. Its entrance is by means of a flight of descending steps. This must have made removal of rubble during excavation difficult: a straight passage at the level of the Lower Church floor would have been much more convenient. Further, it was not the habit, among cave-church masons, to dig below the surface. The location of the Lower Church may best be explained by assuming that the Old Church, and probably also the vestibule, already existed when it was cut.

The plan of the Lower Church appears to be related to that of the New Church, in that it employs the unusual passage preceding the apses. The probability is, therefore, either that the Lower Church was part of the New Church phase, or that it was a later addition modelled partly on the New Church. Since the Lower Church has a funerary function (it contains two grave pits in the nave arcosolia and two more in the floor of the side room) it seems likely that it was part of the New Church phase: the work done for the patrons of the New Church provides a suitable context for the excavation of a funerary crypt.

Finally, the modest niche, about which much has been written and which most authors try to include in reconstructions of the apse of the Old Church. The niche is too close to the north wall of the Old Church to have been part of a centrally placed single apse, and also too high: the remains of the Old Church east wall show that the apse arch closed lower than the level of the niche. Nor is there enough space for a three-apsed east end, so the niche cannot be placed in a lateral apse (and the problem of height would still apply). Jerphanion therefore suggested that the niche belonged to an enlargement of the Old Church apse, carried out some time before the excavation of the New Church.[86] This is improbable, since the decoration of the niche is very crude, and it is unlikely that a fully painted apse (and such was surely part of the Old Church painted scheme) would have been destroyed for an enlargement finished with rustic decoration. Only a project as ambitious as the New Church would have been allowed to bring about the destruction of the most important part of the Old Church. A second solution, that the Old Church had an east end passage, like the New and Lower Churches, with the niche in the north wall of the passage (there are niches so placed in both New and Lower Church passages) was proposed by Restle.[87] This, too, must be rejected since it makes the passage ceiling extremely low. Epstein sites the niche in an asymmetrically placed single apse, thus located in order to overlay the central apse of the Lower Church.[88]

This assumes that the Lower Church was the first structure on the site, an hypothesis that appears untenable for the reasons given above.

The niche was cut in half by the finishing of the west wall of the New Church: it was filled in and plastered over when the New Church was completed, as is evident from the remains of New Church painting visible above and below it. Hence it must precede the New Church. It does not follow, however, that the niche must be part of the Old Church apse: in addition to the structural problems discussed above, the evidence of the painting is against this. First, the niche painting is not in the Old Church style; second, there is no trace of Old Church painting over it, so it cannot be part of a rustic decoration placed in the Old Church prior to the formal decoration. Nor is it plausible that the Old Church workshop would have painted only the nave of the Old Church and left third-rate painting in the apse.

The niche thus has no logical place in either the architecture or the decoration of the Old or the New Churches, and a separate phase must be sought for it. The painting of the niche does not appear to be the work of a professional painter at all, but does fit with the simple 'mason's' painting styles of red-paint ornament or other simple decoration. The niche may, therefore, have been cut while the conversion was in progress. The first action in the excavation of the New Church must have been the digging of a tunnel through the east end of the Old Church, and the niche may have been cut and decorated by the masons engaged in the work. The fragment of rectangular recess above the niche, which led Restle to reconstruct the Old Church east end with a passage, like the New Church, is nothing more than the cutting back of the rough tunnel wall to provide a smooth surface in which to placed the niche. It is not likely that formal liturgical rites continued during the alteration, using the niche as their focus, but it is reasonable to suppose that the niche was a pious gesture on the part of masons working on a particularly venerated site. (Perhaps even a cautious one – there might have been some risk of being crushed by rock-fall in the excavation of a cavity as large as that of the New Church nave.)

To summarize, the sequence of phases in Tokalı Kilise appears to be the following:

I. The excavation of the Old Church, at an unknown date, but probably not long before its decoration with polychrome painting in 913–20.

II. The enlargement of the west end of the Old Church

86 Jerphanion, *Eglises*, I. i, 263.
87 Restle, *Wall Painting*, I, 111.

88 A. W. Epstein, 'The Date and Context of Some Cappadocian Rock-cut Churches' (London University Ph.D thesis, 1975), 56.

to form the vestibule, perhaps not long after Phase I, since this too is decorated with 'archaic' style painting.

III. Excavation of the New Church, starting with a tunnel through the Old Church apse; the masons cut a niche in the tunnel after the destruction of the sanctuary.

IV. Completion of the New Church; the niche was sheared off and its remaining part filled and the New Church was painted. The painting (and probably the excavation also) was the commission of Constantine and Leon. The painting was complete by 963/4, and, allowing for the 'vestibule' phase, was probably started not long before this date. This phase probably included the excavation of the Lower Church as a funerary crypt.

V. Addition of a small number of panels of painting to both Old and New Churches in the eleventh century.

The sequence proposed raises an important question: why did Constantine and Leon excavate the New Church behind the Old Church, rather than in a cone nearby? It would be unnecessary to ask this were a built monument concerned, for alterations to the fabric of a built church are commonplace: alterations, rather than re-building, are more economical of time and resources and often dictated by limitations of the site. This is not so, however, in the case of cave churches. It would have been a simpler matter to excavate the New Church nearby than to take in scaffolding and take out rubble through the relatively narrow Old Church nave, decorated with painting that it was clearly felt necessary to protect, since it was not covered by the New Church programme. This sequence of alterations is, then, unusual, and implies that the Old Church itself had particular importance.

The clumsy, irregular form of the Old Church is also unusual among cave churches, which are generally well carved, and suggests that the church was a modification of an existing cavity. Given the evident importance of the site, it is possible that this existing cavity was a hermit cave.[89] Thus the various phases of development might parallel the pattern seen in other examples: a gradual increase in the importance of the site which attracted patrons. As in Karabaş Kilise, two main phases of patronage are apparent. In the early tenth century an unknown patron commissioned the decoration of the Old Church and then, some 40 to 50 years later, the excava-

tion of the New Church and Lower Church was undertaken by Constantine and Leon.

The nave inscription of the New Church says that Constantine's donation was generated by 'pious love for the monastery (? of the Heavenly Angels)'. Since the term 'monastery' may apply to any establishment of monks, including a hermitage, the most obvious inference from this is that the monastery that grew up around Tokalı Kilise had this dedication. There is, however, a problem concerning the relationship between the nave inscription and the painted narrative cycles: the poem that follows the reference to Constantine declares the programme of decoration to contain twenty episodes. There are more than twenty episodes depicted, however, and the poem lists scenes not present in the cycles.[90] Jerphanion therefore suggested that the poem copied a text written for another church. The quality of the painting indicates that the patrons were wealthy, and the elaborate programme suggests that they were persons of sophistication also. The borrowing of an inscription from another church cannot, therefore, be explained as a short cut on the part of the painter, overlooked by ignorant patrons. Instead, it may have been taken from another church of significance to the patrons. The procedure is not unparalleled, for an inscription in the porch of the Church of Holy Apostles, Sinasos, copies a text from the (now lost) church of St Basil in Kaisareia.[91] If such an explanation for the non-correspondence of text and narrative painting is valid, then it may be that the Monastery of the Heavenly Angels is elsewhere and the reference to it a means of recording the virtue (and, perhaps, the identity), of Constantine. The hypothesis parallels that offered above for the relationship between the Monastery of Panagia and All Saints and Ayvalı Kilise.

There are, of course, rock-cut monasteries near to Tokalı Kilise, described in Chapters 2 and 4, above. These may, however, be attributed to the eleventh century and hence post-date Tokalı Kilise New Church. Constantine's monastery cannot, therefore, be among the rock-cut monasteries of Göreme. It may have been a built structure, but if so then it has vanished without trace. The monasteries of the Göreme crescent probably are, nevertheless, closely connected with Tokalı Kilise: it was argued above that the importance of Tokalı Kilise was such that it generated the eleventh-century monastic development of Göreme.

---

89 *Ibid.* 59–60.

90 Jerphanion, *Eglises*, I. i, 307.
91 Jerphanion, *Eglises*, II, 62.

6

The monasteries and their context

Chronology

The evidence of date given in previous chapters indicates that the hermitages appear earlier on the Cappadocian scene than the monasteries. The earliest phases of most of the hermitages are datable to the late ninth or early tenth centuries: painting dated or datable to the early tenth century is found in Ayvalı Kilise, Tokalı Kilise (Old Church), the Chapel of St Symeon and Karabaş Kilise; an earlier layer still is present in Ayvalı Kilise and Karabaş Kilise. It is among these monuments also that there is evidence of long occupation, such as repainting and structural alteration. Ayvalı Kilise has two phases of painting, Tokalı Kilise and Karabaş Kilise four. Tokalı Kilise, Karabaş Kilise and St Barbara, Soğanlı, each have successive phases of excavation. The dated painting of the latter two churches points to the continued occupation of hermitages into the eleventh century, as do the eleventh-century panels added to Tokalı Kilise and the chapel near the hermitage of Symeon the monk.

Material evidence therefore places the hermitages in a ninth- to eleventh-century bracket, but anchorites may well have inhabited the volcanic valleys before this. If the early date claimed for the Hermitage of Niketas the Stylite is correct, then the chronological bracket begins with the seventh or early eighth centuries.

The monasteries, however, appear to be confined to a much shorter period. The only direct dating evidence among the courtyard group is the inscription in Direkli Kilise which implies a date between 976 and 1025, with the style and programme of the paintings favouring the later years of that bracket. Several monasteries may be dated by the painting in their churches: stylistic analysis suggests a date in the late tenth or early eleventh centuries for Selime Kalesi and a date in the first half of the eleventh century for Eski Gümüş Monastery. A date towards the middle of the eleventh century may be arrived at for Karanlık Kilise Monastery in Göreme, on the basis of

its Column group church. Affinities with churches of the Yılanlı group suggest a date in the second half of the eleventh century for three more complexes: Hallaç Monastery, Bezir Hane and Aynalı Kilise Monastery. Monasteries without painting must be dated by their architecture alone. The inscribed-cross churches of Soğanlı Han, Şahinefendi Monastery and Karanlık Kale place them in the Middle Byzantine period, and it may be significant that the addition of a courtyard complex resembling that of Soğanlı Han was made to the church of St Barbara, Soğanlı, probably in the second half of the eleventh century.

The overall uniformity of layout, architectural detail and room type which is apparent throughout the courtyard monastery group makes a case for placing all the complexes (with the possible exception of Selime Kalesi) within a fairly short chronological period. This would extend from the first quarter of the eleventh century, with Direkli Kilise Monastery and Eski Gümüş Monastery, to the second half of the century, with monasteries linked with the Yılanlı and Column group churches. The complexes of Açık Saray, by virtue of their close architectural parallels with the courtyard monasteries, should probably be attributed to the same period, as secular parallels to the monasteries.

Yusuf Koç Kilisesi Monastery in Avcılar and the refectory monasteries of Göreme may be dated to the eleventh century by their churches, most of which either belong to the Yılanlı and Column groups or may be linked with them. The date of the Archangel Monastery may eventually be established when its paintings have been cleaned and studied; meanwhile, its rooms, refectory and façade are similar to those of both courtyard and refectory monasteries and suggest approximate contemporaneity. In Göreme, the three churches of the Column group are divided between the refectory and courtyard monasteries, indicating that the two monastery types co-existed, or at least overlapped chronologically.

There is evidence of alterations to Eski Gümüş Monastery and possibly to Selime Kalesi while they were still in use as monasteries (at Eski Gümüş the excavation of the side chapel, changes to the tomb recess and repainting; at Selime Kalesi minor changes to Room 1 before it was plastered). These alterations imply a period of use long enough to require them. For the other monasteries of both types, however, several points suggest only brief primary occupation. There is, for example, no instance of repainting. Two monastery churches have only scant painted decorations (Hallaç Monastery, Bezir Hane) and some have none at all (Şahinefendi, Soğanlı Han, Karanlık Kale). At Karanlık Kale the church was plastered but not painted, so it is likely that a painted programme was planned but not undertaken. Similarly, at Direkli Kilise, the church is fully plastered but not fully painted. Had these monasteries been occupied for a long period, the blank plaster would surely have been decorated. At the very least, an accumulation of pious inscriptions, of the kind present in some of the hermitages, might be expected.

Neither is there evidence of planned secondary excavation in the monasteries. What alteration there is to original structures is casual and inept, and may be assigned to the period when abandoned monasteries were converted into pigeon houses, animal houses or peasant dwellings. Again, establishments of long occupation would surely have been altered as the needs of their inhabitants changed. At Hallaç Monastery, the probability that the rough cavity (7) to the east of the courtyard is an unfinished room even suggests that the monastery was abandoned with excavation incomplete.

These signs of brief occupation, in conjunction with the various indications of eleventh-century date noted above, suggest that most of the monasteries were excavated shortly before the Seljuks began their permanent occupation of the area, and abandoned as conditions became unpropitious. The lack of documentary records or references to the monasteries, mentioned in Chapter 1, finds an explanation in such an hypothesis: establishments of brief duration would possess scant archives and the preservation of even these would have been unlikely in circumstances of abandonment under duress.

Architecture

Technique

Excavation is a technique so different from building that it may be useful, before embarking on discussion of the architecture of the Cappadocian rock-cut monasteries, to consider the differences between the two methods. The principal difference, of course, is that excavation is a process of removal, not addition. None of the usual structural considerations of building applies: an excavated dome is in effect weightless, it can rise above thin columns and will stay in place even if these are removed. Excavation requires no elaborate scaffolding, hoists or ramps. No materials need be brought to the site, other than cutting tools, wooden poles for very basic scaffolding, and barrows for carting away the debris.

There is no record of the manner in which rock-cut monuments were excavated, but the only logical procedure would seem to be the following: first, a tunnel would be dug into the rock, to a depth roughly equivalent to, or slightly beyond, the centre of the planned structure; then a cavity would be made by digging outwards from that point, to a roughed-out stage slightly smaller than the finished product. Simple wooden supports would be lodged in shallow holes in the roughed-out surface as the work proceeded upwards (pigeon perches are thus installed today). Architectural details would then be cut in the rough surface, beginning with the vault and working from top to bottom until scaffolding were no longer needed, and then from the farthest point of the cavity back towards the entrance. In this way the debris of carving would fall into areas still in the rough state, and therefore less vulnerable to damage than finished parts. The scaffold poles would be moved down as the work progressed, their sockets cut way in the finishing process.

Some evidence for this order of events is found at Tokalı Kilise (Fig. 42a), where the arch joining the New Church and the Old Church is of irregular form and not concentric with that of the Old Church barrel vault. Probably, when the roughed-out nave of the New Church was finished off, work started at the east end and moved west, towards the Old Church. The shape and position of the connecting arch was thus dictated by the position of the three finished walls of the New Church, and its failure to coincide exactly with the arch of the Old Church could not be remedied. Confirmation that this was the order in which the New Church was finished comes from two crudely painted masons' inscriptions: one dates the finishing of the side chapel to 20 February, the other gives 15 June for completion of the church as a whole.[1] That it took only four months to finish a rather elaborate church (and, allowing for the roughing-out stage, about six months for the whole project) is an indication of the

---

1 'In the name of God, this naos was completed on 20 February' and 'The naos was completed on 15 June. Lord help the *maistor*' (Jerphanion, *Eglises*, I. ii, 302–3, Inscription nos. 32 and 31). The order proposed assumes that both dates refer to the same year, which is surely the case, since it then took a little less than four

months to finish the naos, with its complicated east end and elaborate sculptural decoration. If, however, the nave were completed first, and the side chapel in February of the following year, then it must be supposed that eight months were necessary to complete a small, simple side chapel. The former is clearly the more probable.

swiftness of excavation, as compared with building.[2]

A problem that the excavator encounters, but that the builder generally does not, is that many errors cannot be rectified: if an insufficient mass of rock were allowed for a cavity, or for a detail, such as a column, pilaster or even moulding, then the project must simply have been finished off as well as the physical circumstances permitted. Minor instances of damage during excavation include, at Yusuf Koç Kilisesi, the loss of the southeast column, the stump of which descends from the vault and is covered by the painted decoration; a similar accident must have occurred at Kılıçlar Kilise, where a corner of the southeast capital was broken off and painted over.[3] As described in Chapter 5, more serious problems arose when the north chapel of St Barbara Soğanlı, was excavated as an addition to the original chapel. The excavators seem not to have allowed enough thickness of rock for the new chapel to be completed symmetrically, so it was finished with an off-centre entrance porch and a south wall without the bench and niched decoration of the north wall. Similarly, Çarıklı Kilise probably obtained its curious form (it is an abridged inscribed-cross church with only two columns and seven bays) because the excavators damaged at least one of the western columns. They therefore finished the west end with a single barrel-vaulted arm instead of three bays behind a pair of western columns.[4]

While it is not impossible that some small chapels were cut by monks, much of the work on monasteries and larger churches must have been done by skilled artisans, since the quality of the finished product is, in most cases, as high as the granular rock permits. The number of workers involved was probably quite small compared with the size of a crew needed for a building: for the excavation of a monastery, perhaps two or three skilled masons to do the detailed finishing and a similar number of labourers to do the roughing-out and carting of rubble. Excavation of small chapels could well have been done by one or two masons. Since the monasteries were a late development in the volcanic valley area, it is probable that by the time of their excavation the tradition of rock-cut architecture was sufficiently well established for there to have been a number of skilled masons resident there and able to carry out the work on commission.

A rock-cut church obviously cannot start, as a building does, from a plan laid out on the ground, nor can finishing of the roughed-out form proceed from precisely estab-lished points separated by measured distances. Indeed, the monument cannot be measured at all until it is finished. The quality of the finished product and its fidelity to built models must have depended very much upon the capacity of the masons to work to a mental image of the required structure.

Thus, with few limitations imposed by structural considerations, and with accuracy inhibited by the nature of the process, excavation gives much greater scope for idiosyncrasy than does building. The softness of the rock, which makes it relatively easy to work, must also limit the cutting of fine detail, and doubtless led to the simplification of features such as mouldings and capitals.

It is against this background that the architecture of the monastery complexes must be set: although clearly based on built models, a certain flexibility in the interpretation of those models is to be anticipated. The usual methods of tracing the evolution or relationships of architectural forms by analysis of their elements are also somewhat inhibited. It need not invariably be the case, for example, that those monuments most faithful to built models are earlier than those that are freer interpretations (or vice-versa arguing that the early attempts to produce a new type were inept, followed by greater accomplishment as the masons developed their skills). Quality and fidelity to built models is likely to be a matter of the standard of craftsmanship available for any particular project.

Hermitages

Most of the hermitage chapels described in Chapter 5 are, or were originally, single-naved with longitudinal barrel vaults and single apses. The exception is Ayvalı Kilise, which has two naves; it is not significantly different from the rest, however, since the single-naved form is simply duplicated in order to provide a funerary chapel. Nevertheless the use of a single architectural type for the hermitage chapels is not evidence of close connections between them. The chapels range in quality of execution from the rustic at Tokalı Kilise (Old Church) to the refined at Ayvalı Kilise and Karabaş Kilise. They also differ in their detailing: the church of St Barbara, Soğanlı, for example, has a transverse arch, lacking in the others; both Karabaş Kilise and Ayvalı Kilise have niched interiors, but with niches of differing types.

The single-naved form is common among Cappado-

2 A late nineteenth-century account claims that it took a single man only a month to cut a room 25′ × 13′ and 10′ high. G. Perrot and C. Chipiez, *History of Art in Phrygia, Lydia, Caria and Lycia* (London/New York 1892), 74.

3 N. Thierry, 'Yusuf Koç Kilisesi. Eglise rupestre de Cappadoce',

Mansel'e Armağan (Ankara, 1974), I, 193–206, at 193. In Kılıçlar Kilise the lower part of the image of St Elpidios (on the east face of the south cross-arm) is painted on the area left when the corner of the capital broke away. Restle, *Wall Painting*, I, 132–3.

4 Epstein, 'Rock-cut Chapels', 121.

cian cave churches; it is the type found in most of the painted churches that form Jerphanion's early tenth-century 'archaic' group and also in many of the churches assigned by Thierry to pre-ninth-century dates.[5]

So few built churches have survived in Cappadocia that it is not possible to identify with certainty the models upon which the hermitage chapels depend. Only one built single-naved church in close proximity to the cave churches has been recorded, but no longer survives. This was Ak Kilise, in Soğanlı valley, which was larger than most of the cave chapels (its nave measured 10.80 × 5.30 metres). It had a single apse, the arch and plan of which were slightly horseshoe-shaped; it was probably not vaulted.[6]

There are several more single-naved churches to the north of Hasan Dağı: one, at Anatepe is barrel-vaulted, others (Sarıgöl, Yedikapulu, Gelveri and four in Viranşehir) are too ruined for certainty about their coverings.[7] Further to the southwest, among the 'thousand and one' churches of Kara Dağı, the single-naved form appears to be used only for small funerary chapels, or chapels attached to monasteries.[8] Kara Dağı No. 36 (now destroyed) was part of a complex containing a larger, basilical church. This chapel is of particular interest, since it had applied arcades on its interior axial walls, making, in effect, a niched interior not unlike those of cave churches such as Ayvalı Kilise and Karabaş Kilise.[9]

None of these built churches is securely dated, but they are usually (and reasonably) attributed to the fifth or sixth centuries. They therefore predate the cave chapels by several centuries. The connection between the two groups is probably only generic: the single-naved form is very widespread in church architecture, both geographically and chronologically.[10] The hermitage chapels therefore employ a plan commonly used for minor churches or auxiliary chapels. Since this formula was established in early Christian central Asia Minor, the single-naved cave chapels may perhaps be regarded as Middle Byzantine representatives of a local tradition of long standing, with the built churches among their ancestry.

One church in the hermitage group – the New Church of Tokalı Kilise, added to the original single-naved chapel in the mid-ninth century – does not fit this description, nor very easily the context of central Asia Minor. Jerphanion noted that this church, with its transverse barrel vault, finds its closest parallels in the Tur Abdin Region of Mesopotamia. He suggested that it came to Cappadocia from there, possibly via Commagene, where there is an example in the church of Surp Hagop.[11] Certainly the absence of transverse-naved churches among the built monuments of central Asia Minor suggests that the type is an import.[12] Confirmation of this hypothesis comes from several more transverse nave cave churches found in Göreme valley: none of these matches the size or quality of Tokalı Kilise, which may therefore be seen as an introduction which generated a few copies in its immediate neighbourhood.[13] The mechanism of introduction is open to conjecture: might the patrons, Constantine and Leon, have been Mesopotamians who had their church cut to a model familiar to them? Its decoration with paintings showing a clear Constantinopolitan stamp argues against this, however, as does the probability that their lack of titles shows these patrons to be locally known. Alternatively, one may suppose a member or members of the monastic community around Tokalı Kilise to have come from Mesopotamia, or even an itinerant (and persuasive) master mason who pressed his patrons to accept a novel design. The problem remains one for conjecture.

Monasteries

The courtyard monasteries may not satisfactorily be divided into regional or other sub-categories. Many close architectural parallels between individual monasteries may be cited, but these never extend to all features. Thus, Hallaç Monastery, Kılıçlar Monastery and Bezir Hane may be gathered together, having in common the vestibule decoration of large, shallow, horseshoe-arched blind niches; Hallaç Monastery and Bezir Hane also both

5 For the 'archaic' group: Jerphanion, *Eglises*, I. i, 67–94; II, 414–18; for the Thierry group see Chapter I, note 28.
6 Restle, *Studien*, 24–6, pls. 10–11; Rott, *Denkmäler*, 132–3.
7 Restle, *Studien*, 23–27, pls. 1–23; for Gelveri: Ramsay & Bell, *1001 Churches*, 325–39, figs. 252–67.
8 Ramsay & Bell, *1001 Churches*, 324.
9 *Ibid.* 176–7, figs. 130 and 140; S. Eyice, *Karadağ ve Karaman* (Istanbul, 1971), 59–60, 213.
10 J. Ebersolt, *Monuments d'architecture byzantine* (Paris, 1934), 3–4, 131–2, for a survey of single-nave churches and chapels, to which may be added examples in Lycia, Syria and Pontus: in Lycia, chapels at Alakilise, Dikmen and Muskar, R. M. Harrison, 'Churches and Chapels of Central Lycia', *AnatSt* 13 (1963), 117–52, at 129–31; for Syria, H. C. Butler, *Early Churches in Syria*

(Princeton, N. J. 1929), 187 and Ill. 191; in Pontus, St Akindynos (a single-nave chapel with transverse arches), D. Winfield and J. Wainwright, 'Some Byzantine Churches from the Pontus', *AnatSt* 12 (1962), 131–61, at 146–7, 157–8; also Chapel D, Trebizond; Orta Mahalle, Akcaabat (with a transverse arch); Fetoka (perhaps dated 944–5); St Barbara: S. Ballance, 'The Byzantine Churches of Trebizond', *AnatSt* 10 (1960), 141–75 at 151–52, 166–7, 171.
11 Jerphanion, *Eglises*, I. i, 59. For Surp Hagop, S. Guyer, 'Surp Hagop (Djinndeirmene), eine Klosterruine der Kommagene', *RKW* 35 (1912), 483–508.
12 Restle, *Studien*, 1001–6.
13 A. W. Epstein, 'The Date and Context of Some Cappadocian Rock-cut Churches' (London University Ph.D. thesis, 1975), 69–73.

have basilical halls. On the other hand, the churches of Hallaç Monastery and Bezir Hane, although both of inscribed-cross plan, differ in detail, and Kılıçlar Monastery does not have a basilical, barrel-vaulted hall. In fact, its hall (a flat-ceilinged room with attached columns on the long walls) resembles very closely the hall at Şahinefendi Monastery, and both these monasteries have a decorated façade fronting the vestibule. Here too, however, the similarity is limited since at Şahinefendi Monastery the vestibule has two bays, originally separated by an arcade, and a decoration of deep niches, and therefore differs in several details from the vestibule of Kılıçlar Monastery.

Nevertheless the courtyard monasteries do form a coherent group. They are closely related in their main elements: usually a vestibule forms a common entrance chamber to most of the other rooms of the complex: the basic elements of each monastery include a large hall, a kitchen and a single church; the church has a side chapel and tomb chamber. In most cases the rooms open from a three-sided courtyard (Direkli Kilise Monastery and Karanlık Kale lack the courtyard, but, as noted in Chapter 2, this is probably because they are cut into cliff-sides). This basic formula was evidently modified in some cases by the addition of extra rooms. Thus isolated curiosities, such as the free-cross room at Karanlık Kale (3), the domed room at Hallaç (5), the upper room (21) at Eski Gümüş, with its Aesop paintings, and the galleried hall (18) at Selime Kalesi may be seen as elaborations of the basic scheme, dictated by specific needs of the establishments concerned, or perhaps by the demands of the patrons.

Selime Monastery is somewhat set apart from the others by its size: it is very much larger and more elaborate than the other cave monasteries. If, as seems probable, the aristocratic family depicted on the west wall of the church were its founders, this may have been largely a matter of wealth; except for size it is consistent with the rest, its several 'porch' areas replacing the single vestibule.

Common to all the monasteries is a basic vocabulary of horseshoe-arched blind niches, rectangular-section pilasters and mouldings, linked hood-mouldings over arcades and simplified capitals of slab or tapering block shape. It would seem likely, given the close chronology

proposed for the monasteries, that some teams of masons were responsible for several monuments, but attempts at sub-grouping on the basis of detail also fail: for example, the shallow blind niching which decorates Hallaç Monastery, Bezir Hane, Kılıçlar Monastery and Karanlık Kilise Monastery suggests, at first sight, an 'Avcılar/Göreme' regional style, and the heavier niching of Karanlık Kale and Selime Kalesi a 'Peristrema' group. The division is not consistent, however, since there is also shallow niching in Selime Kalesi, and the modillion-frieze decoration of Karanlık Kale is found also in Hallaç Monastery. No clear workshop groups may be defined, therefore, suggesting perhaps that crews of masons were assembled for each project and did not operate as permanently constituted workshops. It is also apparent that occasionally a mason/sculptor with more flair than most (or perhaps a different background) added unusual details to the basic repertory. Such must have been the case at Hallaç Monastery, which alone of the Cappadocian monuments has animal-head decoration on some capitals, minor piers above the main supports of the crossing, and the enigmatic leaping figure of Room 5.

Monastery churches

All but two of the courtyard monastery churches have inscribed-cross plans. The two exceptions are Aynalı Kilise and Selime Church, both basilicas, which will be discussed below. There are five inscribed-cross churches among the refectory monasteries of Göreme: Chapel 25, Elmalı Kilise, Kızlar Kilise, Çarıklı Kilise and Chapel 20 (these last two have seven-bay plans which may be regarded as incomplete inscribed crosses).[14] The other monastery churches of Göreme have forms common among cave churches: Chapel 21c is single-naved, Chapels 21, 21a and 27 are domed free crosses.[15] Two (Chapels 18 and 28) are of such irregular form that they defy categorization.[16] The churches at the Archangel Monastery are single-naved (St Stephen) and twin-naved (Church of the Archangel). Yusuf Koç Kilisesi in Avcılar has a doubled inscribed-cross plan.

The inscribed cross is therefore the dominant type in the cave monasteries. The churches are uniform in plan but vary in detail. The naos is always a nine-bay square

14 Built two-column churches such as St Amphilochios in Miram, southwest of Konya, have been offered as parallels for this form (Restle, *Studien*, 1029–30). Since, however, Çarıklı Kilise is closely related to two Göreme inscribed-cross churches (Elmalı Kilise and Karanlık Kilise) both by its painting and its architectural details, the resemblance to St Amphilochios, which has only one apse and a single dome over the central eastern bay, is surely fortuitous. St Amphilochios no longer survives: G. L. Bell, 'Notes on a Journey

through Cilicia and Lycaonia', *RA* 9 (1907), 18–37, at 27.

15 As in the case of the single-naved, barrel-vaulted chapels, there are built examples of this type. On Hasan Dağı: Süt Kilise and Yağdebaş: Restle, *Studien*, 84–5, pls. 164–80, figs. 50–1.

16 Chapel 28 is, nevertheless, usually classified as a transverse-nave church (Restle, *Studien*, 1002) which, strictly speaking, it is. It may therefore be one of the crudest chapels based on the form introduced by Tokalı Kilise.

(except in Çarıklı Kilise and Chapel 20, which have abridged forms). Central domes tend to be rather small, often with their sides rising steeply to meet a shallow cap – perhaps the simplified rendering of a drum beneath the dome. Rudimentary pendentives are often cut in the triangular spaces left in the corners of the centre bay ceiling.

The cross-arms are generally barrel-vaulted (Bezir Hane, Şahinefendi, Direkli, Karanlık Kale, Eski Gümüş, Yusuf Koç, Kızlar – in the last example the barrel vaults have shallow calottes cut into them). In some cases arches spring between the crossing supports, making a frame for the vaulting of the centre bay; behind these arches the cross-arms may be barrel-vaulted (Chapel 20, Karanlık Kilise, and probably the lost church of Soğanlı Han) or domed (Hallaç Church, Elmalı Kilise; the east arm of Karanlık Kilise is also domed).

Corner bays are frequently domed (Karanlık Kilise, Chapel 25, Chapel 20, Çarıklı Kilise, Elmalı Kilise, Kızlar Kilise and Şahinefendi). Other treatments include cross vaults (Karanlık Kale), flat ceilings (Direkli Kilise and Yusuf Koç Kilisesi), barrel vaults (Bezir Hane), slightly concave vaults (Eski Gümüş). At Hallaç Monastery there is a combination, surely capricious, of cross vaults and barrel vaults (the northern corner bays are barrel-vaulted, but on different axes, the southern ones are groin-vaulted).

The centre-bay supports are usually columns (slender columns at Karanlık Kilise, Elmalı Kilise, Çarıklı Kilise, Chapel 25, Chapel 20 and Soğanlı Han; heavy columns at Kızlar Kilise and Eski Gümüş). In four churches (Karanlık Kale, Bezir Hane, Direkli Kilise and Hallaç Church) the supports are piers, ranging from slender at Karanlık Kale to massive at Direkli Kilise. Uniquely, at Hallaç Monastery, the main piers carry minor piers, an arrangement for which there appear to be no parallels in built architecture. It may result from the elaboration of a feature often seen in built churches, where a cornice at the springing of the cross-arm barrel vault cuts off a pier-like section between the springing and the capital (this latter feature is reproduced at Bezir Hane Church (Pl. 24)). Şahinefendi Church has piers to the east and columns to the west. Although such an arrangement is occasionally found in built churches, it is probably idiosyncratic here, for similar versatility in the treatment of uprights is found in the hall of the monastery.[17]

Capitals are always very simple, usually slabs (Bezir Hane, Eski Gümüş, Elmalı Kilise, Çarıklı Kilise) or taper-ing blocks (Karanlık Kale, Şahinefendi, Karanlık Kilise, Chapel 25). Both types appear at Hallaç Monastery, some of them decorated with animal heads, scrolls and very stylized foliage. The only other instance of carving on capitals is the rudimentary leaf pattern incised on the tapering block capitals of Şahinefendi Church.

All the churches have three apses, the central one larger than the side apses, sometimes considerably so (Hallaç Monastery, Eski Gümüş, Soğanlı Han, Karanlık Kale). At Karanlık Kilise alone there is an opening between the main and north apses. In all cases the apses open from the three eastern bays of the nine-bay inscribed cross.

The chancel screen common to the great majority of cave churches – a pair of low slabs flanking a central entrance – is found in Bezir Hane, Direkli Kilise and Şahinefendi Monastery; possibly also at Karanlık Kale, where rubble has raised the floor level and obscured the apse furniture. Tall screens, with a central entrance flanked by lateral openings, are present in Karanlık Kilise, Çarıklı Kilise, Elmalı Kilise, Chapel 25, Chapel 20 and Kızlar Kilise. This screen type is interpreted by Epstein, doubtless correctly, as the rock-cut equivalent of the standard Middle Byzantine templon, which has a low parapet slabs from which columns or piers rise to support an entablature.[18] The tall screen also occurs in a form closely resembling the built model at the churches of Açık Saray Complexes No. 1 (Pl. 119) and No. 3 (Pl. 130). At Hallaç Monastery and Eski Gümüş Monastery there are no rock-cut screens of any sort. Probably wooden screens were used: the small corbels placed just inside the apse arch at Hallaç Church may have been cut to take the top beam of the entablature of a tall screen.

Most of the churches with tall screens are in the Column or Yılanlı groups of Göreme, datable to the second half of the eleventh century.[19] It would seem, therefore, that the tall screen was an eleventh-century development in, or introduction to, rock-cut Cappadocia, centred on Göreme, and that in most churches outside the Göreme region the traditional low slab form was retained. As far as built models are concerned, there may be little distinction to be made between the two types. In most cave churches apse entrances are too narrow for a full screen with entablature and columns to be cut successfully. The low slabs may simply have been a necessary curtailment of the standard Middle Byzantine type.

Many of the monastery churches have a narthex of some form, usually rectangular, with a transverse barrel vault (Karanlık Kilise, Kızlar Kilise, Eski Gümüş, Direkli

17 At Mistra, for example: G. Millet, *L'école grecque dans l'architecture byzantine* (Paris, 1916; reprinted London, 1974), 54–6.
18 A. W. Epstein, 'The Middle Byzantine Sanctuary Barrier: Templon or Iconostasis?', *JBAA* 134 (1981), 1–28, at 16–17.
19 Epstein, 'Rock-cut Chapels', 115–26.

Kilise, probably also Elmalı Kilise and Chapel 20). Occasionally the narthex is a small domed room (Chapel 25, Şahinefendi; this is also the case at Açık Saray Church No. 1 and the church of Açık Saray Complex No. 3).

Like the monasteries as a whole, the churches are resistant to sub-grouping. Three churches of Göreme (Karanlık Kilise, Çarıklı Kilise and Elmalı Kilise) have long been united as the 'Column' group, primarily because of the similarity of their painting. Their architecture also makes them a closely linked group, having common features such as the tall screen, domed corner bays, slender columns and centre-bay arches (Çarıklı Kilise has only one centre-bay arch, because it has only two columns). To this group may be added, since they share these features, Chapel 20 and Chapel 25, making a 'Göreme' group. Of the remaining churches, two more (Hallaç Church and Şahinefendi Church) have centre-bay arches but vary in the vaulting of their corner bays and in screen type. Hallaç Church may perhaps be regarded as a rather ostentatious relative of the Göreme group, supplied with enrichments such as animal-head capitals and minor piers by an imaginative (or perhaps non-local) mason.

In the remaining churches the cross-arm barrel vaults meet the centre bay directly, without the intervention of arches. Of these, Karanlık Kale Church is most like the Göreme group, although its supports are slender piers instead of columns. Bezir Hane and Direkli, both with more solid piers, may be loosely bracketed together, as may Eski Gümüş and Kızlar Kilise, both with heavy columns. In neither pair, however, is the similarity sufficient to suggest that the churches were cut by common workshops.

There are several Cappadocian cave churches of inscribed-cross plan that are not attached to monasteries. Two of these are at Açık Saray: Açık Saray Church No. 1, and the church of Açık Saray complex No. 3. Elsewhere there are the following: Göreme Chapel 29a; Sarıca Kilise, southeast of Ortahisar; the Panagia church, near Sinasos; Karlık Kilise, to the east of Cemil; the church 'opposite Munşıl Kilise', in Soğanlı valley;[20] Derviş Akın Kilisesi and Koyunağıl Kilise, both near Selime;[21] Church No. 2 in İsmail Dere,[22] and Çökek Kilisesi, near Çökek, northeast of Ürgüp;[23] also Kılıçlar Kilise, whose relationship to Kılıçlar Monastery is ambiguous, and Ala Kilise, in Belisırma, which may be part of a monastery

complex not fully described here (see Chapter 2).

These churches present much the same variety as those attached to monasteries: a group with centre-bay arches and barrel-vaulted cross-arms comprises Koyunağıl (columns, cross-vaulted corner bays), the chapel 'opposite Munşıl' (columns, barrel-vaulted corner bays), Derviş Akın (piers, barrel-vaulted corner bays), and Açık Saray Church No. 1 (piers, flat-ceilinged corner bays). At Ala Kilise, which also has centre-bay arches, there are piers, domed cross-arms and barrel-vaulted corner bays.

A group with barrel-vaulted cross-arms and no centre-bay arches consists of: Sarıca Kilise (columns, cross-vaulted corner bays), Karlık and Göreme Chapel 29d (both with columns, domed eastern corner bays, and flat western ones). Kılıçlar Kilise is very similar to these two, but also has centre-bay arches running north/south only. Çökek Kilise has piers and assorted corner-bay coverings (northwest domed, southwest cross-vaulted, eastern bays with flat ceilings). Church No. 2 in Haci İsmail Dere has flat-ceilinged corner bays and lacks a central dome, almost certainly a case of incomplete excavation.

These cave churches have the same plan as the monastery churches: the nave is a compact nine-bay square, with small square corner bays; apses open directly off the eastern bays of the nine-bay block. In just one church, the church 'opposite Munşıl Kilise', the apses are linked by lateral openings. There is, therefore, no distinction to be made between the monastery churches and the other Cappadocian cave churches of inscribed-cross plan.

Nor is the plan a peculiarly 'Cappadocian' one, for it appears in two more rock-cut churches distant from the volcanic valley regions. A church known as the Kyriakon, in Şille, northwest of Konya, has crossing arches running east/west, but not north/south, barrel-vaulted cross-arms, domed corner bays and apses opening off the eastern bays of the inscribed cross. It also has a barrel-vaulted narthex decorated with shallow blind horseshoe-arched niches.[24] Still further afield, in Phrygia, an inscribed-cross cave church at Ayazın which has slender piers, centre-bay arches and barrel-vaulted cross-arms also has its apses opening off the eastern bays. It differs somewhat from the Cappadocian examples by having a third pair of piers to the west, below the western cross-arm barrel vault. Its dome is finished on the outside with a drum decorated with double-recessed blind niches.[25]

20 Jerphanion, *Eglises*, I. i, 260–1; II, 47–8; II, 112–13; II, 183; II, 379.

21 N. Thierry, 'Etudes cappadociennes, Région du Hasan Dağı, compléments pour 1974', *CahArch* 24 (1975), 183–90, at 185, figs. 3 & 5.

22 M. Restle, 'Zwei Höhlenkirchen im Haci İşmail Dere bei Ayvalı', *JÖB* 22 (1973), 251–79, at 259–62.

23 L. Rodley, 'Çökek Kilisesi', in preparation.

24 G. L. Bell, 'Notes on a Journey through Cilicia and Lycaonia', *RA* 9 (1907), 18–37, at 26; S. Eyice, 'Akmanastır (St Chariton) in der Nahe von Konya und die Höhlenkirchen von Şille', *Polychordia. Festschrift Franz Dölger* (Amsterdam, 1967), II, 162–83.

25 C. H. E. Haspels, *The Highlands of Phrygia* (Princeton, 1971), 245, pls. 423–31, 577.

43. Karagedik Kilise: view from the northeast (after Restle).

The first inscribed-cross cave churches must have depended upon built models, but once excavated would themselves have been available as models. The centre-bay arches found in some of the cave churches are not normally present in built architecture and may have originated as the invention of cave-church masons.[26] It may be, therefore, that churches with centre-bay arches imitate other cave churches, rather than built ones. No chronology may be developed from this, however, since it is likely that built models continued to be used for some cave churches even after the inscribed-cross plan had been reproduced in rock-cut architecture.

Not all variants seen in the cave churches are attributable to idiosyncrasy. The inscribed-cross cave churches doubtless ultimately depend upon built models which also varied in detail but were consistent in plan. It is probable that the masons who cut the Cappadocian cave churches took for their models built churches in Kaisareia, Koloneia and other towns of the region, but none of these has survived. Indeed, very few built inscribed-cross churches survive anywhere in central Anatolia. In the cave church region itself there is only one: Karagedik Kilise, in Peristrema valley, now a ruin, its west and south sides lost.[27] The exterior of the north wall is decorated with a large double-recessed blind arch which complements the cross-arm barrel vault; this is flanked by two pairs of similar, smaller blind niches (Fig. 43). Triple windows in the centre of the wall beneath the large blind arch are framed by arched recesses; there was a similar decoration on five of the seven facets of the main apse.

The apses here do not open from the eastern bays of

26 Centre-bay arches do appear in much later Armenian churches, such as St John the Baptist, Ktouts, or the church at Aparank (both near Van). The inscribed-cross plan is not typical of Armenian architecture, however, and it is most unlikely that these examples represent an earlier tradition. J. M. Thierry, 'Monastères arméniens du Vaspuraken', *REArm* n.s. 11 (1975–6), 377–421, at 411–14, figs. 18 & 20; *ibid.* n.s. 10 (1973–4), 191–232, at 216–17, fig. 27.

27 Restle, *Studien*, 83 pls. 147–54, Plan 48. Ramsay & Bell, *1001 Churches*, 418, where it is called Ilanli Kilise. The inscribed-cross plan is also found in the church of St Gregory in Nazianzos, which Bell described as 'of much the same type as Ilanli' but this church was heavily restored or perhaps rebuilt in the nineteenth century, and the extent to which it copies an earlier building is unsure (*ibid.* 421–2). Fragments of another built inscribed-cross church are embedded in the later masonry of a mosque in Kaymaklı. The church remains are too fragmentary for reconstruction: H. Gürçay and M. Akok, 'Yeraltı şehirlerinde bir incelme ve Yeşilhisar ilçesinin Soğanlı dere köyünde bulunan kaya anıtları', *Türk ArkDerg* 14 (1965), 35–59, at 37–8.

the inscribed cross, as is the case in the cave churches, but from a row of intercalary bays (i.e. bays separating the apses from the easternmost bays of the inscribed-cross, thus extending the naos eastwards) (Fig. 44a). The crossing supports were slender piers, the cross-arms barrel-vaulted; the intercalary bays and corner bays had barrel vaults on a west/east axis. The main apse is slightly horseshoe-shaped in plan, but all standing arches and decorative ones are semicircular. Although the vaulting and supports of Karagedik Kilise fall within the range of types found in the cave churches, the presence of intercalary bays is an important feature which separates it from them and makes it (or its ilk) unlikely models.

A closer parallel for the cave churches is found in Çanlı Kilise, a little outside the volcanic valley region, near Çeltek, to the southeast of Aksaray.[28] Most of its vaulting has now fallen, but a description by Bell permits reconstruction: the apses open directly off the eastern bays of the nine-bay block (Fig. 44b); the dome, carried on a tall drum, was supported on four piers; the cross-arms were barrel-vaulted, as were the corner bays. The entrance is in the centre bay at the west end; a barrel-vaulted narthex precedes this, but is an addition. Arches are semicircular, as are the plans of the apses.

The exterior decoration of Çanlı Kilise resembles that of Karagedik Kilise: on both north and south walls a large double-recessed blind niche echoes the cross-arm barrel vault and houses two windows; it is flanked by two small, double-recessed arched niches; below, on the south wall, is a row of four triple-recessed niches, each with a narrow window at its centre (Fig. 45). (This was probably the case on the north wall too, obscured by the addition of a single-naved chapel.) Similar blind niches in two registers decorate the facets of all three apses.

Further afield are six inscribed-cross churches in Lycaonia, to the southwest of Cappadocia, four of them in the Kara Dağı region, two near Konya. First, a church at Fisandon, southeast of Karaman, has its central dome carried on slender piers; the cross-arms are barrel-vaulted and the corner bays have cross vaults (Fig. 44c).[29] A large main apse and small side apses open off the eastern bays of the inscribed-cross. The exterior north and south walls are, like those of Karagedik Kilise and Çanlı Kilise, decorated with large blind arches following the form of the cross-arm barrel vaults (Fig. 46). The blind arches shelter three double-recessed, horseshoe-arched blind niches;

below this is a row of seven similar niches, four of them containing windows. The decoration of blind niches continues, at the same level, on the east wall, forming a frieze around the apses.

Çet Dağı Church, north of Madenşehir, and Kara Dağı No. 35, were very ruined when seen by Bell in the early years of this century, but seem also to have been inscribed-cross churches without intercalary bays at their east ends (Figs. 44d & e).[30]

A very irregular building in İbrala, east of Karaman, now in use as a mosque, may have been an inscribed-cross church with intercalary bays (Fig. 44f). Its architectural history is unknown, and it has clearly undergone considerable alteration. It has plain exterior walls and its apse does not project; the cross-arm barrel vaults are trapezoidal in plan.[31] It seems possible, in fact, that this church was originally a basilica to which a dome was added when it was converted into a mosque.

Further west is Ala Kilise on Ali Suması Dağı, above Kilisira, to the southwest of Konya.[32] This has a large main apse, slightly horseshoe-shaped in plan, flanked by very small lateral apses (Fig. 43g). The apses open directly off the eastern bays of the inscribed cross. The vaulting is lost, but fragments of its springing were seen by Bell; the supports were probably piers. The church had a rectangular narthex at its west end, barrel-vaulted and with two transverse arches. The exterior decoration differs from that of the churches just described: the south wall has a shallow blind arcade of three large arches resting on a string course; each arch shelters groups of double-recessed, narrow, horseshoe-arched blind niches, set close together in two lateral groups of three and a centre group of five (Fig. 47); a further bay, probably with three niches, has been lost from the west end of the wall. The niches have small carved cross-medallions below their pronounced horseshoe arches. On the west wall a rectangular entrance is surmounted by a double-recessed horseshoe-arched lunette, flanked by two double-recessed blind niches. Above the entrance are fragments of a window framed by recesses. North and east sides are lost, except for lower fragments largely obscured by rubble on the steep hillside.[33]

Turning back to the east, a final example of the built inscribed-cross church forms the core of a mosque in Sivas.[34] There remain parts of the south, west and east walls and four slender columns, enough to establish that

28 Ramsay & Bell, *1001 Churches*, 404–18; Restle, *Studien*, 84, pls. 155–8, Plan 49.
29 Strzygowski, *Kleinasien*, 154–6; Eyice, *Karadağ*, 84–9, 221–2.
30 Ramsay & Bell, *1001 Churches*, 268–73, fig. 229; 184, fig. 148. Eyice, *Karadağ*, 70–2, 214–15; 61, 213, suggests that they might be basilicas; this is certainly unlikely to be the case at Çet Dağı,

where the piers are L-shaped, bracketing the centre bay.
31 Eyice, *Karadağ*, 81–4, 220.
32 Ramsay & Bell, *1001 Churches*, 399–403.
33 *Ibid.* figs. 325 and 326.
34 S. Eyice, 'Quatre édifices inédits ou mal connus', *CahArch* 10 (1959) 245–58, at 251–3.

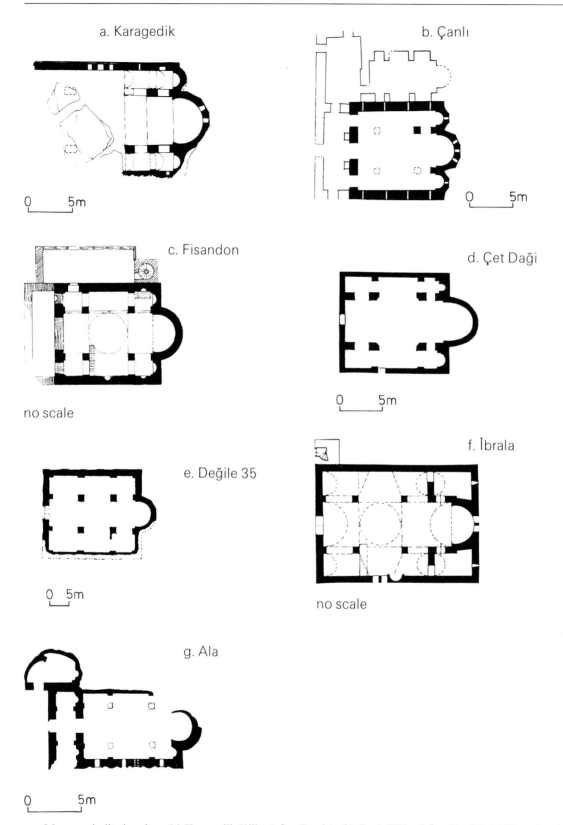

44. Masonry-built churches: (a) Karagedik Kilise (after Restle), (b) Çanlı Kilise (after Restle), (c) Fisandon (after Strzygowski), (d) Çet Dağı (after Bell), (e) Değile No. 35 (after Bell), (f) İbrala (after Eyice), (g) Ala Kilise (after Bell).

45. Çanlı Kilise, near Çeltek: view from the southeast (after Restle).

46. Fisandon Church: view from the southeast (after Eyice).

47. Ala Kilise, Ali Suması Dağı: south wall (after Bell).

the plan was without intercalary bays. Any exterior decoration that exists has been obscured by a cladding of later masonry.

The surviving built inscribed-cross churches of Asia Minor are, therefore, very few, undated and largely ruined; exterior decoration is often their best-preserved feature, and one that has little relevance for comparisons with cave churches. Nevertheless, they do offer two variants of the inscribed-cross plan: one with, one without, east-end intercalary bays. The absence of intercalary bays from the cave churches cannot, therefore, be attributed to simplification engendered by the rock-cut method, since they are also absent from most of the built examples.

The presence or absence of intercalary bays is an important diagnostic feature, more so than variations in corner-bay vaulting or support types. Of the seven built inscribed-cross churches mentioned, only two have intercalary bays: Karagedik Kilise and İbrala (and the irregularities of the latter advise caution about its original form). Although statistical conclusions drawn from such a small number of monuments must be tentative, it would seem that the cave churches follow the more common central Anatolian type. Indeed, they may be seen as confirmation that this was the more common type.

In broad terms, church architecture in central Asia Minor follows the fortunes of the region. The relatively stable and prosperous early Christian period produced the large stone buildings still surviving in Cilicia at sites such as Alahan, Meriamlık and Korykos, in Lycaonia around Kara Dağı and in Cappadocia around Hasan Dağı and scattered elsewhere.[35] From the seventh to the ninth century, territorial losses and the insecurity caused by border raids and fluctuating frontiers cannot have been propitious for architecture. As noted above, the single-naved, rock-cut chapels of Cappadocia probably reflect the rather humble (and largely lost) built-church architectural tradition of Asia Minor during this period. An architectural resurgence, following the return of relative security from the late ninth century onwards, is the context in which to place the appearance of the inscribed-cross church. The plan may thus be seen as a Middle Byzantine import to Asia Minor, but the scarcity and poor condition of surviving monuments hinders the tracing of lines of diffusion or patterns of regional development. It can hardly have been the case that cave-church masons were working to models in areas distant from Cappadocia, so it would seem likely that the buildings arrived first, although the surviving examples are not necessarily among the earliest. Moreover, the variety of detail present in the cave churches suggests that the inscribed-cross plan was well established in the region before the cave churches were cut.

The origin and development of the inscribed-cross church remains controversial, but the type was wide-

35 G. Forsyth, 'Architectural Notes on a Trip through Cilicia', *DOP* 11 (1957), 223–36. For Alahan, M. Gough, Preliminary Reports published in *AnatSt* 1955, 1962–4, 1967. Ramsay & Bell, *1001 Churches*; Restle, *Studien*.

spread by the tenth century and remained important for the duration of the empire.[36] The type is represented in a series of Constantinopolitan churches from the early tenth to the twelfth centuries: the north church of the monastery of Constantine Lips (907),[37] the Myrelaion (920–2),[38] St Saviour Pantepoptes (before 1087),[39] Kilise Camii (eleventh or early twelfth century),[40] and the churches of the Pantocrator Monastery (1118–36).[41] Each of these has (or had) a dome supported on barrel-vaulted cross-arms and four slender columns; the small corner bays are usually covered by cross vaults, occasionally by domes (Kilise Camii). A large main apse and small lateral apses open off intercalary bays.

The intercalary bay appears to be a particularly Constantinopolitan feature; in the provinces the inscribed cross with apses opening directly off the eastern bays is widely established and the appearance of intercalary bays is often associated with a Constantinopolitan connection.[42] The appearance of both types in central Asia Minor therefore suggests the co-existence of a plan with intercalary bays, derived from the capital, and a provincial type with apses opening off the inscribed cross. That the intercalary bay is a rarity in central Asia Minor endorses this view. Further, Karagedik Kilise, which has the intercalary bay, has another 'foreign' feature in its round arches.

Metropolitan influence in central Asia Minor is also evident in churches with plans of the 'provincial' type, however. Attention has been drawn to the Constantinopolitan cast of Çanlı Kilise, manifest in its proportions, building technique, round arches and exterior decoration.[43] And yet this church lacks the intercalary bay of the Constantinopolitan churches. Krautheimer suggests that a mason trained in the capital brought the Constantinpolitan manner to Çanlı Kilise; if so, then this mason was evidently required to retain the local standard for east ends. That the intercalary bay is not found in the cave churches confirms the reasonable expectation that the cave churches depend largely upon established local types. But in the cave churches, too, Constantinopolitan influence has been recognized in the slender

columns of many of the churches, and also in the multiplication of domes. These features were perhaps 'requirements of the patron' grafted on to the standard provincial model, rather than evidence of the importation of whole architectural schemes; once arrived, such details would easily become part of the cave-church masons' repertory.

Several degrees of 'importation' may therefore be supposed, encompassing the introduction of an entire scheme at Karagedik Kilise, the use of a largely introduced, but locally adapted, form at Çanlı Kilise, and, in the cave churches, the use of specific metropolitan features in schemes that otherwise depend on local models.[44] Whether any of these 'imports' came directly from the capital is, of course, uncertain, and the manner of the introductions must be a matter of conjecture. One possibility is that the military campaigns of the ninth to eleventh centuries brought metropolitan visitors to central Anatolia, some of whom may have sought divine benevolence for their endeavours by commissioning churches.

As noted above, Selime Kalesi and Aynalı Kilise Monastery have basilical churches. This departure from the formula common to the other courtyard monasteries requires explanation. One possibility, given the association of the basilica with the early Christian architecture of Asia Minor, is that these two are substantially different in date from the other monasteries. However, Aynalı Kilise has the tall screen which seems to be an eleventh-century development in cave-church architecture and its extensive red-paint decoration makes it a close relative of the Yılanlı group churches, especially Chapel 20. Similarly, there are several indications of an eleventh-century date for Selime Church: the single layer of painting, its style, and the iconography of the donor image.

Basilicas were still being built in the provinces in the eleventh and twelfth centuries so the form itself is not a guide to date.[45] A certain heaviness of form at Selime Church does, however, bring to mind the rather solid basilicas of Hasan Dağı and Kara Dağı. Possibly, then, the church is a copy of an early basilica, commissioned by patrons who chose to model their monastery church

36 R. Krautheimer, *Early Christian and Byzantine Architecture* (3rd edn, Harmondsworth, 1979), 59–61; C. Mango, *Byzantine Architecture* (New York, 1976), 178–80.

37 T. Macridy, A. H. S. Megaw, C. Mango, E. J. W. Hawkins, 'The Monastery of Lips (Fenari Isa Camii) at Istanbul', *DOP* 18 (1964), 249–315, at 279–300.

38 C. L. Striker, *The Myrelaion (Bodrum Camii) in Istanbul* (Princeton, 1981) fig. 19.

39 T. F. Matthews, *The Byzantine Churches of Istanbul. A Photographic Survey* (Pennsylvania, 1976), 59.

40 *Ibid.* 386–7.

41 *Ibid.* 71–2.

42 Millet, *L'école grecque*, 56–9.

43 Krautheimer, *Early Christian and Byzantine Architecture*, 423–4; C. Delvoye, 'L'architecture byzantine au Xe siècle', *Proceedings of the XIIIth International Congress of Byzantine Studies, Oxford, 1966* (London, 1967), 225–34 at 230.

44 Further evidence of imported architectural types is available in Üçayak, a ruined church near Kırşehir, to the north of Aksaray. This is a brick church with two domed naves, probably datable to the late tenth or early eleventh century; like the inscribed-cross churches, it has extensive double-recessed blind niche decoration. S. Eyice, 'La ruine byzantine dite 'Üçayak' (= Utch-aiak) près de Kırşehir en Anatolie Centrale', *CahArch* 18 (1968), 137–55.

45 Delvoye, 'L'architecture byzantine', 232–3.

upon an existing monument of particular importance, either general or personal. In the context of architectural revival following the centuries of disruption, such a procedure is plausible. No obvious model is available, however: the alternation of piers and columns in the nave arcades inhibits derivation of the type from the known built basilicas of central Asia Minor, or, for that matter, anywhere else.[46] Two undated basilicas in Greece, at Goudi-near-Athens and Kalabaka (Thessaly) have alternating columns and long rectangular piers, but this is only loosely comparable with the scheme of columns and piers, of equal thickness seen at Selime.[47] The coherence of the church interior, with its complex piers and complementary mouldings, makes it unlikely in this case that the unusual features are another instance of inventiveness on the part of the mason. Selime Church is doubtless a copy of a built church, but the date and location of the model remains elusive.

Derivation from an early model is not likely for Aynalı Kilise, however, whose slender columns and generally rather delicate appearance link it firmly to the eleventh-century monuments of Göreme. Possibly these two are evidence of the continued use of the basilica in Middle Byzantine central Anatolia.

Decoration and façades

Carved ornament is rare in the cave monuments, so much so that where it appears it is likely to be either intrusive or idiosyncratic. Thus, as noted in Chapter 2, the animal and human figure sculpture in Hallaç Monastery is perhaps the work of an Armenian mason, brought to Cappadocia in the eleventh-century migration, who drifted to the volcanic valley region from the areas of settlement further north.

A firmer link is possibly to be found with the highlands of Phrygia, which contain a number of rock-cut dwellings and churches of the Byzantine period.[48] Most of these are rather crudely cut compared with the Cappadocian monuments, but there are notable exceptions, such as the church at Ayazın, mentioned above. Their decorative vocabulary of linked hood mouldings, simplified capitals and shallow blind horseshoe-arched niches, is similar to that of the Cappadocian monuments. Here, too, are parallels for the stables of Açık Saray, Yusuf Koç Kilisesi

Monastery and Selime Kalesi.[49] The area also contains many ancient rock-cut tombs with decorated façades, including some with confronted lions carved in high relief, not unlike the confronted bulls of Açık Saray No. 7; other monuments have shallow-relief animal carving, recalling that in Rooms 1 and 28 of Selime Kalesi.[50] The connection with Phrygia is doubtless a loose one; the number of Christian monuments there is much smaller than that in Cappadocia and their quality is generally poor. The inscribed-cross church at Ayazın does, however, indicate approximate contemporaneity with the Cappadocian monasteries and raises the possibility that itinerant masons worked in both areas and brought to Cappadocia a few exotica derived from ancient sculpture.

More prosaically, a local parallel for the meandering stem with stylized foliage on the lintel above the entrance to Selime Kalesi Room 13 is provided by decoration on the north wall of Yağdebaş Kilise, on Hasan Dağı.[51] A similar pattern also appears on a Roman tomb-façade in Gümüşören, south of Erciyes Dağı, the arched opening of which has the same elements as the hooded arched window above the Selime lintel.[52] No close connections are to be supposed; rather it would seem that cave masons occasionally took inspiration from locally available remnants of late antique or early Christian ornament. Something similar may explain the crude scroll-work on the façade arcade at Eski Gümüş, which has no obvious progenitor. Fragments of carved sixth-century capitals in the monastery courtyard, brought there in recent times for safekeeping, testify to the availability of such material to the Cappadocian mason with an inclination towards ornament.

The façades which front the cave monasteries and the Açık Saray complexes are the most conspicuous features of Cappadocian rock-cut architecture. Parallels have been sought in the architecture of Mesopotamia and Persia, in late antique stage-fronts, and Islamic palace façades.[53] While it may be reasonable to see the Cappadocian façades as part of a long tradition of Near Eastern architectonic exterior decoration, it is unlikely that the masons working in the volcanic valleys in the tenth and eleventh centuries were familiar with the façade of Ctesiphon or even the exteriors of Islamic palaces. Further, the Cappadocian façades do not resemble very closely the decorated fronts of monuments beyond the

46 J. Lafontaine-Dosogne, 'La Kale Kilisesi de Selime et sa représentation des donateurs', *Zetesis. Album Amicorum E. de Strijcker* (Antwerp/Utrecht, 1973), 741–53, at 745. This author mentions several churches in which groups of slender columns alternate with single heavy piers, but none of these resembles the arrangement at Selime.

47 For Goudi, Millet, *L'école grecque*, 44–5. For Kalabaka, G. Lampakis, *Mémoire sur les antiquités chrétiennes de la Grèce*

(Athens, 1902), 31.

48 Haspels, *The Highlands of Phrygia*, 225–54.

49 *Ibid.* pl. 418.

50 *Ibid.* For example: pls. 96, 132, 474–5.

51 Restle, *Studien*, pl. 178.

52 *Ibid.* pl. 219.

53 Ramsay & Bell, *1001 Churches*, 448–50; Jerphanion, *Eglises*, I. i, 44; Kostof, *Caves of God*, 69–75.

Euphrates. A common vocabulary of arches, pilasters, niches, and mouldings may be loosely defined, but this is the general inheritance of all architecture derived ultimately from that of the Hellenistic world.

The outstanding decorative motif among cave churches and monasteries is the horseshoe-arched blind niche, the sources of which are local. Whatever their origin, horseshoe arches were well established in early Christian Cappadocia, appearing for example, in the fifth- or sixth-century churches at Yedikapulu, Eski Andaval and Sivrihisar, and in many Kara Daği churches.[54]

A further important contribution to the development of the Cappadocian façade, generally overlooked in the hunt for exotic sources, must surely have been made by the introduction of the built inscribed-cross church with decorative niching on its exterior walls. The scheme on the south wall of Ala Kilise, on Ali Suması Daği with small, closely set horseshoe-arched niches enclosing medallions, strongly recalls both the motif and arrangement so widely used in rock-cut façades (Fig. 47).

Finally, a decorated façade is a very predictable development in an architecture denied, by its nature, any other form of exterior embellishment. The masons of Cappadocia should perhaps be credited with the inventive use of locally available forms and motifs, rather than with highly improbable grand tours of Near Eastern antiquities.

The monasteries in use

Monasticism

No documentary record of the Cappadocian monasteries has yet come to light and very probably none ever will. The nature of monastic life in the volcanic valleys may therefore only be conjectured by setting the material evidence against what is known of Byzantine monasticism elsewhere in the empire. The following brief summary is centred upon those aspects of Byzantine monasticism most relevant to its material culture, rather than its spiritual aspects.[55]

The earliest monks were hermits, who withdrew from the world to live in solitude, prayer and contemplation, seeking to diminish the importance of the flesh by austerity of diet and living conditions. Thus, in 313, St Anthony of Egypt went to the edges of the desert to live as a recluse for twenty years. He was joined by followers who regarded him as their spiritual father, but also lived in individual seclusion.[56] During the next two centuries the Nile valley attracted great numbers of such hermits living in natural caves or small cells, often rock-cut, in semi-desert areas. Such hermitages survive in the desert near Esna, each consisting of a few small rooms for sleeping, cooking and food storage, and a small oratory.[57]

The term 'solitude' in this context has more than one application. For some monks it was the near-total avoidance of human contact, but for many it meant living alone for most of the time but occasionally joining others at a gathering place. The term *laura* for this loose association of monks emerged in Palestine, where a development similar to that of Egypt took place. In practical terms the laura was a scatter of cells occupied by solitaries, within reach of a church and kitchen where the anchorites would assemble weekly, for celebration of the eucharist and other religious ritual.[58]

Communal religious life, an alternative to the laura, is found in Egypt, Palestine and Asia Minor by the second half of the fourth century. In a permanent settlement, the *coenobium*, monks might live and work together, their work including agricultural labour and other activities necessary to sustain the community. The coenobium was to some extent a predictable development from the habit of followers to congregate around an ascetic of famed piety. St Euthymios, in Palestine, for example, sought solitude of the strictest kind, but nevertheless attracted followers to such an extent that a laura grew up around him; before dying, he left instructions that it should be made into a coenobium.[59] Such a community required more material substance than the anchorite groups: the fourth-century coenobium of St Pachomios at Tabennesis, on the Nile north of Thebes, had an enclosing wall, a gatehouse and guest house, an assembly hall for worship, a refectory, a kitchen and bakehouse, a hospital and a number of houses, each holding between twenty and

54 For Yedikapulu, Eski Andaval and Sivrihisar, see Restle, *Studien*, pls. 19, 48, 119; for Karaman, see Ramsay & Bell, *1001 Churches*, 316–17. The problem of the origins and diffusion of the horseshoe arch need not be taken up here; suffice it to say that it was well established before the Middle Byzantine period.

55 For broader treatments of the subject: ch. 2 in D. M. Nicol, *Meteora. The Rock Monasteries of Thessaly* (London, 1975), 18–45; C. Mango, *Byzantium. The Empire of New Rome* (London, 1980), 105–24; J. M. Hussey, 'Byzantine Monasticism', *CMH* (Cambridge, 1967), IV. 2, 161–84.

56 D. J. Chitty, *The Desert a City* (Oxford, 1977), 2–6.

57 J. Jacquet and S. Sauneron, *Les ermitages chrétiens du désert*

d'Esna, Fouilles de l'institut français d'archéologie orientale du Caire (4 vols., Cairo, 1972), II, *Descriptions et plans*. The excavators date these hermitages to the late sixth or early seventh centuries, but the type appears much earlier; it is described in the *Historia Monachorum* (B. Ward and N. Russell, *The Lives of the Desert Fathers* (Oxford, 1981), XX, 9, 106). For a comprehensive guide to the remains of early monasticism in Egypt, C. C. Walters, *Monastic Archaeology in Egypt* (Warminster, 1974).

58 Chitty, *Desert*, 14–16; Ward & Russell, *Lives* XX, 7, 8, 106.

59 D. J. Chitty, 'Two Monasteries in the Wilderness of Judaea', *PEFQ* (1928), 134–52, at 135.

forty monks, housed in individual cells.[60]

Coenobitic life in Asia Minor was to take its definitive form with St Basil of Kaisareia. Well born and well educated, Basil visited Palestine and Egypt in 357–8. On his return he removed himself and his family to Annesi, in Pontus, where he established a small community on the banks of the river Iris. His sister Makrina set up a similar establishment for women on the opposite bank. Basil stressed the importance of personal solitude but saw the coenobium as the structure within which a monk might best isolate himself from the mundane, since the company of others of similar vocation would curb self-indulgence. The 'rules' which Basil drew up defined the life style and comportment of the monk: simplicity of dress, and of diet, the shedding of personal property, restraint and compassion when dealing with others, the necessity for labour. Communal life required an administrative structure: the coenobium would have a superior (*higumenos*) and a second-in-charge (*deuteros*).[61] In time a series of other offices evolved, and in later centuries were often specified, as were other aspects of organization, in the *typikon*, or foundation charter of the monastery.[62]

The anchoritic and coenobitic habits that co-existed in early Christian times continued to do so throughout the Byzantine period. They were, from the outset, often complementary: a monk might spend part of his life as a hermit and part in a community. Anchoritism was seen as a particularly exalted form of piety, not to be undertaken without preparation. Extreme asceticism, wherein the concept of austerity was warped to encompass self-injury, was generally rejected.[63] It became usual for a monk to begin his religious life in a community and later, having proved his fitness for the solitary life to the satisfaction of his *higumenos*, become an anchorite. The council of Trullo (692) specified that the solitary life might be taken up only after at least three years in a coenobium.[64]

In the early Christian centuries, monasteries spread across the empire. There were over seventy monasteries in and around Constantinople by the end of the sixth century, and the urban monastery is also known elsewhere.[65] Most monasteries, however, were in rural areas.

Monasteries varied considerably in size, some with monks in their hundreds, others with just a few. The very large were exceptional; most monasteries seem to have had from ten to twenty monks and few had more than fifty.[66]

The notion of physical removal from the world embraced by the desert fathers endured to the extent that wildernesses remained attractive to monastic settlement. The monastic 'centre', an accumulation of monasteries in a single, geographically isolated area, became an important feature of the Byzantine world. The development seen in early monasticism is repeated in the histories of monastic centres of the Middle Byzantine centuries. Mount Olympos, in Bithynia, south of the Sea of Marmara, first colonized by solitaries in the fourth century, became an important Middle Byzantine monastic centre from which records of over sixty monasteries have survived.[67] The monastic settlement of Latmos, on the coast of southwest Anatolia, was started, possibly as early as the seventh century, by refugee monks who lived in loose association; by the mid ninth century there were both coenobia and hermitages.[68] Mount Athos, in the first half of the ninth century, was the site chosen by a recluse, Peter the Athonite, who was joined there by a small group of followers. In the tenth century St Athanasios, with imperial benevolence, established the first coenobium of Athos.[69] The pattern occurs again in the last centuries of the Byzantine empire at Meteora, in Thessaly.[70] Most of these centres had a range of monastic institutions: hermitages, laurai and coenobia.

Isolation from the world did not, of course, exclude charity. Many solitaries were famed for their abilities to heal and counsel, and the philanthropic opportunities available to a monastic community were quickly recognized: when St Basil left Pontus to return to Kaisareia, soon to become its bishop, he founded a coenobium outside the city which, in addition to a church and housing for the community, had a hospital and hospice for travellers. The twelfth-century Pantocrator Monastery in Constantinople had a large hospital with a permanent medical staff and separate wards for different classes of ailment.[71] This degree of organization is exceptional, but most monasteries had the giving of

60 Chitty, *Desert*, 20–3.
61 W. K. L. Clarke, *Basil the Great. A Study in Monasticism* (Cambridge, 1913), 19ff., 48ff., 59ff.
62 R. Janin, 'Le monachisme byzantin au moyen age. Commande et typika (Xe–XIVe siècle)', *REB* 22 (1964), 5–44, at 28–9.
63 C. Butler, *The Lausiac History of Palladius* (Cambridge 1898), 241; I. Pena, P. Castellana, R. Fernandez, *Les reclus syriens* (Milan, 1980), 103–6.
64 *Mansi* XI, 964.
65 P. Charanis, 'The Monk as an Element in Byzantine Society', *DOP* 25 (1971), 61–84, at 64–5. For Constantinople: R. Janin, *La*

géographie ecclesiastique de l'empire byzantin (Paris, 1953), 3–4.
66 Charanis, 'The Monk', 69–72.
67 R. Janin, *Les églises et les monastères des grands centres byzantins* (Paris, 1975), 127–31.
68 T. Wiegand, *Der Latmos (Milet. Ergebnisse der Ausgrabungen und Untersuchungen seit dem Jahre 1899)* (Berlin, 1913), III. i, 178–80.
69 K. Lake, *Early Days of Monasticism on Mount Athos* (Oxford, 1909), 11.
70 Nicol, *Meteora*, 81–3.
71 P. Gautier, 'Le typikon du Christ Sauveur Pantocrator', *REB* 32 (1974), 1–145, at 83–7.

alms and of hospitality to travellers, shelter for the needy, including orphans and the elderly, as an established part of their work, frequently defined in their *typika*.[72]

Much of this elementary philanthropy concerned the poor, but the charitable services that the monastery as an institution could provide were of interest to the wealthy also. Patrons had various reasons for founding or endowing monasteries, among them provision for retirement in old age and, eventually, of a place for burial and the assurance of prayers said for the soul of the departed. The monastery could also be a place of refuge for, or disposal of, those running foul of political life: much of what is known of the monasteries on the islands in the Sea of Marmara, just beyond the Bosphoros, comes from references to their role as places of imprisonment for those out of favour with the court of Constantinople.[73]

The secular world from which the monks sought to isolate themselves was always reluctant to be abandoned. From the fifth century onwards, church and state passed a series of edicts which were designed to control aspects of monastic life. The following selection offers glimpses of the problems that generated them: the Council of Chalcedon (451) prohibited monks from entering the army, marrying and concerning themselves in secular affairs, and required that episcopal approval be sought for new foundations. Justinian, in a series of novellas, defined standards for the domestic conditions of a coenobium but acknowledged the right of anchorites to live apart; the superior (*higumenos*) was to be elected by the community, or appointed by a bishop; double monasteries (having sections for men and women) were prohibited. The Council of Trullo (692) set ten years as the minimum age for entry to a monastery; the second Council of Nicaea (787) attempted to regulate the migration of monks from one monastery to another.[74] The repetition of these directions and prohibitions in subsequent acts suggests, however, that they were often violated.

Monastic ownership of land, the main source of revenue in the medieval world, engendered exploitation and clashes of interests. In the tenth century, the emperors Nikephoros Phokas and Basil II sought to restrict the acquisition of peasant land by monasteries.[75] Attempts were made to inhibit the foundation by the laity of new monasteries. Nikephoros Phokas' often quoted novella of 964 attacked the worldliness and wealth of monasteries and prohibited the foundation of new ones. Intending patrons were directed to use their largesse to repair existing monasteries that were in a state of decay. An exception was made, however, for hermit cells and laurai, provided that their land-holdings be very modest. Although Nikephoros' prohibition on new foundations was repealed twenty-four years later, continuing problems with the establishment of small monasteries, many of which endured only as long as their founders, are apparent from the 996 novella of Basil II, which refused to recognize as a monastery any foundation with less than eight monks.[76] As a revenue-producing property, the monastery might have greater temporal than spiritual interest for the layman. From at least the eighth century, possibly earlier, monasteries could be bought and sold, bequeathed and inherited.[77] However close individual monks might have been to the spiritual concerns that led the early anchorites to the desert, the monastery became a significant element in Byzantine materialism.

Hermitages

The Cappadocian hermitages are easily placed against the background of Byzantine monasticism sketched above. They were clearly the establishments of anchorites. Niketas, the hermit of Güllü Dere, is called 'the stylite' and apparently lived in a cell at the top of his cone, as did the monk Symeon of Zelve. The stylite habit – literally living on top of a column – originated with St Symeon the Stylite in fourth-century Syria and was adopted by a series of others in later centuries.[78] Parallels for the equation of a suitable natural feature with a stylite's column are found in the early tenth-century hermitage of Paul of Latmos, which was a cave at the top of a rocky crag, and the similar fourteenth-century hermitage of Athanasios at Meteora.[79] Most of the other hermitages described above also probably began as anchorite dwelling places. Some, like the Karabaş Kilise complex, either were, or became, the sites of small communities: possibly a gathering of disciples around a founder hermit.

The excavation and decoration of chapels on at least three of these sites (Karabaş; St Barbara, Soğanlı; Niketas the Stylite) were the work of lay patrons. The

72 D. Constantelos, *Byzantine Philanthropy and Social Welfare* (New Jersey, 1968), 90–1.

73 Janin, *Centres*, 63–71.

74 Janin, 'Le monachisme byzantin', 6–7.

75 P. Charanis, 'The Monastic Properties and the State in the Byzantine Empire', *DOP* 4 (1948), 51–118, at 55.

76 *Ibid.* 63.

77 P. Lemerle, 'Un aspect du rôle des monastères à Byzance: les monastères donnés à des laïcs, les charisticaires', *CRAI* (1967), 9–28, at 11–12.

78 H. Delehaye, *Les saints stylites* (Brussels/Paris, 1923), cxvii–cxliii.

79 Wiegand, *Latmos*, 233–4; Nicol, *Meteora*, 94–5. Also G. P. Schiemenz, 'Die Kapelle des Styliten Niketas in den Weinbergen von Ortahisar', *JÖB* 18 (1969), 239–58, at 254–5.

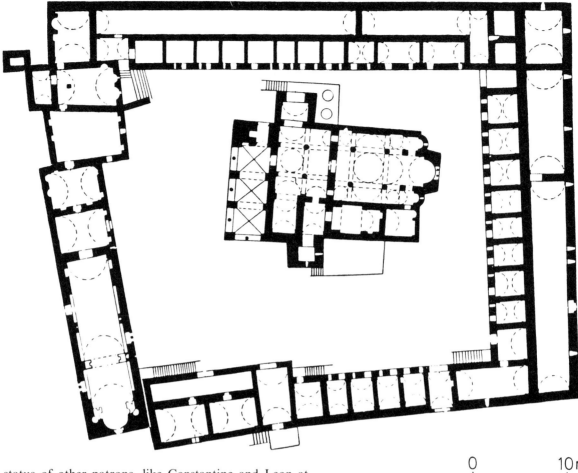

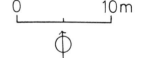

48. Monastery of St Meletios, near Megara (after Orlandos).

status of other patrons, like Constantine and Leon at Tokalı Kilise and John, the founder of the Monastery of Panagia and All Saints, at Ayvalı Kilise, is unknown. Beyond Cappadocia, there are documented examples of the patronage of hermitages. For example, the church of St Barbara, on the site of the hermitage of St Luke of Phokis, was built by the *strategos* Krinites Arotras, who had turned to the hermit for counsel.[80] Similarly, in Paphos, Cyprus, the bishop Basil Kinnamos caused the expansion of the hermitage of St Neophytos to form a laura and probably commissioned the painting of the hermit's cave-dwelling.[81] A considerable difference of degree separates these from the minor benefactions that were received by the Cappadocian hermits, but the principle is likely to have been similar. The laura that grew up around Neophytos' cave survived into the post-Byzantine period and the saint left writings; the hermitage of St Luke became an important monastery with imperial benefactors. Cappadocia was a less propitious ground for the survival of permanent records.

Monastery plans

The study of Byzantine monastic architecture is hindered by several factors: the monasteries that have survived (most of these are in Greece) have done so because they continued in use into the post-Byzantine period. They have thus accumulated alterations and rebuilding over several centuries, and their original forms are often uncertain. Those that perished with the empire, or before it, have fallen into ruin, or been lost entirely. In particular, there are very few remains of small monasteries, such as the Cappadocian ones. Saints' lives, *typika* and other sources of monastic history seldom describe the physical circumstances of the monasteries to which they refer in sufficient detail for reconstruction. Further, there must

80 E. G. Stikas, *To oikodomikon chronikon tes mones tou Hosiou Louka Phokidos* (Athens, 1970), 6–7.

81 C. Mango and E. J. W. Hawkins, 'The Hermitage of St Neophytos and its Wall Paintings', *DOP* 20 (1966), 119–206, at 124 and 205–6.

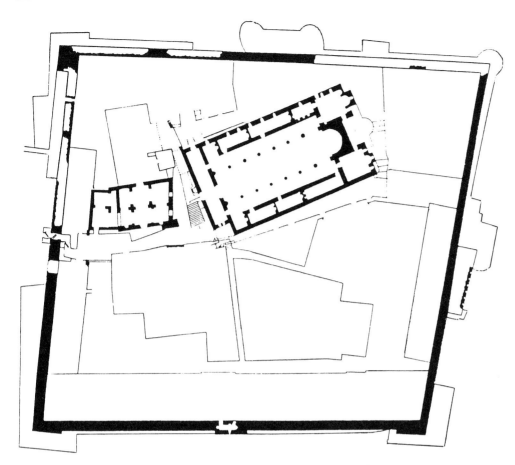

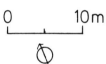

49. Monastery of St Catherine, Mt Sinai (after Forsyth).

have been considerable variety in the architecture of the Byzantine monastery: an establishment with half a dozen monks would obviously have been materially different from one with a large number of monks and extensive charitable functions; there were doubtless also differences between urban and rural monasteries. Monasteries are likely to be architecturally organic, adding structures as needed. Finally, the monastic principle of material simplicity is not one to encourage architectural refinement.

The most familiar Middle Byzantine monastery plan, found in many of the monasteries of Greece, consists of an enclosed courtyard with its perimeter wall lined with rooms: cells, store rooms, offices, often on two or more floors. The monastery church occupies the centre of the open courtyard and the refectory is frequently at the west side, opposite the church entrance. The complex is entered by a gatehouse and the courtyard likely to contain a fountain and a well.[82] The monastery of St Meletios, near Megara, will serve as an example (Fig. 48).[83]

The courtyard plan with free-standing church is found centuries earlier in the sixth-century monastery of St Catherine on Mount Sinai (Fig. 49).[84] It is not, however, typical of early monasteries. The plan at Mount Sinai is essentially that of a modified fortress and its recurrence in later centuries is likely to have been a matter of parallel development rather than inheritance. In general the early monasteries of the east were less regular in their arrangement. The monastery of St Euthymios, in Palestine, for example, had its church set against the eastern enclosing wall (Fig. 50). The plan shows rooms of several periods and the original arrangement might not have been so haphazard. Nevertheless, the contours shown on the site

82 P. M. Mylonas, 'L'architecture monastique du Mont Athos', *Le Millénaire du Mont Athos* (Venice, 1964), II, 229–46, at 234–5; A. K. Orlandos, *Monasteriake architektonike* (Athens, 1958), 13–16.

83 A. K. Orlandos, *Archeion ton Buzantinon mnemeion tes Hellados*

5 (1935–40), 34–118.

84 G. H. Forsyth, 'The Monastery of St. Catherine at Mount Sinai: the Church and Fortress of Justinian', *DOP* 22 (1968), 1–19, fig. 1.

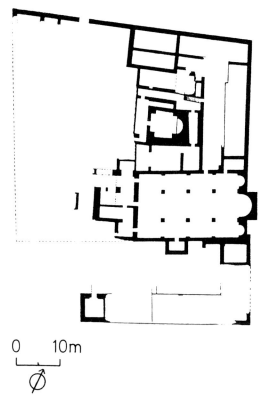

0   10m

50. Monastery of St Euthymios, Palestine (after Chitty).

plan make it unlikely that the church was ever central.[85]
The Coptic monasteries of the Wadi 'n Natrun, are virtually villages enclosed within walls, with little formal
arrangement (Fig. 51). Their walls form irregular rectangles, within which blocks of cells and other rooms are
both set against the walls and free-standing. These
monasteries were founded between the late fourth and
mid sixth centuries. They now have no buildings earlier
than the ninth century and some later still, but it is
unlikely that the present informal plans replace formal
earlier ones.[86] Early monasteries in Syria consisted of
churches with residential buildings grouped nearby.
Occasionally a symmetrical scheme is found: the
monastery of Id-Dêr, for example, has its basilical church
opening off the west side of a square colonnaded atrium,
around which is a regular series of rooms on two floors
(Fig. 52).[87] Others are less orderly: the seventh-century
monastery of Sameh has an open courtyard with blocks

of rooms on north and south sides, with the church
appended to the south block (Fig. 53).[88] Lack of formal
planning is also the case in the few monasteries of Asia
Minor that have survived as substantial ruins or been
excavated. The fifth/sixth-century buildings of Alahan
Monastery, to the south of Karaman, straggle along an
artificial terrace on a hillside (Fig. 54).[89]

In the Kara Dağı region, Değile site 35/45 has a zig-zag
of rectangular blocks, each containing several rooms. A
church to the east has no formal architectural connection
with the complex, and in fact appears to be walled off
from the open area which fronts the rooms (Fig. 55).[90]
Fragments of three sides of a courtyard with rooms
around it remain at Değile site 32/39/43 (Fig. 56), and a
basilical church is placed to one side of it.[91] Another
Değile site, which includes a basilical church (33) and a
single-naved chapel (36), has a rectangular courtyard,
with the church at the west side and the chapel in the
centre of the courtyard (Fig. 57). Rooms are irregularly
grouped to the north of the church. The church entrance
is on the perimeter of the complex as recorded by Bell,
so there was probably a further part of the complex to
the west, in front of the church.[92] It is not even certain
that these complexes were monasteries, they were in ruins
when first described and are even more so now. Eyice suggests that 39/43 may be an episcopal palace rather than
a monastery, and that 45 may be a house.[93] Closer to the
volcanic valley region, on Hasan Dağı, is what Bell described as 'the single instance of the square plan in central
Asia Minor'.[94] This was a complex known as the *Han*,
which had a square courtyard with a single-naved church
set into its southeast corner (Fig. 58). The plan also shows
a rectangular room of uncertain date and function; the
other monastery buildings are lost.

Fragmentary though the evidence is, it seems that there
was no standard plan for the early monasteries of Asia
Minor, nor, perhaps for early monasteries in general. For
the Middle Byzantine monastery in Asia Minor there is
even less evidence. Several monasteries in Bithynia, on
the Sea of Marmara, have been identified, but they are
so ruined or overbuilt that their original forms are indis-
tinguishable. One of them, the Monastery of St John of
Pelekete, had, when seen in 1910, a rectangular courtyard
lined with rooms, and a central church. The latter had
been rebuilt in 1838, however, and the original form of

85 D. J. Chitty, 'The Monastery of St Euthymios', *PEFQ* (1932), 188–
    203, at 191.
86 H. G. Evelyn-White, *The Monasteries of the Wadi 'n Natrun. Part
    III: The Archaeology and Architecture* (New York, 1933), 5, pls. 4,
    35, 50, 80.
87 H. C. Butler, *Early Churches in Syria* (Princeton, 1929), 85–8.
88 *Ibid.* 89–90.

89 M. Gough, 'Alahan Monastery. Fourth Preliminary Report',
    AnatSt 17 (1967), 37–47.
90 Ramsay & Bell, *1001 Churches*, 183–93.
91 *Ibid.* 199–209.
92 *Ibid.* 164–78.
93 Eyice, *Karadağ*, 53–5 (211–12) and 62–3 (213–14).
94 *Ibid.* 463–4.

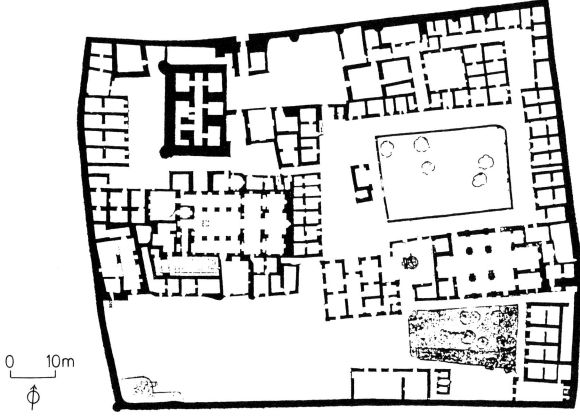

51. Monastery of Baramûs, Wadi'n Natrun, Egypt (after Evelyn-White).

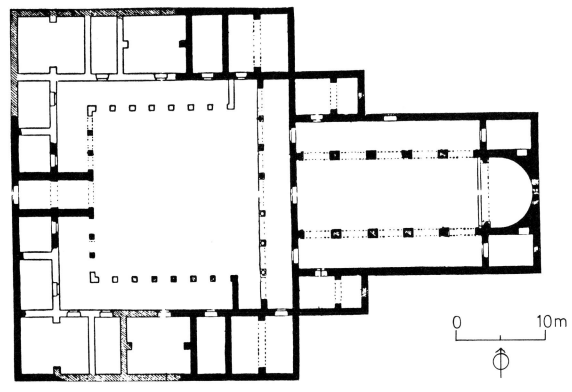

52. Monastery of Id-Dêr, Syria (after Butler).

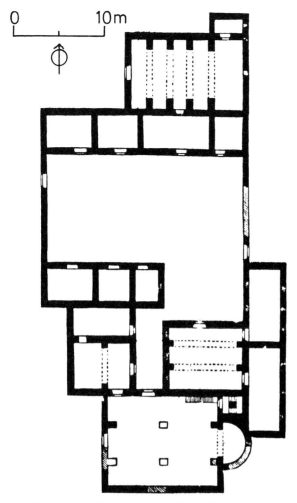

53. Monastery of Sameh, Syria (after Butler).

the whole is uncertain.[95] In the monasteries of Latmos, on the Carian coast, fortified walls enclose churches, cell blocks and other monastic buildings, generally without formal arrangement. Churches are often free-standing, but the schemes lack the compactness of the Greek plans: the enclosing walls follow the lines of the irregular hill sites.[96]

In the east, several monasteries survive in the Tur Abdin, in Mesopotamia. Some of these were founded in the fourth century and are still in use, so their buildings span several centuries. Nevertheless, there seems to have been no impulse towards orderly architectural planning.

The monastery of Saints Samuel, Symeon and Gabriel, near Kartmin, is typical in having a cluster of buildings within surrounding walls.[97]

The Armenian Monastery of Hogeac'vank', near Van, has its buildings, including the church, grouped in one corner of a square enclosed by the walls (Fig. 59). The foundation date of the monastery is uncertain, but it was probably in existence by the second half of the ninth century; it was restored in the seventeenth century.[98] The monastery of Srkhouvank also had its church embedded within other monastery rooms. Again the foundation date is unknown and the present buildings may date only from the rebuilding after the earthquake of 1648.[99] The plan of the monastery of Etchmiadzin does resemble those of the Greek monasteries, with its central, free-standing church enclosed by a square of domestic buildings. This arrangement is unusual in Armenian monasteries, however, and most of the monastic buildings are recent.[100] The form of the fourteenth-century monastery of Sumela, outside Trebizond, is largely dictated by its mountain-side site. It has a series of narrow rectangular courtyards, running north/south at different levels. The rooms run along the eastern side and the church is on the west side of the main courtyard.[101]

No conclusions as to the form of the Middle Byzantine monastery in central Anatolia may be drawn from such scant evidence. In view of the lack of architectural formality in the early monasteries of the east, however, it seems likely that the scheme found in the Greek monasteries was not ubiquitous, but was a development of the western part of the empire.

Courtyard monasteries

To some extent, the courtyard monasteries resemble the Greek monasteries as they now appear, with rooms arranged around a courtyard. The principal divergence from this plan is that the Cappadocian monastery has its church to one side of the courtyard, rather than in its centre, and the courtyard is generally three-sided, rather than completely enclosed. Both these features are, of course, attributable to the rock-cut method: the church cannot, in such a context, be free-standing, and the excavation of a four-sided courtyard would have been very laborious. It may also have been the case that the

95 C. Mango and I. Ševčenko, 'Some Churches and Monasteries on the Southern Shore of the Sea of Marmara', *DOP* 27 (1973), 235–77, at 247.

96 Wiegand, *Latmos*, figs. 19, 60, Supplements 1, 3, 4.

97 G. L. Bell, *Churches and Monasteries of the Tur Abdin and Neighbouring Districts* (Heidelberg, 1913), 64–70.

98 J. M. Thierry, 'Monastères arméniens de Vaspurakan', *REArm* n.s.

4 (1967), 167–86, at 171–4.

99 *Idem, REArm* n.s. 8 (1971), 215–27, at 218, pl. 42.

100 J. Strzygowski, *Die Baukunst der Armenier und Europa* (Vienna, 1918), 247–8.

101 D. Talbot Rice, 'Notice on Some Religious Buildings in the City and Vilayet of Trebizond', *Byzantion* 5 (1929–30), 47–81, at 73–5.

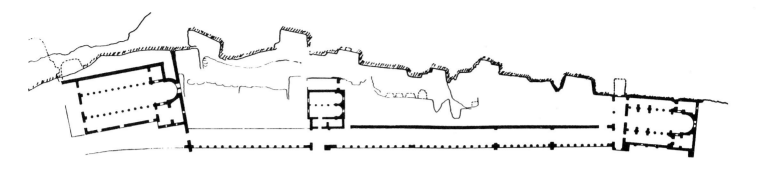

0 10m

54. Alahan Monastery (after Gough).

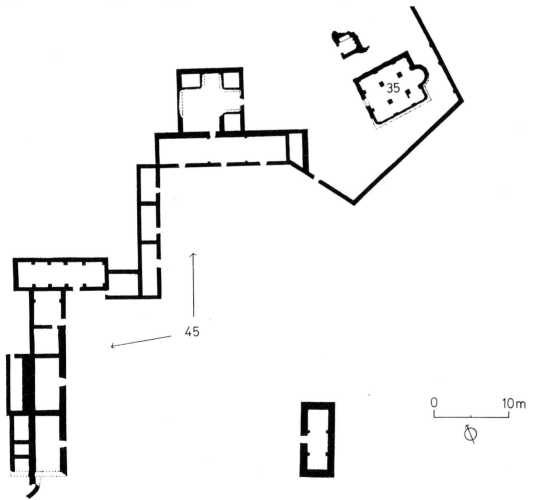

0 10m

55. Değile 35/45 (after Bell).

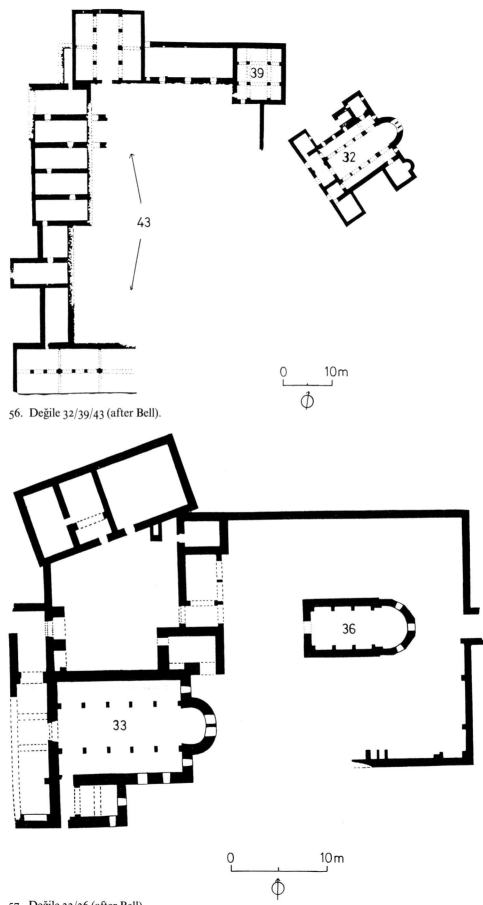

56. Değile 32/39/43 (after Bell).

57. Değile 33/36 (after Bell).

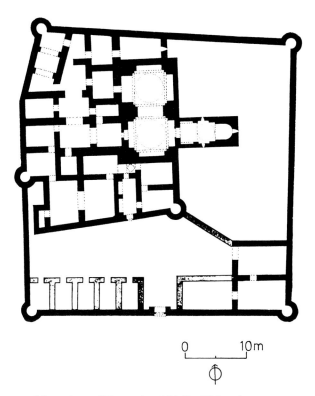

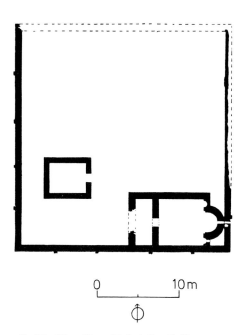

58. The Han, Kara Dağı (after Bell).

59. Monastery of Hogeac'vank' (after Thierry).

fourth side of the cave monastery courtyard was closed by a masonry wall. Perhaps, therefore, the regular lines of the cave monasteries are to be related to the Greek square plan: conceivably the currents that brought the inscribed-cross church to Cappadocia carried the regular monastery plan also. This is, however, only speculation, since it will be evident from the discussion above that so little is known of the architecture of the Middle Byzantine monastery in central Anatolia that no assessment of the architecture of the cave monasteries in this context is possible.

The attribution of functions to the individual rooms of a courtyard monastery is also largely a matter of speculation. Some rooms have obvious functions: the kitchens (square rooms with wide domes, conical or pyramidical vaults, and smoke holes at the centre) are of a type traditional in the Greek monasteries and probably generally.[102] The large halls present in all the courtyard monasteries were probably refectories, supplied in most cases with wooden rather than rock-cut furniture. The traditional refectory plan, again known chiefly from Greek examples, but probably much more widespread, is a rectangular room with a recess at the far end to mark the head of the table, or to provide a place for the reader

of psalms at mealtimes.[103] This form is found in Hallaç Monastery, Şahinefendi Monastery, Karanlık Kale and Eski Gümüş Monastery. In the last of these there are fragments of a rock-cut table and benches. At Selime Kalesi, the main contenders for identification as the refectory are the large halls, 13 and 18; Room 18 is closer to the kitchen, but its galleries have no obvious function in a refectory, so perhaps the simpler Room 13 had this function.

Sleeping accommodation for the monks is more problematic. The Greek monasteries housed their monks in small cells, arranged in blocks, often on more than one floor.[104] Such is also the case in the Coptic monasteries mentioned above. There are no comparable structures in the cave monasteries, however. It is most unlikely that cell blocks were free-standing, built structures, since no trace of such blocks remains and cells could so easily have been rock-cut. Another possibility is that the monasteries were *laurai*, with their monks living as solitaries using the monastery for occasional assembly. Then, however, a collection of hermitages in the vicinity of each monastery should be present. Even given the difficulty of identifying such dwellings among the rough cavities of post-Byzantine agriculture, some should be recognizable, from

102 Orlandos, *Monasteriake architektonike*, 61–8.   103 *Ibid.* 43–55.   104 *Ibid.* 31–37.

carved or painted crosses, or inscriptions, and this is not the case.

Alternatively, some of the smaller monastery rooms may have been dormitories. Cell blocks of the Greek type also appear to be absent from the monasteries of Asia Minor mentioned above. There may indeed have been a difference of tradition in this respect between the monasteries of the western part of the empire and those of central and eastern Anatolia. Accommodation in dormitories was specified in a novella of Justinian; perhaps this recommendation was not always ignored.[105] At Hallaç Monastery, the two small rooms flanking the hall (3 and 4) may have been dormitories, since they are less public than the others, having no entrance direct from the vestibule or courtyard. At Bezir Hane, Rooms 3 and 4, at the west side of the vestibule, may have had this function; at Kılıçlar Monastery Room 3; the upper rooms 7 and 8 at Karanlık Kilise Monastery; Rooms 3 and 4 at Aynalı Kilise Monastery; Rooms 1–4 at Selime Kalesi; Rooms 4 and 8 at Karanlık Kale; Rooms a–c at Şahinefendi Monastery; perhaps Room 3 at Direkli Kilise.

In most cases the limited capacity of these rooms suggests that the number of monks was small: perhaps as few as ten in many of the monasteries, and as many as thirty in the larger Selime Kalesi. Such small numbers do not appear consistent with the size of the refectories, which seem to provide for larger numbers. Karanlık Kilise Monastery, in which furniture survives, has a table that would seat about forty-five if closely packed, perhaps thirty more comfortably. The table fragment at Eski Gümüş would have seated fifteen to twenty, but may originally have been longer. If the other refectories had tables commensurate with the room size than they, too, could have catered for similar numbers. Certainly the existence of large kitchens in most of these monasteries implies a larger community than the available housing suggests. Some of this capacity may, however, have been provided to accommodate guests. Most of the courtyard monasteries probably had a population in the ten-to-twenty bracket cited above for the majority of Byzantine monasteries, occasionally swelled by visitors. The problem then arises as to where the guests stayed. In some monasteries there are a few well-finished rooms in excess of those that met domestic needs. Some of these may have served as hospices. Room 5 at Hallaç Monastery and Room 18 at Selime Kalesi may, for example, have had such a function. In general, however, there are no such

extra rooms. Perhaps visitors stayed in the villages, visiting the monasteries only for meals and services. Very little is known of the habits of Middle Byzantine travellers in central Anatolia, but one ancient practice, still employed, may be considered: they may have used tents.[106]

Underground cavities, probably storage basements, are found at Eski Gümüş Monastery, Hallaç Monastery and Kılıçlar Monastery, and perhaps remain undiscovered in others. Only one complex, Eski Gümüş Monastery, has a 'secret' room (Room 21). Given its difficulty of access, this was probably for the storage of valuables, including books, perhaps – its deep niches may have held cupboards (and the scenes from Aesop painted on the walls are perhaps evidence of the discreet perusal of secular literature in this room). It is not necessary to conclude from the lack of such rooms elsewhere that the other monasteries were without valuables. In the convoluted landscape of the volcanic valleys it would be safest to excavate a treasury chamber outside the main complex, with a hidden entrance. The hypothesis may provide inspiration for the explorer.

One feature, the tomb chamber, is of particular importance in assessing the function of the courtyard monastery. At Hallaç Monastery a chamber to the south of the church contains three graves and space for two more; at Şahinefendi and Karanlık Kilise Monastery tomb chambers open to the south of the narthex, each containing two graves; at Aynalı Monastery a chamber opening off the east of the narthex contains an arcosolium with space for one grave pit; at Selime Kalesi a chamber to the north of the narthex contains a single grave; at Eski Gümüs Monastery a tomb chamber with two graves, cut at different times, opens off the north wall of the naos; at Karanlık Kale the side chapel contains a single arcosolium and Room 3, opening off the hall, contains two graves; at Direkli Kilise Monastery the side chapel contains an arcosolium with two graves. In all cases, the tomb chamber is clearly designed to give prominence to a small number of interments only, it is not the general burying-place for the community.

It is clear, therefore, that these monasteries had a memorial purpose. The tomb chambers were to receive either the remains of the founders themselves or those of persons whose memory the founders sought to preserve. One possibility that arises, given that hermitages gathered importance as successive patrons paid them pious attention, is that the courtyard monasteries represent a final

---

105 Novella 5 (535): C. E. Zacharie von Lingenthal, *Imp.Iustiniani PP.A. Novella quae vocantur* (Leipzig, 1881), 63.
106 Temporary shelters are, of course, associated with the Turkish and Arab peoples of the east Mediterranean and central Asia, rather than with the Byzantines. The suggestion here is simply that the

Byzantines of central Anatolia may have adopted the habits of their nomadic neighbours for journeys such as pilgrimages. For a recent survey of the forms of temporary shelter used by the peoples of the east Mediterranean and central Asia, see T. Faegre, *Tents. Architecture of the Nomads* (London, 1979), chapters 1–3.

stage in the process – they were excavated to take the remains of holy men. But none of the courtyard monasteries contains any reference to a venerated hermit. The evidence of the hermitage sites is that original structures, however humble (the ill-cut Old Church of Tokalı Kilise is an example) were preserved, but no such structures are found on the monastery sites. More probably, therefore, the courtyard monasteries were founded to be the memorials of their patrons. The hermitages may be a factor, however, in the sense that sanctity given to the volcanic valley area by the presence of hermits was doubtless a reason for siting memorial establishments there. This interpretation is consistent with the indications that the numbers of monks were small: the founders provided for their own, or their families' interment and for a small monastic community to run them. One exception, Selime Kalesi, so much larger than the rest, was probably not founded with this function only. The single grave in its tomb chamber was probably, however, for a member of the family depicted on the west wall of the church.

Refectory monasteries

A separation of function between the courtyard and refectory monasteries is implied by their different architectural forms. The refectory monastery does not have the range of rooms of the courtyard monastery, it consists simply of church, refectory and a number of rough rooms. A difference in burial arrangements is also evident. There are no elaborate tomb chambers, graves are often found in narthexes, but in larger numbers than in the courtyard monasteries and without special architecture to shelter them. The refectory monasteries do not, therefore, appear to have been established as memorials.

Again, there are no cells, so accommodation must have been in dormitories. A large number of rough cavities exists in the Göreme Park area, and around Yusuf Koç Kilisesi Monastery and the Archangel Monastery in Cemil. Subsequent use of the monuments for agricultural purposes may account for many of the cavities, but some must be original. A few, such as cavities (b) and (c) in Göreme Unit 2 are certainly so, for they have decorated entrances. But since it is impossible to know how many of the cavities are original, population size may not be estimated from them.

Most of the refectory tables could seat thirty to forty people. Since there are at least ten refectories associated with monastery units in Göreme valley, a population of 300 to 400 could have been provided for. This is an upper limit, of course, reached only if all refectories were in full

use at the same time, which need not have been the case. As suggested in connection with the courtyard monasteries, it may have been that the resident communities were much smaller than the refectory tables suggest, and that extra seating space was provided for visitors. The absence of rooms clearly identifiable as kitchens perhaps also argues for small permanent communities occasionally swelled by numbers of visitors. Even so, both permanent residents and visitors must have needed feeding, and there must have been kitchens of some sort. They evidently did not employ the formal architecture of the courtyard monastery kitchens, but must have been much rougher cavities whose function is no longer identifiable.

The boundary lines drawn in Fig. 30 to divide the Göreme structures into 'monastic units' are largely a matter of archaeological convenience. It is impossible to define accurate limits for the units, or to know what relationship existed between them. For reasons given in Chapter 4, however, it is probable that the Göreme structures constitute several institutions, rather than a single monastery. The two monastery types are, therefore, differently distributed: the courtyard monasteries are spread throughout the volcanic valley area, whereas the refectory monasteries are concentrated in Göreme valley. The two exceptions are Yusuf Koç Kilisesi Monastery, two kilometres away as the crow flies, and the Archangel Monastery in Cemil. Particular importance, therefore, must have been attached to the Göreme site to encourage such density. When the immediate vicinity is scanned for a suitable focus, that which presents itself is, of course, Tokalı Kilise, the most elaborate of all the cave churches. Jerphanion interpreted Tokalı Kilise as the *katholikon* of a monastery in Göreme valley.[107] The chronology of the monuments of Göreme valley does not support this, however, since the refectory development post-dates all phases of Tokalı Kilise. I have suggested above that this church, with its several phases of alteration and two phases of high-quality painting, marks the site of an important hermitage. Rather than being the *katholikon* of a single Göreme monastery, therefore, it may have been the *raison d'être* for the later series of Göreme refectory monasteries. Increasing veneration of the site may have caused an eleventh-century development of the valley and the large refectory tables were to accommodate pilgrims coming to visit Tokalı Kilise. The number of resident monks may, as in the case of the courtyard monastery, have been small. The pilgrims would have had the same rough dormitory accommodation as the monks, in cave rooms nearby, or, as suggested above, in tents.

The Archangel Monastery may have had a similar

107 Jerphanion, *Eglises*, I. i, 43.

function, catering to pilgrims to the *hagisma* or holy spring on the site. Yusuf Koç Kilisesi Monastery is perhaps to be connected with the Göreme development, since it is not far away. Alternatively it may have had an attraction of its own: perhaps the small room (3) behind the large porch and façade contained a venerated relic.

A final difference between the refectory and courtyard monasteries appears to have been one of wealth. The labour involved in carving out a whole series of rooms for a courtyard monastery implies the availability of more lavish patronage than that which endowed the refectory monasteries. The painting in courtyard monastery churches, too, is generally of higher quality than that found in refectory monasteries. There is some overlap between the groups in this respect, since a single workshop probably painted Karanlık Kilise (part of a courtyard monastery) and Çarıklı Kilise and Elmalı Kilise, which are part of the refectory monastery development. Even here, however, it is noticeable that the painted programme of Karanlık Kilise, with its lavish use of blue, an expensive pigment, must have been far more costly than the more modest programmes and largely earth-colour paintings of Çarıklı and Elmalı Kilise.

A general difference of function between the two monastery types may be summarized thus: the courtyard monasteries were probably established by wealthy patrons, primarily as their own memorials; they were probably sited in the volcanic valleys because of the existence there of hermitages and small monastic communities, but were not directly associated with such establishments. The refectory monasteries, on the other hand, seem to have had a direct connection with venerated sites, particularly the site of Tokalı Kilise in Göreme, probably acting as custodians and providing for visitors. Karanlık Kilise Monastery, a courtyard monastery in Göreme valley, may have had a dual role.

Patronage

Some information concerning the patrons of Cappadocian cave monasteries is available from painted inscriptions and donor images. Most of the these are found in the hermitage group of monuments. Eustathios the *Kleisourarch* of Zeugos and Klados(?), at the hermitage of Niketas the Stylite, was a military commander, in charge of a frontier area.[108] If Zeugos is to be identified with Zygos, in Antitaurus, then his area of operation was some 170 km from the cave chapel he commissioned and he was a visitor to the volcanic valley region.[109]

John, the patron of Ayvalı Kilise, is described as 'the builder of the monastery of Panagia and All Saints', which was probably not the hermitage itself (see above, Chapter 5). The location of the Monastery of Panagia and All Saints cannot be determined; it cannot have been one of the cave monasteries since Ayvalı Kilise, cut in the late ninth or early tenth century, predates these. Among the ruins of built architecture in the region there is none that may be identified as a monastery; thus if the Monastery of Panagia and All Saints were local, it has vanished without trace. Alternatively, it may have been outside the area and therefore John may also have been a visitor.

Constantine and Leon, who redecorated Tokalı Kilise in the mid tenth century, are without titles, but the quality of the work commissioned by them suggests that they were both wealthy and sophisticated. Here, too, there is a reference in the dedicatory inscription to a monastery (of the Heavenly Angels?) which may be elsewhere than Göreme, since part of the inscription may have been copied from another church (see Chapter 5). The eleventh-century redecoration of Karabaş Kilise was the commission of the Skepides family, headed by Michael Skepides, the *Protospatharios*. Two members of the family, Catherine and Nyphon, are described as *monachos* and *monache* but, as noted above, they were probably not members of the community of Karabaş Kilise. They may have taken the monastic habit on retirement or *in extremis* and the monastic presence in the volcanic valleys may have prompted Michael Skepides to decorate Karabaş Kilise to commemorate these events in his family.

Another member of this family is commemorated in Gök Kilise, also in Soğanlı valley, where a painted inscription reads: '[Kind Lord] protect your servant John Skepides, *Protospatharios* of the *chrysotriklinion*, *Hypatos* and *Strategos*'.[110] The style of the painting in Gök Kilise seems to place it in the eleventh century, but a more precise dating is impossible: John Skepides' panel may have preceded or followed the painting of Karabaş

108 N. Oikonomedes, *Les listes de préséance byzantines des 9e et 10e siècles* (Paris, 1972), 342.
109 N. Thierry, 'Les enseignements historiques de l'archéologie cappadocienne', *TM* 8 (1981), 501–19, at 508.
110 Gök Kilise has twin barrel-vaulted naves with a single apse in each, the south one closed by a tall screen. The church is undecorated except for two panels of painting of high quality in the north nave: one panel contains figures of Kosmas and Damianos, the other,

on the west wall, shows St Eustathios on horseback pursuing a stag. The inscription mentioned runs along the top of the panel. Jerphanion, *Eglises*, II, 369–72, Inscription no. 206; Rott, *Denkmäler*, 144–5; Grégoire, 'Rapport', 98. The qualification 'of the *chrysotriklinion*' is derived from the monogram XPE which is commonly used in ancient inscriptions for *chreophylakion* and was so interpreted by Jerphanion and Rott, but Grégoire's interpretation, given here, is certainly right.

Kilise, but is probably not chronologically distant from it.[111] Skepides is one of the very few names occurring in cave churches that may also be found in documentary sources.[112] One Eustathios Skepides, *Strategos*, was in south Italy in 1042, where he may have been the administrator of the theme of Lucania.[113] What, if any, be his relationship to the others is, of course, unknown, as is his age in 1042. He might have been of the same generation as Michael Skepides, or his senior.

The social level of the Skepides family was probably that of provincial gentry: the portraits of the two men in Karabaş Kilise (Michael and an unidentified other) show them to be luxuriously dressed; John (in Gök Kilise) and Michael have formal titles. Both *Protospatharios* and *Hypatos* (consul) were, by the eleventh century, widely conferred titles of modest rank.[114] John Skepides' title, *Strategos*, denotes a military commander, again, by the eleventh century, of middle rank.[115] The occurrence of two chapels in the cave church area endowed by members of the Skepides family perhaps indicates that the family was Cappadocian, but it is equally possible that John and Michael were posted there – as their possible relative Eustathios was apparently posted to Italy.

Basileios the *Domestikos* (of the theme?), who was responsible for the painting (and probably excavation) of the church of St Barbara, Soğanlı, was probably a military officer of low rank.[116] His purpose in commissioning the church seems to have included the provision of a funerary chapel for a child, in the charge, perhaps, of a small community of monks.

Little enough is known of the patrons of hermitages but for the patrons of monasteries there is even less. Among the courtyard monasteries, only three have donor images or inscriptions. Selime Kalesi appears to be the foundation of the family painted on the west wall of the church, unidentifiable because the inscriptions that doubtless once existed were lost when the painting was burned. From their ornate dress and the iconographic parallels with images of exalted families, the Selime group would seem to be aristocratic.

At Karanlık Kilise Monastery, in Göreme, eight persons are represented. Chief among them is John, the *Entalmatikos*, perhaps a minor official or agent of the Patriarchate. The others, Genethlios, Nikephoros the

Priest and Bassianos, and four juveniles, may be members of his family or, since no women are represented in the church, perhaps members of a confraternity. At Direkli Kilise there is only an inscription, probably mentioning a single donor, the name lost.

The scarcity of references to donors in the courtyard monasteries may be a matter of chance, since areas likely to contain such references are frequently damaged. Of the monasteries without evidence of patronage, several are without polychrome decoration: Aynalı Kilise Monastery, Şahinefendi Monastery, Soğanlı Han, Karanlık Kale monastery. As noted above, the church in the last of these was plastered and a painted decoration was probably planned; had it been executed it might have included a donor reference. Another group does have painting in its churches, but still no donor images or inscriptions. Even here, however, there is the possibility of losses: the damaged apse panel of Hallaç Church might have had a kneeling figure; in Eski Gümüş there may have been an image or inscription on the lost back wall of the tomb chamber; in the church of Bezir Hane the painting of the apses, which might have included a cornice inscription, is entirely lost. Finally, brief occupation and possibly abandonment before completion may include lack of donor inscriptions and portraits among its symptoms.

Donors are generally rather modestly represented in refectory monasteries. Those depicted are identified by their first names only, without titles, except for Ignatios the monk in Chapel 18. The others are: Theognostos, Leon and Michael in Çarıklı Kilise; Anna in Chapel 21; Theodoros in Chapel 28; Theodoros and two others in Yusuf Koç Kilisesi. All patrons wear ornate secular dress, including Ignatios, who perhaps therefore became a monk at the end of his life. Others (?Harmoloikos in Chapel 21, Falibon and Leon Marulines (?) in Chapel 27) are recorded in inscriptions that are part of the painted decoration; Thamades and Michael in Chapel 27 only by very simple red-paint inscriptions on the rock.

The donor panel in Çarıklı Kilise is part of a full painted programme of high quality and the three donors represented were probably the founders of this complex. Such is probably also the case of the donors depicted in Yusuf Koç Kilisesi, again part of a full programme. The other refectory monastery donor images, which appear

111 Only the right side of the scene (the stag, a piece of hillside, the forelegs of the horse) is preserved. The strong highlight system which is used suggests an affinity both with Karabaş Kilise and with St Barbara, Soğanlı, discussed above, so an eleventh-century date is likely; such a date is supported by the presence of a tall screen in the south chapel.

112 The others are in the Pigeon House Church, Çavuşin: Nikephoros, Leon and Bardas Phokas, Theophano, Melias the *Magistros*; see L. Rodley, 'The Pigeon House Church, Çavuşin', *JÖB* 33 (1983),

301–39.

113 He appears as signatory to a legal judgement on a land-title dispute: A. Guillou, 'La Lucanie byzantine', *Byzantion* 35 (1965), 119–49, at 122.

114 R. Guilland, *Recherches sur les institutions byzantines* (Berlin/Amsterdam, 1967), II, 49–50 and 106–10.

115 Oikonomedes, *Listes*, 345–6.

116 *Ibid.* 341.

in painted panels of modest quality, perhaps record not founders but patrons who made gifts to the monasteries, and perhaps even became members of the communities themselves. Such may be the explanation for the depiction, in Chapel 18, of the donor Ignatios the monk, in secular dress.

With the exception of the family represented in Selime Kalesi Church, who may have been aristocratic, the patrons of monasteries in the volcanic valleys would appear to belong to the gentry, rather than the upper ranks. Some of those represented as small figures in panels by mediocre painters may have been even less.

Conclusion

The analysis given above supposes three sorts of monastic presence in the volcanic valleys: solitaries, communities primarily concerned with the provision of memorials for their founders, and communities serving as custodians of venerated sites and acting as centres for the reception of visitors. A final question that arises is the nature of the relationships between these three types of monastic establishment. In the Middle Byzantine period with which we are concerned, anchoritism was largely an adjunct of the coenobitic system. Monks who felt themselves called to the ascetic life would first spend time in a community and then, usually after being given the blessing of the superior, remove themselves to a place of solitude. The chronology of the Cappadocian caves does not, however, permit the conclusion that the hermitages were occupied by anchorites who began their religious lives in the Cappadocian cave monasteries, since the hermitages pre-date the monasteries, sometimes by as much as a century. Nor is there any evidence that the volcanic valleys had monasteries of built masonry, earlier than the rock-cut ones, which might have been the source of hermits. It must be, therefore, that the hermits came from elsewhere – perhaps from monasteries in the environs of Kaisareia and Koloneia, perhaps from much further afield. They were the religious pioneers of the volcanic valley region.

It is probably valid to assume a larger hermit population than the material evidence suggests. Some anchorites, more successful than others in their search for solitude, may have managed to avoid the pious attentions of patrons seeking to excavate and decorate cave churches on their sites. Possibly too, dwelling caves close to churches have been overlooked, being difficult to distinguish among the many cavities cut for agricultural

purposes in the post-Byzantine centuries. Church sites, especially those of the 'archaic' group churches, with their early tenth-century painting, and the small chapels with rustic painting assigned by Thierry to pre-ninth-century dates, need to be examined more thoroughly for evidence of contemporaneous cavities.[117] Study so far has been largely limited to the painting of these churches. If the chapels of the Thierry group are as early as claimed, the poor quality of their decoration might be evidence that only rustic work was available before the late ninth- to late eleventh-century period of security brought wealthy patrons to the region. This bracket, into which most of the known hermitages fall, may thus be that of the availability of patronage rather than of the anchorite habit itself.

Hermitages and monasteries account for only a small fraction of the number of cave monuments. Most of these are 'solitary' churches, having no complexes or cave rooms attached to them other than those accountable to post-Byzantine agriculture. As noted above, some of these 'solitary' churches may be found to be less solitary when their sites have been properly explored, but this is unlikely to apply to a majority. It is unlikely, too, that built structures existed alongside these 'solitary' cave churches. There is no material evidence of this and, as noted above in respect of monastery cells, it is unlikely that subsidiary structures would be built, or made of scarce timber, when rock-cut architecture was considered adequate for churches. Further, there are no obvious monastic implications in the painted programmes of the 'solitary' churches. Some contain images of monk saints, but these are very few and in any case do not indicate that a church is monastic.[118] It is striking that most of the cave churches are very clean: their paintings are not blackened by soot or damaged by candle grease. The few churches that were in use until the evacuation of the Greek population of the 1920s are, on the contrary, heavily blackened. The church of the Archangel in Cemil is an example. It would seem, therefore, that most of the cave churches were not used by regular congregations. Instead, they may have been commissioned by pious visitors, who perhaps re-visited from time to time, but for the most part intended their monuments to mark their sojourns in the volcanic valleys. The churches were not, therefore, monastic in the usual sense, but it is likely that monks had a custodial function.

In the late ninth/early tenth century the Byzantine frontier was being pushed eastwards, leaving Cappadocia less vulnerable to raiding than it had been for several cen-

---

117 For the 'archaic' group: Jerphanion, *Eglises*, I. i, 67–94; II, 414–18. For the Thierry group: see Chapter 1, note 28.
118 A count of saints in a sample of 35 churches produced the following

figures: martyrs – 360; bishops – 168; women – 83; monks – 37; only 18 of the 35 churches had any monk saints at all.

turies. Increased security does not of itself provide a reason for the proliferation of cave churches at this time. Nor is there reason to suppose a general population increase in the volcanic valley region. An increased transient population is, however, likely. The roads between Koloneia, Kaisareia and Nakida (Niğde) were doubtless used by troops and, with increasing security, merchants and other travellers. A detour to visit holy men in the volcanic valleys might well have become a pious gesture, undertaken particularly willingly, perhaps, by those about to engage in battle.

The ancient notion that spiritual (or other) benefit is to be derived from visiting holy places was assimilated into Christianity very early. Most major Christian pilgrimage sites were either the holy places of the Bible or the shrines of saints. Several of the latter were in Asia Minor: the shrine of St Thekla, at Seleukeia on the coast south of Cappadocia; the shrine of St Polyeuktos at Melitene, of St Theodoros at Euchaita. Kaisareia attracted pilgrims for its association with St Basil and for the relics of the Forty Martyrs of Sebaste and of St Mamas that were held there.[119] No such hallowed site is known in the volcanic valleys. The region does have its local saint: St Hieron, born in Matiana (Avcılar) in the time of Diocletian, captured in Korama (Göreme) and martyred in Melitene.[120] Usually represented as a military saint, he was in fact an early conscientious objector. He does not, however, seem to have been much venerated in the volcanic valleys, for he is depicted in only four cave churches.[121] One of these is Tokalı Kilise, where Hieron is part of the New Church programme, but not a major part: his panel is rather casually placed on the north wall of the Old Church, overlaying the original decoration. Hieron was not, therefore, the inducement to patrons of the valleys, and, in passing, it may be noted that this failure to embrace a home-grown martyr is a further indication, if any be needed, that the rock-cut monuments were not part of a tradition continuous from early Christian times.

Minor pilgrimages are also known, however: to icons, holy men, shrines, relics, holy springs and wells, in search of cures, solace, advice, or just general insurance against censure in the hereafter.[122] Such minor pilgrimages in Cappadocia were undertaken until recent times, especially to Nazianzos where paralytics were taken to be cured at the Church of St Gregory.[123] Venerated relics may have accumulated in the volcanic valleys, but probably the hermits themselves were the initial attraction. Their setting, too, a spectacular and unearthly landscape which still astonishes the traveller, must also have had its part in making the region a place of minor pilgrimage.

The large number of cave churches of the tenth and eleventh centuries is itself testimony that the cave church region gathered importance at this time. Three other fragments of evidence endorse this. First, there is the Pigeon House Church, Çavuşin, which may have been commissioned by members of the Phokas family to celebrate the accession to the throne, in 963, of their relative, the usurper Nikephoros.[124] If this is so, then by the second half of the tenth century there was a certain pious prestige attached to establishing a monument in the area. Further, the church contains an inscription referring to a general, Melias the *Magistros*, who fought in the tenth-century campaigns of a series of emperors. A significant distortion to the account of his death as written by Matthew of Edessa may have been generated by the misreading of images painted in the church.[125] This rather unimposing monument would therefore have been known to wider circles than those of the volcanic valleys.

Next, there is the record of church administration in Cappadocia. Lists (*notitiae*),of metropolitanates and their dependent bishoprics show that there were three metropolitanates in Cappadocia: Tyana, Mokissos and Kaisareia. In *notitiae* attributable to dates between the seventh and ninth centuries, the lists of bishoprics for each of these remains constant. They are: for Kaisareia – Basilika Therma, Nyssa, Theodosioupolis, Kamouliana, and Kiskisos; for Tyana – Kybistra, Phaustinoupolis, Sasima; for Mokissos – Nazianzos, Koloneia, Parnassos, Doara.[126] None of these is in a region where cave churches are dense, although Koloneia

119 B. Kotting, *Peregrinatio Religiosa* (Regensberg, 1950), 139, 160.
120 *ActaSS Novembris*, III, 329–38.
121 Göreme Chapel 2a (Saklı Kilise): Restle, *Wall Painting*, II, pl. 21; Tokalı Kilise: Jerphanion, *Eglises*, I. i, 268; Göreme Chapel 29b: *ibid.* I. i, 257; Ayvalı Kilise: N. & M. Thierry, 'Ayvalı Kilise ou pigeonnier de Gülli Dere. Eglise inédite de Cappadoce', *CahArch* 15 (1965), 97–154, at 125.
122 For pilgrimages to shrines of saints: S. Vryonis, *The Decline of Medieval Hellenism in Asia Minor* (Berkeley/Los Angeles/London, 1971), 38–40.
123 D. Petropoulis and H. Andreadis, *La vie réligieuse dans le région d'Akseray-Ghelveri* (Athens, 1970), 42ff.
124 L. Rodley, 'The Pigeon House Church, Çavuşin', *JÖB* 33 (1983), 301–39.
125 H. Grégoire, 'Notes épigraphiques', *Byzantion* 8 (1933), 49–88, at 80–2. (Some accounts of the death of Melias tell of his execution in Baghdad with forty officers, at a date near to that of the death of Nikephoros Phokas in 969. In fact, Melias lived for at least a further ten years. Grégoire suggests that the 'forty officers' are derived from the images of the Forty Martyrs of Sebaste in the Pigeon House Church, and the erroneous date from the association of the church with Nikephoros Phokas, whose image is in the north apse.)
126 J. Darrouzès, *Notitiae Episcopatuum Ecclesiae Constantinopolitanae* (Paris, 1981), *notitia* I: 206, 209, 212; *notitia* II: 219, 223, 227; *notitia* III: 233, 236, 237; *notitia* IV: 251, 255, 259. *Notitia* III contains three additions, but these are attributable to scribal error: *ibid.* 24–5.

and Nazianzos are on the fringes of the cave-church region. In *notitia* VII (Darrouzès), attributable to the administration of Leo VI and Nikolaos Mystikos (901–907), the lists for Tyana and Mokissos remain as before, but there are changes for Kaisareia: in some recensions four more bishoprics appear (Evaissa, Seberaias, Ariaratheia, Dasmendron) and in others these four plus another six (Aipolioi, Aragena Manda, Sobesos, Hagios Prokopios, Tzamandos, Siricha).[127] Of these, three (Hagios Prokopios, Sobesos and Dasmendron) are in areas associated with cave churches. In subsequent *notitiae* the group of six does not reappear.

Evaluation of this information is problematic: the *notitiae* are difficult to date and of uncertain provenance. It would appear that *notitia* VII records an expansion of ecclesiastical administration in Cappadocia, coinciding with the period of territorial recovery mentioned above. There is no consistent revision of metropolitanates, however. Although there are changes to the bishoprics of Iconium (Konya), the lists for Melitene and Sebasteia, also in areas of eastern Anatolia affected by the new circumstances, remain unchanged, as do the lists for Mokissos and Tyana, the other two metropolitanates of Cappadocia. The 'new' bishoprics may therefore have existed before and perhaps after *notitia* VII, but gone unrecorded.[128] Whatever the explanation for the isolated and brief appearance in the lists of bishoprics in the volcanic valley areas, however, it may be significant that the documents in which they appear record ecclesiastical administration at just the moment, the early tenth century, when the cave church development was beginning its expansion.

In lists following *notitia* VII, there are only minor changes for Cappadocia, but one of these may be significant for the cave monuments. This is the addition of the bishopric of Matiana (Avcılar) to the list for Mokissos, which appears in *notitiae* X and XIII (XI and XII list metropolitanates only).[129] *Notitia* X is of uncertain date; it may be a tenth-century list, incorporating later revisions, but the date of the establishment of Matiana as an episcopal seat cannot be established with precision. Once again, however, its appearance seems to coincide with the flourishing of the volcanic valleys.

Finally, there is the brief aside by Leo the Deacon, mentioned in Chapter 1: he describes Cappadocia as the place where the people once were troglodytes. This sounds like hearsay rather than first-hand knowledge and Leo's source may have been centuries old and not even referring to the volcanic valleys.[130] But something must have prompted him to add this parenthesis to his account. Might it not have been more recent travellers' tales about the strange landscape and its hermits and chapels?

The context proposed for the rock-cut monuments is therefore one of a rapidly developing centre of minor pilgrimage. The association of some of the early painted churches with hermits or small communities of monks suggests that it was they who provided the initial inspiration for acts of patronage, and may, indeed, have been doing so for centuries, but on a very limited scale while the area was insecure. The return of Cappadocia to Byzantine control in the late ninth century brought security and patrons to the region. Most of these patrons were probably transients, who visited holy men and commissioned cave churches as acts of piety. The development of this custom led to the growth in the eleventh century of the series of refectory monasteries in Göreme, probably catering to visitors to Tokalı Kilise and perhaps other hermitage sites, and also to the foundation of the courtyard monasteries, commissioned by patrons wishing to take their eternal rest in an area of pious reputation.

This development in the volcanic valley area was relatively brief: by the latter part of the eleventh century the period of peace was ended by the incursions of the Seljuks. It is unlikely, of course, that all trace of Christian life left the valleys, but it is probable that religious communities no longer flourished, their sites forming obvious targets for plunder. In addition, distaste for the invader may have been less important than the decreased availability of patrons.

It is a commonplace that history records the deeds of a minority: emperors, generals, patriarchs and saints – and Byzantine sources are often rather thin even for some of these. The manner of life and deeds of the majority are usually glimpsed only when they impinge upon the activities of the great. For all their intrinsic interest, the cave churches and monasteries of Cappadocia are humble monuments when set against the built architecture of the empire. Had they been built, they would doubtless have been brushed away in the tedious struggles that have taken place for the unpromising land of Central Anatolia. As it is, they endure as material evidence of a generally unchronicled Byzantine class: monks who lacked hagiographers; soldiers too low in rank to be given credit for victories; minor officials who did nothing good, bad, or important enough to bring them to the attention of historians.

127 *Ibid.* 274, 278, 283.
128 *Ibid.* 67–8.
129 *Ibid.* 324, 361.

130 Troglodytes, both legendary and observed, are mentioned by Strabo and Xenophon, see Chapter 1, notes 19 and 23.

SELECT BIBLIOGRAPHY

Most of the works included here are concerned with cave churches, not monasteries, and contain descriptions rather than general discussions of the material. The literature on Cappadocian monuments is, however, so scattered that this compilation may be useful.

Archelaos, I. S., *E Sinasos, etoi thesis, istoria, ethike kai dianoetike katastasis . . . tes en Kappadokia komopoleos Sinasou . . .* (Athens, 1899).

Brehier, L., 'Les églises rupestres de Cappadoce et leur témoignage', *RA*[5] 25 (1927), 1–47.

Idem, 'Les peintures des églises rupestres de Cappadoce. L'oeuvre archéologique du R. P. Guillaume de Jerphanion', *OCP* 4 (1938), 577–84.

Budde, L., *Göreme. Höhlenkirchen in Kappadokien* (Dusseldorf, 1958).

Idem, 'Die Johanneskirche von Göreme', *Pantheon* 19 (1961), 263–71.

Cormack, R. S., 'Byzantine Cappadocia. The Archaic Group of Wall Paintings', *JBAA* 30 (1967), 19–36.

Diehl, C., Review of Jerphanion, *Eglises*, in *JSav* (1927), 97.

Epstein, A. W., 'Rock-cut Chapels in Göreme Valley, Cappadocia: The Yılanlı Group and the Column Churches', *CahArch* 24 (1975), 115–35.

Idem, 'The Date and Context of Some Cappadocian Rock-cut Churches' (London University Ph.D. thesis, 1975).

Idem, 'The "Iconoclast" Churches of Cappadocia', *Iconoclasm. Papers Given at the Ninth Spring Symposium of Byzantine Studies* (Birmingham, 1977), 103–11.

Idem, 'The Fresco Decoration of the Column Churches, Göreme Valley, Cappadocia', *CahArch* 29 (1980–1), 27–45.

Giovannini, L., *Arts of Cappadocia* (Geneva, 1971).

Gough, M., 'The Monastery of Eski Gümüş. A Preliminary Report', *AnatSt* 14 (1964), 147–61.

Idem, 'The Monastery of Eski Gümüş. Second Preliminary Report', *AnatSt* 15 (1965), 157–64.

Idem, 'The Monastery of Eski Gümüş', *Archaeology* 18 (1965), 254–63.

Grégoire, H., 'Notes épigraphiques', *Byzantion* 8 (1933), 49–88 (78–88).

Holzmeister, C. and G., and R. Fahrner, *Bilder aus Anatolien. Höhlen und Hane in Kappadokien* (Vienna, 1955).

İpşiroğlu, M. S., and S. Eyüboğlu, *Saklı Kilise, une église rupestre de Cappadoce* (Istanbul, undated).

Jerphanion, G. de, 'La date des peintures de Toqale Kilisse en Cappadoce', *RA*[4] 20 (1912), 236–54.

Idem, 'Inscriptions byzantines de la Région d'Urgub en Cappadoce', *MélUSJ* 6 (1913), 305–400.

Idem, 'Le rôle de la Syrie et de l'Asie Mineure dans la formation de l'Iconographie chrétienne', *MélUSJ* 8 (1922), 331–83.

Idem, *Une nouvelle province de l'art byzantin. Les églises rupestres de Cappadoce* (Paris, 1925–42).

Idem, 'La date des plus récentes peintures de Toqale Kilisse, en Cappadoce', *La Voix des Monuments* (Paris/Rome, 1938), 208–36.

Idem, 'Les noms des Bergers dans la scène de la Nativité en Cappadoce', *BIABulg* 10 (1936), 91–2.

Idem, 'Sur une question de méthode. A propos de la datation des peintures cappadociennes', *OCP* 3 (1937), 141–60.

Idem, 'Les caractéristiques et les attributs des saints dans la peinture cappadocienne', *AnalBoll* 55 (1937), 1–28.

Jolivet, C., 'La peinture byzantine en Cappadoce de la fin de l'iconoclasme à la conquête turque', *Le Aree omogonee della civiltà rupestre nell'ambito dell'Impero bizantino: La Cappadocia* (Galatina, 1981), 159–97.

Lafontaine, J., 'Note sur un voyage en Cappadoce (été 1959)', *Byzantion* 28 (1958) *(sic)*, 465–78.

Lafontaine-Dosogne, J., 'Sarıca kilise en Cappadoce', *CahArch* 12 (1962), 263–84.

Idem, 'Nouvelles notes cappadociennes', *Byzantion* 33 (1963), 121–83.

Idem, Review of N. and M. Thierry, *Nouvelles églises*, *Speculum* 40 (1965), 555–7 (in English), and *BZ* 58 (1965), 131–6 (French).

Idem, 'L'église aux trois croix de Güllü dere en Cappadoce', *Byzantion* 35 (1965), 175–207.

Idem, 'Une église inédite de la fin du XIIe siècle en Cappadoce: La Bezirana kilisesi dans la vallée de Belisirama', *BZ* 61 (1968), 291–304.

Idem, 'La Kale Kilisesi de Selime et sa représentation des donateurs', *Zetesis (Album Amicorum E. de Strijcker)* (Antwerp/Utrecht, 1973), 741–53.

Idem, 'Rospisi tserkvi, nazyvaemou Chemlekchi Kilise, i problema prisutstviya Armyan v Kappakokii', *Sbornik statey v chest' V. N. Lazareva* (Moscow, 1973), 78–93.

Levides, A. M., *Ai en monolithois monai tes Kappadokias kai Lykaonias* (Constantinople, 1899).

Millet, G., 'Les iconoclastes et la croix. A propos d'une inscription de Cappadoce', *BCH* 34 (1910), 96–109.

Pallas, D. I., 'Une note sur la décoration de la chapelle de Haghios Basileios de Sinasos', *Byzantina* 48 (1978), 208–25.

Restle, M., *Byzantine Wall Painting in Asia Minor*, trans. I. R. Gibbons (Shannon, 1969); first published as *Die byzantinische Wandmalerei in Kleinasien* (Recklinghausen, 1967).

Idem, 'Zwei Höhlenkirchen im Haci İşmail Dere bei Ayvalı', *JÖB* 22 (1973), 251–79.

Rodley, L., 'Hallaç Manastır. A Cave Monastery in Byzantine Cappadocia', *XVI. Internationaler Byzantinistenkongress. Akten* 11/5, *JÖB* 32/5 (1982), 425–34.

Idem, 'The Pigeon House Church, Çavuşin', *JÖB* 33 (1983), 301–39.

Schiemenz, G. P., 'Eine unbekannte Felsenkirche in Göreme', *BZ* 59 (1966), 307–33.

Idem, 'Verschollene Malereien in Göreme: die "archaische Kapelle bei Elmalı Kilise" und die Muttergottes zwischen Engeln', *OCP* 34 (1968), 70–96.

Idem, 'Die Kirche bei Katırcı Camii. Eine Neuentdeckung in Göreme', *AA* 84 (1969), 216–29.

Idem, 'Die Kapelle des Styliten Niketas in den Weinbergen von Ortahisar', *JÖB* 18 (1969), 239–58.

Idem, 'Zur Chronologie der kappadokischen Felsenmalereien', *AA* 85 (1970), 253–73.

Idem, 'Ein Neufund byzantinischer Wandmalerei in Güzelyurt', *RQ* 67 (1972), 153–74.

Idem, 'Nachlese in Göreme', *AA* 87 (1972), 307–18.

Idem, 'Die Kreuzkirche von Açık Saray', *IstMitt* 23/24 (1973/74), 233–62.

Idem, 'Herr, hilf deinem Knecht. Zur Frage nimbierter Stifter in den kappadokischen Höhlenkirchen', *RQ* 71 (1976), 133–74.

Sterrett, J. R. S., 'Troglodyte Dwellings in Cappadocia', *The Century* 60 (1900), 677.

Thierry, N., 'Iconographie inédite en Cappadoce. Le cycle de la conception et de l'enfance de la Vierge à Kızıl Tchoukour', *Akten des XI. Internationalen Byzantinistenkongresses, Munich 1958* (Munich, 1960), 620–3.

Idem, 'Quelques églises inédites en Cappadoce', *JSav* (1965), 626–35.

Idem, 'Eglises rupestres de Cappadoce', *CorsiRav* 12 (1965), 579–602.

Idem, 'Le costume épiscopal byzantin du IXe au XIIIe siècle d'après les peintures datées (miniatures, fresques)', *REB* 24 (1966), 308–15.

Idem, 'Les peintures de Cappadoce de la fin de l'Iconoclasme à l'Invasion turque (843–1082)', *Revue de l'Université de Bruxelles* n.s. 19–20 (1966–8), 137–63.

Idem, 'Etude stylistique des peintures de Karabaş Kilise en Cappadoce (1060–1061)', *CahArch* 17 (1967), 161–75.

Idem, 'Notes critiques à propos des peintures rupestres de Cappadoce', *REB* 26 (1968), 337–66.

Idem, 'Peintures paléochrétiennes en Cappadoce, l'église No. 1 de Balkan dere', *Synthronon, Art et Archéologie de la fin de l'Antiquité et du Moyen Age* (Paris, 1968), 53–9.

Idem, 'Un décor pré-iconoclaste de Cappadoce: Açıkel Ağa Kilisesi', *CahArch* 18 (1968), 33–69.

Idem, 'Un style schématique de Cappadoce daté du XIe siècle d'après une inscription', *JSav* (1968), 45–61.

Idem, 'Quelques monuments inédits ou mal connus de Cappadoce, centres de Maçan, Çavuşin et Göreme', *Information de l'histoire de l'art* (Jan.–Fev. 1969), 14–25.

Idem, 'Les peintures murales de six églises du Haut Moyen Age en Cappadoce', *CRAI* (1970), 444–79.

Idem, 'Un atelier de peintures du début du Xe siècle en Cappadoce', *BAntFr* (1971), 170–8.

Idem, 'Art byzantin du Haut Moyen Age en Cappadoce: l'église No. 3 de Mavrucan', *JSav* (1972), 233–69.

Idem, 'La basilique de S. Jean Baptiste de Çavuşin', *BAntFr* (1972), 198–213.

Idem, 'Iconographie et culte de la croix en Asie Mineure, en Transcaucasie et en Syrie et Mesopotamie byzantines', *Annuaire de l'E.P.H.E.* 82/3 (1973–4), 209–12.

Idem, 'Yusuf Koç Kilisesi. Eglise rupestre de Cappadoce', *Mansel'e Armağan* (Ankara, 1974), I, 193–206.

Idem, 'A propos des peintures d'Ayvalı köy (Cappadoce). Les programmes absidaux à troix régistres avec Deisis en Cappadoce et en Géorgie', *Zograf* 5 (1974), 5–22.

Idem, 'Etudes cappadociennes, Région du Hasan Dağı, compléments pour 1974', *CahArch* 24 (1975), 183–90.

Idem, 'L'art monumental byzantin en Asie Mineure du XIe siècle au XIVe', *DOP* 29 (1975), 75–111.

Idem, 'Art byzantin du Haut Moyen Age en Cappadoce: l'église peinte de Nicétas Stylite et d'Eustrate Clisurarque, ou fils de Clisurarque en Cappadoce', *Communications, 14e Congrès international des études byzantines, Bucharest 1971* (1976), 451–5.

Idem, 'Les plus anciennes représentations cappadociennes du costume épiscopal byzantin', *REB* 34 (1976), 325–31.

Idem, 'Mentalité et formulation iconoclastes en Anatolie', *JSav* (1976), 81–119.

Idem, 'L'archéologie cappadocienne en 1978. Ses difficultés. Son intérêt pour les mediévistes', *CahCM* (Jan–Mars 1979), 3–22.

Idem, 'Le culte de la croix dans l'empire byzantin du VIIe siècle au Xe dans ses rapports avec la guerre contre l'infidèle. Nouveaux témoignages archéologiques', *Miscellanea Agostino Pertusi* (Bologna, 1981), I, 205–28.

Idem, 'Monuments de Cappadoce de l'antiquité romaine au Moyen Age byzantin', *Le Aree omogenee della civiltà rupestre nell'ambito dell'Impero bizantino: La Cappadocia* (Galatina, 1981), 39–73.

Thierry, N. and M., 'Eglise de Kızıl-Tchoukour: chapelle iconoclaste, chapelle de Joachim et d'Anne', *MonPiot* 50 (1958), 105–46.

Idem, 'L'église du Jugement Dernier à Ihlara (Yılanlı Kilise)', *Anatolia* 5 (1960), 159–68.

Idem, 'Voyage archéologique en Cappadoce', *REB* 19 (1961), 419–37.

Idem, *Nouvelles églises rupestres de Cappadoce. Région du Hasan Dağı* (Paris, 1963).

Idem, 'Une nouvelle église rupestre de Cappadoce: Cambazlı Kilise à Ortahisar', *JSav* (1963), 5–23.

Idem, 'Haçlı kilise, l'église à la croix, en Cappadoce', *JSav* (1964), 241–64.

Idem, 'Ayvalı Kilise ou pigeonnier de Gülli Dere, église inédite de Cappadoce', *CahArch* 15 (1965), 97–154.

Thierry N., and A. Tenenbaum, 'Le cénacle apostolique à Kokar Kilise et Ayvalı Kilise en Cappadoce: Mission des apôtres, pentecôte, jugement dernier', *JSav* (1963), 229–41.

Verzone, P., 'Gli monasteri de Acık Serai in Cappadocia', *CahArch* 13 (1962), 119–36.

Vryonis, S., 'Another Note on the Inscription of the Church of S. George of Beliserama', *Byzantina* 9 (1977), 11–22.

Wagner J., and G. Klammet, *Göreme. Felsentürme und Höhlenkirchen im türkischen Hochland* (Vienna/Munich, 1979).

White, J. E., 'The Cavate Dwellings of Cappadocia', *Records of the Past* (Washington) 3 (1904), 67–73 and 128.

Wiegand, E., 'Zur Datierung der Kappadokischen Höhlenmalereien', *BZ* 36 (1936), 337–97.

Wood, D., 'Byzantine Military Standards in a Cappadocian Church', *Archaeology* 12 (1959), 38–46.

Yanagi, M., *Kappadokya. Höhlenkloster in der Türkei* (Tokyo, 1966).

ICONOGRAPHIC INDEX

Archangels, 23, 24, 31, 50, 53, 55, 90, 92, 112, 116, 156, 159, 165, 166, 176, 181, 182, 186, 198, 200, 205, 211, 212

Christ, 43, 90, 146, 156, 159, 165, 172, 173, 175, 176, 178, 181, 190, 197, 204, 205, 211, 216

Virgin, 23, 24, 43, 50, 53, 90, 94, 112, 116, 117, 156, 166, 176, 178, 186, 190, 192, 206, 207, 211, 220; *Deesis* (Christ with the Virgin and John the Baptist), 44, 53, 90, 116, 156, 166, 173, 176, 181, 198, 205, 207, 211

Holy Cross, 159, 166, 167, 186

Mandylion, 53, 181, 205

LIFE OF CHRIST
Annunciation, 43, 53, 71, 116, 156, 159, 176–7, 179, 198, 205, 210, 215, 216
Visitation, 43, 159, 179, 205, 210, 215, 216
Proof of the Virgin, 43, 179, 205, 210, 215, 216
Reproaches of Joseph, 205, 216
Journey to Bethlehem, 53, 177, 205, 210, 215, 216
Nativity, 43, 44, 53, 71, 116, 159, 166, 176, 198, 205, 210, 215, 216
Adoration of the Magi, 43, 53, 71, 159, 166, 176, 210, 215, 216
Dream of Joseph, 43, 159, 210, 216
Flight into Egypt, 43, 71, 159, 210, 215, 216
Massacre of the Innocents, 71, 210, 215
Pursuit of Elizabeth, 71, 215
Murder of Zacharias, 215
Presentation, 43, 116, 159, 179, 198, 210, 215, 216
Angel and John the Baptist, 43
John the Baptist and Christ, 43, 215, 216
Calling of John the Baptist, 71, 215, 216
Prophecy of John the Baptist, 215
Baptism, 43, 53, 71, 159, 166, 176, 210, 215, 216
Christ in the Temple, 216
Temptation, 216
Christ and Zaccheus, 43
Miracle at Cana, 215, 216
Calling of the Apostles, 215, 216
Miracle of the Loaves and Fishes, 215
Healing the Blind, 43, 215, 216
Healing Lepers, 216
The Widow's Mite, 216
Healing the Withered Hand, 216
Healing the Possessed, 216
Healing the Nobleman's Son, 216
Raising the Daughter of Jairus, 159, 216
Healing the Paralytic, 159, 216
Transfiguration, 53, 146, 159, 166, 176, 198, 210, 215
Raising of Lazarus, 43, 53, 146, 166, 176, 210, 215, 216
Entry into Jerusalem, 43, 53, 146, 159, 166, 176, 210, 215, 216
Christ with Martha, 146
Last Supper, 43, 53, 159, 164, 166, 176, 177, 211, 215, 216

Washing the Feet, 43, 159, 210, 216
Communion of Apostles (Divine Liturgy), 43, 159, 198
Betrayal, 43, 53, 159, 166, 176, 211, 215, 216
Christ before Anaias and Caiaphas, 43
Christ before Pilate, 43, 215, 216
Denial by Peter, 43
Way of the Cross, 43, 166, 176, 215, 216
Crucifixion, 43, 53, 146, 159, 166, 176, 186, 198, 211, 215, 216
Deposition, 43, 211, 215, 216
Entombment, 43, 159, 176, 177, 211, 215, 216
Myrophores, 43, 53, 159, 166, 176, 198, 211, 215, 216
Anastasis, 43, 53, 146, 159, 166, 176, 198, 205, 207, 211, 215, 216
Benediction of Apostles, 43, 53, 216
Mission of Apostles, 216
Ascension, 43, 53, 71, 146, 159, 166, 176, 210, 215, 216
Pentecost, 43, 146, 216
Last Judgement, 159
Second Coming, 211, 212

LIFE OF THE VIRGIN
First Steps of the Virgin, 71
Virgin Blessed by Priests, 71
Presentation of the Virgin in the Temple, 71
Virgin Fed by an Angel, 71, 159
Dormition, 43, 71, 159, 211

OLD TESTAMENT SUBJECTS
Adam and Eve, 204
Daniel and the Lions, 190
Elijah and the Chariot, 211, 212
Elijah and the Fire, 211, 212
Elisha and the Mantle, 211
Hospitality of Abraham, 53, 166, 176, 216
Joshua and the Angel, 159
Joshua Stopping the Sun, 159
Sacrifice of Abraham, 211
Three Hebrews, 156, 176, 190

PROPHETS AND PATRIARCHS
Abraham, 53
Daniel, 31, 156, 186, 190, 205
David, 186, 190, 205
Elias, 181, 205
Ezekiel, 190, 205, 211, 216
Habbakuk, 211
Hosea, 211
Isaiah, 90, 190, 205, 211
Jeremiah, 205, 211, 216
Joachim, 211
Joel, 211

Jonah, 211
Moses, 181
Nahum, 211
Obadiah, 211
Solomon, 190, 205
Zacharias, 90, 117, 211

SAINTS
Abibos, 177, 212
Aetios, 211
Agape, 215
Agapios, 211
Akakios, 44
Akindynos, 90, 198, 211
Alypios, 44, 216
Amphilochios, 116, 211
Anastasia, 146, 205, 211, 215
Andrew, 156
Andronikos, 166, 206
Anempodistos, 198
Aniketos, 177
Anna, 90, 94, 186, 198
Antonios, 212, 213, 216,
Aphthonios, 90, 198, 212
Archipas, 212, 213
Arsenios, 212, 213, 216
Athanasios, 43, 211
Athenogenes, 116, 198, 204
Auxentios, 177, 198
Bakchos, 33, 90, 94, 156, 177, 198
Barbara, 166, 175, 177, 190, 205, 212
Bartholomew, 156
Basil, 23–4, 26, 31, 90, 92, 116, 156, 166, 173, 181, 198, 204, 216; Life
    of Basil, 216
Blasios, 43, 116, 166, 198, 204, 216
Catherine, 90, 175, 178, 190, 198, 205, 215
Christina, 212
Christopher, 156, 190, 192, 205, 212
Constantine and Helena, 146, 156, 166, 173, 181, 190, 205, 211, 215
Damianos, 31, 90, 166, 186, 198, 205, 211
Daniel the Stylite, 204, 207
Demetrios, 156, 177, 198, 211
Dometianos, 215
Eirene, 177
Eleutherios, 198
Elpidios, 90, 212
Elpidiphoros, 198, 206
Ephraim, 44
Epiphanios, 90, 116, 198, 216
Eudokia, 166
Eugenios, 177, 198
Eunoikos, 211
Euphemia, 90, 159, 160n, 212
Euphrosyne, 211
Eupraxia, 146, 212
Eusebios, 211
Eustathios, 90, 159, 205, 211, 212, 220; Martyrdom of Eustathios and
    family, 220
Eustratios, 177, 198
Euthymios, 186, 189, 216
Eutychios, 211
Flavios, 211
Forty Martyrs of Sebaste, 216
George, 31, 90, 94, 146, 156, 166, 173, 175, 178, 182, 192, 198, 205;
    Martyrdom of George, 146, 181
George (bishop), 116
Gourias, 146, 177
Gregory of Nazianzos (the Theologian), 43, 116, 156, 166, 181, 190,
    198

Gregory of Nyssa, 43
Gregory *Thaumaturgos*, 90
Helena, 212
Hermolaos, 205
Hesychios, 211
Hieron, 212, 215
Hypatios, 166, 211
Ignatios, 211
Jacob, 156, 186
Jason, 116
John the Baptist, 116, 159, 186, 190; *see also* **Virgin**, *Deesis*
John Chrysostom, 90, 156, 166, 181, 190, 198, 204
John the Evangelist, 165, 186, 204
John *Kalibites*, 205
Joulitta, 190, 211
Justus, 211
Karterios, 212
Kattidios, 215
Klaudios, 211
Klemes, 211, 212
Konon, 211
Kornoutos, 198, 204
Kosmas, 31, 33, 90, 166, 186, 198, 205
Kyriaka, 177
Kyriakos, 156, 198
Kyrillos, 211
Lauros, 156, 177, 198
Leontios (of the Forty Martyrs), 44, 205, 211
Leontios (bishop), 43, 190, 204
Loukianos, 212
Luke, 156, 165, 190, 204
Mamas, 177
Mardarios, 177, 198
Marina, 90, 215
Mark, 156, 165, 186, 204
Mary the Egyptian, 216
Matthew, 156, 165, 204
Menas, 198, 206
Merkourios, 90, 198, 205
Modestos, 198
Nikandros, 211, 216
Nikephoros, 159, 206
Niketas, 177, 181, 182, 205, 211
Nikolaos, 31, 116, 156, 166, 204, 211
Olympia, 212
Onesimos, 173
Onouphrios, 173
Orestios, 177, 198, 211
Pachomios, 212
Panteleemon, 90, 186, 198, 205, 215
Paraskeve, 166, 190, 205
Paul, 90, 156, 186
Paul *ho homologitis*, 211
Pegasios, 90, 198, 212
Peter, 90, 156, 211
Philoktemon, 211
Phloros, 156, 177, 198
Phokas, 212
Photios, 177
Priskos, 211
Probos, 146, 166, 177, 206
Proklos, 212
Prokopios, 90, 156, 166, 190, 198, 205
Romanos, 205
Sabas, 205, 207
Sakerdon, 211
Sergios, 33, 90, 94, 156, 177, 198
Seven Sleepers of Ephesos, 205, 207
Simon, 156, 186

Simon of Cyrene, 166
Sisinnios, 44, 181, 182, 211
Smaragdos, 211
Sophia, 146
Sozon, 190
Spyridon, 211
Stephanos, 116, 205, 211
Symeon the Stylite, 186, 190, 205, 207, 216; Life of Symeon, 190
Tarachos, 146, 166, 177, 206
Thekla, 190, 211
Theodoros, 92, 156, 166, 173, 175, 178, 181, 198, 205, 215, 220
Theodota, 146, 190, 205

Theophilos, 211
Theophylaktos, 204
Theopiste, 159, 205, 212
Thomas, 173, 186, 190, 211
Timotheos, 216
Tryphon, 156, 212
Vales, 211
Vikentios, 198, 206
Viktor, 206
Xanthios, 211
Zosimas and Mary the Egyptian, 216

GENERAL INDEX

Abbas, 197, 201, 202

Açık Saray, 9, **121–50**, 228, 229, 236, 256, 257; Figs. 18–27; Pls. 117–42a

Açıkel Ağa Kilisesi (Belisırma), 8n., 256

Aesop, 112, 227, 248

Aipolioi, 254

Ak Kilise (Soğanlı), 226

Aksaray (= Koloneia), 2, 5, 63, 120, 150, 230, 231, 235n., 252, 253; Fig. 1

Ala Kilise (Ali Suması Dağı), 231, 237; Figs. 44g, 47

Ala Kilise (Belisırma), **119–20**, 229

Alahan Monastery, 234, 242; Fig. 54

Alakilise (Lycia), 226n.

Ali Suması Dağı, Ala Kilise, 231, 237; Figs. 44g, 47

Amida, 4

Anatepe, church, 226

Annesi, 238

Anthony of Egypt, 237

Aparank, church, 230n.

aplekta, 5, 150

Aragena Manda, 254

'archaic' group, 43n., 193, 220, 226, 252, 255

Archangel Monastery (Cemil), 151, **157–60**, 183, 223, 227, 249, 252; Pl. 150

architecture

  altars, 22, 30, 39, 52, 61, 70, 71, 89, 100, 131, 146, 164, 169, 181, 189, 195, 204, 216, 219; Pls. 82, 157, 176

  capitals, 15, 17, 19, 20, 23, 27, 30, 36, 38, 50, 52, 61, 69, 100, 112, 134, 146, 164, 169, 176, 181, 189; Pls. 6, 8–10, 12–17, 19, 23, 25, 32, 33, 47, 49, 50, 60, 96, 97, 112, 122, 129, 130, 156, 228

  carved decoration: bosses, 20, 59, 112, 122, 123, 130, 138, 139, 144, 179, 181; Figs. 11a, 17, 19, 20, 22, 25; Pl. 47; figural, 19, 20, 22, 26, 65, 82, 144–5, 227, 236; Fig. 26; Pls. 10, 11, 11a, 13, 14, 17, 54, 75; non-figural, 15, 17, 19, 20, 22, 65, 68, 77, 95, 101, 103, 106, 112, 120, 125, 134, 144, 151, 187, 189, 192, 193, 236; Pls. 6, 8, 9, 12, 15, 33, 53, 64–7, 93, 101–2a, 106, 121, 130, 140, 145, 181

  chancel screens: low, 29, 39, 47, 70, 89, 115, 169, 173, 175, 176, 178, 195, 204, 208, 216, 219, 228; Pls. 60, 80, 82, 176; tall, 52, 61–2, 123, 134, 164, 169, 172, 176, 181, 204, 228, 235; Figs. 12c, 39c; Pls. 50, 119, 157

  church plans: basilica, 8, 61, 69–71, 219, 235–6, 242; Figs. 11, 13, 49, 50, 52, 54, 56, 57; Pls. 49, 50, 60; free-cross, 147, 170–2, 181, 182; Fig. 27b; inscribed-cross, 20–2, 29–31, 38–9, 43–5, 47–8, 52–3, 88–9, 100–1, 112–14, 119, 120, 134, 146, 152, 164, 169–70, 175, 176, 181, 227–35; Figs. 2, 5, 6, 8, 9a, 15–17, 21, 27a, 28, 31, 43–8; Pls. 12, 13, 16, 20, 23–5, 33, 37, 79–81, 96, 97, 112–15, 129–31, 142, 156; single-nave, 123, 131, 159, 181, 182, 184, 189, 195, 204, 215, 225–6, 242; Figs. 15–17, 19, 20, 34–6, 39, 57, 58; Pls. 119, 127, 169, 170, 176; transverse-nave, 173, 179, 216, 226; Fig. 42; Pls. 184, 185; twin-nave, 208–10, 225; Fig. 40a

courtyards, 9, 11–14, 33, 45, 65, 81, 103, 122, 125, 129, 132, 137, 140, 144, 148, 203, 241, 242, 244; Figs. 2, 6, 8, 9, 11, 13, 17, 19–25, 31, 36, 39a–b, 47–59; Pls. 3–5, 29, 30, 38, 46, 103a–105, 117, 128, 133, 137, 138, 140, 151, 174

façades, 15, 33, 40, 45, 50, 56–9, 65, 69, 85, 95, 103–5, 118, 119, 122, 123, 125, 132, 137, 142, 144, 148, 151, 157, 162, 167, 173, 177, 203, **236–7**; Fig. 39b; Pls. 4, 5, 30, 34, 38–41, 46, 46a, 65, 76, 96, 101–5, 116, 117, 128, 133, 138, 140, 143, 146, 150, 151, 154a

galleries and upper floors, 50–2, 60–1, 68, 79–81, 85–7, 109–12, 125–8, 134–7, 162; Figs. 9b, 11b, 13, 15, 17, 20, 21b, 31b

halls, 15, 27–8, 36–8, 41, 59, 77–8, 80, 85–7, 95, 123, 125, 129–30, 134, 138, 140–1, 142, 144, 148, 158, 193, 203, 206, 247; Figs. 2, 5–8, 11, 13, 15–17, 19–26, 36, 39a; Pls. 6, 23, 32a–c, 47, 69, 70, 77, 78, 91, 92, 106, 132

kitchens, 19, 38, 81–2, 98, 109–10, 128, 130, 132, 143, 148, 237, 247, 249; Figs. 2, 6, 13, 16, 17, 20 21; Pls. 73, 108

millstones, 6, 7, 52, 60, 61, 100, 110, 116; Figs. 9, 11, 17

plaster, 66, 77, 78, 103, 105, 131; Pls. 52, 53, 66, 67, 69, 96; *see also* polychrome painting

refectories, 9, 43, 51, 109, 151, 157, 160, 164, 165, 167, 169, 170, 173, 174, 178, 179, 181, 247, 249; Figs. 9a, 28, 32, 33; Pls. 144, 152, 155, 158, 161, 167

seats, 22, 39, 47, 52, 70, 114, 115, 123, 164, 169, 189, 195, 216, 219; Pls. 18, 114

side chapels, 43–4, 70, 89, 101, 115, 117, 195, 204, 216; Figs. 15–17, 36, 39a, 42a; Pls. 37, 82, 100

stables, 82, 129, 140, 148, 150, 152, 236; Figs. 20, 22, 28; Pls. 74, 136, 147

storage areas, 15, 43, 98, 100, 109, 110

tomb chambers, 22–3, 39, 52, 55, 61, 74, 103, 114, 117, 118, 192–3, 196, 248–9; Figs. 2, 6, 9, 11, 13, 15, 17, 36; Pls. 19, 44, 59, 113, 115; graves, 23, 39, 42, 52, 69, 89, 98, 101, 114, 115, 131, 146, 169, 172, 173, 175, 178, 181, 182, 183, 184, 188, 189, 192, 204, 207, 208, 219; Figs. 2, 6, 9, 13, 15–17, 20, 27a, 39a, 42b

Ariaratheia, 254

aristocracy, 4, 5, 73, 251

Armenians, 4, 26

Athanasios of Meteora, 239

Athanasios the Athonite, 238

Avanos (= Venasa), 5, Fig. 1

Avcılar (= Maçan, Matiana), 5, 8, 11, 26, 32, 151, 223, 227, 253, 254; Fig. 1; *see also* Bezir Hane, Durmuş Kilisesi, Yusuf Koç Kilise Monastery

Ayazın (Phrygia), 229, 236

Aynalı Kilise Monastery (including Göreme Chapel 14), 11, **56–63**, 84, 100, 103, 118, 119, 175, 181, 223, 235, 236, 248, 251; Figs. 11, 12; Pls. 46–50

Ayvalı Kilise (Güllü Dere), 117, 193, **207–13**, 215, 216, 218, 223, 225, 226, 240, 250, 257; Figs. 40, 41; Pls. 180–2

Ayvalı Köy, 256

Balkan Dere, 8n., 149n., 256
Baramûs, Monastery of (Wadi'n Natrun), 242; Fig. 51
Barbara, Church of St (Göreme), *see* Göreme Chapel 20
Barbara, Church of St (Soğanlı), 48, 94, 156, **203–7**, 223, 225, 239, 251;
    Fig. 39; Pls. 177–9
Basil I, 4
Basil II, 4, 94, 206, 239
Basil Kinnamos, 240
Basil the Great, 2, 4, 23, 24, 238, 253
Basileios of Melitene, scribe, 5n.
basilica, *see under* architecture
Basilika Therma, 253
Belisırma, 11, 63, 255; Fig. 1; *see also* Açıkel Ağa Kilisesi, Ala Kilise,
    Bezirana Kilisesi, Direkli Kilise Monastery, Kırk Dam Altı Kilise
Bezir Hane (Avcılar), 8, 11, **26–33**, 39, 45, 84, 103, 223, 224, 226, 227,
    228, 248, 251; Fig. 5; Pls. 21–8
Bezirana Kilisesi (Belisırma), 255
Bithynia, 8, 238, 242
Botaniates, 4

Caesarea, *see* Kaisareia
Cambazlı Kilise (Ortahisar), 257
Çanlı Kilise (Çeltek), 231, 235; Figs. 1, 44b, 45
capitals, *see under* architecture
Caria, 244
Çarıklı Kilise (Göreme Chapel 22), 25, 50, **162–7**, 175, 179, 182, 225,
    227, 228, 229, 250, 251; Fig. 31; Pls. 151–3
Catherine, Monastery of St (Mount Sinai), 241; Fig. 49
Çavuşin, 6, 7, 207; *see also* John the Baptist (Church of), Pigeon House
    Church
Çeltek, Çanlı Kilise, 231, 235; Figs. 1, 44b, 45
Cemil, 157; Fig. 1; *see also* Archangel Monastery, Karlık Kilise,
    Stephen (Chapel of St)
Çet Dağı church, 231; Fig. 44d
Chalcedon, Council of, 5, 239
chancel screens, *see under* architecture
Cilicia, 234
coenobium, 9, 237, 238
Çökek Kilisesi, 229
'Column' group, 26, 48, 56, 119, 164, **182–3**, 223, 228, 229, 255
Commagene, 226
Constantine VII, 212
Constantine VIII, 94, 117, 206
Constantine X, 73
Constantine Lips, Monastery of (Constantinople), 235
Constantinople, 4, 5, 213, 218, 238, 239; *see also* Constantine Lips
    (Monastery of), Kilise Camii, Myrelaion, Pantocrator Monastery,
    Pantepoptes (St Saviour)
courtyards, *see under* architecture
Ctesiphon, 236

Dasmendron (= Ovacık), 5, 254
Değile, 242; Figs. 55–7
Derinkuyu (= Malakopea), 5, 150; underground city, 6
Derviş Akın Kilisesi (Selime), 229
Deuteros, 238
Digenes Akrites, 4
Dikmen, church, 226n.
Diokaisareia (= Tilköy), 4
Direkli Kilise Monastery (Belisırma), 11, 33, 84, **85–95**, 103, 117, 223,
    224, 227, 228, 229, 248, 251; Fig. 15; Pls. 76–89
Doara, 253
documentary evidence, lack of, 2, 5, 8–9
Domestikos, 206–7, 251
dormitories, 247, 249
Durmuş Kilisesi (Avcılar), 8

Edessa, 4
Egypt, 237, 238

Elmalı Kilise (Göreme Chapel 19), **176–7**, 182, 227, 228, 229, 250
Elpidios, *Memorophylax*, 5
Entalmatikos, 54–5, 251
Erciyes Dağı, 2, 7, 236
Eski Andaval, church, 4, 237
Eski Gümüş Monastery (Gümüşler), 11, 22, 47, 84, 95, **103–18**, 223,
    224, 227, 228, 229, 236, 247, 251, 255; Figs. 1, 17; Pls. 101–15
Etchmiadzin Monastery, 244
Euchaita, Shrine of St Theodoros, 253
Eustathios Skepides, 251
Euthymios the Great, 237; Monastery of, Palestine, 241; Fig. 50
Evaissa, 254

façades, *see under* architecture
Fisandon, church, 231; Figs. 44c, 46
Forty Martyrs of Sebaste, 253; Church of (Şahinefendi), 8n., 33
free-cross church plan, *see under* architecture (church plans)

galleries, *see under* architecture
Gelveri, church, 226
Gök Kilise (Soğanlı), 250
Göreme (= Korama), 5, 26n., 48, 56, 151, **160–83**, 213, 222, 223, 226,
    227, 228, 236, 249–50, 253, 254, 256; Figs. 1, 30–3; Pls. 154a–167;
    Chapel 1: 193; Chapel 2a (Saklı Kilise): 255; Chapel 6: 183, 193;
    Chapel 7: *see* Tokalı Kilise; Chapel 8: 183; Chapel 9: 183;
    Chapel 10: 25, 26, 182; Chapel 11: 183; Chapel 11a: 182; Chapel
    13: 183; Chapel 14: *see* Aynalı Kilise Monastery; Chapel 16: 179,
    183; Chapel 17 (Kızlar Kilise): 25, 118, 181, 182; Pl. 20; Chapel
    17a: 181, 182; Chapel 17b: 181, 183; Chapel 18: 25, 178, 182,
    227; Chapel 19: *see* Elmalı Kilise; Chapel 20 (St Barbara): 25,
    63, **173–6**, 182, 183, 227, 228, 229, 235; Pl. 162; Chapel 21: 25,
    63, **181–2**, 227, 251; Chapel 21a: 182, 183, 227; Chapel 21b: 181,
    183; Chapel 21c: 182, 183, 227; Chapel 21d: 182, 183; Chapel 22:
    see Çarıklı Kilise; Chapel 22a: 182; Chapel 23: *see* Karanlık
    Kilise; Chapel 25: 167, **169–70**, 183, 227, 228, 229; Pls. 154a, 156,
    157; Chapel 27: 25, 63, **170–2**, 182, 183, 227; Pl. 159; Chapel 28
    (Yılanlı Kilise): 25, 26, **172–3**, 227; *see also* Yılanlı group; Chapel
    29: *see* Kılıçlar Kilise; Chapel 33 (Mereyemana Kilise): 43
Goudi (near Athens), 236
graves, *see under* architecture (tomb chambers)
Gregory of Nazianzos, 4; Church of, 230n., 253
Güllü Dere, 184, 188, 207, 239, 254, 257; Pls. 1, 168; *see also* Ayvalı
    Kilise, Haçlı Kilise, Niketas the Stylite (Hermitage of)
Gülşehir (= Zoropassos), 5, 8n., 121, 147, 150; Fig. 1
Gümüşler, 11, 103; *see also* Eski Gümüş Monastery
Gümüşören, 236

Haci İşmail Dere, Church No. 2: 229, 256
Haçlı Kilise (Güllü Dere), 257
Hagios Prokopios, *see* Ürgüp
Hallaç Monastery (Ortahisar), 9, **11–26**, 30, 33, 39, 42, 43, 45, 48, 118,
    223, 224, 226, 227, 228, 247, 248, 251, 256; Figs. 2–4; Pls. 3–19
halls, *see under* architecture
Halys river (= Kızılırmak), 5, 121n.
Han, the (Kara Dağı), 242; Fig. 58
hans, 149–50
Hasan Dağı, 2, 4, 226, 234, 235, 236, 242, 256, 257
Hatuniye Medrese (Kaisareia), 4
Heavenly Angels, Monastery of, 218, 222, 250
hermitages, 2, 9, 44, **184–222**, 223, 225–6, 239–40, 252
hermits, 187, 192, 237, 254
Hieron of Matiana, 5, 26n., 253
Higumenos, 238, 239
Hogeac' Vank' (Van), 244; Fig. 59
Holy Apostles, Church of (Sinasos), 149n., 193, 215, 222
Hosios Loukas, Monastery of, 44, 240
Hypatos, 250, 251

İbrala, 231, 234

Iconium, *see* Konya
Id-Dêr Monastery (Syria), 242; Fig. 52
İhlara, 11, 63, 256; Fig. 1; *see also* Karanlık Kale, Kokar Kilise,
    Michael (Church of St), Sümbüllü Kilise
Inscriptions, 23, 31–2, 44, 54–6, 73–5, 94, 156, 167, 172, 175, 176, 178,
    182, 187, 192, 196–7, 198–200, 204, 206, 211–12, 216–18; Pls. 45,
    63a–b, 84b
Istanbul, *see* Constantinople

John the Baptist, Church of (Çavuşin), 8, 256
John of Pelekete, Monastery of (Bithynia), 242
John Tzimisces, 4
Justinian, 239, 248

Kaisareia (Anatolia), 1, 2, 4, 5, 7, 150, 222, 230, 252, 253, 254; Fig. 1;
    Church of St Basil, 222
Kaisareia (Palestine), 4
Kalabaka (Thessaly), 236
Kamouliana, 253
Kara Dağı, 226, 231, 234, 235, 237, 242
Karabaş Kilise and complex (Soğanlı), 117, 188, **193–202**, 203, 206,
    207, 222, 223, 225, 226, 239, 250, 251, 256; Figs. 36–8; Pls. 174–6
Karagedik Kilise (Peristrema valley), 230, 231, 234, 235; Figs. 43, 44a
Karaman, 231, 242
Karanlık Kale (İhlara), 11, 84, **95–103**, 148, 223, 224, 227, 228, 229,
    247, 248, 251; Fig. 16; Pls. 90–100
Karanlık Kilise (Göreme Chapel 23) and Monastery, 11, **48–56**, 62,
    109, 118, 148, 160, 162, 167, 176, 177, 182, 223, 227, 228, 229, 248,
    250, 251; Figs. 9–10; Pls. 41–5
Karlık Kilise (Cemil), 229
Karşı Kilise (near Açık Saray), 8n., 73, 147
Kartmin, Monastery of Saints Samuel, Symeon and Gabriel, 244
Kaymaklı: mosque, 230n.; underground city, 6
Kayseri, *see* Kaisareia
Kiev, Church of St Sophia, 73
Kılıçlar Kilise (Göreme Chapel 29), 39, **43–5**, 225, 229; Pl. 37
Kılıçlar Monastery, 11, **39–43**, 226, 227, 229, 248; Fig. 7; Pls. 34–6
Kilise Camii (Constantinople), 235
Kilisira, 231
Kırk Dam Altı Kilise (= St George) (Belisırma), 8n., 257
Kırşehir, 235n.
Kiskisos, 5n.
kitchens, *see under* architecture
Kızıl Çukur, 8n., 184n., 256
Kızılırmak (= Halys river), 5, 121n.
Kızlar Kilise, *see* Göreme Chapel 17
Klados, 187, 250
Kleisoura, 4, 187
Kleisourarch, 187, 188, 189, 250
Kokar Kilise (İhlara), 257
Konya (= Iconium), 229, 231, 254; Sultanate of, 4
Korama, *see* Göreme
Korykos, 234
Koyunağıl Kilise (Selime), 229
Krinites Arotras, 240
Ktouts (Armenia), 230n.
Kybistra, 253
Kyriakon (Şille), 229
Kyzistra, 5

Latmos, 8, 238, 239, 244
laura, 9, 237, 238, 240, 247
Leo VI, 254
Leo the Deacon, 1, 254
Lucania, 251
Lucas, Paul, 1, 7
Luke of Phokis, 44, 240
Lycaonia, 231, 234
Lycia, 226n.

Maçan, *see* Avcılar
Madenşehir, 231
Magistros, 251n., 253
Maistor, 32, 224n.
Makrina the Younger, 238
Malakopea (= Derinkuyu), 5, 150
Maleinos, 4
Mamas of Kaisareia, 253
Manzikert, 4
Marmara, Sea of, 238, 239, 242
Matiana, *see* Avcılar
Matthew of Edessa, 253
Mavrucan, 8n., 256
Melendiz river, 63
Meletios, Monastery of St (Megara), 241; Fig. 48
Melitene, 4, 254; Basileios of, scribe, 5n.; Shrine of St Polyeuktos, 253
Meriamlık, 234
Mesopotamia, 226, 236
Meteora, 8, 238, 239
Michael VII, 73
Michael, Church of St (İhlara), 117
millstones, *see under* architecture
Mistra, 228n.
Mokissos, 253, 254
monasteries: plans of built monasteries, 240–4; post-Byzantine use of
    cave monasteries, 11, 15, 19, 20, 24, 26, 40, 42, 45, 50, 61, 77, 85,
    105, 112, 116, 118, 151, 162, 204, 208; size of population in, 248,
    249
monastic centres, 8, 238
monasticism, 8, 9, **237–9**
Mount Athos, 8, 238, 241n.
Mount Olympos (Bithynia), 8, 238
Mount Sinai, Monastery of St Catherine, 241; Fig. 49
Munşil Kilise, church opposite (Soğanlı), 229
Muskar, 226n.
Myrelaion (Constantinople), 235

Nakida, *see* Niğde
names (from inscriptions)
    Anna (Göreme Chapel 21), 182, 251
    Bardas [monk] (Karabaş Kilise), 196; Fig. 37b
    [Bardas Phokas] *Caesar* (Pigeon House Church), 251n.
    Basileios, *Domestikos* (St Barbara, Soğanlı), 206–7, 251
    Basileios, priest (Karabaş Kilise), 200, 201; Fig. 38e
    Bassianos (Karanlık Kilise), 54, 55, 251; Fig. 10b
    Bathystrokos, *Abbas* (Karabaş Kilise), 197, 201, 202; Fig. 37c
    Catherine, nun (Karabaş Kilise), 198, 200, 201, 250; Fig. 38a
    Constantine (Tokalı Kilise), 218, 222, 240, 250
    Demna (Ayvalı Kilise), 211, 212; Fig. 41a
    Eirene (Karabaş Kilise), 198–9; Fig. 38b
    Eudokia (Karabaş Kilise), 198, 200, 250; fig. 38d
    Eustratios, *Kleisourarch* (Hermitage of Niketas the Stylite), 187, 188,
        250
    ?Falibon (Göreme Chapel 20), 175–6, 251
    Gen[eth]lios [Karanlık Kilise], 54, 55, 251; Fig. 10a
    [?H] armoloikos (Göreme Chapel 21), 182, 251
    ?Ignatios [monk] (Göreme Chapel 18), 178, 251, 252
    John (Ayvalı Kilise), 212, 213, 240, 250
    John, *Entalmatikos* (Karanlık Kilise), 54, 55, 251; Fig. 10a
    John Skepides (Gök Kilise), 250, 251
    Kosmas (Karabaş Kilise), 197, 201, 202
    Leon (Çarıklı Kilise), 167, 251; Pl. 153
    Leon Marulines (Göreme Chapel 20), 175–6, 251
    [Leon Phokas] *Curopalates* (Pigeon House Church), 251n.
    Leon, son of Constantine (Tokalı Kilise), 218, 222, 240, 250, 251
    Makar [monk] (Ayvalı Kilise), 212, 213; Fig. 41b
    Maria (Karabaş Kilise), 198–9; Fig. 38b
    Melias, *Magistros* (Pigeon House Church), 251n., 253
    Michael (Çarıklı Kilise), 167, 251; Pl. 153

Michael (Göreme Chapel 27), 172, 251
Michael Skepides, *Protospatharios* (Karabaş Kilise), 198, 199, 200, 201, 250, 251; Fig. 38f
Nikephoros [painter] (Tokalı Kilise), 218
Nikephoros Phokas (Pigeon House Church), 5, 251n.
Nikephoros, priest (Karanlık Kilise), 54, 55, 251; Fig. 10b
Niketas, *Maistor* (Bezir Hane), 32–3
Niketas the Stylite, 187, 188, 239, 250
Nyphon, monk (Karabaş Kilise), 198, 200, 250; Fig. 38d
Photios [monk] (Karabaş Kilise), 196; Fig. 37a
Roustiakos [monk] (Karabaş Kilise), 197, 201, 202
Symeon, monk, 192, 193, 239
Thamades (Göreme Chapel 27), 172, 251
Theodora, Empress (Pigeon House Church), 251n.
Theodoros (Ayvalı Kilise), 211, 212
Theodoros, (Göreme Chapel 28), 173, 251
Theodoros, (Yusuf Koç Kilisesi), 156, 251; Pl. 155
Theognostos (Çarıklı Kilise), 167, 251; Pl. 153
Za[charias] [monk] (Karabaş Kilise), 196; Fig. 37d
Nazianzos, 5, 253, 254; Church of St Gregory, 230n., 253
Neophytos of Cyprus, 240
Nevşehir, 6, 56, 121, 147
Nicaea, Council of, 239
Niğde (= Nakida), 2, 5, 6, 11, 103, 253; Fig. 1
Nikephoros Phokas, 1, 4, 5, 239, 253; *see also* names (from inscriptions)
Niketas the Stylite, Hermitage of (Gülü Dere), 8n., **184–9**, 193, 202, 207, 223, 239, 250, 256; Fig. 34a; Pls. 168–71
Nikolaos Mystikos, 254
notitiae, episcopal, 5, 26, 33, 253–4
Nyssa, 4, 253

Ortahisar, 6, 7, 11, 149n., 229, 257; Fig. 1; *see also* Cambazlı Kilise, Hallaç Monastery, Sarıca Kilise
Osk Vank, 26
Ovacık (= Dasmendron), 5, 254

Pachomios of Egypt, 237
painting
    donor images, 24, 44, 53–5, 71, 73, 156, 166–7, 178, 182, 198–200, 211–12, 251; Figs. 10, 14, 29, 38, 41; Pls. 62, 149, 153
    monochrome (usually red), 15, 17, 19, 22, 23, 30, 36, 38, 39, 41, 42, 50, 51, 52, 59, 60, 61, **62–3**, 92, 101, 103, 118, 125, 131, 140, 151–2, 162, 167, **169–70**, 172, 173, **175**, 181, 192, 197, 204; Fig. 12; Pls. 6–9, 14, 17, 19, 20, 33, 41–3, 47, 48–50, 96, 100, 151, 154a, 156
    polychrome, 23–4, 30–1, 43–4, 48, 50, 52, 53–5, 71–3, 89–94, 112, 115–16, 117, 119, 131, 146–7, 159, 165–7, 172, 175, 176–7, 178, 179, 181, 182, 186–7, 190, 192, 196–200, 204–6, 210–12, 215–18, 220; Fig. 4; Pls. 18, 26–8, 37, 41, 44, 45, 60, 61a–b, 80–2, 84a–89, 110–11, 112–15, 142–3, 170–1, 173–73a, 176, 178–9, 182, 183–5
palaces, 149
Palestine, 237, 238; Monastery of St Euthymios, 241–2; Fig. 50
Panagia and All Saints, Monastery of, 211, 212, 213, 222, 240, 250
Panagia Church (Sinasos), 229
Pantepoptes, St Saviour (Constantinople), 235
Pantocrator Monastery (Constantinople), 235, 238
Paphos, Cyprus, 240
Paris: Bib. Nat. Ms. Gr. 922 (*Sacra Parallela*), 73; Bib. Nat. Coislin 79 (*Homilies of St John Chrysostom*), 73
Parnassos, 253
patrons, 250–2, 254; *see also* names (from inscriptions); painting (donor images)
Paul of Latmos, 239
Paulicians, 4
Peristrema valley, 2, 4, 8n., 11, **63**, 85, 95, 117, 119, 120, 227; Fig. 1; *see also* Belisırma, İhlara, Karagedik Kilise, Selime
Peter the Athonite, 238
Phaustinoupolis, 253
philanthropy, 238–9

Phokades, 4, 5, 251n., 253
Phrygia, 229, 236
Pigeon House Church (Çavuşin), 5n., 85, 218, 220, 251n., 253, 256
pigeon houses, 6, 7, 8, 100; *see also* monasteries, post-Byzantine use
pilgrimage, 253, 254
Polyeuktos, Shrine of St (Melitene), 253
Pontus, 226n., 238
population movements, 1, 160
Protospatharios, 198, 200, 250–1

refectories, *see under* architecture
refuge, 7
Romanos I, 4

Şahinefendi (= Sobesos, Söviş, Suveş), 5, 11, 22, 33, 254; Fig. 1; *see also* Church of the Forty Martyrs
Şahinefendi Monastery, **33–9**, 43, 45, 223, 224, 227, 228, 229, 247, 248, 251; Fig. 6; Pls. 29–33
Saklı Kilise (Göreme Chapel 2a), 255
Sameh Monastery (Syria), 242; Fig. 53
Samuel, Symeon and Gabriel, Monastery of Saints (Kartmin), 244
Saniana, 150n.
Sarıca Kilise (Ortahisar), 229, 255
Sarıgöl, church, 226
Sasima, 253
sculpture, *see under* architecture (carved decoration)
Sebasteia, 254
Seberaias, 254
Seleukia, Shrine of St Thekla, 253
Selime, 11, 63, 229; Fig. 1; *see also* Derviş Akın Kilisesi, Koyunağıl Kilise
Selime Kalesi, 11, **63–85**, 95, 148, 223, 224, 227, 235, 236, 247, 248, 249, 250, 252, 255; Figs. 13–14; Pls. 51–75
Seljuks, 4, 26, 95, 103, 254; *hans*, 149–50
side chapels, *see under* architecture
Şille, Kyriakon church, 229
Sinasos, 149n., 160n., 222, 229, 255; *see also* Holy Apostles (Church of), Panagia Church
single-nave churches, *see under* architecture (church plans)
Siricha, 254
Sivas, 231
Sivrihisar, 237
Skleros, 254
Sobesos, *see* Şahinefendi
Soğanlı, 6n., 11, 45, 193; Fig. 1; *see also* Ak Kilise, Barbara (Church of St), Gök Kilise, Karabaş Kilise, Munşil Kilise (Church opposite)
Soğanlı Han, 11, **45–8**, 84, 103, 118, 223, 224, 228; Fig. 8; Pls. 38–40
Söviş, *see* Şahinefendi
Srkhovank Monastery, 244
stables, *see under* architecture
Stephen, Chapel of St (Cemil), **159–60**, 183, 210n., 227
storage areas, *see under* architecture
Strabo, 7, 254n.
Strategos, 250–1
Sümbüllü Kilise (İhlara), 120
Sumela, 244
Surp Hagop, 226
Suveş, *see* Şahinefendi
Symeon the Monk, Hermitage of (Zelve), 188, **189–93**, 202, 223, 239; Fig. 35; Pls. 172a–73
Symeon the Stylite, 239
Syria, 226n., 239, 242; Id Dêr Monastery, 242; Fig. 52; Sameh Monastery, 242; Fig. 53

Tabennesis, 237
Tağar, triconch church, 8on.
Tephrike, 4
Thebes, 237
Thekla, Shrine of St (Euchaita), 253

Theodora, Empress, 177
Theodosioupolis, 253
Tilköy (= Diokaisareia), 4
Tokalı Kilise (Göreme Chapel 7), 32, 85, 160, 210, **213–22**, 223, 224,
    225, 226, 240, 249, 253, 254, 255; Fig. 42; Pls. 183–8; Lower church,
    219; New church, 216–19; Old church, 215–16; Vestibule, 219–20
tomb chambers, *see under* architecture
Trebizond, 226n., 244
troglodytes, 1, 7, 254
Trullo, Council of, 238, 239
Tur Abdin, 226, 244
twin-nave church plan, *see under* architecture (church plans)
Tyana, 253, 254
typika, 5, 238, 239, 240
Tzamandos, 254

Üçayak, church, 235n.
Üçhisar, 6, 7
underground cities, 6
upper floors, *see under* architecture (galleries)
Ürgüp (= Hagios Prokopios), 2, 5, 6, 33, 45, 56, 229, 254
Ürgüp façade, 118–19

Van, 244
Venasa (= Avanos), 5

Venice: Bib. Marciana Cod. Gr. 538 (*Job*), 43n.
vestibules, *see under* architecture
villages, rock cut, 5, 6, 7, 8
Viranşehir, churches, 226

Wadi'n Natrun, Egypt, 242
water supply, 2

Xenophon, 6n, 254n.

Yağdebaş Kilise, 236
Yaprakhisar, 120
Yaroslav the Wise, 73
Yedi Kapulu, church, 226, 237
Yeşilhisar, 6n.
Yılanlı group, 25, 26, 33, 62, 63, 95, **182–3**, 223, 228, 235, 255
Yılanlı Kilise, *see* Göreme Chapel, 28
Yusuf Koç Kilisesi Monastery (Avcılar), **151–7**, 183, 223, 224, 227,
    228, 236, 249, 250, 251, 256; Figs. 28–9; Pls. 143–9

Zelve, 6, 189, 193; Fig. 1; *see also* Symeon the Monk (Hermitage of)
Zeugos, 187, 250
Zoropassos, *see* Gülşehir
Zygos, 187